Mountain Photography

Philip R. I. Smith

Rocky Mountain Books
Calgary–Victoria–Vancouver

This book is dedicated to my wife, Karen, and to our kids, Joshua and Julia, for their unbounded spirit of adventure and infinite patience.

Printed in China

We acknowledge the financial support of the Government of Canada through the Book Publishing Industry Development Program (BPIDP) and the support of the Alberta Foundation for the Arts for our publishing program.

RMB

Published by
Rocky Mountain Books
#108, 17665-66A Avenue
Surrey, BC V3S 2A7

Library and Archives Canada Cataloguing in Publication

Smith, Philip R. I. (Philip Raymond Ives), 1960-
Mountain photography / Philip R.I. Smith.

Includes bibliographical references and index.
ISBN 1-894765-44-3

1. Photography of Mountains--Canada. I. Title.

TR787.S64 2004   778.9'36143   C2004-904077-4

Contents

Foreword – 5
Preface – 6
Introduction – 8

Choosing a Camera — 10
The Digital Debate – 11
Digital Debate Arguments… – 12
…And Answers – 14
Size Matters – 16
Digital Camera Essentials – 17
Single–Lens Reflex (SLR) or Rangefinder? – 18
How Automatic Should Your Camera Be? – 20
Good Mountain Camera Features – 22
Not–to–be–missed Functions – 23

Accessories — 24
Shopping for Lenses – 24
Zoom or No Zoom? – 26
Mountain Camera Bags – 27
Camera Bag Alternatives – 28
Essential Accessories – 29
Don't Chintz on Film! – 30
Filters to Correct Color – 32
Other Useful Filters for Color Photography – 34
Filters for Black & White – 35

Getting Started — 36
Loading and Unloading Film – 37
If the Film Doesn't Advance – 38
Light Leakage – 39
Holding Your Camera Properly – 40
Steadying Your Camera – 42

Metering Exposures Correctly — 43
Meter Calibration Scale – 43
Metering for Results – 44
Incident Meters vs. Reflected Light Meters – 45
Bracketing – 46
Advanced Exposure Control – 47
Exposing Correctly on Snow and Ice – 49
Overexposing and Underexposing for Effect – 51

Choosing Shutter Speeds — 53
Stopping Motion Entirely – 55
Avoiding Camera Shake – 56
Choosing Depth of Field – 57
Maximizing Depth of Field – 58
Depth of Field Preview – 59
Depth of Field Applications – 61
Aperture Priority – 64
Shutter Priority – 65

Tripods And Releases — 66
Lighter is Not Always Better – 68
Choosing the Ideal Tripod – 69
Choosing a Tripod Head – 70
C–clamp Supports – 71
Monopods – 72
Mini–tripods – 72
Cable and Remote Releases – 73
Becoming Too Dependent on Your Tripod – 75
Tripods, Releases and Mountain Safety – 77

Color, Black & White, Or...? — 79
Shooting Slides vs. Prints – 81
Slow Films vs. Fast Films – 83
Color Films – 85
Color Harmony and Complimentary – 87
Black and White Films – 88
Black and White Graduated Tones and Contrast – 90
Sepia Printing and Hand Coloring – 92

Alternative Film Treatments — 93
Cross–Processing Color Film
Tungsten Film – 95
Color Infrared Film – 97

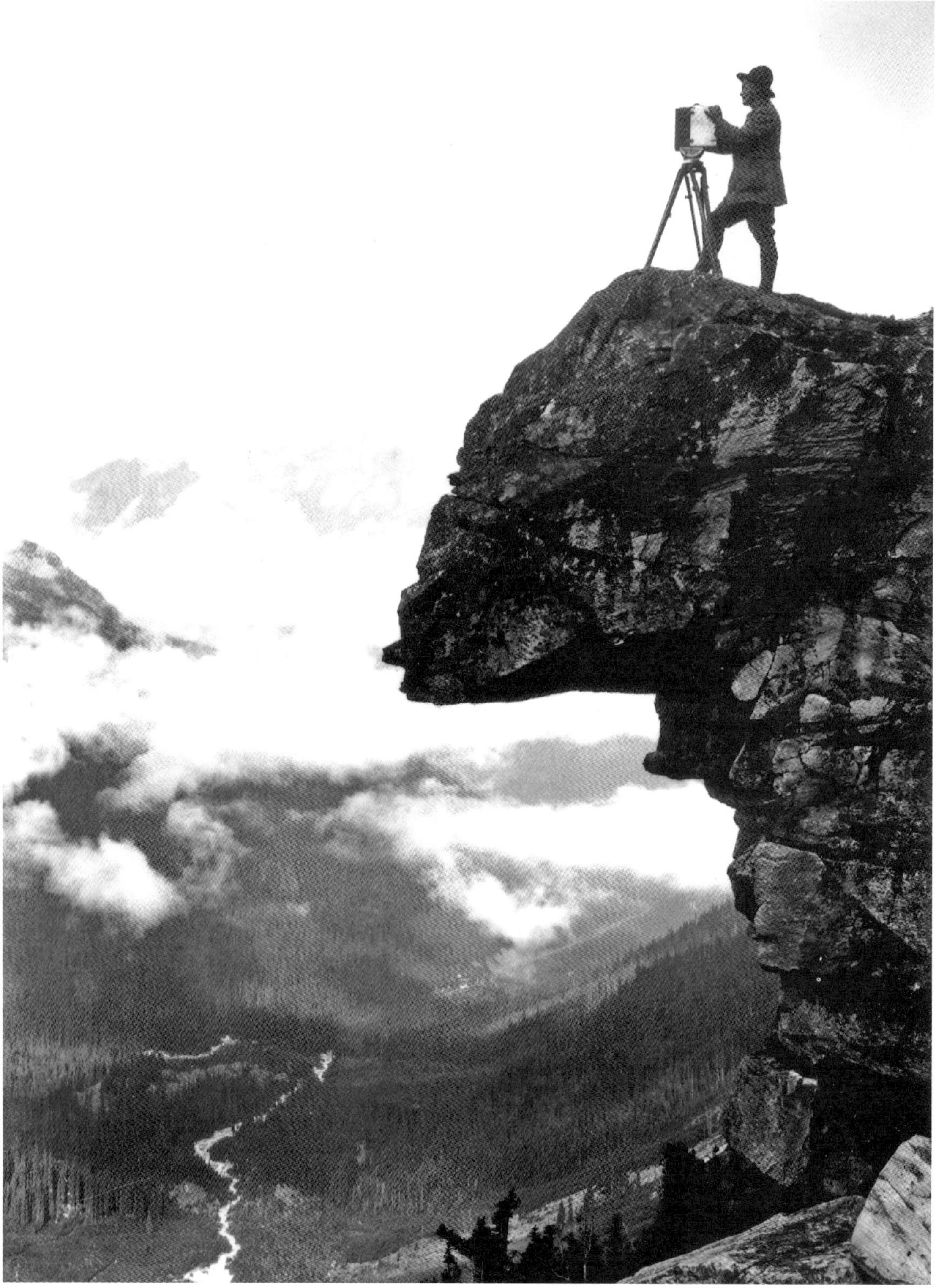

Rockies photographer, Byron Harmon at work on a rocky promontory above the Illecillewaet Valley in the early 1900s.

The Creative Eye — 99
The Art of Seeing… – 100
…And Being Flexible – 101
To the Craft of Visual Communication – 102
Lines, Shapes and Patterns – 103
Texture, Tone and Contrast – 104
The Rule of Thirds – 106
Variations of The Rule of Thirds – 107
Disregarding The Rule of Thirds – 108
Dead Centre Positioning: Static Shooting – 109
Dead Centre Positioning: Motion – 111

Cropping Your Subject — 112
Very Tight Crops – 114
Small Man–Big Environment – 115
Radical Cropping – 116
Horizontal Framing – 118
Vertical Framing – 119
Tilted Framing – 121
Horizon, or Horizonless? – 123
Light and Dark Backgrounds – 125
Sharp or Fuzzy Backgrounds – 126
Foreground as Interference – 127

Finding a Perspective — 129
Level (normal) Perspective – 131
Direct Overhead Perspective – 132
Ground Level Perspective – 134
Oblique Perspectives – 136
Dramatic Viewpoints – 137
Emphasizing Steepness – 139
Tricks for Enhancing Perspective – 141

Capturing & Creating Motion — 143
Control Motion with Shutter Speed Selection – 144
Panning Action Scenes – 146
Attaching Your Camera to Moving Objects – 148

Mountain Light — 150
Radiant Light; an Overview – 152
Choosing Time of Day & Time of Year to Shoot – 153
Frontal Lighting – 155
Sidelighting – 156
Backlighting – 158
Creating Silhouettes – 159
Shooting on Overcast Days – 160
Bright Overcast Lighting – 162
Partially Cloudy Weather – 163
Fill–in Light – 165
Reflecting Light Purposely – 167
Filling with a Flash – 169
Creative Flash Use – 170
Dealing with Haze and Lens Flare – 172
Faithfully Recording Skies at Sunset and Sunrise –174
Shooting Comfortably (and Safely!) During Stormy Weather – 176
Recording Twilight Glow, Lightning and Star Patterns – 178
Shooting in the Dark: Some Ad Hoc Lighting Ideas – 180

Specialized Shoots — 182
Photographing Wildlife – 184
Close–up Photography – 187
Panorama Formats – 190
Who Wants to "Model"? – 192
Self–portrait Shooting – 194
Rigging a Climbing Shot – 196
Speed Kills! Protect Yourself – 198

Big Trip Photography — 200
High Mountain Expeditions – 201
Shooting in Very Cold Weather – 204
Hot Tropical Extremes – 206
World Travel – 208
Creating Effective Slide Shows – 211
Publishing Your Mountain Stories – 213
Building Multimedia and Digital Presentations –215

Troubleshooting – 217
References – 219
Glossary – 220
Acknowledgements – 222
Index – 223

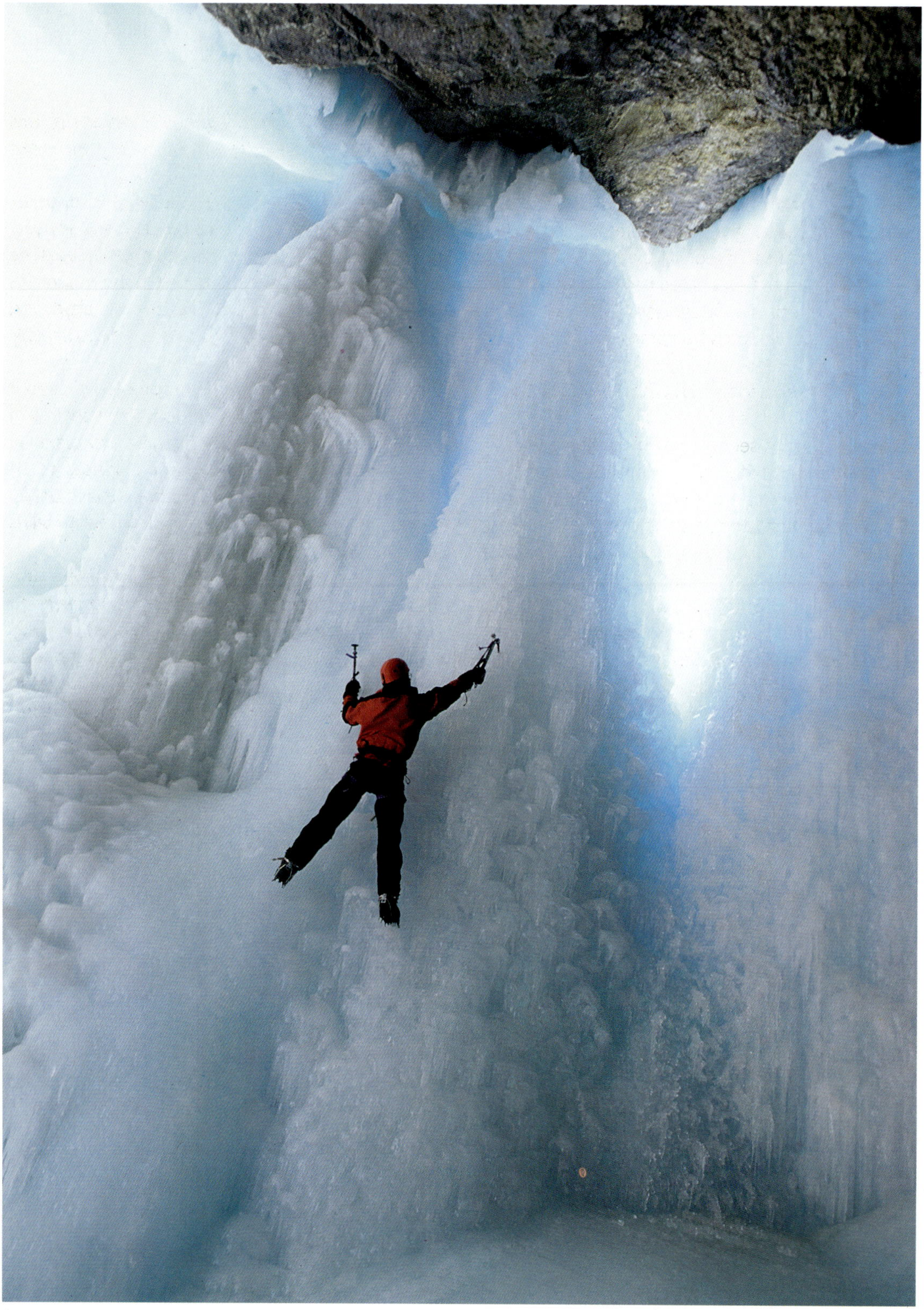

Preface

I chose photography as a career path, and life-style, in an act of absolutely blind faith. A good friend had unexpectedly met up with me in the midst of a solo trip to the Patagonian mountains. He needed a break before finishing his last year of geography studies; I had likewise postponed my last year of geology for reasons of "mental health", or whatever it was called back then.

While traversing the Patagonian Icecap on a third day of cloudless weather, he sprang a most pivotal question: would I consider postponing university studies a couple of years longer and form a business with him to produce and sell our mountain imagery?

Outrageous as it seems to me now, there was, if I recall correctly, no hesitation in my response. No other option seemed relevant or even possible at the time. And though our first commercial efforts together were a nearly complete disaster, I still had few doubts about the choice we'd made.

His tragic death from unrelated incidents later that year left me without a partner to muscle along with. I considered leaving our newly formed "business" behind and going back to university. But I dismissed the thought almost as quickly. Photography and mountains—the "canvas" I'd chosen to create with—were both deeply entrenched in my psyche and could not be cast aside that easily.

Photography had been a formative passion long before that time though. I still remember buying my first "point-and-shoot"—a sandwich-sized 110 format—when I was 11, followed by a Vogtlander 35 mm a couple of years later. When the barely used Vogtlander tumbled spectacularly from a cliff during an ill-fated outing, splintering into hundreds of bits and pieces, I resolved to become more serious about camera equipment, and camera handling.

I spent all the money I'd accumulated from paper routes and other odd jobs on a Leica IIIf, and as many Leitz lenses as I could afford. This equipment joined me on every new mountain outing, first in the mountains close to home, then in the St. Elias, the Himalayas and the Alps. I had few other possessions for years, certainly none so mightily valued.

Looking back, I think what first captivated me about photography was how all-encompassing it seemed. I could use my camera for pure creative expression in a literally infinite number of ways if I wanted to, or I could simply employ it to preserve rich mountain experiences. It's largely this versatility that still makes photography so deeply rewarding for me.

Friends have long suggested that I, and others who make their living from photography, must have an exceptional "eye" for picture taking. While I certainly believe talent is important to creating exciting images, it's not everything. Much of what passes for God-given ability can be learned through patient determination and practice.

Moreover, I'm now of the belief that one can sometimes discover an "eye" where none was thought to exist. It's partially for this reason that I'll always stress gaining a thorough knowledge of camera fundamentals with anyone who asks my opinion. To paraphrase a famous remark, knowledge such as this can, I believe, truly set the mind free, for both creative and intuitive visual exploration.

Opposite: Look for unusual locations to shoot. I discovered a gigantic cave behind this frozen waterfall on one outing, and reasoned it would be a great place to return to with camera and climbing friend. This shot was taken from inside the cave, looking out. Banff National Park, Canada. Kodak E100VS, 28 mm lens.

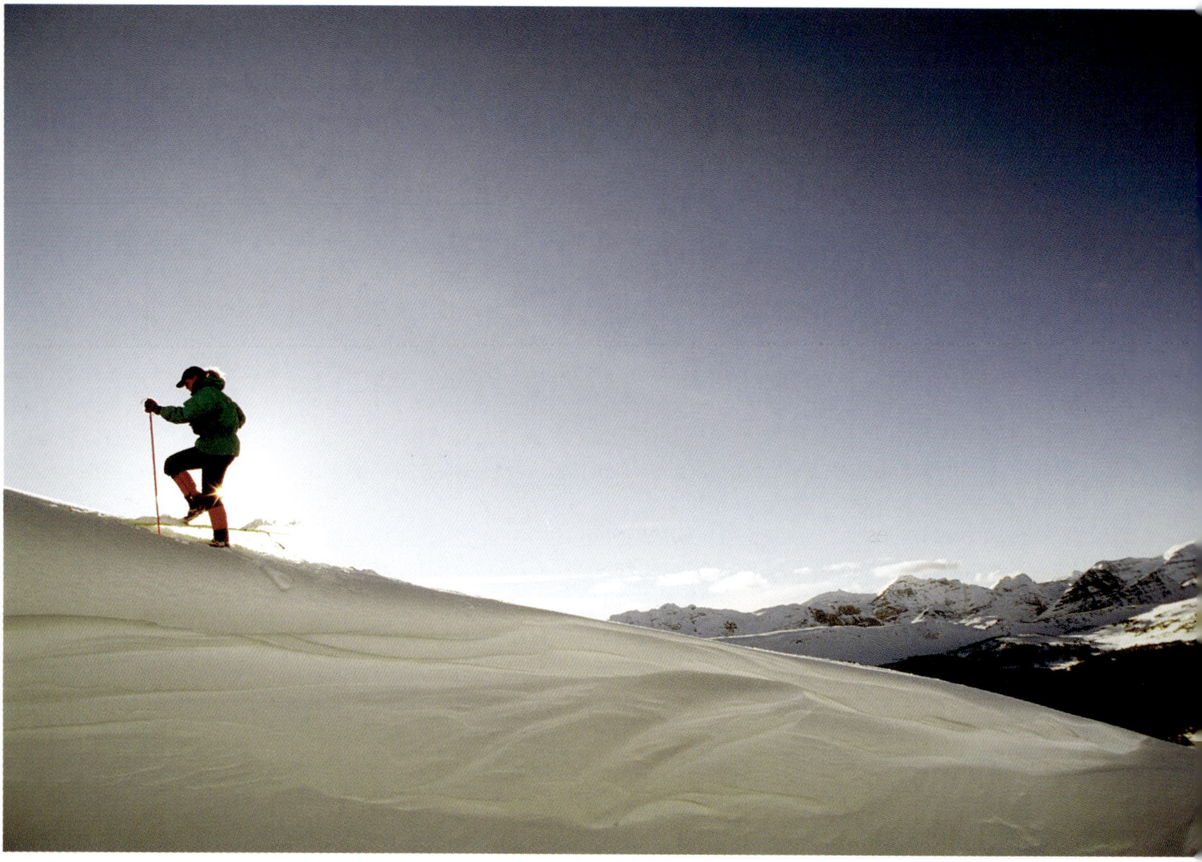

Having a companion merely change position, or flick snow off a ski, will sometimes creatively enhance a shot in ways you may not even think of. Banff National Park, Canada. Fuji Velvia, 35-70 mm zoom lens.

Introduction

"Mountaineers are sometimes charged with making the most of their gymnastic feats. Those I have known have been, for the most part, modest and precise, not to say prosaic persons—at any rate in their writings. But I cannot claim as much for their cameras. These little instruments are given to sensationalism of the crudest kinds. They make the easiest rocks look highly dangerous, and difficult cliffs impossible. Let wives and mothers take heart—mountaineering is not nearly so bad as it is photographed."

Douglas Freshfield, from Climbers and Painters

Were it always so. Written nearly a century ago, these sentiments are more often the antithesis of those expressed by today's alpine travellers.

The intensity of mountain experiences, and the majesty of mountain landscapes, are often rendered dull and lifeless on film. All too commonly such failures are blamed on equipment. What is usually needed though is not a better camera, but a few good pointers on photography fundamentals.

Photography, at best, strives towards a near-perfect blend of science and art. It is this combination of polar opposites that makes good photography so compelling to view, yet elusive to create.

By extension, any photographer—whether casual or serious—will improve their skills dramatically by paying close attention to technical and artistic fundamentals. Thankfully, this is not rocket science. Just as failing to understand what makes a computer run doesn't have much bearing on your ability to operate it, so too with the camera.

What is of importance, for those of us whom are neither a technical whiz nor a creative genius, is to acquire a good working knowledge of cameras and photography, from both the artistic and scientific sides of the equation.

There are countless photography courses available for those aspiring to achieve more with their cameras. Although few, if any, will specifically address issues unique to shooting in the mountains.

Unlike most courses and several current photography books, *Mountain Photography* will favor an exploration of field technique over a lengthy discussion of glitzy new technology. There are two reasons for this.

First, technology changes; digital camera technology is changing especially fast and any discussion about the latest gear will quickly lose relevance. Second, field technique is well geared to mountain environments, where successful photography depends more on working with topography, weather, and other physical constraints than it does on having the right camera.

I've drawn, to some extent, from the experiences and comments of other photographers while compiling this book. What has been interesting to discover is that these often-accomplished individuals tend to lean toward one of two philosophical camps on the subject of mountain photography.

There are those for whom it is most important to capture a scene or experience. For such people, the expression "f-8 and be there" might be an accurate sentiment. F-8, one stop on the lens diaphragm, relates to a fairly wide depth of field, to keep things of interest mainly in focus. And being there? Enough said.

The other perspective emphasizes creativity over capturing. Individuals of this "camp" will often return to the same location to recreate scenes for the main purpose of perfecting the finished photograph. They share a belief that good locations are few and far between; therefore, why tear all over the country looking for them?

As with those whose orientation is mainly capturing, however, most of us are drawn to the mountains to explore new places and enjoy fresh experiences. We are not likely to return repeatedly to the same spots, unless they are favorite haunts.

What we need is a basic level of knowledge that can travel into the mountains with us. And, considering weight and load restrictions, a methodology that allows for the best possible results with the fewest pieces of equipment.

The following pages will address this need. I would encourage every aspiring photographer to shoot and re-shoot the same locations, and even make notes, while exploring new techniques or testing new ideas; there is no better way to learn what works, and what doesn't. Moreover, this is probably the best way to determine what time of day, or time of year, lighting conditions render the most exciting results on film.

Thanks to the digital camera, such experimentation has become easier, and cheaper, than ever. Easier, because you can refer to an image you've just shot more or less instantaneously, rather than having to wait until processed film returns from the lab. Cheaper, because it costs virtually nothing to shoot an image; if you don't like it, you simply erase it from memory. If you do, you merely save it on disk or transfer it to a hard drive.

Over the years I've learned, both through observation and by trial and error, techniques that save time and eliminate the need for extraneous equipment. Such short cuts can often mean the difference between getting a great shot or not. To the best of my ability as first a photographer and then a writer, I have included them all in the pages to come.

My hope is that these tidbits of knowledge and experience will be insightful for each of you, whether your mountain outings mean hanging off the end of a rope, waiting for a break in summit storm clouds, or simply watching the mist roll off an alpine pond.

Choosing a Camera

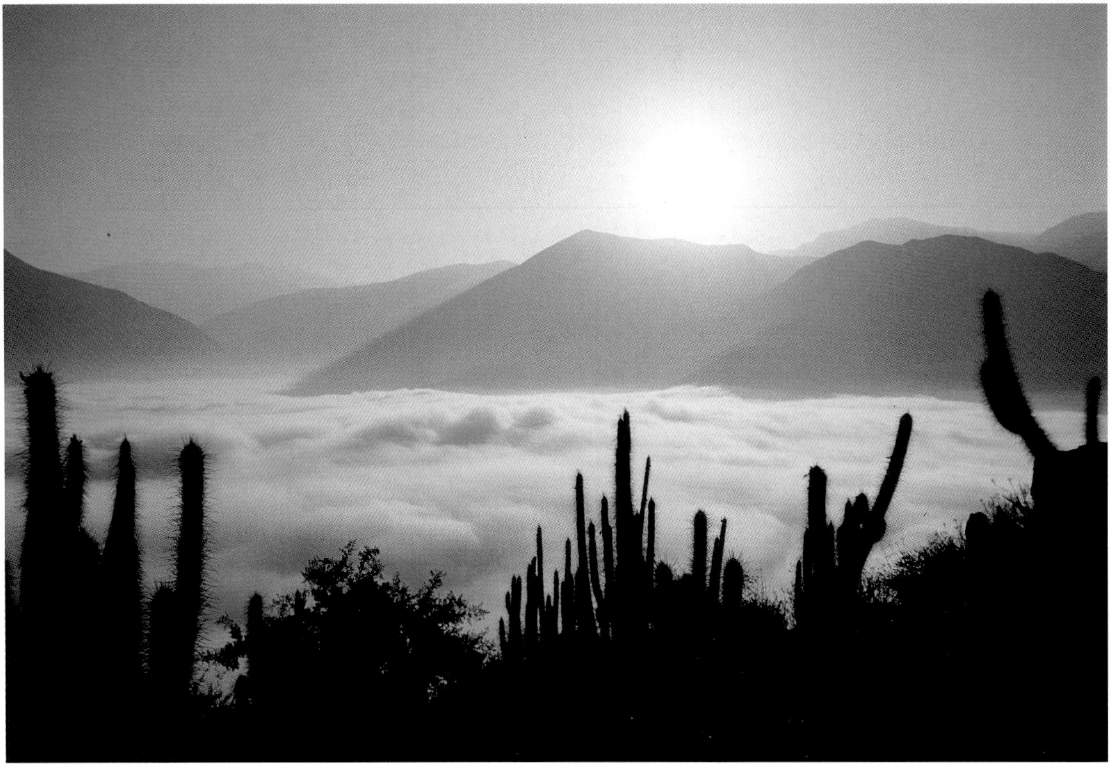

Better optics will certainly result in better pictures, particularly when shooting directly into the sun.
Andes mountains, Valle de Elqui, northern Chile. Fuji Velvia, 35 mm lens.

Consumers are faced with a bewildering choice of cameras these days. Digital and traditional film models might be either fully automatic or capable of manual operation; format choices range from ABS to 35 mm, medium and larger still; camera functions vary from gimmicky to quite basic; and so on…

Most modern cameras produce acceptable results; many will help you produce stunning pictures. With certainty, it's no longer enough, when shopping for a new camera, to simply walk into a camera shop and say, "I want a great camera". Chances are you'll be steered towards one that is more expensive, and has more bells and whistles, than you'll ever need, while perhaps lacking some of the functions that might be most useful.

The real trick is to find exactly the right camera for your own needs. In order to do so, you first have to be quite honest about your photographic intentions. Do you intend to shoot mainly mountain scenery, or perhaps wildlife or sporting activities instead? Are you a "point and shoot" person, or do you prefer to take your time and carefully compose most shots? Do you need a very small and lightweight camera for high-mountain travel? Or not?

The list of essential questions is a good deal longer than this. In the end you may have to compromise your ideals to acquire a camera that will do everything you need it to, but is not so feature-laden that your chosen model becomes a liability through size, weight, cost or complexity.

I'll try to address the most pertinent issues throughout this chapter. Perhaps, though, your first thoughts should focus around photography's rampaging digital debate.

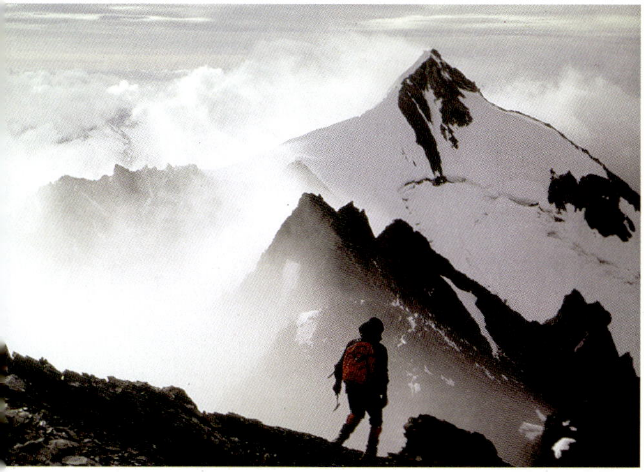

Any camera you invest in should join you on all your mountain outings, no matter how far afield. St. Elias mountains, B.C.-Yukon border, Canada. Fuji Velvia, 55 mm lens.

The Digital Debate

The question of whether or not to shoot digital is almost certainly the most controversial one amongst photographers these days, whether old hands at the medium or relative newcomers.

The advancement of digital technology has been both swift and impressive. Many of the digital cameras introduced lately have achieved similar levels of resolution as film. Several camera manufacturers maintain that their digital resolutions will soon even bypass those achievable on typical film stock.

Moreover, the resolution of a digital photo can be improved upon further using interpolation software that adds pixels to an image by examining existing adjacent pixels.

Digital cameras are good for the environment. Relatively scarce raw materials such as silver that are used in the manufacturing of film are not required and a digital camera's processing functions don't rely on toxic chemical.

Digital cameras are particularly suited to shooting candid snaps, such as this one. You can quickly review the image you've managed to capture and re-shoot if necessary. Alberta Rockies, Canada. Kodak E100VS, 28 mm lens.

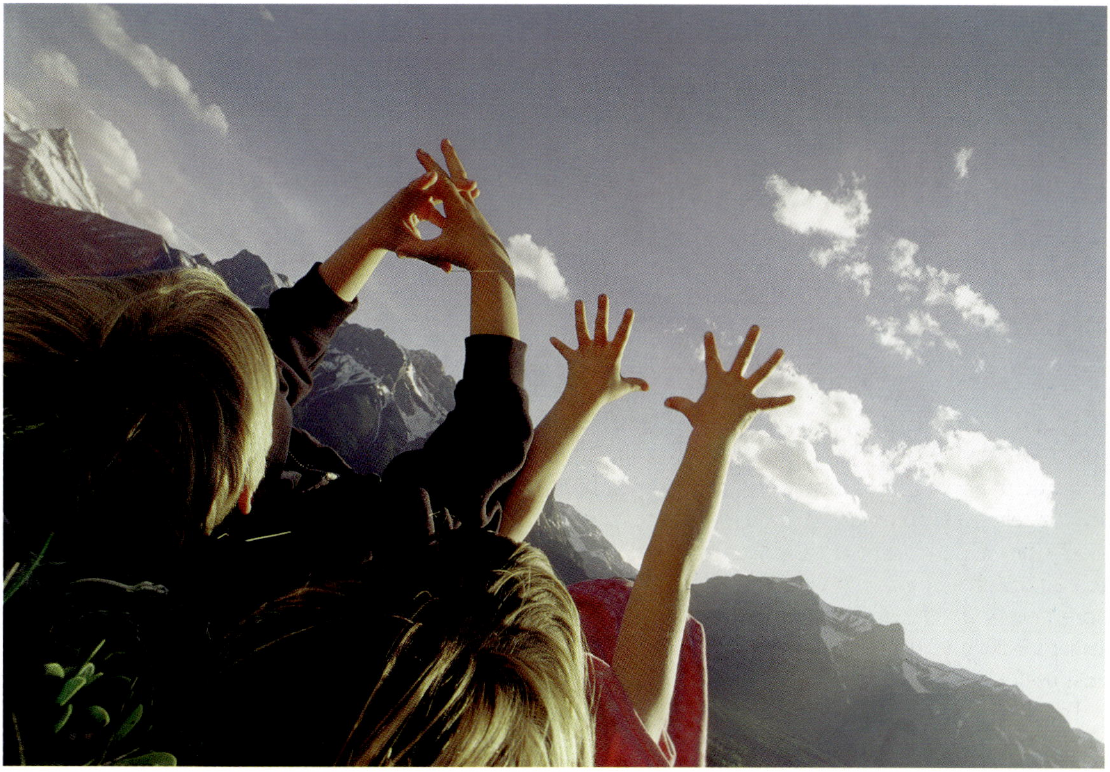

There's no question that mountain-friendly digital cameras have now arrived on the scene. Whether you should go out and buy one, stick with your tried and true film camera, or even purchase a new analog model is difficult to say. The decision is certainly a very personal one.

Consider the following arguements carefully before committing cash in either direction. If you decide to go digital, review "Digital Camera Essentials" on page 17 for a rundown on features and specs that shouldn't be missed.

Digital Debate Arguments...

Unquestionably there are phenomenal advantages to the digital medium. For one thing, an image can be viewed immediately after having been shot, allowing the photographer the opportunity to re-shoot it if needed. No longer do you have to wait for the results to be returned from the lab in order to see if they worked out or not.

And this is just the beginning. With most digital cameras, a captured image can easily and instantly be changed from color to another format, say black & white or sepia. Manipulation or alteration is relatively straightforward, especially with a software program like Photoshop.

Digital images can also, with the help of an appropriate cable attachment, be uploaded to your web site, sent to a friend electronically, or printed off using your computer's printer.

Unlike prints and transparencies, digital photos are not subject to scratches or dust as they sit in your "collection". They just require file space, whether on a CD, disk or hard drive.

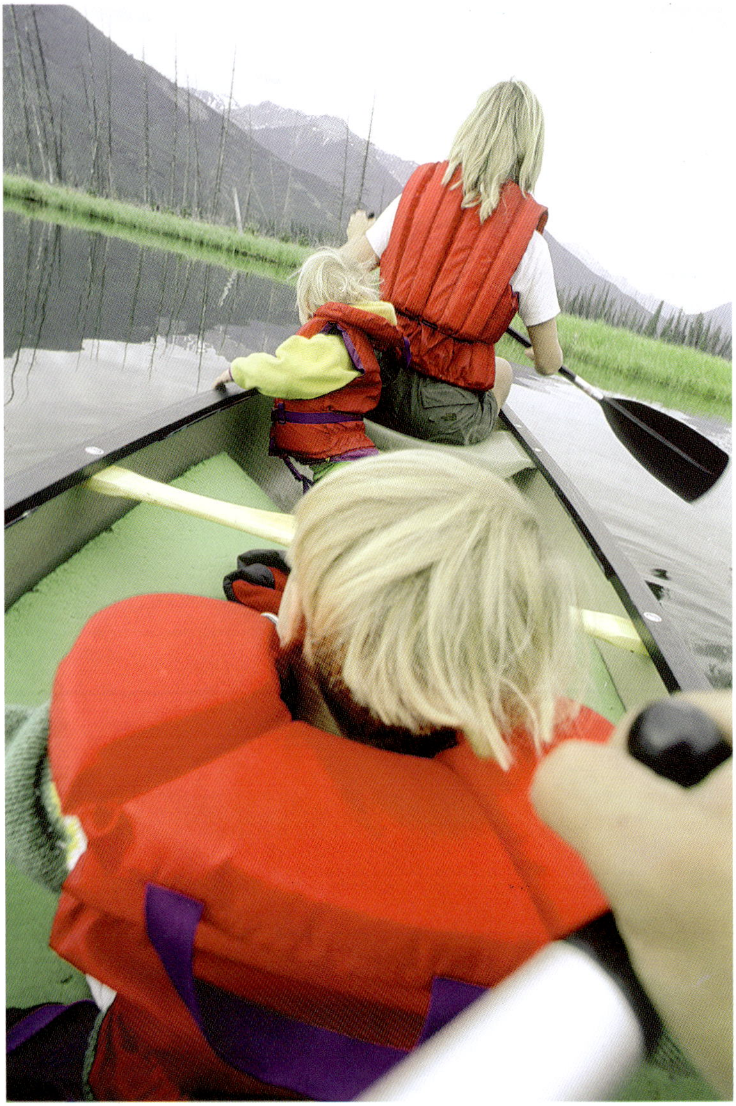

All but the most expensive digital cameras are still unable to provide the complexity of color that characterize shots such as this one. Banff National Park, Canada. Fuji Velvia, 20 mm lens.

While travelling in the mountains, the use of a digital camera can lighten your load significantly. Film never needs to be carried (although heavy replacement batteries may have to be); digital memory chips—film's replacement—are lightweight by comparison. As well, some of the precautions while using film in, say, warm humid environments or exceedingly cold climates can be forgotten (see later chapters).

Finally, there's the issue of cost. Once you've acquired a digital camera and its accessories, there really are no other costs. No processing or film purchases to make. The only additional expense will likely be the cost of black & white or color ink cartridges and photo-grade paper if you're printing a lot of your digital work.

Nonetheless, digital cameras are not for everyone, and probably never will be. Partially this has to do with the fact that not every photographer sees image creation as having anything to do with computers. Photography at its best is, an art form not simply technology at work. Many of us photographers will probably go out of our way to disassociate the two.

There are good technical reasons, too, why digital cameras will likely never replace analog cameras altogether. One is that as digital technology improves, so does analog technology. New film stocks have greater resolutions, higher color densities and wider latitudes than their predecessors. Practically every digital camera currently on the market still produces an inferior resolution compared to an analog camera at the same price point, although this may soon change.

Speed is also a factor. Only very expensive digital cameras can deliver the kind of rapid shooting that a good motor drive can provide while shooting traditional film stock. At the time of writing, few can match the eight frames per second achievable with the Nikon F5 say, or the Canon EOS.

Color reproduction continues to be one of the major criticisms of new digital camera technology. Although it has improved dramatically with the development of the newest digital cameras, color palettes still fall short of those rendered by the best traditional film stock.

With certainly, digital technology can't yet answer to the subtleties of color and tone that separate one analog film stock from another, say the difference between a portrait film and a slightly more saturated version. Until it does so, many professional still photographers and, for that matter, most Hollywood film directors will not be abandoning analog film. The bulk of new blockbuster movies and TV commercials are currently shot on traditional film stock and are only then digitally mastered.

Make sure any camera you invest in, digital or analog, is up to the rigors of travel in harsh and remote locations, if such areas will be part of your mountain itinerary. St. Elias mountains, Canada. Kodachrome, 85 mm lens.

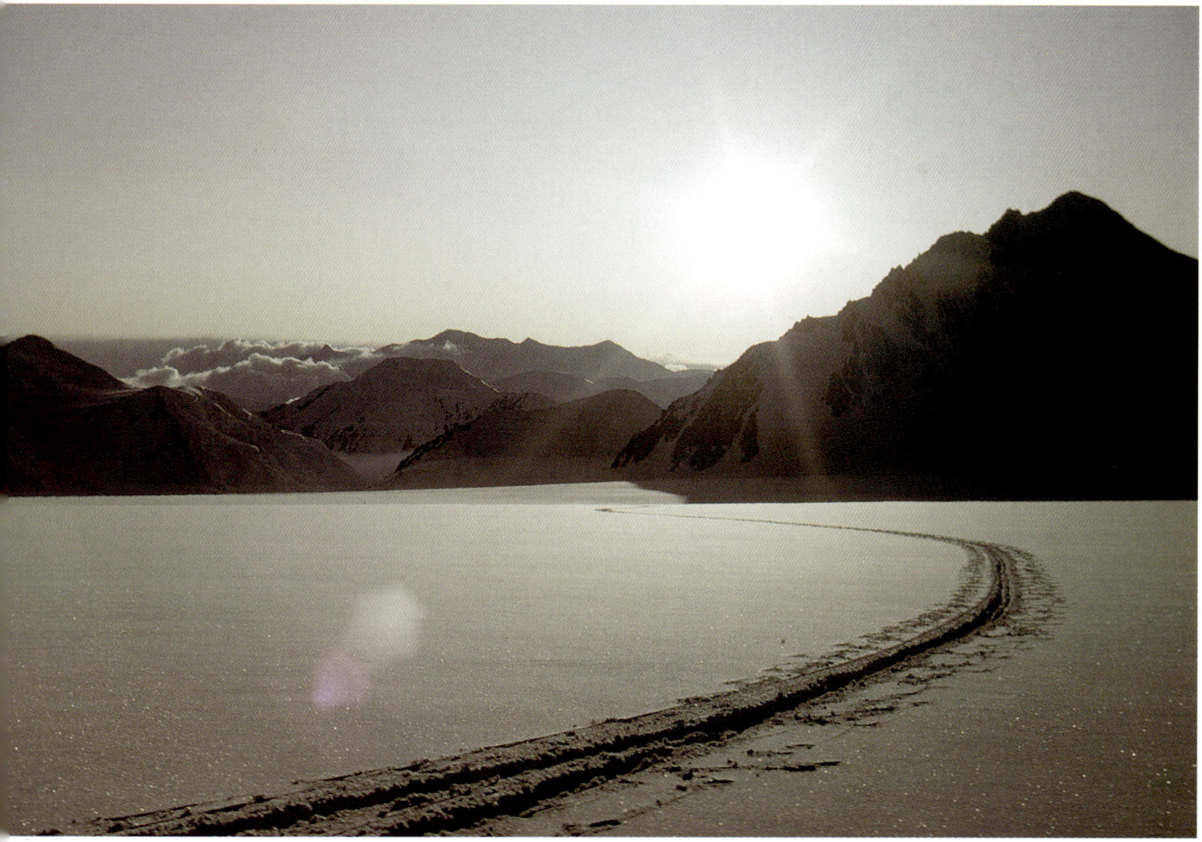

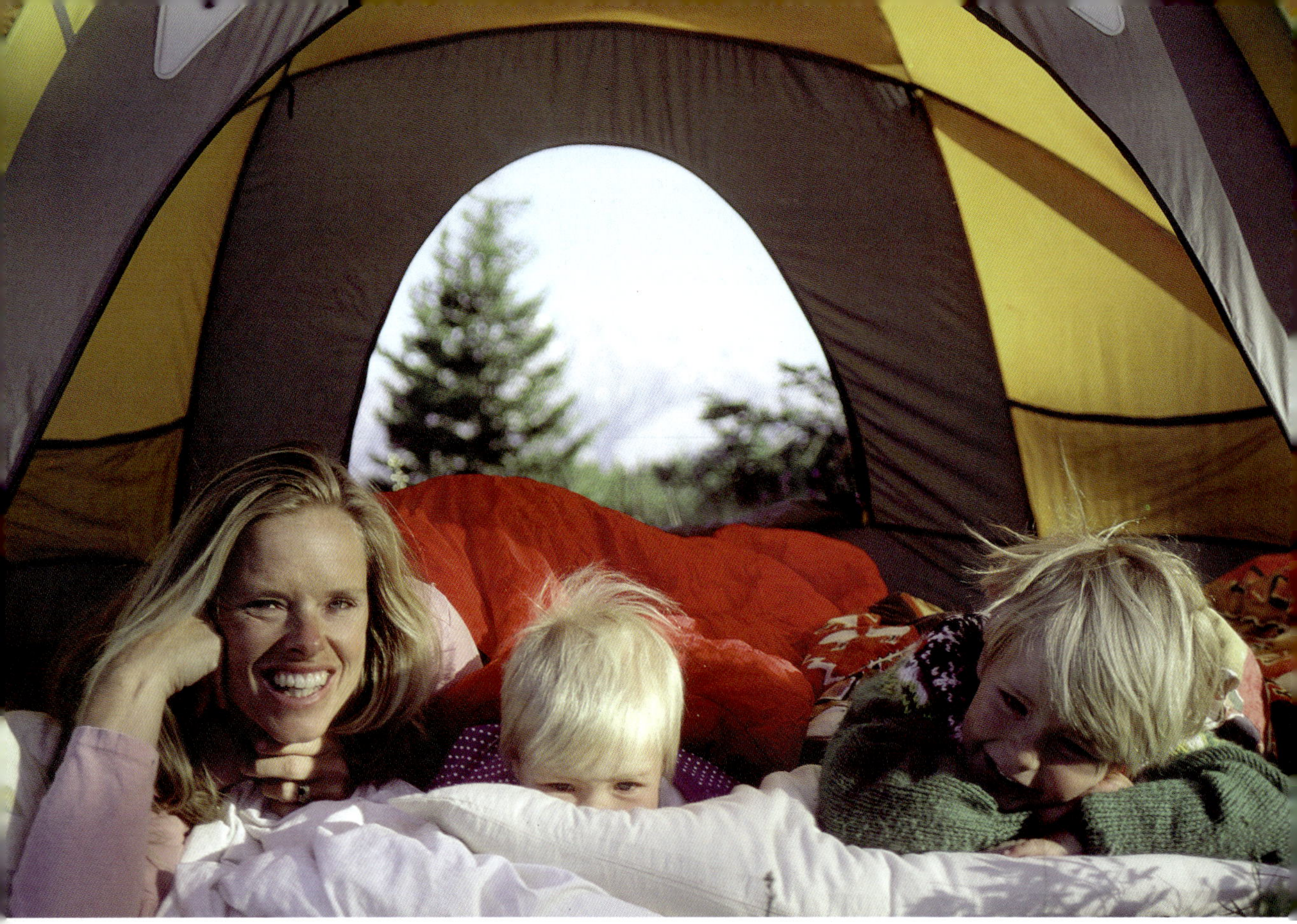

You'll often need to take many snaps to get just the right one with subject matter such as this. A digital camera can reduce costs while also providing instant feedback on results. Canadian Rockies. Fuji Velvia, 35-200 mm zoom lens.

...and Answers

Before any of us can properly decide the answer to the dilemma of film versus digital, we must ask ourselves a fundamental question: what do we intend to do with our photos, once shot?

If your main objective is to easily send them over the Internet, produce prints for your friends or review them instantly after shooting, a digital camera is almost certainly best for you. If, on the other hand, creating fine prints or producing transparencies for slide shows is your primary intention, and instant results are not really required, an analog camera may be more suitable.

Remember the argument about rapid shooting. If sports action sequences are your forte, you'll need to shoot several frames per second. Should ski or wildlife photography be amongst your chief interests, these sequences may have to last several seconds. Make sure any camera you invest in (digital or analog) is up to the task.

Consider a digital's battery requirements. The weight you'll save by not having to carry film can be easily lost by having to lug around extra batteries. Rechargers are likely to be useless if long forays into the mountains are planned; that is, unless you're planning to carry a solar panel or some other device to power one.

If you're cost sensitive more than anything else, a digital camera will be well worth looking at. Although you might have to pay more for a camera body and digital accessories at the time of initial purchase, think of the money you'll save in the long run by not having to continually cover the cost of new film and processing.

These are relatively straightforward scenarios. But what if, like many of us, you want to create beautiful images that are both suitable for slide shows and also easily deliverable over the Internet or to your web page? Again, you need to sort out the pros and cons of each option and think about the arguments presented above. In the end, though, your best answer might well be to invest in a good analog camera.

Why? Ask any computer savvy photographer how easy and cost effective it is now to convert existing analog images, in both print and transparency forms, into digital files. The new scanners, such as Nikon's Coolscan 5000 ED transparency scanner (currently retailing at around $1,500 USD), used for scanning the photos in this book , can do comparable work to that performed by quarter-million-dollar drum scanners 10 years ago. Three hundred dollars can buy you a print scanner that will deliver really phenomenal results.

Of course, you don't even need to have this technology at home or office in order to make the conversion. Most film labs, for a reasonable fee, will transfer your analog images to CD or disk at the time of processing. If not, it's generally easy to find someone to do so after prints or transparencies are created.

The point is that it's possible to have your cake and eat it too;as long, that is, as you're willing to wait for the inevitable processing and then conversion. If you're not, and you want to see results sooner, why not go digital? You'll have the company of many shooters in the reporting field who need to deliver just-in-time images to their news desks, as well as a growing number of other professionals across the photography spectrum.

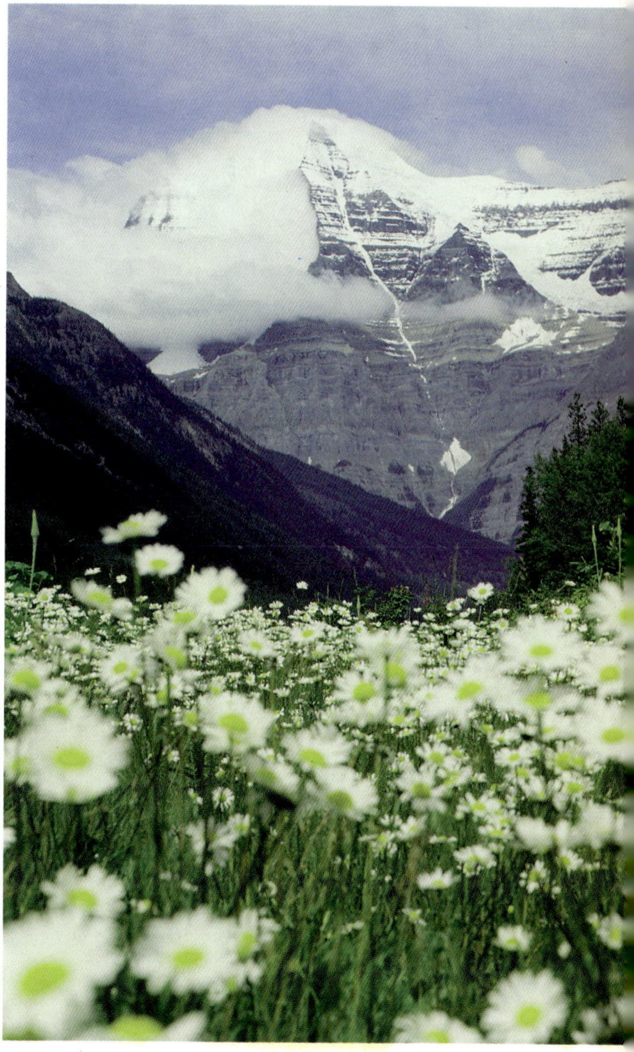

Mountain scenery is best shot on analog film and then scanned into digital form, unless your digital camera produces extremely good resolution. Mount Robson, Canadian Rockies. Fuji Velvia, 35 mm lens.

Size Matters

Ask anyone who's climbed a big peak to carry out a commercial photo or film shoot: it's really a pain to carry too much—or excessively large—camera equipment, at least without the help of a dozen porters.

And the story is really the same for any of us mountain travellers, even though we might only be of the day–outing variety. Dragging along cameras that are inordinately big and heavy simply doesn't make any sense.

That being said, it is certainly possible to err in the opposite direction. You should never expect to get the same quality of results from a tiny point–and–shoot camera as from a larger single–lens reflex, especially one that has been outfitted with particularly fine lenses.

Likewise, cameras using small film formats, such as 110 or ABS, will simply not give you as good pictures as large and medium format cameras will. This is why the larger—and more expensive—equipment continues to be sold to serious amateur and professional photographers.

However, the contrasts between formats have often been seriously overstated. Unless your intention is to create very large prints from your work, you will probably never see the difference between a photo created on 35 mm film and one shot with a 6x7 camera. Even while using ABS film (with its substantially smaller negative), you might not see a substantial quality loss, by comparison to larger formats, until your prints reach 5x7 size or bigger.

My personal view is that the 35 mm format is pretty hard to beat, particularly while shooting most mountain subjects. Even for those who plan on doing most of their photographic work while hanging on the end of a rope, or climbing to the highest summits, 35 mm cameras make good sense, since they can be remarkably small and yet produce high–quality results.

Obviously my opinion is not an exceptional one; the vast majority of new analog cameras are still created in a 35 mm format. This means that the lion's share of accessories and film types, manufactured by any of the large camera companies, will continue to be geared to it. ABS and medium formats, by contrast, lack an expansive array of add-ons. Hence, users might sometimes feel limited by the available selection.

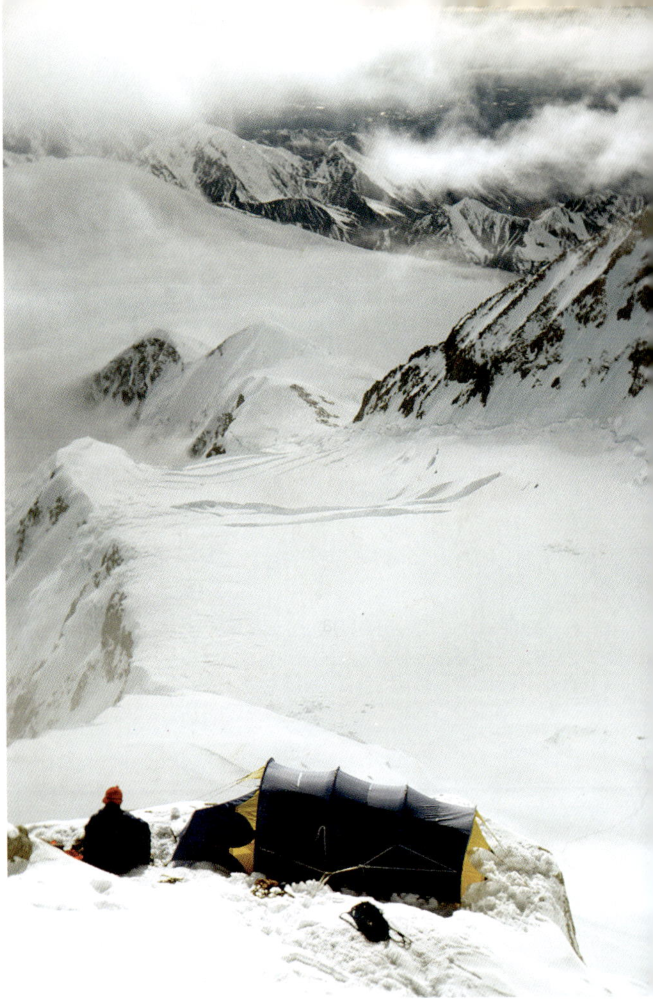

Pat Morrow took this photo with a little Rollei point-and-shoot. Such cameras are particularly well suited to ultralight expeditions and vertical wall climbs.

One of the reasons the 35 mm format has not lost its popularity since it was first introduced as an offshoot of the movie industry early in the 20th century, is because of the dramatic color and resolution improvements of its film medium through time. Modern 35 mm films probably produce better quality results than were possible in medium formats 30 years ago.

Another reason is that it's something of a standard within the photographic industry. It would be quite unthinkable to re-create the home slide show with either a larger or smaller transparency format, for example. Likewise, processing labs, most of which currently offer relatively low–cost and speedy 35 mm photofinishing, would find a large–scale transition to any other format difficult, probably resulting in reduced services to us, their customers.

Digital Camera Essentials

As with traditional analog cameras, the challenge while shopping for just the right digital camera for mountain use is to find something that is neither overly cumbersome, nor limited through tininess.

A 3 megapixel camera is, at the very least, what you'll need to record decent digital images. I reccommend a 4 megapixel camera if you can afford it, especially if your'e hoping to produce good quality 8x10 or 11x14 prints from favourite shots. or have you pictures published in books or magazines.

An optical zoom is much better than a digital one. An optical zoom enlarges the image before it reaches the sensor, while digital zooms just interpolate the middle part of the sensor's image to mimic the zoom effect.

Check battery requirements. In practice you'll want to record at least 250 images before having to change batteries. This is particularly important if you plan to venture into places where this might be difficult to do.

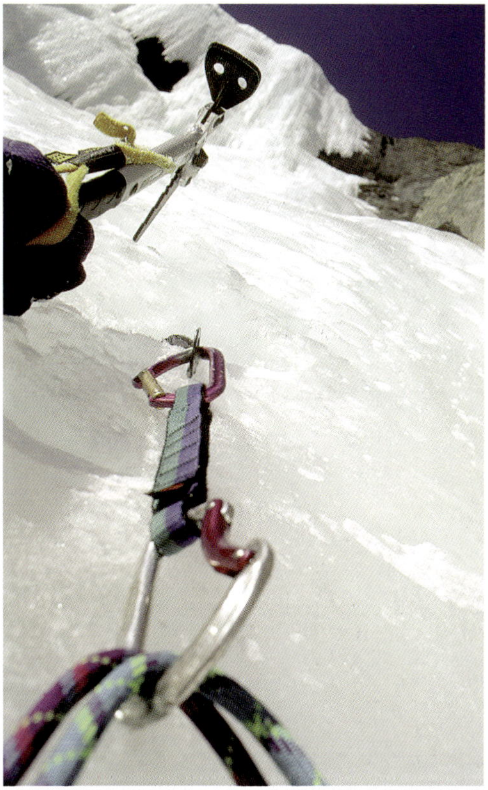

With a camera always close at hand, you can record great point of view shots such as this one. Spray Falls, Canadian Rockies. Fuji Velvia, 20 mm lens.

For the lightest of mountain outings, small cameras are often indispensable. Garibaldi Lake, Coast mountains, Canada. Kodachrome, 35-70 mm lens.

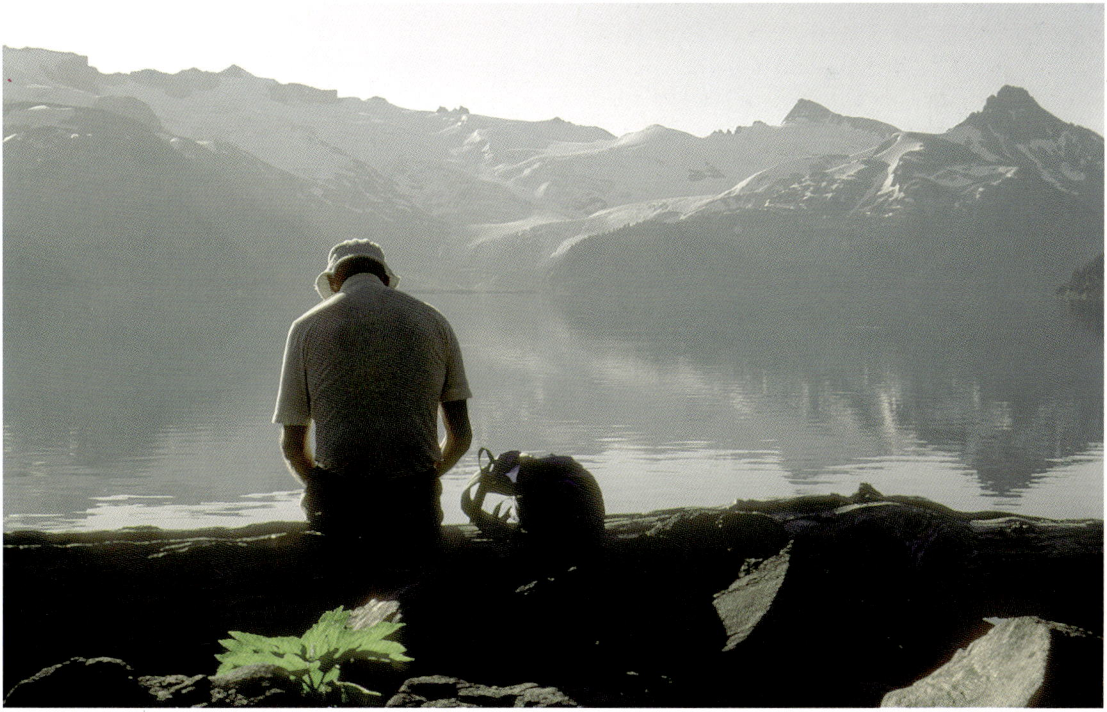

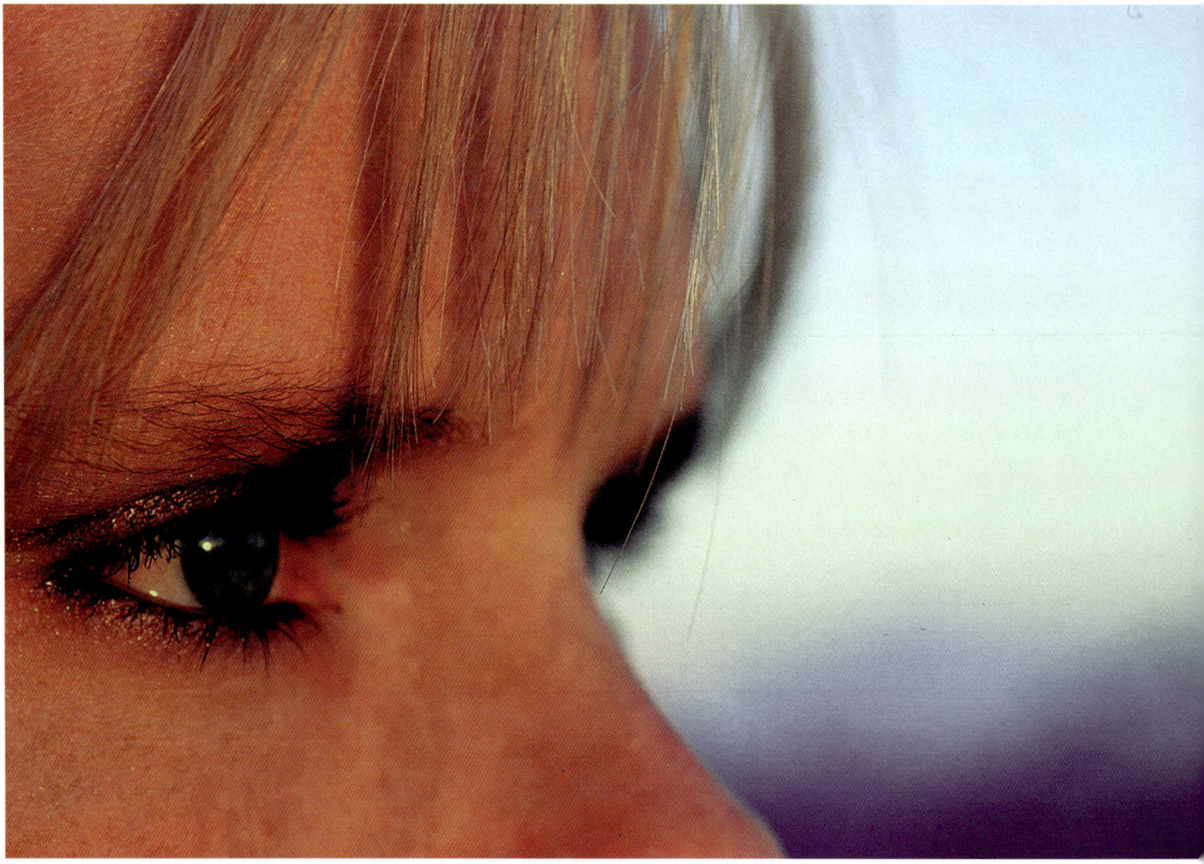

While shooting really close views such as this one, parallax error becomes problematic with a rangefinder camera, but not with an SLR. Coast mountains, Canada. Kodak Ektachrome, 55 mm macro lens.

Single-Lens Reflex (SLR) or Rangefinder?

At one time all cameras were rangefinders, meaning that it was not possible to view directly through the camera lens. Early Leica models, for example, some of which are still in use today, were built as rangefinder cameras.

The comparatively recent advent of single-lens reflex technology revolutionized 35 mm photography, and, to a lesser extent, medium format photography as well. SLRs soon became the most popular type of camera on the market, which indeed they remain to this day.

SLR cameras use a series of ingeniously placed mirrors, which flip up when the camera shutter is released, to permit the user to look directly through any camera lens. This gives them three obvious advantages over rangefinder cameras. First, they allow faster focusing. Second, they permit depth of field preview. Third, they overcome a problem known as "parallax error" —the difference between what you see through the viewfinder and what you get on film—which occurs at short focusing distances no matter how close the viewfinder and lens are placed together.

The issue of focusing used to be the paramount one. Early rangefinder models made focusing something of a guessing, or manual measurement, game. At close range, camera–to–subject distances often could not be precisely determined; hence, depth of field ranges would have to be widened to ensure that subjects would be in focus at all.

Recent rangefinder technology has made improvements in this regard. However, I doubt that any rangefinder camera could match the focusing speed and accuracy of most SLR cameras.

More important now are issues of depth of field preview and parallax error. Both crop up routinely while shooting in the mountains, or anywhere else for that matter.

Nonetheless, for the true camera connoisseur there remains a subtle quality difference in favor of rangefinder cameras. This is perhaps why they are still made. An SLR's internal mirrors can introduce tiny amounts of light when the camera shutter is released, even though these mirrors flip up out of the line of view. Such internal light will degrade image quality, if only slightly.

Probably the bigger plus for rangefinders has to do with their quietness. Relative to SLRs, their shutter mechanisms operate with barely discernible "clicks", as there are no mirror movements. This can be a big plus while photographing wildlife which may be spooked by any excessive noise. It can also be advantageous while taking candid snaps of people in remote mountain villages.

The continued popularity of SLRs, though, owes to the belief that their benefits greatly outweigh their disadvantages. Only a handful of photographers would argue differently. Most references to cameras in this book will thus concern SLRs. If you're shooting with a rangefinder camera, you may want to keep this in mind and make mental adjustments as necessary.

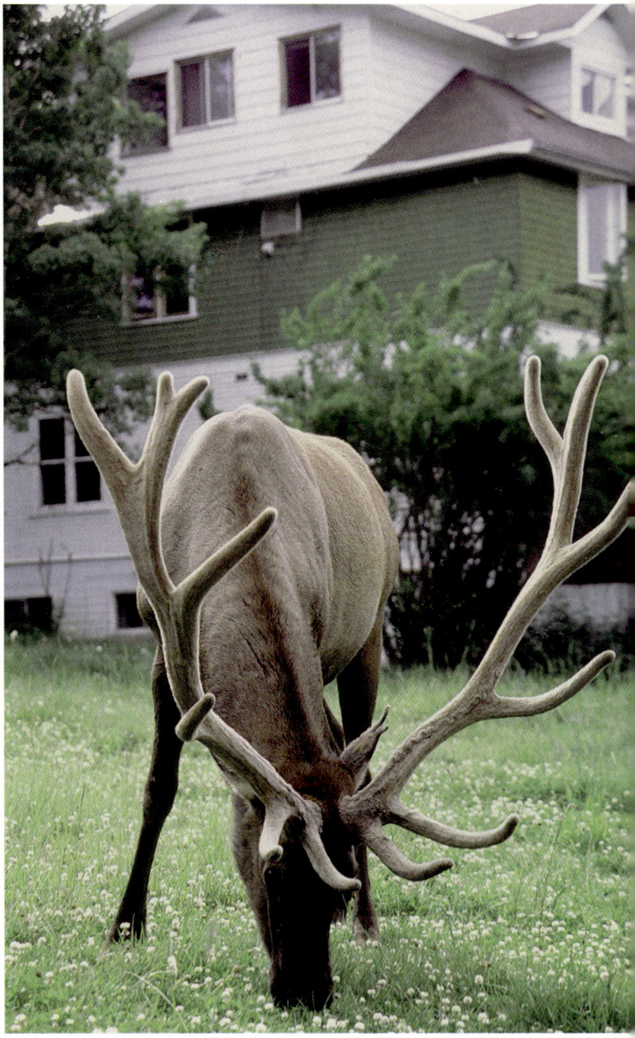

Using a rangefinder allowed me to get several shots of this bull elk without spooking him, or even alerting him to my presence. Banff, Canada. Fuji Velvia, 85 mm lens.

How Automatic Should Your Camera Be?

Photography never comes easier than with a simple point-and-shoot camera. Mountain travel certainly presents great moments for using them too, such as quickly grabbing a candid snap of a woebegone companion, or when trying to catch a fleeting moment of really intense action.

If your intent is to record all of your mountain experiences on film, it probably makes sense to keep a small, and easily accessible, point–and–shoot camera on you at all times. There's no better way to guarantee a good cross-section of results.

The key to this strategy, however, is your camera's accessibility. If you keep it buried somewhere in your rucksack, any camera will be of little use when required immediately. So it's important to devise a system of carrying the camera—a pocket dedicated to the task, for example, or a strap you can hang it from, that always keeps it within easy reach.

Small, fully automatic cameras come in either 35 mm, ABS, or smaller film formats. I would recommend sticking with the 35 mm size, not just because your resulting images will tend to be of slightly better quality, but also because more labs will be able to process your film. If your choice is digital, a point–and–shoot with a resolution of 3.2 million pixels per frame or more should create pictures that satisfy most users.

For truly creative photography, however, point-and-shoot cameras are prone to several shortcomings. Although many have zoom lenses, the range of these will always be fairly limited. Sooner or later you'll wish for either wider or longer settings. Unfortunately, in almost all cases the lenses are fixed to the camera body, which means you can't make substitutions.

The existing selection of accessories is also generally limited. Their lens barrel size is normally too small for attaching the filters and hoods created for larger SLR lenses. Quite often they lack a cable release screw mount and other desirable attributes.

An autofocus camera resulted in this "completely defocused" result. Autofocus cameras, or settings, are usually incapable of doing their job properly in very low light conditions. Canadian Rockies, Kodak E100VS, 28 mm lens.

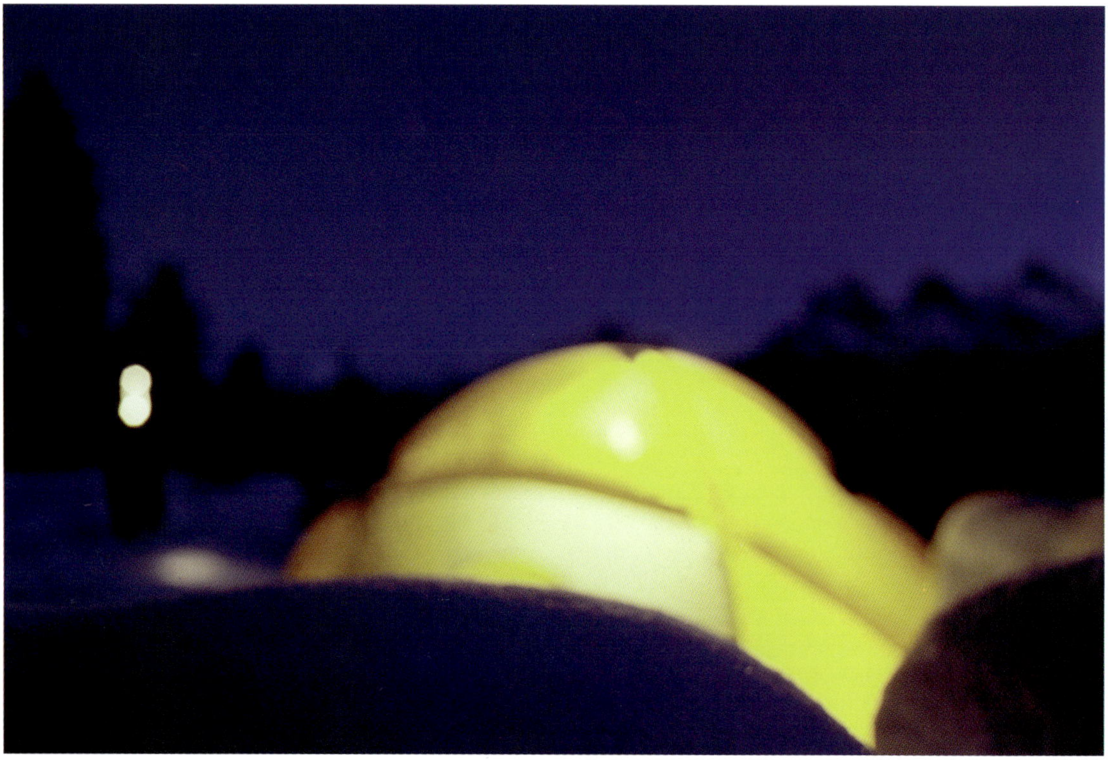

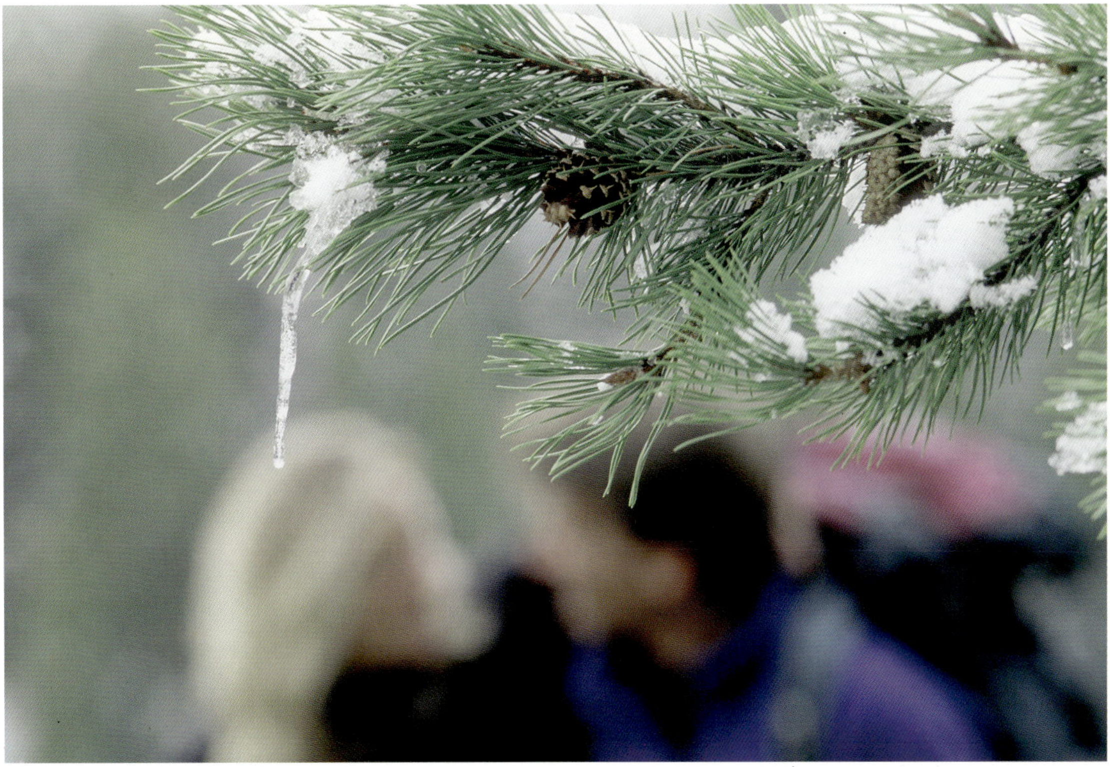

Some point–and–shoot cameras restrict your ability to focus creatively. Look for one with a manual override setting for those creative moments. Canadian Rockies, Fuji Velvia, 105 mm lens.

Two further setbacks come to mind. The first, discussed in the previous section, has to do with the quality of images they produce. This is not as important as many people make it out to be, mainly because point-and-shoot lenses have improved dramatically in recent years. But, if you're thinking of creating large prints from your negatives, transparencies or digital files, the quality issue will have some relevance.

The other rather irritating characteristic of many point-and-shoot cameras has to do with speed. Their electronics just work too slowly sometimes to allow the user to instantly stop motion the split second the shutter is released.

This seems to be caused by attempts to eliminate "red eye", a problem caused by placing the camera flash too close to the lens. Several point-and-shoot manufacturers have deduced that the way to get around "red eye" is to use an initial flash to constrict eye pupils, which inadvertently delays the shutter release. Somehow this delay often shows up during daytime photography too, even when the flash is not functioning.

The best way to get around the speed issue is, of course, to shop for a camera that is simply fast enough. With a little hunting, it shouldn't be too hard.

Bear in mind while shopping that an automatic SLR with removable lenses may be only a little larger than a point-and-shoot, and so still be convenient enough for mountain travel. There are several great chest harnesses on the market these days to help carry them in the mountains, so that they're always handy when you need them most. The somewhat larger size of these cameras might be more than compensated for by the extra creative options they allow.

Or, if you have the budget, consider buying both a point-and-shoot, which you can take along whenever you head out to the mountains, and also a larger SLR for specific photo outings. You can always add lenses and accessories to the latter as time goes by or as your skills evolve.

Good Mountain Camera Features

Any camera you purchase should—like most other items of personal equipment—feel right to you. By "feel" I mean it should fit nicely and securely in your hand.

The inherent dangers of mountain travel demand good handling characteristics; maintaining a firm grip can help to avoid dropping a camera from considerable height, especially if the neck strap is used improperly. Some cameras just make a better personal fit than others.

Along with being of suitable size and feel, your camera should be sturdy. No matter how carefully you stow it away, how hard you try to keep it from brushing against rocks or how much you protect it from rain and snow, chances are it will be subject to a good deal of abuse.

Given the choice between a camera loaded with bells and whistles and one that has fewer functions but a rock solid body, I would always opt for the latter. Having a really tough camera may make all the difference between getting great shots and not, especially on longer trips where a simple breakdown can mean disaster. You'll likely get many years of trouble-free service out of it, too, meaning lower maintenance costs and fewer hassles even when warranties would have you think otherwise.

In any event, several of the functions packed inside many modern cameras, both SLR and point-and-shoot varieties, simply don't make sense for mountain photographers. Some of these functions are intended for indoor and studio operation. Others probably wouldn't make sense regardless of what, or where, you are shooting.

As with any mechanical device, the more gimmicks there are on board, the greater the likelihood is of breakdown. Without a doubt, new electronic cameras are more prone to problems than are older manual cameras.

Modern cameras consume far greater amounts of power, which means that batteries need to be replaced more often and spare batteries carried on longer trips. Avoid cameras with proprietary rechargeable batteries if you plan to be away from civilization for extended periods.

Most new cameras don't work at all without adequate battery power. Many older ones did, albeit at a limited number of settings. An old Nikon F2 can be a real lifesaver if you have to shoot in really tough conditions. By no means am I suggesting that you should go out and buy an old camera versus something newer. Many up-to-date camera functions are actually very useful. But you need to know which ones, as well as the ones to skip.

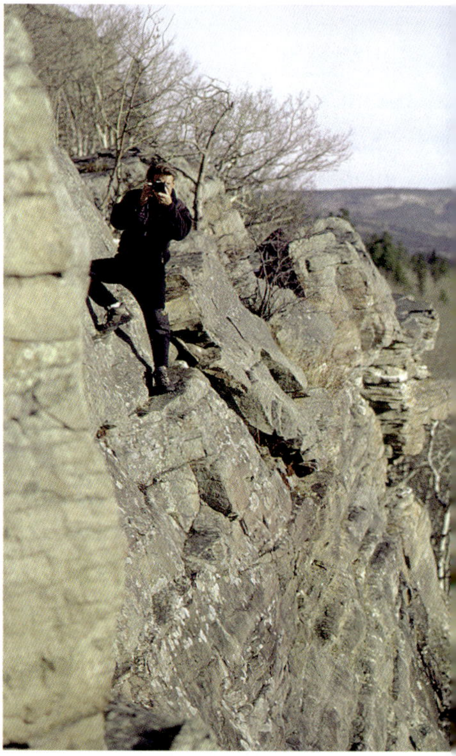

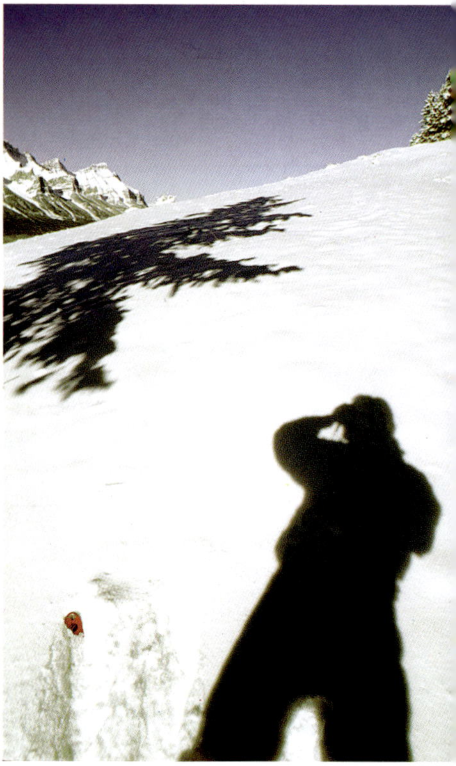

Top: Every camera has a certain physical "feel", in much the same way a pair of boots or ice axe will. Finding the right fit may be very important while shooting in precipitous terrain. Canadian Rockies, Kodak E100VS, 35 mm lens.

Bottom: Simpler cameras rarely break down in cold weather and have far fewer battery requirements. Canadian Rockies, Kodak E100VS, 20 mm lens.

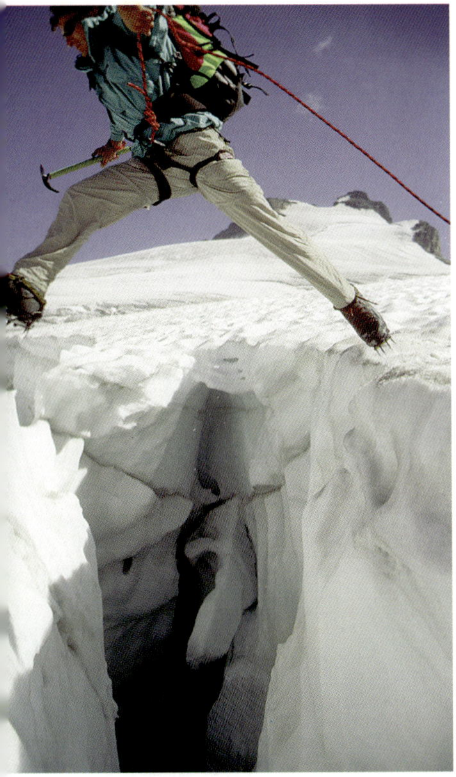

A motor winder is essential for recording the best action, at the precise moment it occurs. Even the fastest fingers can't begin to keep pace with a mechanized winder. Banff National Park, Canada. Fuji Velvia, 35-70 mm zoom lens.

Not-to-be-missed Functions

Here are some not-to-be-missed camera functions for creative photography. Your selection will no doubt vary and will likely expand as your skill level increases or your interests change.

- A tripod socket and cable release attachment. Many electronic cameras now come with electronic releases, instead of the old cable. This is fine, but make sure that the electronic release has a long enough range, so that you can stand away from the camera and still trigger it with ease. Also, make sure you carry a spare set of batteries for the release.
- A self-timer can be useful in two ways. It allows you to join your companions, or to simply stand alone, in a composition before the shutter goes off. It can also be used as a replacement for a cable release should you forget yours at home, or if your electronic one runs out of battery power.
- A depth of field preview button. More will be said of this later. It allows you to see what elements of your composition will be kept in focus and which ones won't. You can judge this for yourself by looking at the relevant marks on your camera lens, but the depth of field preview offers a quick and easy method by comparison.
- A bracketing dial, or at least some easy method of bracketing. Again, more will be said of bracketing in a later chapter. Since you often don't want to be slow while trying to bracket a scene, the bracketing mechanism on a good camera should be easy to reach and quick to employ.
- A plug–in for a remote flash, in case you want to attach a flash, by cable, to your camera from a distant position. This can be a useful approach to nighttime or low light photography.
- If your intention is to do lots of night photography, and you plan to use a SLR camera while doing so, a device for locking up the camera's mirror assembly is fairly important. Without one, you might record blurriness from mirror vibration, no matter how sturdy your tripod is.

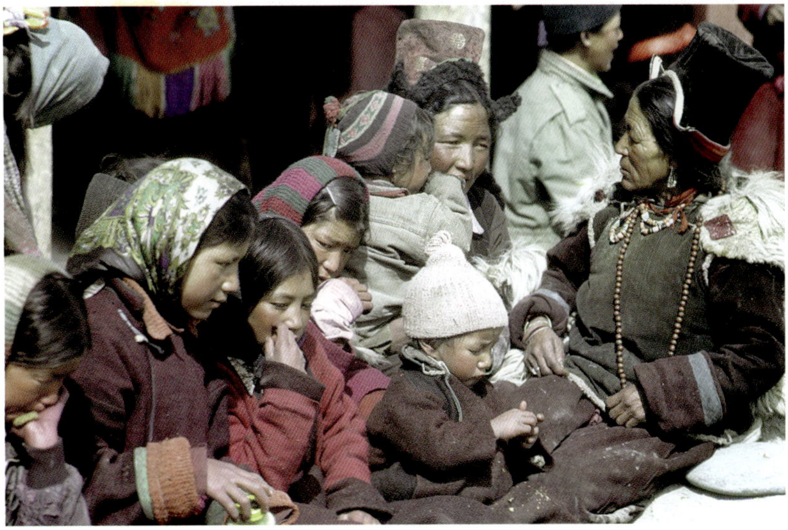

Some cameras allow you to remove the top viewing mirror so that you can compose shots while looking down. This feature can be invaluable in some travel situations. Picture taking was forbidden at this festival, but I ventured a few snaps with my camera's viewfinder removed. Nobody noticed me because my head remained bowed. Stok Monastery, Ladakh, India. Kodachrome, 85 mm lens.

Accessories

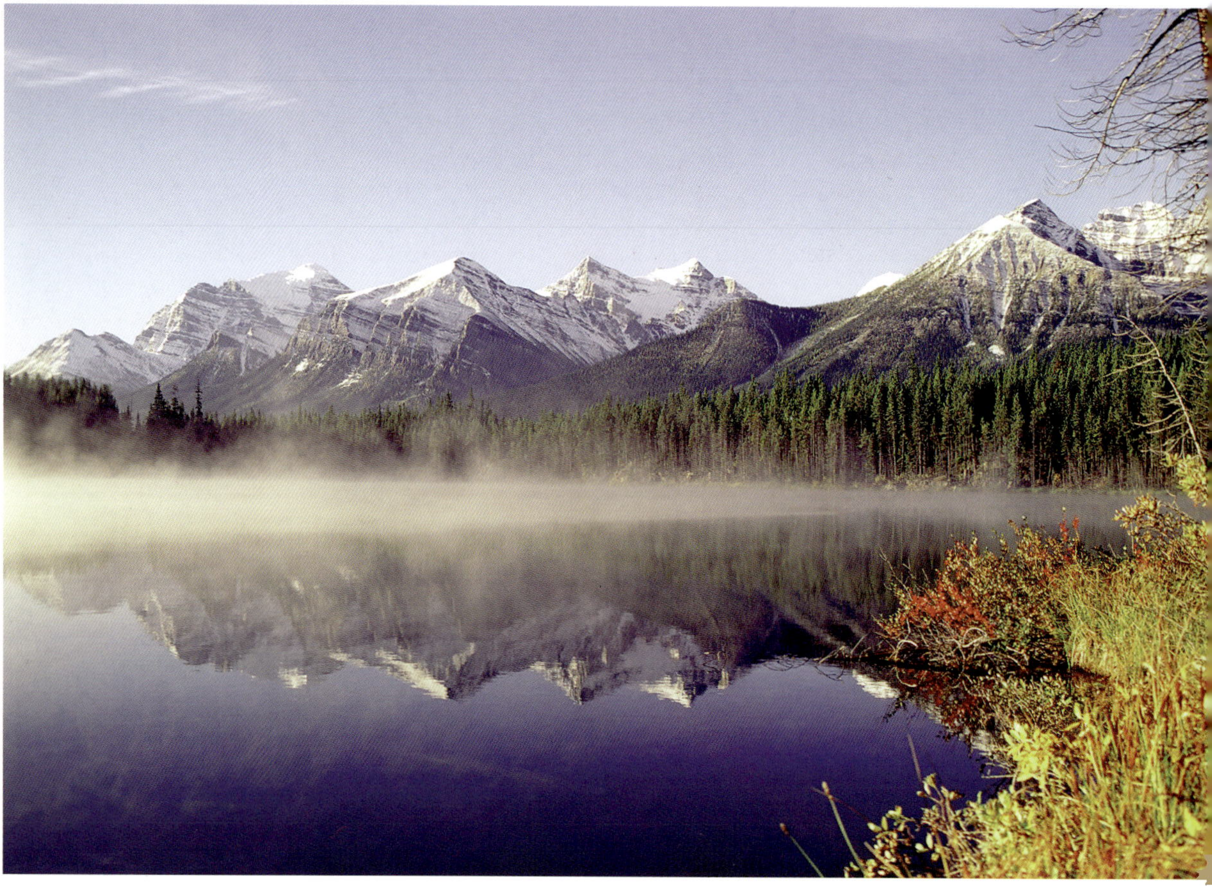

Shopping for Lenses

Like cameras, there's a huge choice of lenses on the market these days, especially for 35 mm SLR cameras (and their digital equivalents). Before buying one or more, it's again important to think carefully about your current photography interests and perhaps any new subject matter you'd like to work with as well.

For example, if you think you might want to try shooting wildflowers close-up, make sure any lens you buy has a macro capability that will allow you to focus at very close range. If, on the other hand, high-speed sporting activities intrigue you, consider buying a lens with a wider maximum aperture that will allow you to shoot at faster speeds in low light conditions.

Both of these choices will cost you more than if you simply buy the standard versions of each lens. Sometimes the comparable price will be double, or even triple. Knowing that you will probably upgrade in the future, you would be better off making a heftier up-front investment rather than spending money on a less useful lens.

It is easy to go overboard with this way of thinking though. The photographer who buys a 1000 mm lens for 35 mm camera equipment to occasionally shoot a moonrise behind mountains needs to consider whether the investment is really worthwhile. So too does someone who buys a 15 mm wide angle for the odd extreme panorama view.

These somewhat obscure lens choices—at the extreme ends of the focal length spectrum—are also incredibly expensive ones. It's unlikely that such equipment will be called into use very often. When they are, it is almost always better to hunt out a place to rent them for a day or two.

Think carefully before buying any particularly expensive lens when one of slightly inferior quality, from the same manufacturer, costs half as much, or less. Nikon, for example, for years has marketed three grades of 35 mm lenses: the E series, at the bottom of the heap; the R series, a step up; and the ED series, their very best ones.

Although the difference in price between the lower two grades is not great, probably making the R lenses a generally better investment overall, the ED lenses tend to be comparably far more expensive. Moreover, their somewhat improved optical features typically add extra weight and size to each lens, making them less suitable for mountain travel.

If you do want the very best lenses money can buy, or ones in the most expensive categories, and your budget simply doesn't allow for new ones, consider buying them used. Most reputable used camera dealers do thorough technical checks before listing used equipment and extend a free trial period for you to test any piece that you buy. It's very unlikely that any such tested lens will break down soon after the trial period—unless subjected to the most extreme mountain "stresses", of course.

These two shots were taken at nearly the same time. One was shot with a 20 mm lens, the other with a 28 mm lens. Although exposures stayed the same, one appears brighter than the other, mainly because of additional dark areas included by the wider lens.
Banff National Park, Canada. Fuji Velvia, 20 and 28 mm lenses.

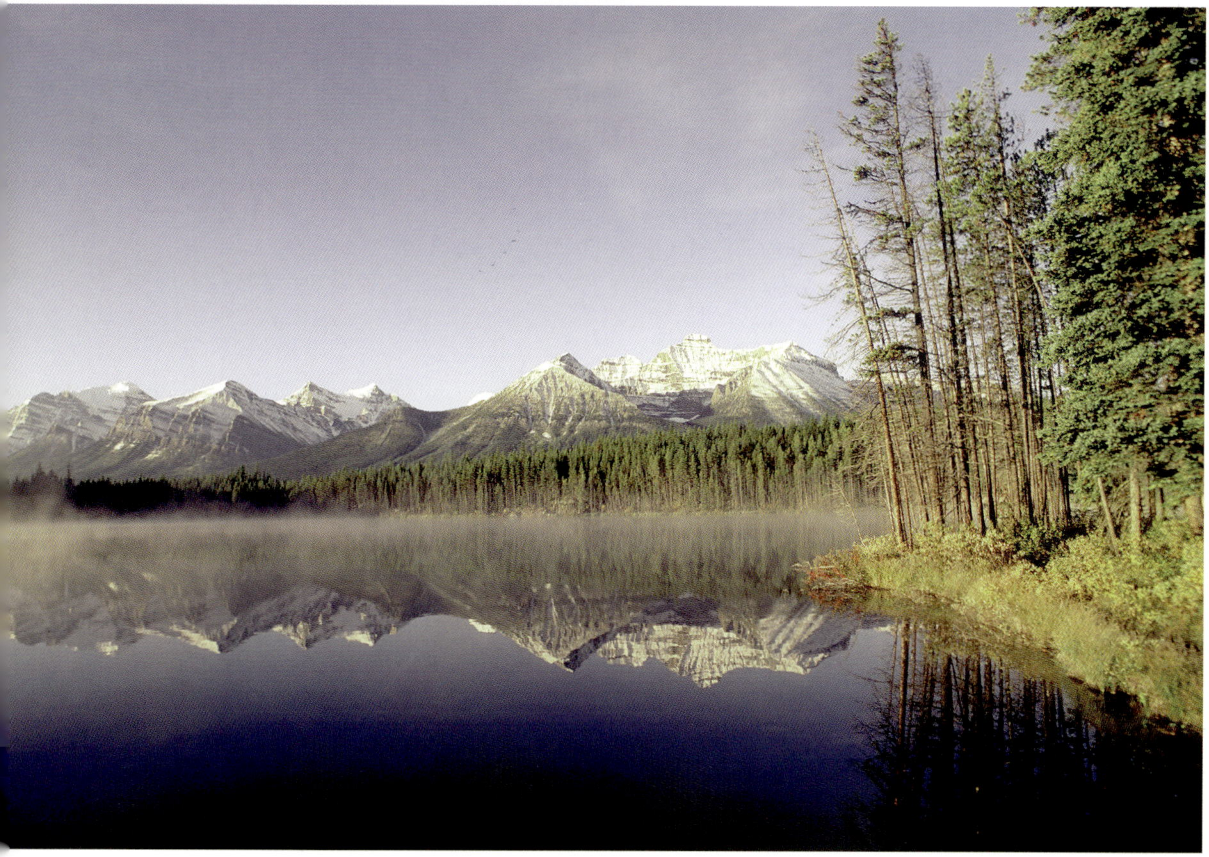

Zoom or No Zoom?

There was a time, 15 or 20 years ago, when zoom lenses were all noticeably inferior in quality to fixed focal length lenses. This is really no longer the case. Unless you're pointing your camera directly into the sun, in which case the extra lens elements of a zoom lens will likely exaggerate lens flare, it has become very difficult to spot any significant quality differences between the two types of lenses.

The biggest downside to zoom lenses probably has to do with the way they're used. Although designed to allow a virtually unlimited choice of focal lengths within a particular range, many zoom lens users tend to shoot at either the highest or lowest focal lengths only (according to manufacturers and industry experts alike). So, with a 70-200 mm zoom lens, for example, the 70 or 200 setting might be chosen—but little, if anything, in between.

This is a shame, for it misses the point entirely. Zoom settings are most useful when geared to a chosen scene, and not the other way around.

Of course, it's not hard to correct this tendency and get the most out of any zoom lens you acquire. Simply compose a scene, mentally, before you even get the camera out of its bag. Then move your zoom lens dial to where it matches your visualized composition.

Once you've jumped this small hurdle, your zoom lens(es) become a nearly indispensable photography tool. Several photographers I know use them exclusively in their photography work.

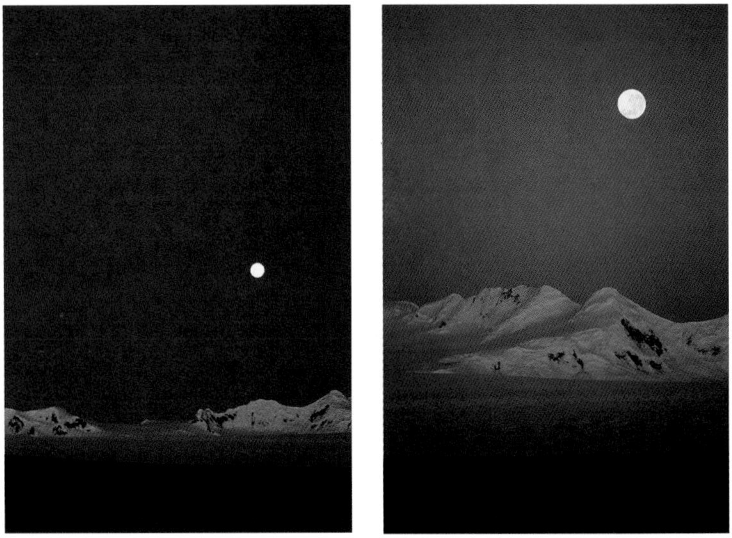

A long zoom lens accounted for both of these shots. The first frame was taken at the zoom's minimum setting, then the camera was turned vertically and shot at the maximum setting. Patagonia Icecap, Argentina. Kodachrome, 35-200 mm zoom lens.

Eliminating the need to change lenses is of particular advantage while photographing in the mountains. If you are climbing, skiing, or even hiking, it's easy to appreciate the benefit of not having to lower your camera bag, screw a new lens on and then re-hoist the bag. In fact, you'll likely end up getting more great pictures since the process of changing lenses might make you think twice about expending the effort, or potentially compromising group safety.

If you can get by with just one zoom lens and a few accessories, a waist or shoulder camera bag might not be necessary. This can be a big plus when you need to carry lots of mountain gear in a knapsack. Most strap-on chest camera bags, discussed in the next section, are large enough to fit typical zoom lenses; some will even accommodate large ones.

One is not always enough though, as no zoom lens has the flexibility to facilitate every composition. Sometimes you'll want a second zoom, or perhaps a fixed focal lens or two. This is particularly true if you need a fast lens, a good macro lens, or one reaching to the widest and longest ends of the lens spectrum. It would be difficult, for example, to find a zoom reaching as wide as 16 mm or one longer than 300 mm.

In fact, it's probably not worth the effort to hunt one out. If you need a really wide or long lens, say to shoot radically wide panoramas or moonscapes, you'd be better to buy them as fixed focal length lenses.

As mentioned earlier, they will certainly be expensive enough as such, particularly if they're good quality lenses. Any decent zoom lens capable of reaching the focal length extremes would be absolutely exorbitant by comparison. So don't break the bank in order to get the most distance from your zoom lens. Buy one that will cover most contingencies, and purchase a fixed lens or two to complement it if need be.

Mountain Camera Bags

It probably goes without saying that a good camera bag is absolutely essential for mountain travel. What is likely not as obvious is that its functionality will determine, to a large extent, how much you use your camera, where and when.

Practically every photographer has a personal opinion on how the best ones ought to work. This variety of opinion stems partly from different gear requirements. If encumbered with a couple of camera bodies, say, as well as several lenses and other accessories, a fairly large, comprehensive case or bag would certainly be needed. On the other hand, if travelling with just a few items of gear, a scaled down version of some sort makes far better sense.

Personal opinions are most varied about how a bag should be carried. Some people like carrying camera equipment on their backs; others prefer it in a waist pouch or harnessed to their chest. While using the really small automatic cameras, many of us would opt to just stash it in a zip pocket.

In the mountains, though, it's often the chosen activity that will dictate the kind of bag that is best. Usually a rucksack full of weather and other mountain gear needs to be carried; hence, a dedicated camera backpack will be ruled out for all but the shortest outings. Simply stashing a camera in that pack might be an option, but it would likely not work optimally if you need to access it quickly, or fetch it without adjusting your body stance.

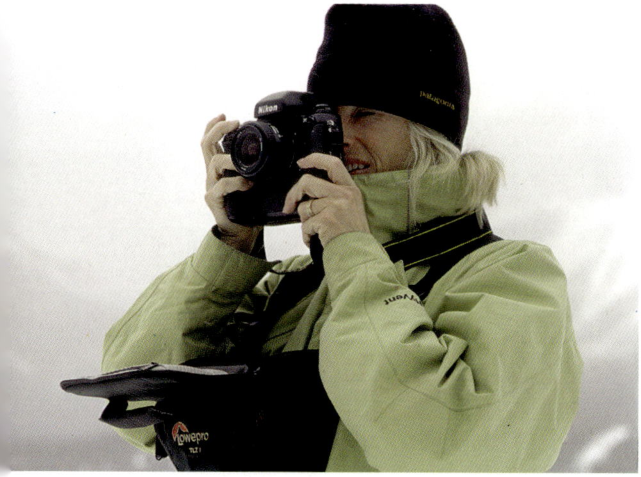

Chest bags are great while climbing or skiing, allowing easy access to your camera without altering your body position. Banff National Park, Canada. Kodak E100VS, 105 mm lens.

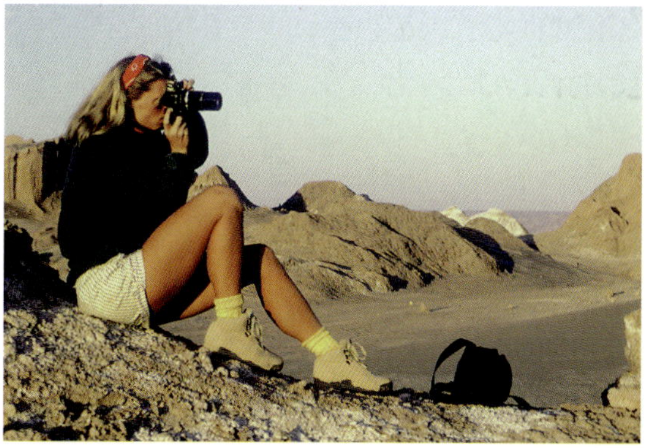

An advantage of chest camera bags is that they remain strapped to you, even while you're shooting. This way they won't collect debris or moisture as would a camera bag lying on the ground. Valley of the Moon, Chile. Kodachrome, 85 mm lens.

Similarly, a waist bag would make little sense if you need to wear a climbing harness for all or part of the time. Even if you don't, but you find yourself carrying a backpack, a waist bag would likely get in the way. You may find it downright irritating to use, in fact.

This leaves, by default, camera bags that are harnessed around the chest. For almost any mountain activity I can think of, it will likely be your best option.

The beauty of the chest bag is that it keeps your camera accessible without compromising body movement at all. Hands can quickly and deftly reach inside the main pouch, your camera remains attached to your neck with the strap at all times, and you can keep your eyes trained on a chosen subject or activity at hand and the chest bag won't interfere with climbing harnesses, backpacks, or anything else for that matter.

Most are large enough to accommodate a fairly sizeable zoom lens. Before buying any chest bag, though, it would be wise to first purchase the camera and lens combo you intend to take with you, and then shop around.

Their only downside is that they generally can't carry more than one camera body and lens. Hence, for creative outings, when you might want a couple bodies loaded with different film, and several lenses, you'll likely find chest bags a little limiting.

Just as with cameras themselves, it may make sense to have more than one bag, at least if you plan to do a lot of varied photography. One could perhaps be a larger, pack version, capable of carrying a lot of gear on dedicated photography outings. The other might be a smaller chest bag to be used on ski, climbing, or hiking trips.

Camera Bag Alternatives

A number of shooters I know use a specialized photographer's vest instead of, or in conjunction with, a camera bag. Some mountain friends use nothing at all, preferring to simply hang the camera around their necks, usually tucked inside a shirt or jacket.

Vests can certainly be useful for commercial photography assignments, when you need to grab film, filters or different lenses in a hurry. In my opinion they're not the best for most kinds of mountain travel though.

For one thing, they need to be worn on the outside of other garments to be of any use. This is fine when photographing close to, say, your car, a trailhead, or on short jaunts in warm sunny weather. But it's not so good when hiking hard, dealing with fast changing weather, or on long day or multi-day outings.

We typically add or subtract clothes often on our mountain outings. A photographer's vest is just not that well suited to being taken off, thrown aside, and then put back on. Also, it generally won't fit over cold weather garments that may need to be worn at higher altitudes or in wintry conditions, at least not without seriously constricting user motion.

Finally, these vests don't offer the same degree of protection that a padded camera bag will. Consider the rough terrain often encountered on mountain travels, especially while climbing or biking. Vests simply won't insulate gear from sudden bangs, hard scrapes, or falling objects.

For the casual hiking or sight-seeing trip, a vest might just be ideal, however. You can cram an amazing amount of gear and film into them and still not feel too weighed down. And they do allow for much faster access, say to change film or lenses, than a backpack will.

Tucking a camera inside your shirt or jacket for anything more than a few moments is, by comparison, probably never a good idea. In addition to offering little protection for your camera, the inner shirt environment tends to be a sweaty one, especially during times of exertion. More often than not your viewfinder will be steamed up and completely unusable when you retrieve your camera from inside your shirt. Your lens may quickly follow suit too, particularly when the outside environment is a good deal colder than the one close to your chest.

If anything, you may want more protection for your camera gear than that offered by a simple bag. This is particularly true while taking part in some watersport, such as canoeing or kayaking, or for travelling in wet climates (see "Hot Tropical Extremes" page 206). But it may also be a requirement if the mountain terrain you're heading into is prone to extreme dustiness, or blowing sand.

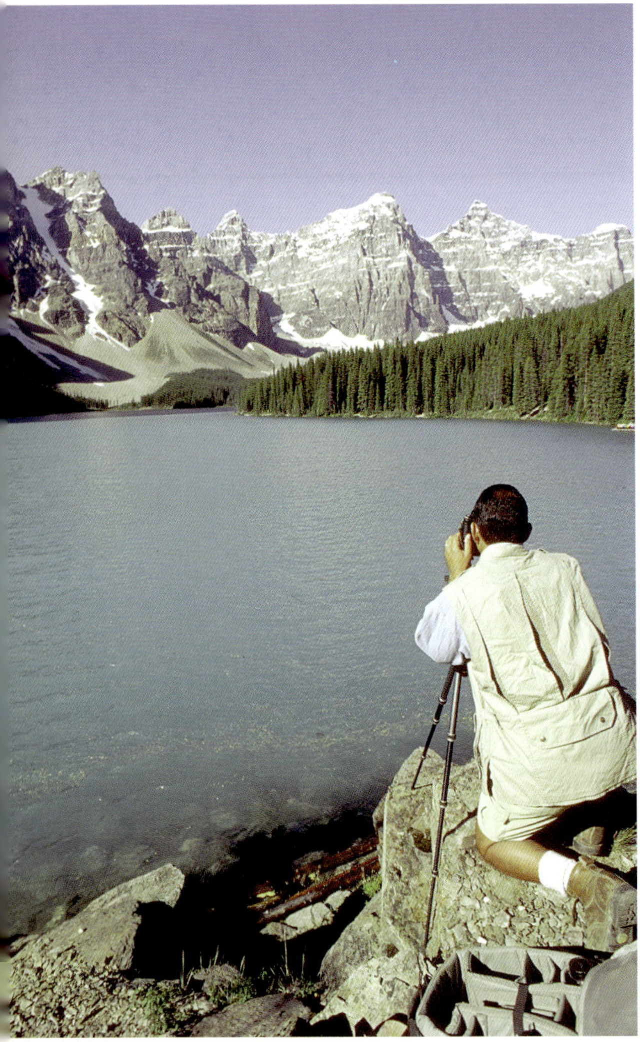

This photographer is using both a large backpack-style camera bag and a photographer's vest. Although great while shooting close to your car or a trailhead, neither are suitable for long treks into the backcountry. Moraine Lake, Banff National Park, Canada. Kodak E100VS, 28 mm lens.

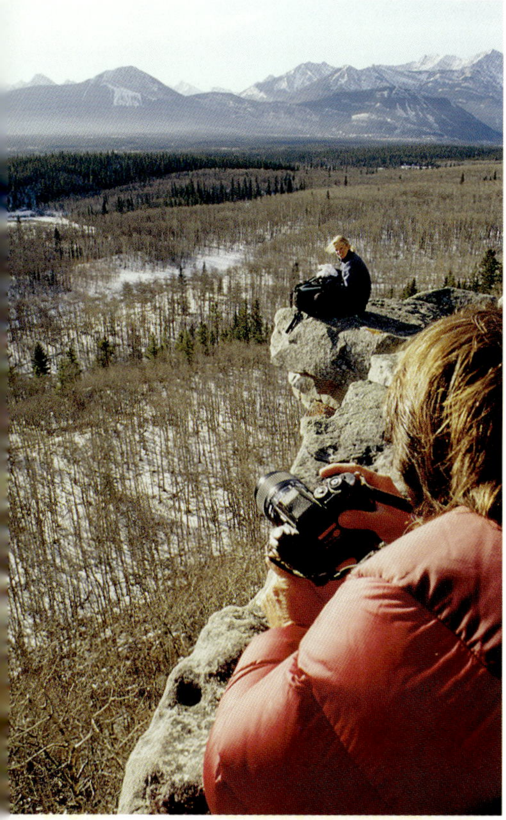

Simply tucking a camera into your jacket may be an acceptable alternative for a moment or two, especially when shuffling onto an edge or tenuous ledge to shoot from. Better still to use a chest-harnessed bag though. Canadian Rockies. Kodak E100VS, 20 mm lens, 81B filter.

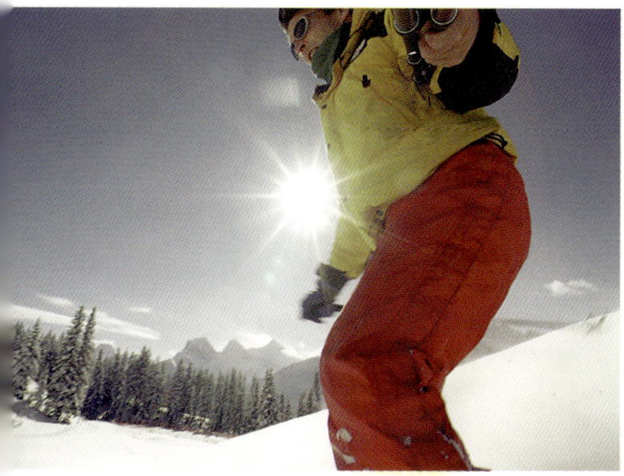

A tripod may serve more uses than that of a static stand. Here the author is employing a lightweight one as an arm extension in a moving camera set-up. If the camera had been pointed a little lower, boots and flying snow would have been captured and the tripod wouldn't have been visible. Banff National Park, Canada. Kodak E100VS, 20 mm lens.

If you are planning any such trip, buy a padded waterproof case. These sealed, high-impact plastic protective containers can be found both in camera and mountain or watersport specialty shops. They will probably have to be carried in a backpack while trekking, since they generally come equipped with a handle, not carrying straps. But unless of a larger size, this requirement will likely not be too onerous for you.

Another option is to get a waterproof housing for your camera and lens combo. The best of these are light in weight and yet able to provide great protection from dampness and even total immersion in water. One downside is that they have to be completely opened for lens or film changing but, again, this may not be a particularly grave problem if your requirements are not too demanding.

Essential Accessories

A good tripod will probably be your most important accessory of all. More will be said in a later section (see "Tripods and Cable releases" page 66) on the best kinds of tripods for mountain shooting, with an emphasis on the kinds of photography you want to do. Make sure your budget allows for a decent one, even if it means cutting back on other camera costs.

Motor winders are quite essential for both sports action and wildlife work. If the camera you've bought or are intending to buy doesn't come outfitted with one, and you're keen to photograph these types of subjects, consider buying one suited to your camera. Ideally it should be able to shoot off at least five frames per second (fps) when higher shutter speeds are selected.

Sooner or later, you'll probably want to have a decent flash as well. This should be capable of operating either on your camera, or remotely off, with a cable attachment. Look for one that has these additional features: an adjustable head, both sideways and up and down; manual and TTL settings; ASA control; filter holder; and a wide angle to telephoto adjustment.

I won't delve into the complexities of flash photography to explain these features quite yet; the importance of them will likely become evident when flash photography is discussed in more detail later on. As well as shopping for features, ensure that, like your other camera equipment, the flash is sturdily made and capable of withstanding some bashing around.

If you're planning to photograph wildlife or do self-portraiture, consider investing in a remote triggering device if your camera doesn't come with one. Although you can perhaps get by without it, say by using a self-timer or long cable release, a remote can be extremely handy in some cases. And it may help to keep things safer too, if your camera and you are separated by a precipitous gully, say, or by several meters along a knife-edged ridge.

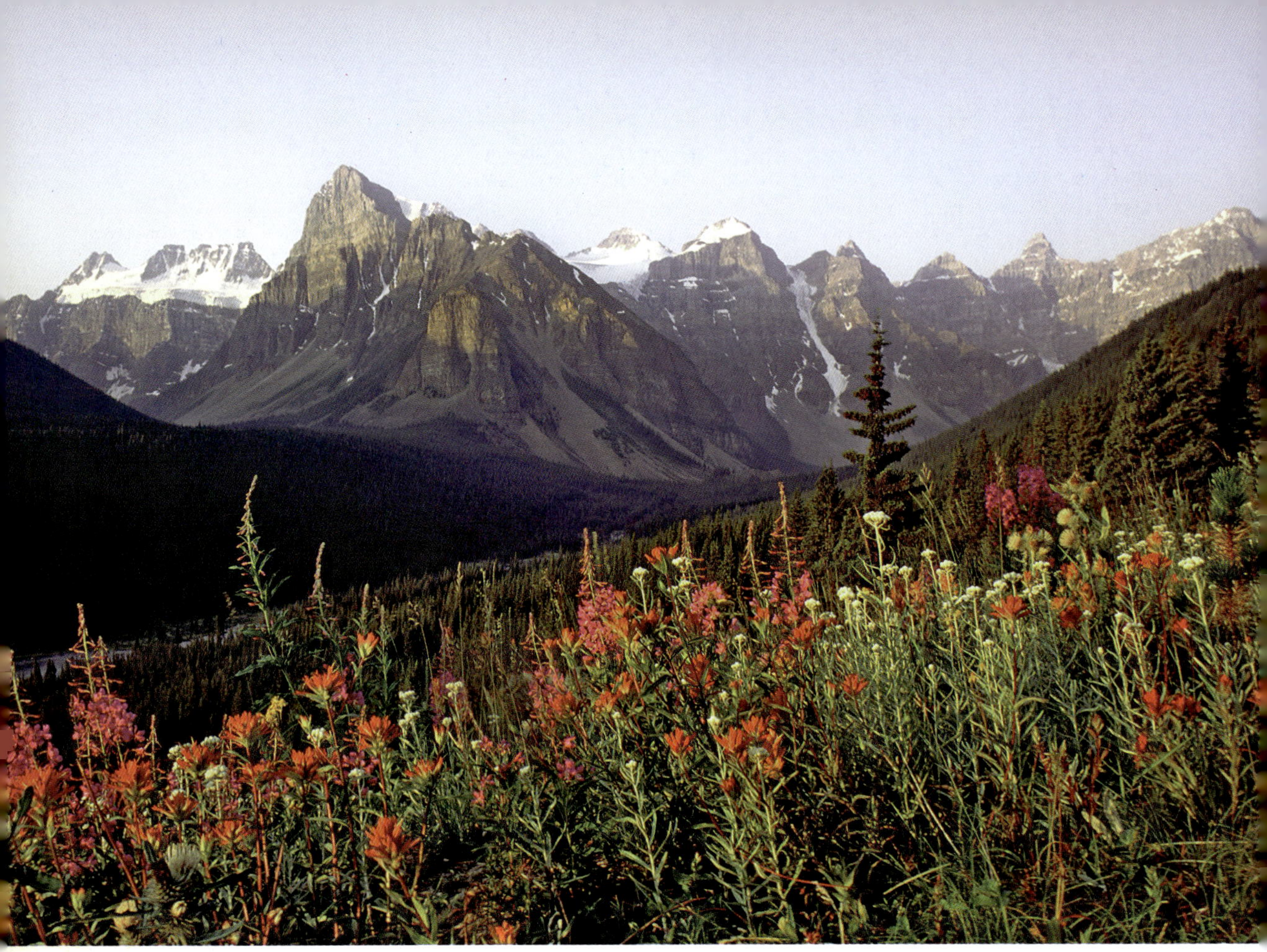

Colors simply turn out richer and more defined, when captured on better films. Canadian Rockies. Fuji Velvia, 28 mm lens.

Don't Chintz on Film!

Especially not on quality! Once you've spent good money on a camera, lenses and accessories, why go cheap on film—and hence compromise your quest for really stellar results?

Of course, if you're using a digital camera, this admonishment isn't really necessary. You've already decided upon the quality of output—by choosing a camera with a given resolution—and the difference between one brand of memory chip and another is not worth worrying about.

But for analog camera users, beware! There are better and worse film varieties you need to watch for. The color performance, grain characteristics and overall look of prints or transparencies, once you've developed them, are all factors that vary widely between films.

The best ones are the professional brands, mainly made by Kodak, Fuji, Ilford and Agfa. Often these will only be available through camera stores and professional labs.

They need not cost more than consumer varieties. Check prices for bulk-film purchase at your favorite lab or camera dealer. If it won't provide a discount of at least 10 percent for 20 or more rolls, consider shopping for film through one of the reputable camera mail-order companies.

Look for the film's ASA rating (also called the ISO rating). More will be said later, in the section entitled "Color, B&W, or…?" page 79, about which speed of film to use and when. ASA values should be printed clearly on the side of any film box, often as part of the particular brand name.

Fuji 100, for instance, denotes a 100 ASA rating; Agfa 400 a 400 ASA, and so on. At times, such as with Fuji Velvia, this number may not be too evident. When it isn't, simply check the film's fine print for the right value.

With color films—transparency or print—look also for the saturation rating of the film, or ask a knowledgeable salesperson. A very saturated film (also referred to as "vivid color" film) will deliver very rich or "saturated" color. They tend to be the best ones for most outdoor shooting, but this judgement is something of a personal one. A less saturated film, by comparison, will deliver less vibrant color but truer skin and earth tones (saturated films sometimes make skin areas look red).

Check to make sure any film you buy has not exceeded the expiration date, marked usually in faint lettering on the film box. It's not the end of the world if it has, but know that color rendition might not be the best when you process expired film.

It should, at very least, be seriously discounted by your retailer, say by 30 percent or more. I sometimes buy cheaper, outdated film for shoots where I'm cross-processing, because I anticipate color distortion in final results anyway (see later section on "Cross Processing Color Film" page 93).

The expiration date may be less critical with color films—and some B&W ones like SCALA—than how film is stored during its shelf life. Make sure any film you purchase from a professional dealer is taken from a refrigerator. If it's color infrared you are buying, it should actually be coming from a freezer.

On this note, bear in mind that you too should store your purchased film in a refrigerator or freezer (better). By doing so, you'll maintain the film's chemistry beyond its normal expiration period. If you can't actually chill the film, such as when shooting in a warm climate, try at least to protect it from extreme heat and humidity.

Contrast tolerances evident in this photo would not be nearly so pronounced if shot on an inferior film. Bow Lake, Banff National Park, Canada. Fuji Velvia, 28 mm lens.

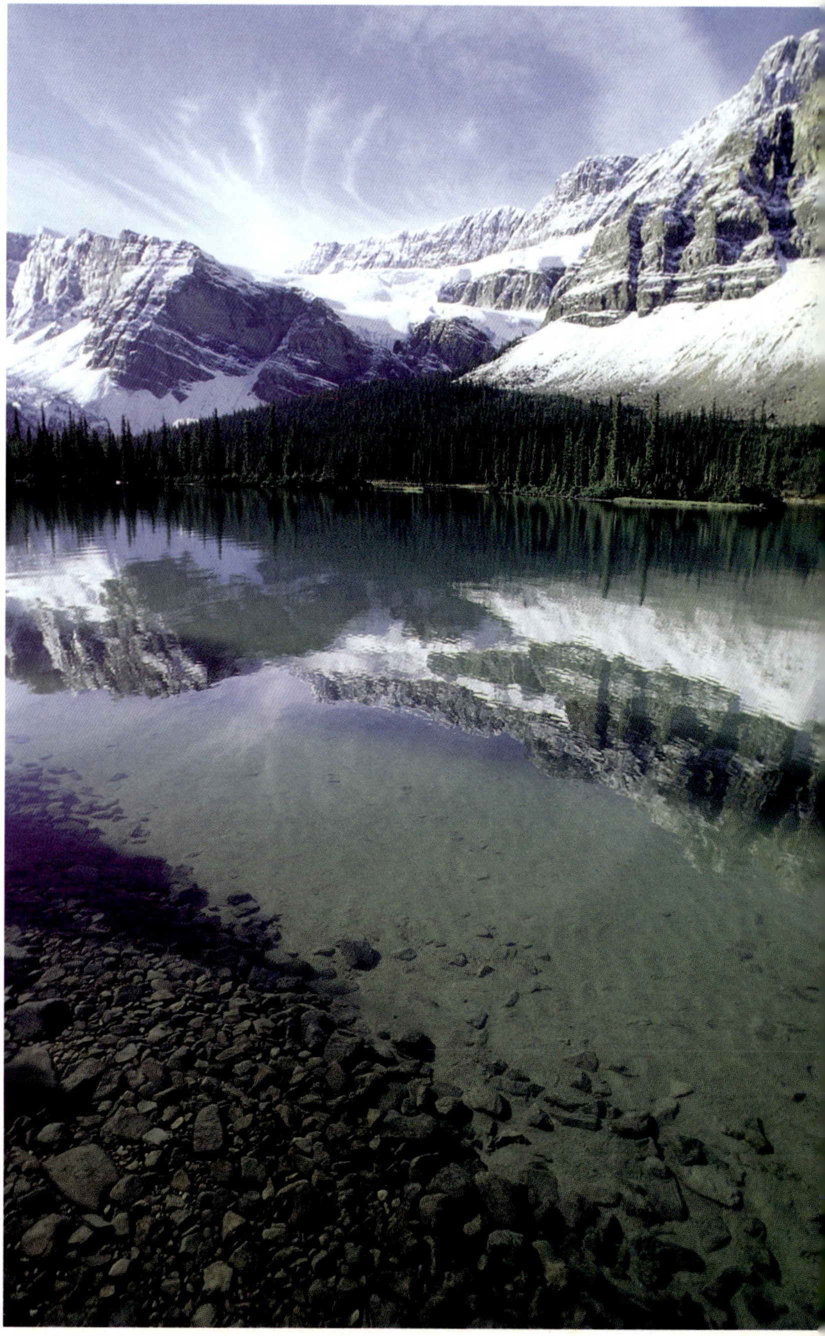

Filters to Correct Color

I would hesitate to go overboard in buying filters to use when shooting in color, especially while using digital equipment where color alteration is generally better left until after shooting. Nevertheless, there are a few useful filters for mountain photography.

These come in two different categories. The first, referred to as color conversion filters, change the color temperature of light striking film. Available in a variety of blue and amber shades, they are especially useful for trying to render acceptable color tones while using, say, tungsten lighting sources, or tungsten films (see discussion on "Tungsten Films" page 95).

Alternatively, they can be used to create a tungsten or amber effect. Blue conversion filters will render a bluish color cast, making things look colder than might be the case. They are especially effective for exaggerating wintry weather or landscapes.

Amber filters, on the other hand, enhance warmth. They're often useful for warming a scene photographed in flat, overcast light, as long as sparingly applied (with nice early morning or evening light, amber filtration is often over-the-top, and so should probably be avoided unless this is your intended effect).

Graduated amber filters do much the same, but only across one part of the field of view. They could be used, for example, to warm a sky that comprises the upper half of your frame, while not changing colors in the bottom half at all. Since filtration is graduated, the most color change will occur towards the upper frame edge.

Filters in the second category work differently. Color compensation filters, as their name implies, are intended to compensate for color deficiencies, either in film emulsions or with a light source other than mid-day sun. Filter colors range from blue, green and red through yellow, magenta and cyan, and shades vary from deep to rather subtle.

You are not likely to have much use for these particular ones, since most such compensation can be better achieved with computer software whenever it's needed. However, other compensating filters that are designed to enhance color by reducing haze and white light reflection may sometimes prove invaluable. The two best ones are polarizing and ultraviolet (UV) filters.

Polarizing filters are particularly successful at improving the look of mountain skies. If used in full light while shooting views at right angles to the sun, they will often heighten contrast enormously between blue areas and clouds. The resulting effect can be dramatic.

Be careful not to overuse them though. Too deep a blue shade will look, at very least, unnatural. This is particularly true while shooting with an extreme wide-angle lens that takes in a lot of sky. If heavily polarized,

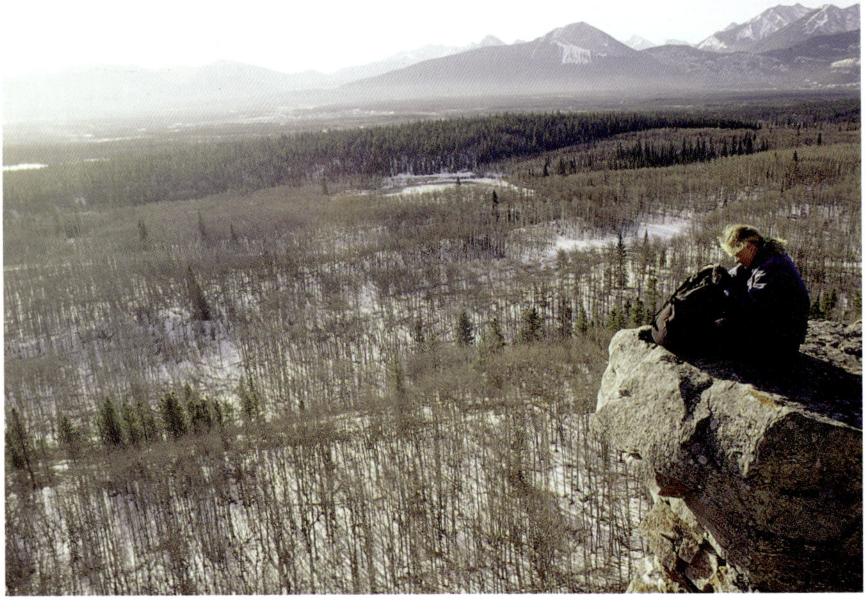

This scene, on the other hand, benefited enormously from subtle warming. The forested areas would otherwise look bluish-grey, and filtering did not really effect sky colors. Canadian Rockies. Kodak E100VS, 28 mm lens, 81B filter.

the sky will invariably range from light on one side to extremely dark on the other when there is no good reason for it to do so.

In practise, it is easy to control the extent of polarization, and hence prevent such overuse. By simply rotating the filter in either direction once it's mounted on your camera lens, you can readily observe an increasing or decreasing polarization effect.

UV filters are perhaps even more useful. They reduce the blue hazy look often noticed in the mountains, particularly at higher elevations and across distant views. They are most effective while shooting with long telephoto lenses, which compress ambient haze.

Almost any shot taken with a UV filter will be less bluish than if no filter is used, since haze has an overall blue cast. This is generally a good reason to always have one either mounted to a long lens, or at least easily accessible in your camera bag.

If your camera is not an SLR, or if you are taking light readings with an off-camera meter, pay close attention to the instructions that come with a new filter concerning ASA modifications. All filters will reduce incoming light to some extent; some much more than others. In order to get proper exposures while using filters, some modification to either the f-stop or shutter speed will be necessary.

Be aware that all color filters will render subtly different results with even fairly similar film stocks. Their effect will vary widely depending on light characteristics too, such that a certain look will be rendered under a mid-day sun and quite another earlier or later in the day. The best advice for using any is to simply experiment and make written notes if you can.

Finally, when shopping for any filter, remember to pay a few extra dollars for one that's at least the same optical calibre as the lens it's to be mounted on.

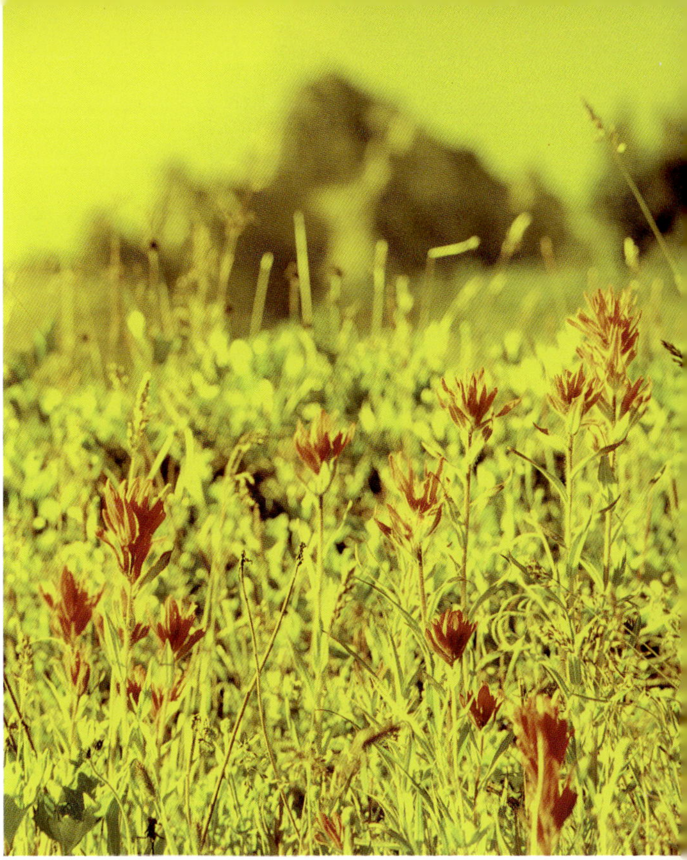

Whoops! Bad filter choice! Overwarming a scene is often a poorer option than not warming it at all. Banff National Park, Canada. Kodak E100VS, 28 mm lens.

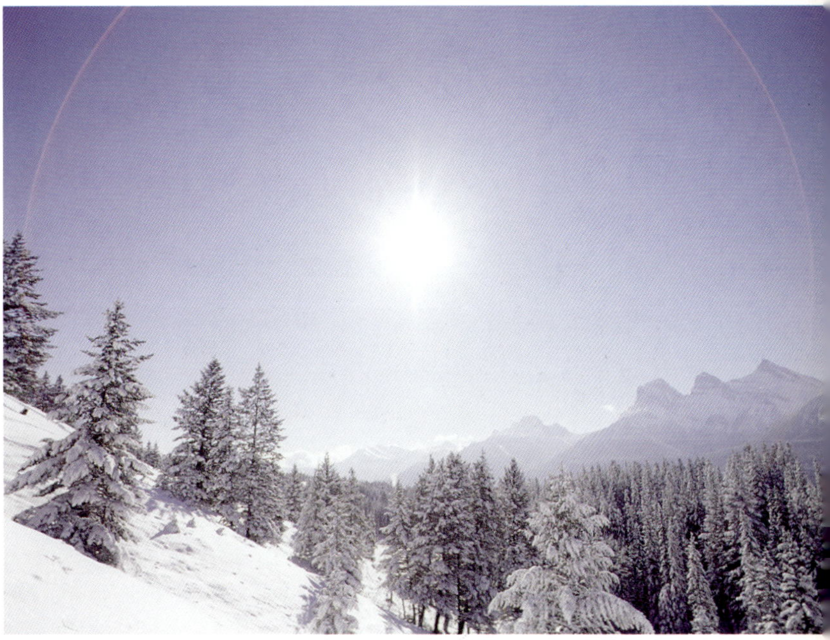

A UV filter used to reduce the distant hazy look was responsible for this unexpected development: an almost perfectly concentric ring around the sun. Canadian Rockies. Kodak E100VS, 20 mm lens.

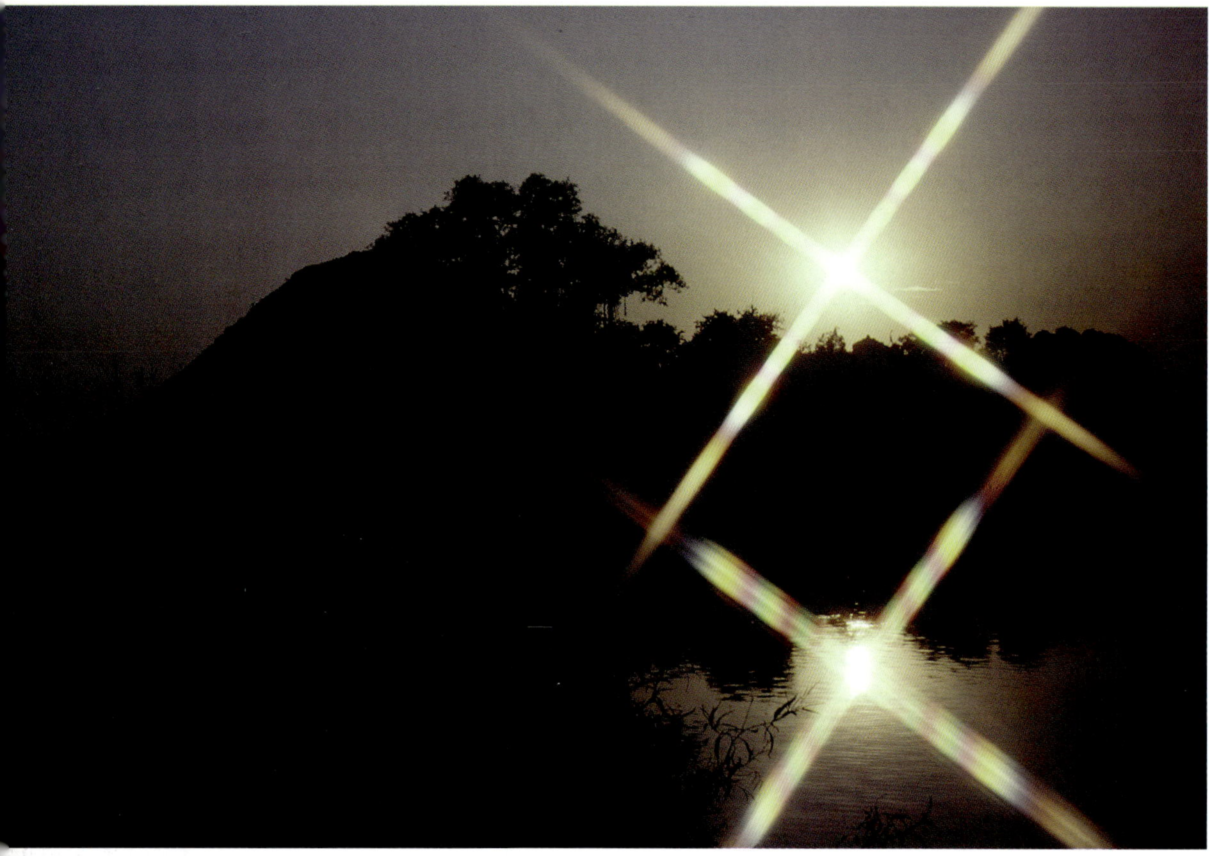

"Star" filters render somewhat gaudy effects, as seen in this shot. They are probably best left to using in night clubs or on the Vegas strip. Rajasthan, India. Kodachrome, 35 mm lens.

Other Useful Filters for Color Photography

Just as UV and polarizing filters aim to improve the quality of ambient light itself, neutral density filters are used to reduce the amount of light entering the camera lens. In one sense, they do by design what all filters inadvertently do to some extent.

This reduction of light can be useful with especially brilliant subject matter or backgrounds. Say you want to pan a skier's descent to show blur, but the bright surroundings won't allow you to choose a shutter speed slower than 1/125 second. A neutral density (ND) filter that reduces incoming light by one or two stops might make all the difference.

Or, perhaps your intention is simply to maintain a shallow depth of field. Consider the above example. If background areas of your composition were really cluttered, it would be preferable to render them completely de-focused. Yet the ambient brightness might not allow you to, since an impossibly fast shutter speed would have to be selected to maintain proper exposure. Here, again, an ND filter can be put to good use.

Most ND filters will reduce incoming light by one, two or three stops. A two-stop filter will likely be adequate for most mountain situations, although a three-stop filter might be even better if you're travelling amongst lots of snow and ice.

Like color conversion filters, ND filters may be purchased with graduated tones. Maximum effects are realized at one edge of these filters, whereas the extreme other edge is usually without effect at all. They can be great light-"equalizing" filters with compositions that have dark areas at the bottom of the frame and very bright ones on top, such as a scenic view that shows poorly lit forest presided over by snow-capped peaks and bright sky.

Other filters will likely be of less interest to most mountain shooters. They range from star filters, which render somewhat gaudy "star effects" with point light sources, and soft focus filters, intended to do much as their name implies, to multiple-image filters, which generate ghostlike images.

If, however, any of these effects are of interest to you, by all means experiment with them. You might want to discuss these and other filters further with knowledgeable salespeople at your favorite camera store, or try some web sites listed in the reference section for more information.

Filters for Black & White

Several of the filters used for color photography will also be beneficial while shooting in black & white. Polarizing and haze filters serve much the same purposes across the two mediums, with the minor difference being that grey tones are purposely selected and improved upon, instead of colors. Neutral density filters do exactly the same thing to black & white images as they do to color ones.

Colored filters do very different things to black and white shots though. Their chief effect is to block light from any color but their own, a characteristic that can be usefully applied in many mountain situations.

For example, say your companion is wearing a red parka while travelling in a dark forest. You'd like to shoot the scene, but are concerned that he won't contrast well against the background since both are evenly illuminated.

A red filter is likely your answer. It will permit more red light through while blocking that from the foliage. A black & white image shot with a red filter will show a relatively bright parka set well apart from a dark forest.

Selective color filtering of this sort is perhaps most dramatic with mountain skies. Often blue skies will record a lackluster light grey color on black and white film, owing mainly to the nature of most black & white film chemistries. By applying yellow or, more dramatic still, red filtration, the effect is to block blues and deepen sky tones.

As with polarizing though, be careful not to overdo the filter effect. Remember, it's just for enhancement and, as such, the final look has to be believable.

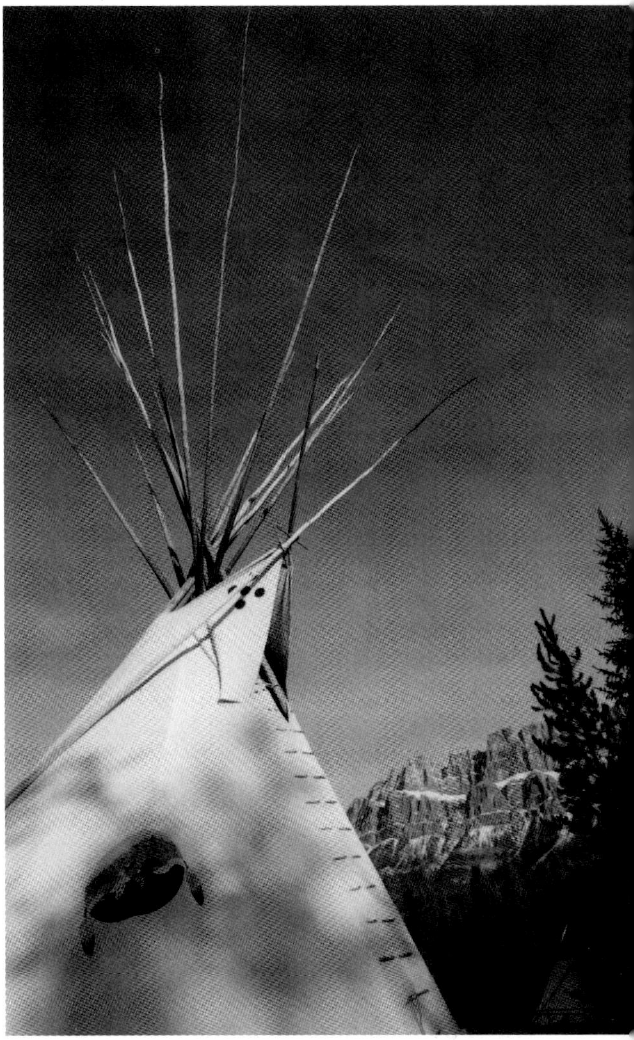

A yellow filter helped to subtly darken the skies above the teepee, heightening contrast in that part of the frame. Banff National Park, Canada. Kodak CN100, 24 mm lens.

Getting Started

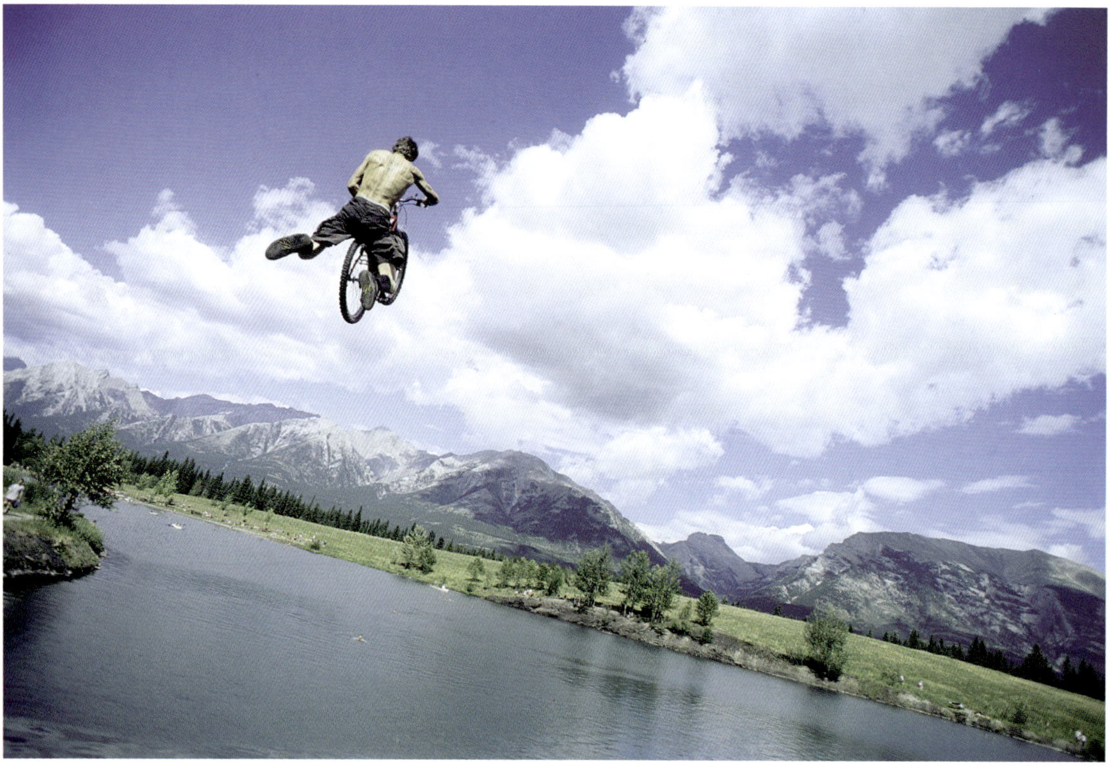

I managed to get into position just before this rider became airborne during a "big air" mountain bike contest. He performed the most spectacular jump of all the riders, as it turned out. Canmore, Alberta. Kodak E100VS, 20 mm lens.

Nothing is quite so disappointing as seeing hard-earned film results completely ruined. Light streaks, camera shake, bad exposures and wrong focus are a few of the problems that even seasoned photographers have to grapple with now and then.

Yet these things can generally be easily avoided. Simply turning your back to the sun, holding your camera a different way, closing in on your subject to meter properly, or just thinking carefully for a moment about focusing intentions might make all the difference between recording a lackluster shot and a great one.

Mountain situations often demand complete attention from us while, say, climbing or skiing. Providing a decent belay or properly assessing an avalanche slope should be foremost in our thoughts at such times, not the question of whether an envisioned shot will be properly exposed.

Even when picture taking is intended to be the primary focus, difficult weather and fleeting light may need to be reckoned with quickly while composing or planning a shot.

So, for the mountain photographer to best capture and deliver any given situation on film, it's imperative that camera basics become as routine as putting on mountain gear. Habits should be developed that support and encourage good technique.

This section will look at habits that many successful shooters take for granted and rely upon in almost any conceivable situation. Some are very simple; others require more thought and, sometimes, a little practise.

No amount of time—or rolls of film—however, would be wasted by developing a really good set of camera habits. With the mastery of them comes the real thrill of mountain photography: creating and capturing, in the most eye-catching way, dramatic viewpoints and action.

Loading and Unloading Film

Load carefully! Dust, grit and hair inside your camera's body can really create nightmares. Not only do they play havoc with moving pieces and precision parts, they can also, if caught in the wrong places, completely degrade film without your knowledge—at least until results return from the lab.

Grit that lodges onto the film pressure plate, for example, may leave deep scratches embedded throughout an entire roll of film (and others, if it's not removed between rolls). And even fine hairs that get stuck in, say, the flip-up reflex mirror that lies between lens and shutter may show up, in exaggerated form, on the film if they're not pulled before shooting.

So it's wise to examine the internal workings of your camera before ever loading a new roll. A simple blower brush, available at any camera store, is very useful to remove light dust and dirt particles that are evident inside.

More forceful blasts from a pressurized air canister might be required to deal with stubborn grit. Note, however, that this device should be used sparingly and very carefully, especially around shutter elements, which are quite prone to damage.

Dirt on the pressure plate, mirror assembly and lens surfaces are most likely to show up on film. Particles that are trapped within the lens will likely not effect results, unless you're shooting directly into the sun, in which case they exaggerate camera flare (discussed in a later section). These, and other unsightly bits lodged in your camera's viewfinder or internal meter, should only be removed by a specialized camera technician.

A quick camera reflex resulted in this shot. Within 10 seconds of observing the prominent "rays of God" effect, light faded rapidly and the scene turned a nondescript gray. Mount Rundle, Banff National Park, Alberta. Fuji Velvia, 85 mm lens.

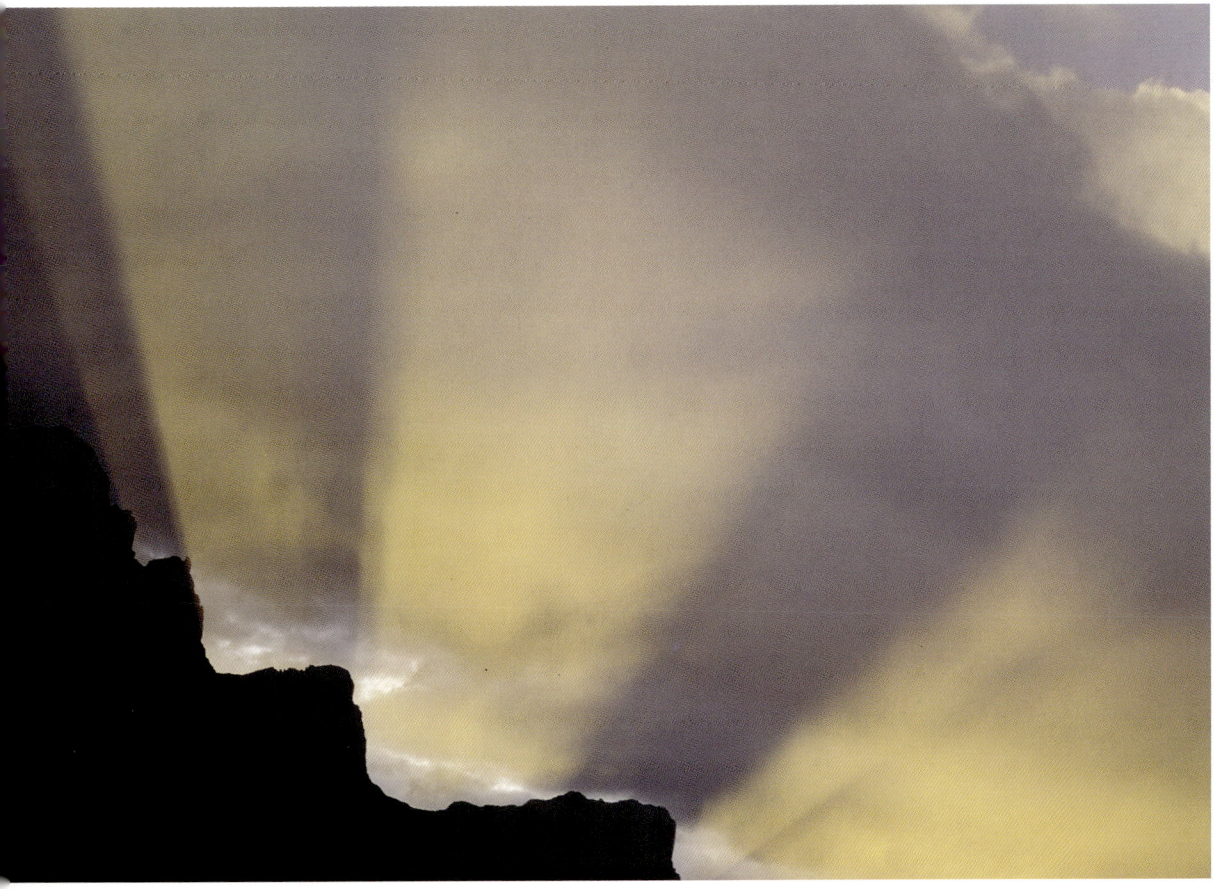

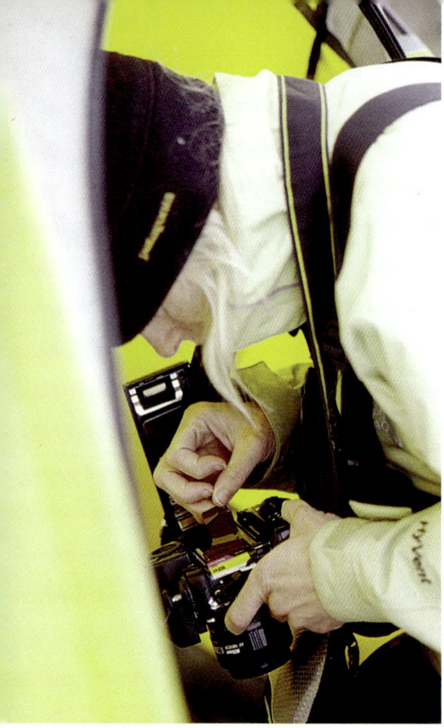

Try to load film in a relatively dark place, or away from the direct sun. A tent interior is a good choice, since it provides protection against both wet weather and direct sunlight. Canadian Rockies. Kodak E100VS, 105 mm lens.

As important as checking and cleaning your camera between rolls is, so too is being careful not to introduce more grit during the process of loading and unloading film. Try to choose a fairly clean location before opening your camera. If a wind is blowing dust around, endeavour to find or create shelter to protect yourself and your camera from the blast.

The same goes for the introduction of moisture into your camera. If it's raining or snowing, find or create shelter to protect the inside of your camera—and film surfaces—from droplets of rain and dustings of snow. Otherwise, these may show up on processed film. They may also encourage the growth of fungus or mould inside your camera, especially if you're shooting in a tropical mountain environment (see later section).

Most new cameras either automatically read a newly loaded roll of film for its ASA or DIN number, or they allow you to peek through a window to see the actual roll of film you're working with.

If your camera is an older one, however, another good habit to get into while loading is to insert the film carton end into the metal jacket on the backside of your camera. Not only can you keep track of its all-important ASA setting this way, but you will also know whether the loaded roll is color film, black & white, tungsten, or something else.

If the Film Doesn't Advance

A common snag while loading film, which has been largely corrected in modern auto-loading cameras, is that sprockets on the drive mechanism inside your camera simply don't mesh with the row of holes (or "perfs") on the sides of the film. In other words, the film leader does not catch on the camera's take-up reel.

This situation can be extremely maddening, especially if you think you've almost finished a great roll of shots when, in fact, not a single frame has been exposed.

If yours is an old-style camera that needs to be manually loaded, there is a way to ensure this never happens: once you've carefully loaded a roll of film and closed the camera back, wind and then shoot one frame. Wind again, then gently take in any slack with your camera's manual rewind lever (located above the film you just loaded and usually on the left side of the camera, as you're looking at it from behind).

Follow the arrow and be careful not to pull up on the lever while you're doing this, otherwise you may open the camera back. Once the film is tightly wound, take another shot. If the lever moves abruptly a half rotation or so, the film is properly loaded. If not, and especially if you hear a halfhearted crunching sound, chances are you need to try loading it again.

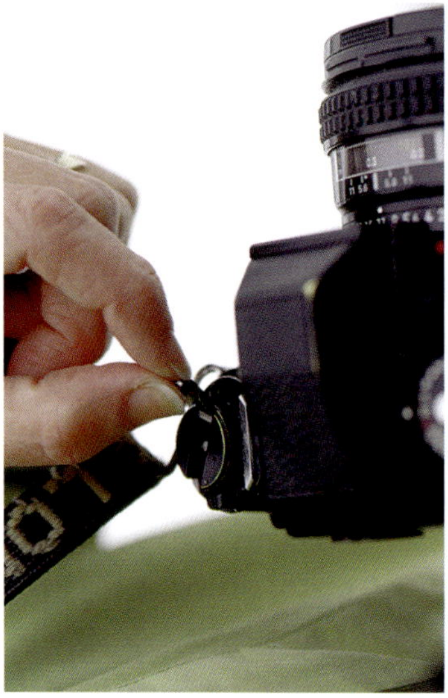

While using older cameras, gently take in any film slack with the rewind lever after loading. Then you will be able to confirm that the film is advancing properly. Canadian Rockies. Kodak E100VS, 55 mm macro lens.

Light Leakage

Light leakage created many frustrating moments in my early photography days. At one point, I think I'd actually concluded that it was the inevitable result of working with an inferior camera.

Undoubtedly, it partially resulted from trying to eke too many frames out of a roll. If I recall correctly, I was of the belief that 39, or even 40, frames could be squeezed from a 36 exposure roll, mainly by not allowing for a sufficiently long film leader (as a rule of thumb, 38 frames are probably the most you should expect from a 36 roll, and 25 or 26 from a 24 roll).

But neither my camera nor my thrift was really to blame. The real issue was that I insisted on loading and unloading my camera while fully enjoying the sun.

Light leakage onto film makes good sense when you consider that film chemistry has to be highly sensitive to light. And direct sunlight in the mountains, or even reflected light from snow or bright, rock surfaces, is particularly intense. Film canisters, while manufactured to block the majority of incoming light, are nonetheless somewhat permeable to really intense light.

So DON'T ever load or unload film facing the sun! Turn your back to it, and open your camera in the shade thus created. Or take advantage of the relatively dark surroundings of a mountain hut, or of the shady interior of your car, to load and unload film before heading out.

Once you've removed a roll from the camera and placed it in its plastic packaging tube with the lid on, it's also wise to protect it from further exposure to sunlight or—if you can manage it—heat, dust and dampness.

I make it a habit to immediately open a dark pouch inside my camera bag to drop in the exposed roll. Unexposed film that I'm intending to use right away, on the other hand, is kept in a separate compartment on the outside of my bag where I can access it quickly if need be.

The actual organization of film within your own bag, as with camera equipment, is open to personal taste. But the endeavour should always be to protect film as much as possible, and especially from any direct sunlight.

Light leakage can destroy otherwise good photos if care is not taken to ensure proper film loading and unloading. Canadian Rockies. Kodak E100VS, 105 mm lens.

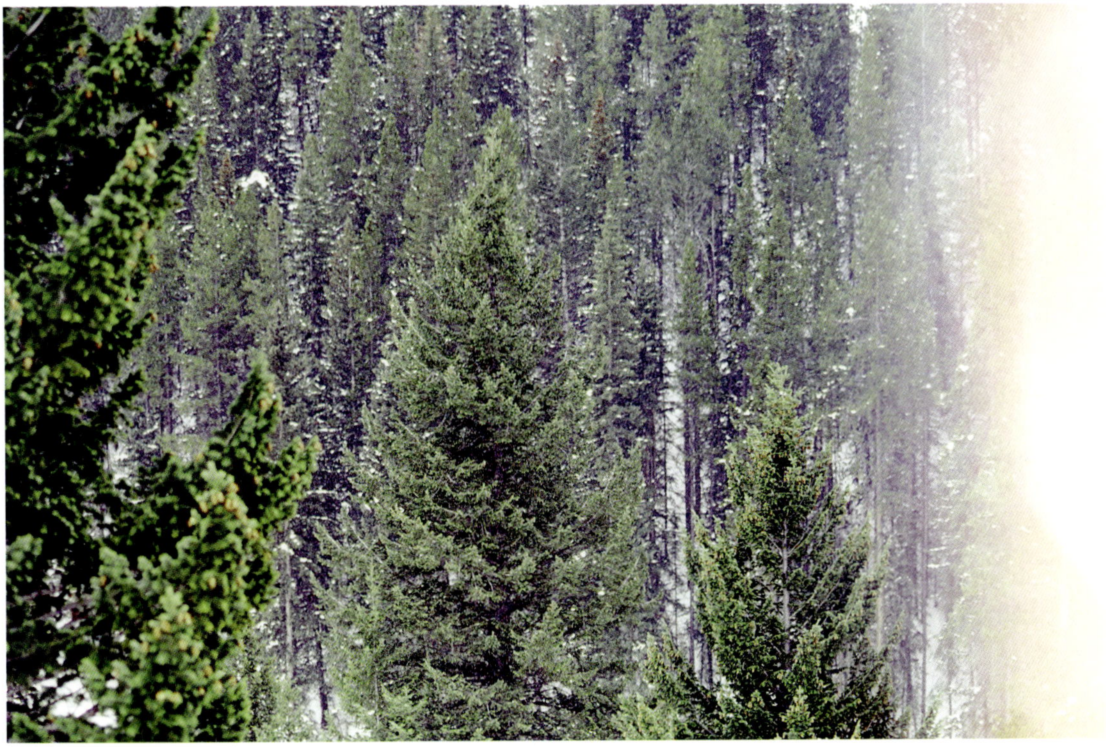

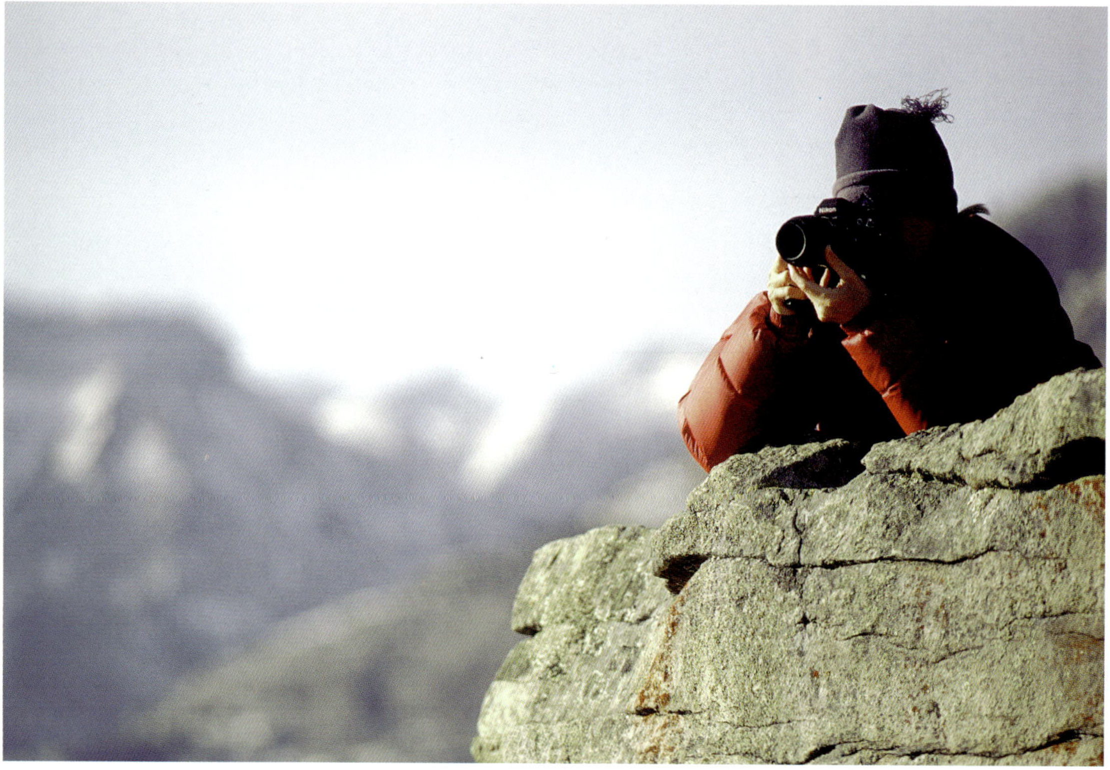

These three shots demonstrate different camera stances that all work well. At the edge of a cliff, the "belly" position, where resting elbows prop a camera up to eye level, is by far the safest one. Canadian Rockies. Kodak E100VS, 105 mm lens.

Holding Your Camera Properly

Frustrating for many of us, when results arrive back from the lab, are photos that look "shaky", or ones that show half a thumb. More often than not these problems owe to holding the camera incorrectly. Employ correct techniques, and problems quickly become history.

First, while hand-holding any camera, it's important to find a steady body position. One of the best of these resembles a two-legged tripod, where legs are spread wide apart and the camera is held at eye level.

In the event that a lower, ground-level position is desired, say in order to photograph wildflowers up close or to capture a mountain biker zooming by overhead, elbows can be used in the same two-"legged" position. Your camera bag or backpack might make a useful additional support while using long lenses in this position.

For something in between—photographing kids at an adult's navel height, for example—a crouching position, with preferably one knee resting on the ground and an elbow resting on the other knee, will usually suffice. Alternatively, sitting cross-legged on the ground with both elbows resting on your knees will provide an even more stable position.

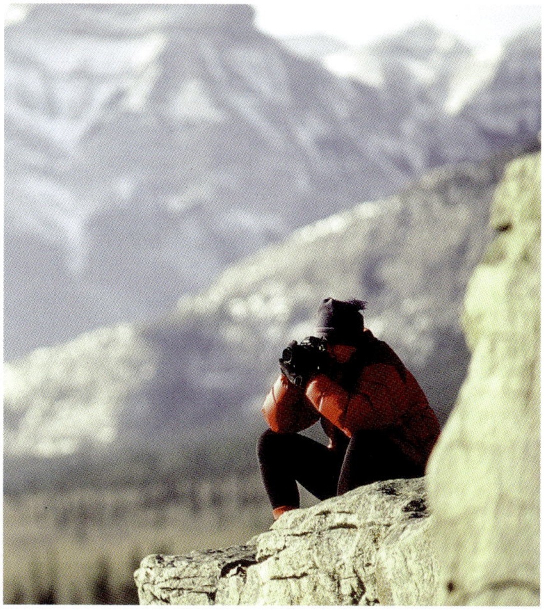

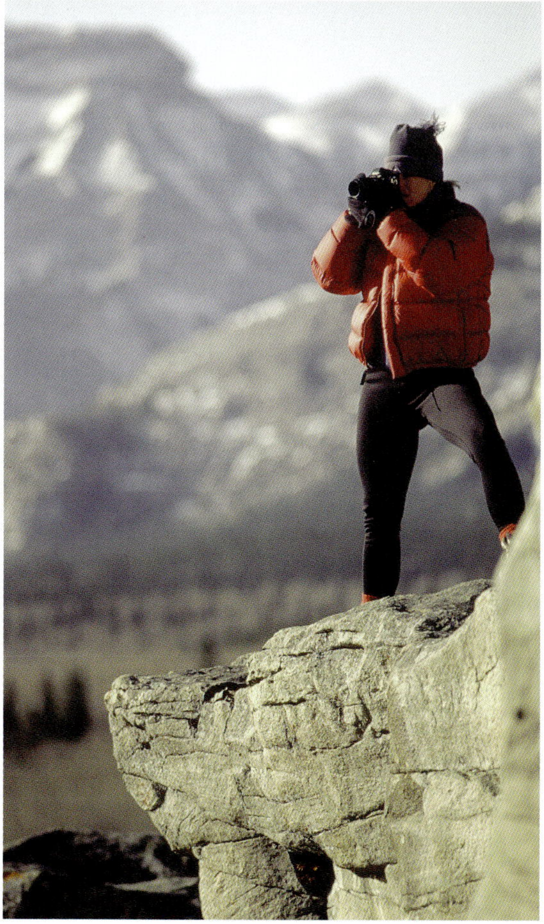

Holding a camera properly becomes routine after a very short time. While shooting horizontally, the right hand is nearly always used to trigger the camera shutter, and so it rests against—and grips—the right-hand side of the camera (except on specially developed left shutter models, for some left-handed people, where the reverse is true). The left palm cups the bottom of the camera, while fingers are used to adjust the focus and the diaphragm opening, or f-stops.

If the camera is aligned vertically instead, to shoot vertical frames, then generally it is the right hand that supports and grips the bottom of the camera and operates the shutter, while the left hand is free to work the lens.

Always squeeze the shutter carefully, never with a jabbing motion. This point is often overlooked by beginners and is probably the most common cause of camera shake.

After a shot is taken, use your right thumb to cock the film advance lever before shooting again. If you're using a motor winder or automatic camera, your thumb need not move at all between frames.

As long as the fingers of your left hand are kept on the lens to make adjustments, they should never wander into the line of view where they might be inadvertently recorded along with the rest of the scene. Other incidental body parts may, however, creep into the frame from time to time. No matter how carefully you look through your viewfinder, you may not see, for example, a wisp of long hair blowing in front of the lens—which can easily happen if a strong wind is blowing from behind.

The best advice in situations such as these is, of course, to tie your hair back and try to be aware of anything else that may fall into your camera's field of view.

Steadying Your Camera

The best device any photographer has in his or her arsenal to really provide camera stability is, of course, the tripod or some other mechanical camera support. A full discussion of when to best use these, and which are of most use to the mountain photographer, will follow in "Tripods And Cable Releases" on page 66.

When a tripod is inappropriate, or if you don't happen to be carrying one, and you need additional stability for whatever reason, here are some tricks you can easily employ.

The first is to simply press the camera into your face, while shooting in either a vertical or horizontal position, hold your breath and squeeze the shutter extra slowly. For additional support, wrap your camera's strap around your left wrist. It will still be secured around your neck—where it should be for safety at all times while shooting in the mountains, unless fastened to a tripod or other support—and it shouldn't be overly uncomfortable unless tightened too much.

Next, keep in mind natural features that might be handy supports in lieu of a tripod. Mountains are especially well endowed with them.

Rocks and stumps are useful while shooting from ground-level or mid-height positions. Tree trunks or cliff edges are likewise handy when standing fully upright. The important thing is to always first recognize the need for additional support, and then quickly survey the landscape or your belongings to determine what might be most appropriate.

Pushing a camera into your face while slowly squeezing the shutter enables you to get sharper results at slower shutter speeds. This is particularly true with longer lenses or while panning an action scene. Canadian Rockies, Kodak E100VS, 85 mm lens.

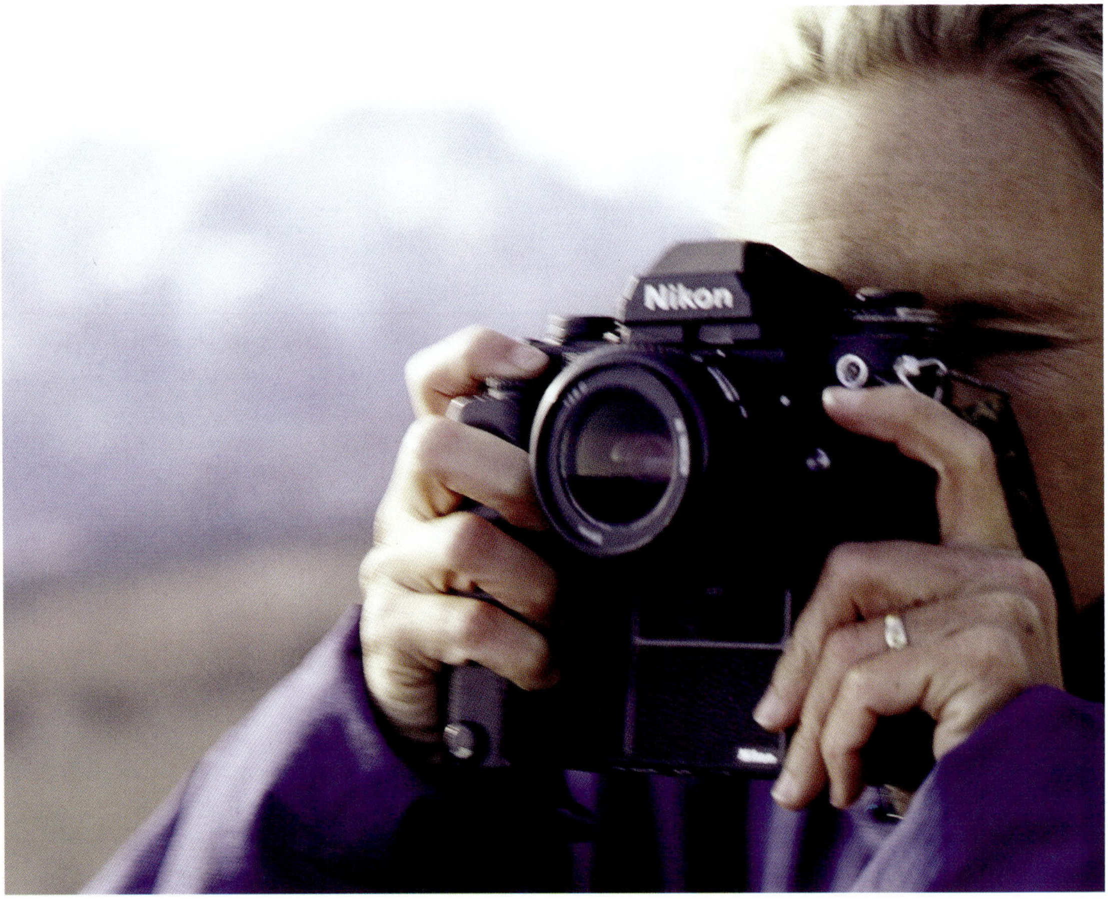

Metering Exposures Correctly

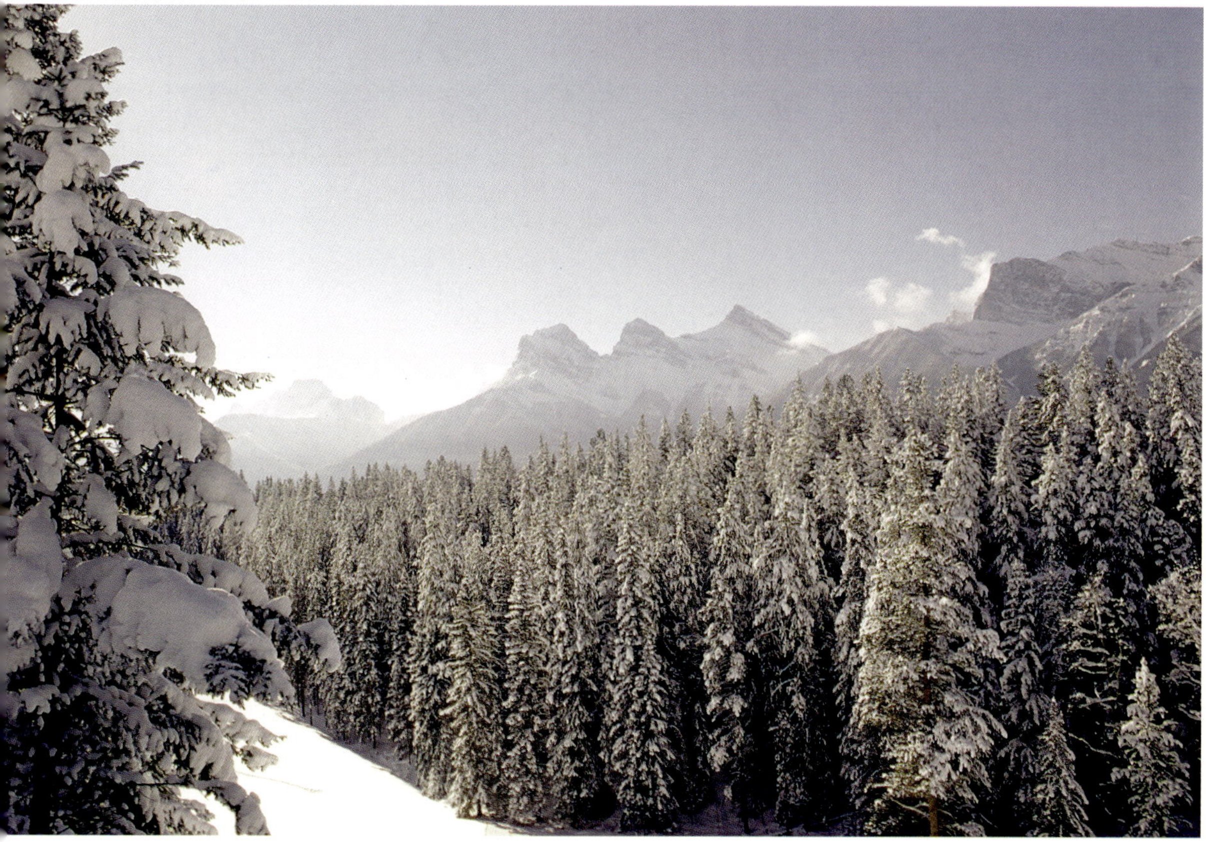

Metering this shot properly proved to be difficult. I wanted to record detail in nearby forest areas while preserving blue sky tones. Several exposures were required to get a best compromise. Canadian Rockies. Kodak E100VS, 28 mm lens.

Manufacturers have focused a tremendous amount of attention on exposure metering while constructing steadily more computerized and high-tech cameras. Yet, for all the merits of the many metering systems a photographer now has at his or her disposal—spot metering, centre-weighted metering, 3D color matrix metering and so on—probably the most important exposure decisions will rely upon a photographer's thought and knowledge, not a sophisticated meter.

Many metering situations in the mountains will be very straightforward and can be handled by almost any internal camera meter. However, more complex lighting or more unusual subject matter forces one to mentally articulate a desired final result on film before correct exposures can be determined.

Meter Calibration Scale

Nearly all meters are calibrated to provide results based on what is called an "18 percent gray scale." What this means is that if all surfaces were a certain shade of gray, cameras would record exposure perfectly every time.

The mountain environment, of course, looks anything but a tedious and uniform shade of gray, at least most of the time. An alpine meadow in midsummer is a kaleidoscope of color. And contrasts are particularly striking here: there are dark evergreen forests and

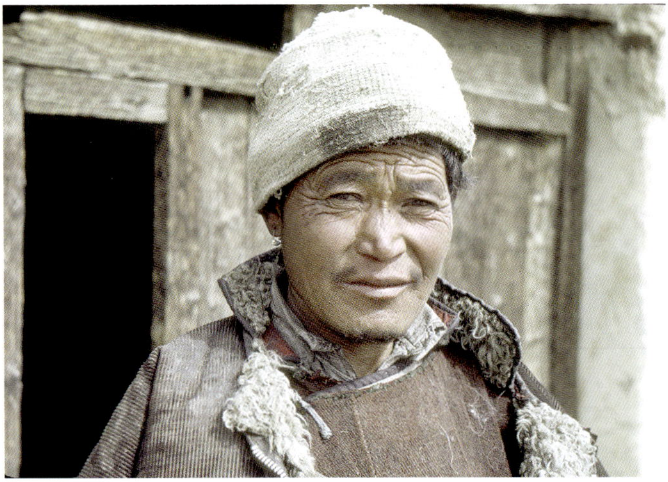

This portrait of a Buddhist monk was relatively easy to determine the exposure for. Almost every part of the scene closely approximates an 18 percent gray standard. Lamayuru monastery, Ladakh, India. Ektachrome, 85 mm lens.

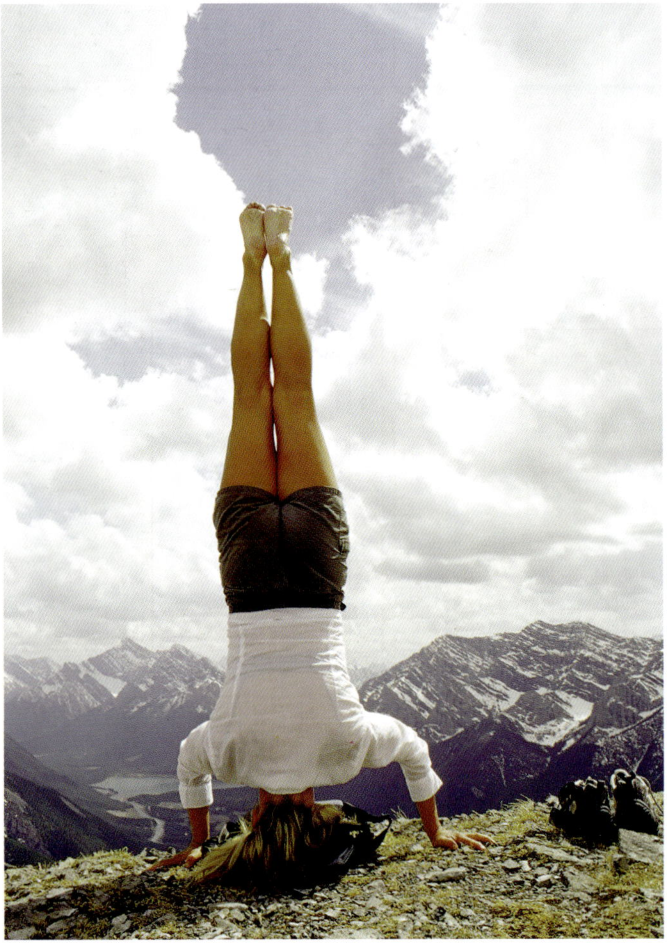

deep blue skies, but there are also brilliant snowfields, bright cascades of water and lofty white clouds.

Some surfaces do approximate the 18 percent gray standard quite faithfully though. Limestone and most granite cliffs in overcast weather, but not necessarily when fully sunlit, are two of them. Midrange blue skies often come close, as do sometimes the blues and greens of mountain lakes.

Handily, moderate skin tones often do so as well. More will be said about metering exposure from skin in the next sections. What is immediately important to recognize is that judging "ideal" exposure from especially light Caucasian skin or from really dark skin will distort results, either by underexposing or overexposing.

You will probably want to read the next sections carefully, and experiment on yourself, before deciding whether your skin tones, or those of your subjects, fit the 18 percent gray standard or not.

Metering for Results

Mountain contrasts will often record faithfully on film, providing fairly uniform lighting conditions exist, but just as often, exposures have to be geared to chosen subjects, not the entire scene.

Eyes adjust much more readily to high contrast than film does, even films with a high contrast tolerance. Hence, they may not truthfully indicate the full extent of contrast that will later appear on film.

In situations where the subject is dark relative to its surroundings—say a climber ascending a shady rock ridge in front of a brightly lit background—the photographer has to make a decision: does he or

Always have a clear idea of what you want to expose for. A blanket exposure reading of this scene would have darkened my subject significantly, perhaps eroding the value of the shot completely. Canadian Rockies. Kodak E100VS, 28 mm lens.

she want to record the entire scene faithfully as he or she sees it?

If so, the choice would be to meter for the climber's surroundings. The climber will appear silhouetted against the mountain backdrop, even if the photographer's eyes see the climber clearly, not as a silhouette.

Depending on composition and drama, this can render a very nice effect. Alternatively, the photographer may choose to expose correctly for the climber and allow the surroundings to "burn" out, or overexpose (if so, chances are that he or she will use a longer lens to get closer to the subject, and show less of the surroundings, a method that will be dealt with later).

Neither approach is right or wrong—just different—but any attempt to compromise between the two by choosing some middle value will probably be met with disappointment.

Incident Meters versus Reflected Light Meters

Most internal exposure meters, also known as "light" meters, measure reflected light; that is, the amount of light reflected off the surface of a particular subject, or of an entire scene. These are, unsurprisingly, termed reflected light meters.

There is another type of meter, called an incident light meter, which measures the amount of light actually reaching the surface of a subject. These usually handheld meters are commonly used by studio and fashion photographers. In general, they more faithfully record correct exposures for smallish subjects, such as still-life objects and people, and at times they do so for larger scenes too.

In the mountains they can be quite useful, providing, for example, a much more accurate light reading while shooting wildflowers in the forest (reflected light meters will often either overexpose or underexpose flower blossoms, depending on whether the sun is out or not), or for metering light on faces, hands, feet, etc., when the surroundings are brighter or darker than a chosen subject.

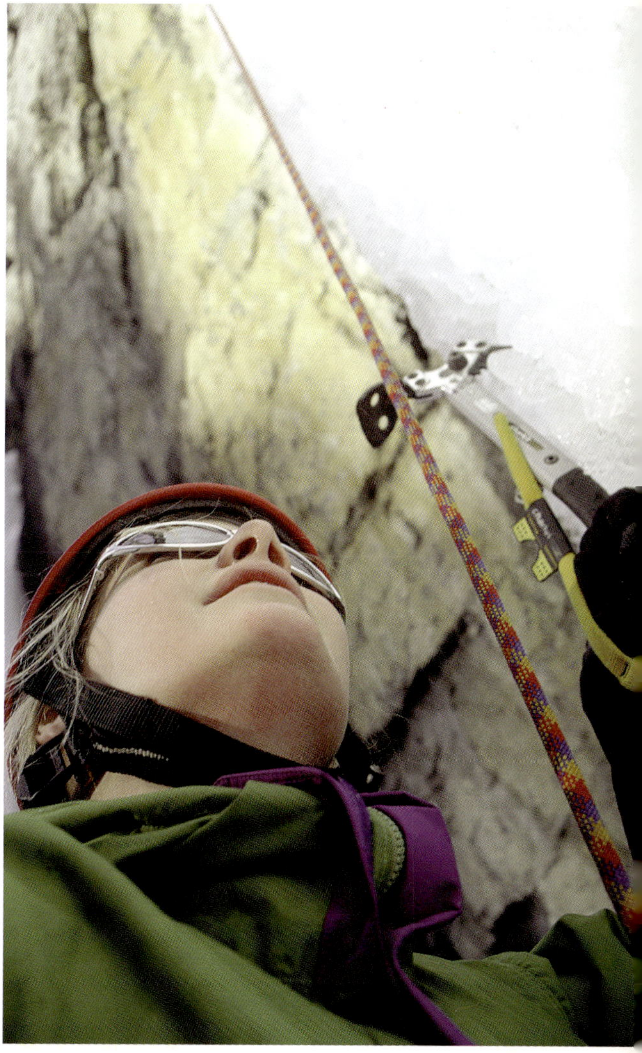

An incident light meter was very useful for this shot. It allowed me to judge an accurate exposure for skin areas, which a reflected light meter may have missed owing to the bright and darker surrounding areas. Canadian Rockies. Ektachrome EPN, 35-70 mm zoom lens.

They are, however, not infallible. Incident meters will almost definitely give a misleading measurement for an entire scene if exposed to more, or less, light than other components of that scene. In situations such as these, your camera's built-in reflected meter may be just as—or more—useful than a handheld incident meter, especially when combined with careful thought.

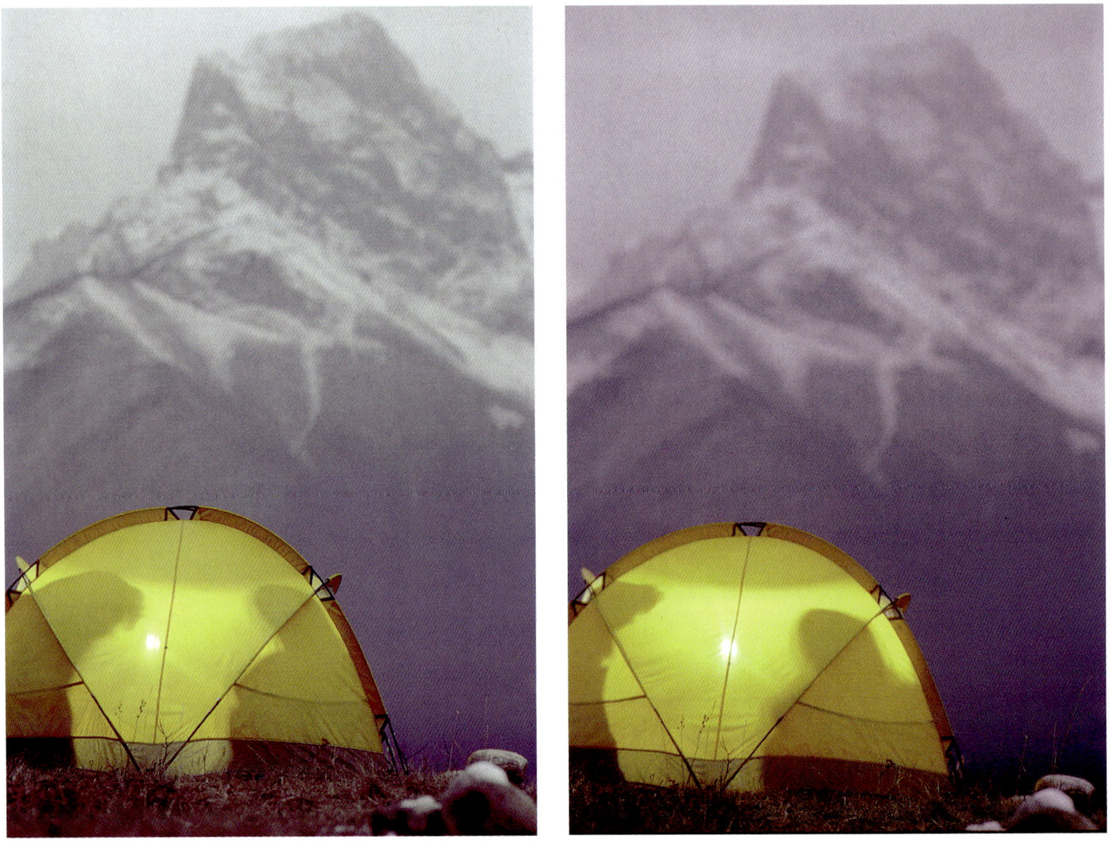

Twilight shooting often necessitates some bracketing. It is usually difficult to shoot consistently perfect exposures when light is either rapidly fading, or quickly building. Canadian Rockies. Fuji Velvia, 105 mm lens.

Bracketing

Another approach to ensure you get the right exposure is to simply bracket a scene. In other words, you would shoot a variety of frames at, and then both above and below, your best exposure guess.

Most commonly, bracketing is done at half or full f-stop intervals. Sometimes shutter speeds are adjusted up or down instead of f-stops. The idea is to ensure that you get a perfectly exposed shot; in essence, you've decided not to risk missing the best one.

I'm not a big fan of bracketing as a rule, unless light conditions are really difficult to judge, or when shooting for clients (where very slight changes in exposure can mean the difference between a successful shoot and a bomb). In these types of situations fast bracketing becomes an important skill to learn.

More often than not, though, bracketing is a habit-forming crutch. Here are some arguments I would raise against excessive bracketing: great photo opportunities may be lost if you're dependent on bracketing, especially while photographing wildlife or unique high-mountain situations where every single frame is unique. Bracketing as well, particularly at half-stop intervals, wastes a tremendous amount of film, which may not be in great supply considering the weight conscious nature of many of us heading out to the mountains.

Also, if you're maximizing the depth of field, bracketing can really wreak havoc on results, unless you're paying close attention to the focusing dial to ensure that you make changes with every bracketed frame.

But, most of all, an ingrained bracketing habit will discourage the process of evaluating exposure, as discussed above. This process, perhaps more than any other technical one, is essential to master in order to build photography competence and confidence.

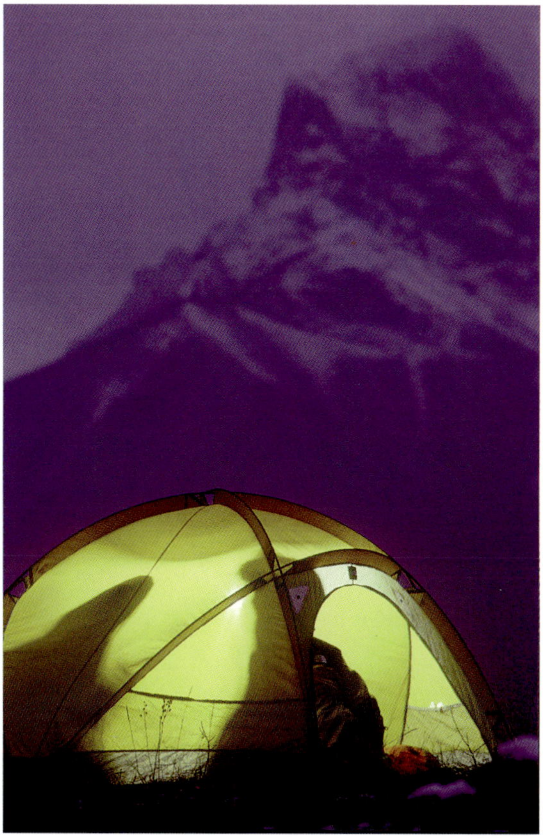

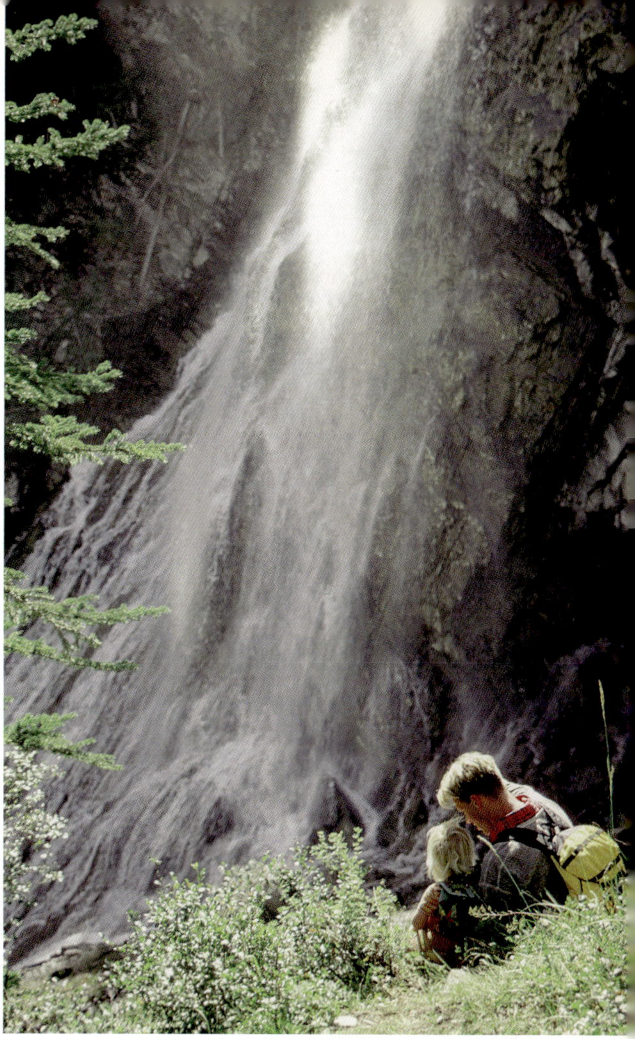

Two exposure readings were taken to ensure proper exposure for both subjects and background areas. Happily, they gave similar enough readings that no other lighting was required. Banff National Park, Canada. Fuji Velvia, 28 mm lens.

Advanced Exposure Control

For most of us, carting around an incident meter when most cameras come equipped with perfectly good built-in ones is simply not likely, nor even particularly desirable. So, when you need more precise readings from smaller subjects, here is a quick and dirty method of measuring with your camera's internal reflective meter that comes close to approximating results produced with an incident meter.

Turn the backside of your hand (NOT your palm) toward and mainly filling the camera lens, in the same direction, and at roughly the same angle, that you're planning to shoot your picture. If you've ensured that the light on your hand is a close approximation to the light on your subject and that your hand is not, for example, half cast in shadow, the exposure readings thus produced should be quite accurate.

With a little practise and experimentation, this approach may prove to be one of the best to determine exposure, especially while working with only a modicum of equipment.

Here is an example of where it can be used to great effect: an alpine brook cascading between luxurious mosses presents a beautiful nature subject. If a camera is pointed directly at the cascade and the exposure is then taken, chances are that the resulting photo will be underexposed—i.e., dark. This owes to the fact that the meter is judging the overall scene on the basis of very bright cascading water.

If, on the other hand, exposure is read from the surrounding dark mosses, the opposite will likely be true: the shot will be overexposed. By metering off the back of your hand, an intermediate value will be

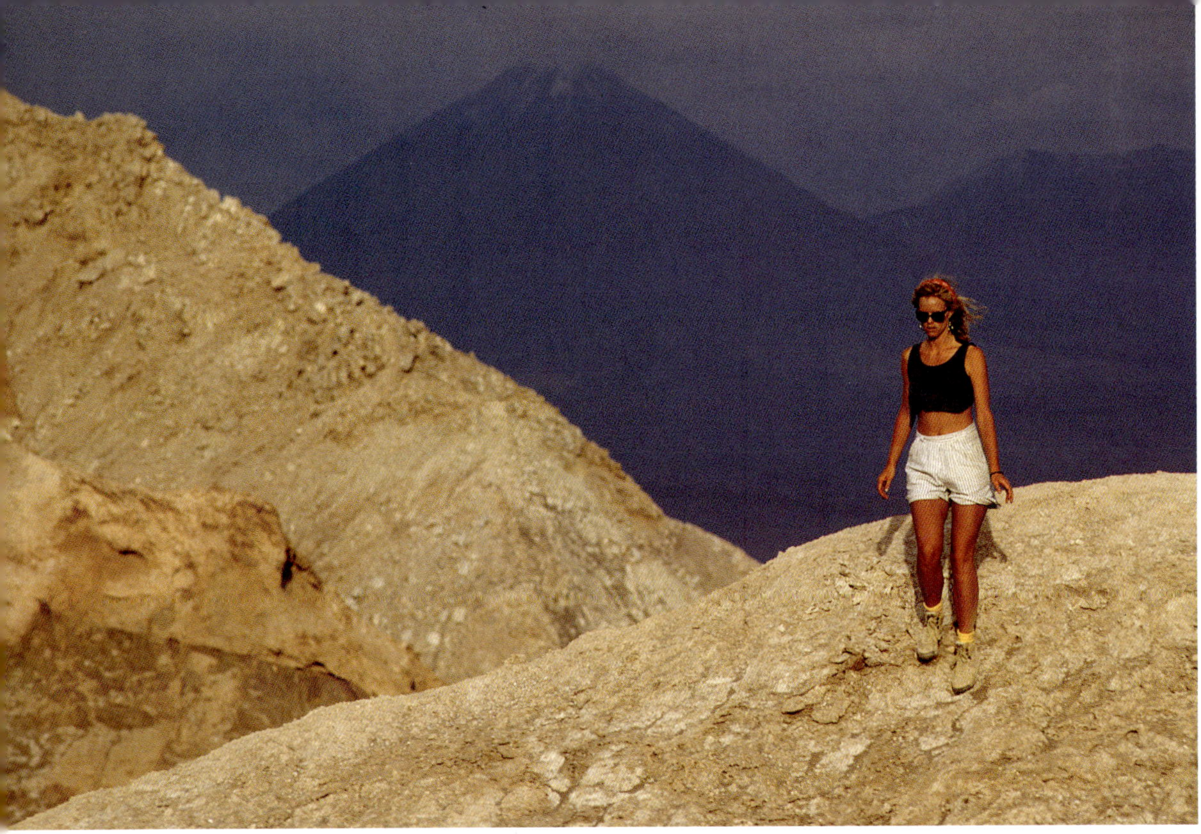

My intent was to preserve a dark, moody backdrop in this shot. Hence exposure was geared to the subject's skin areas, and then darkened by a half stop. San Pedro de Atacama, Chile. Kodachrome, 35-70 mm zoom lens.

provided that will almost certainly be more accurate than either of the two extremes.

Now consider photographing your mountaineering companion surrounded by ice and snow and wearing a navy parka and black climbing pants. You may be fortunate enough to get an accurate exposure reading by simply pointing your camera at the scene, as your camera's meter averages values from the entire field of view and automatically provides you with a middling one.

Chances are better, though, that your picture will end up either overexposed or underexposed, depending on whether you've included more bright background or dark clothing in your frame. This is where the back of your hand comes in handy, especially if the skin tones of your subject's face are really what you want to have properly exposed.

Note, however, that although measuring off the back of your hand—when done properly—gives consistently accurate readings for nearby subjects, and ones that dominate a composition, it doesn't always produce the best readings for a larger or more complex scene. This is not to say the back of your hand is of no use in such situations; rather, that it's best used in conjunction with other methods.

One other approach I frequently use, especially to judge exposure for a wide scene that includes sky and distant scenery, is to point my camera at a piece of cloudless blue sky that represents neither the brightest nor darkest part of the sky, take a reading, then take a reading off the back of my hand, and finally simply point my camera in the direction of the scene.

If all three readings are more or less in agreement, I am content that the exposure chosen will be the correct one. If not, I am forced to think about which is probably going to render the most accurate results. Keep in mind that if your hand's skin color is either lighter or darker than average, you might want to emphasize readings from the other methods more.

Although it sounds like a lot of work to meter exposure in three different ways for the same scene, it should, with practise, just take a few seconds. And the exercise is a great confidence builder that your final choice will be the correct one.

Exposing Correctly on Snow and Ice

Many mountain friends have expressed their disappointment to me over photographs taken while shooting amongst lots of snow and ice. Almost always the problem has been that pictures turned out too dark.

While shooting in such very bright environments is not particularly tricky, it is true that your camera's light meter will usually give you wrong exposure readings. These have to be adjusted in one of two ways if shots are to avoid that disappointing "dark" look.

The simplest method, and one normally recommended by camera manufacturers, is to compensate by adding two full stops of exposure. That is, either adjust your f-stop from say f-22 to f-11, or lower the shutter speed by two settings, perhaps from 1/1000 to 1/250 second.

Here's an example to illustrate this method. Say you're skiing across an icefield, and you stop to take a shot of your companions a rope length away against a distant, bright mountain backdrop. With 100 ASA film in your camera, your light meter reads 1/500 second at f-16.

If you'd like to maintain a wide depth of field to, say, include a nearby section of your rope in focus, then you should lower the shutter speed to 1/125 second and leave the aperture at f-16. If not, and you just want to be sure that you get a sharp photo, then simply drop the aperture to f-8 and make no changes to shutter speed (this would be a particularly good choice if your chosen lens is a long one).

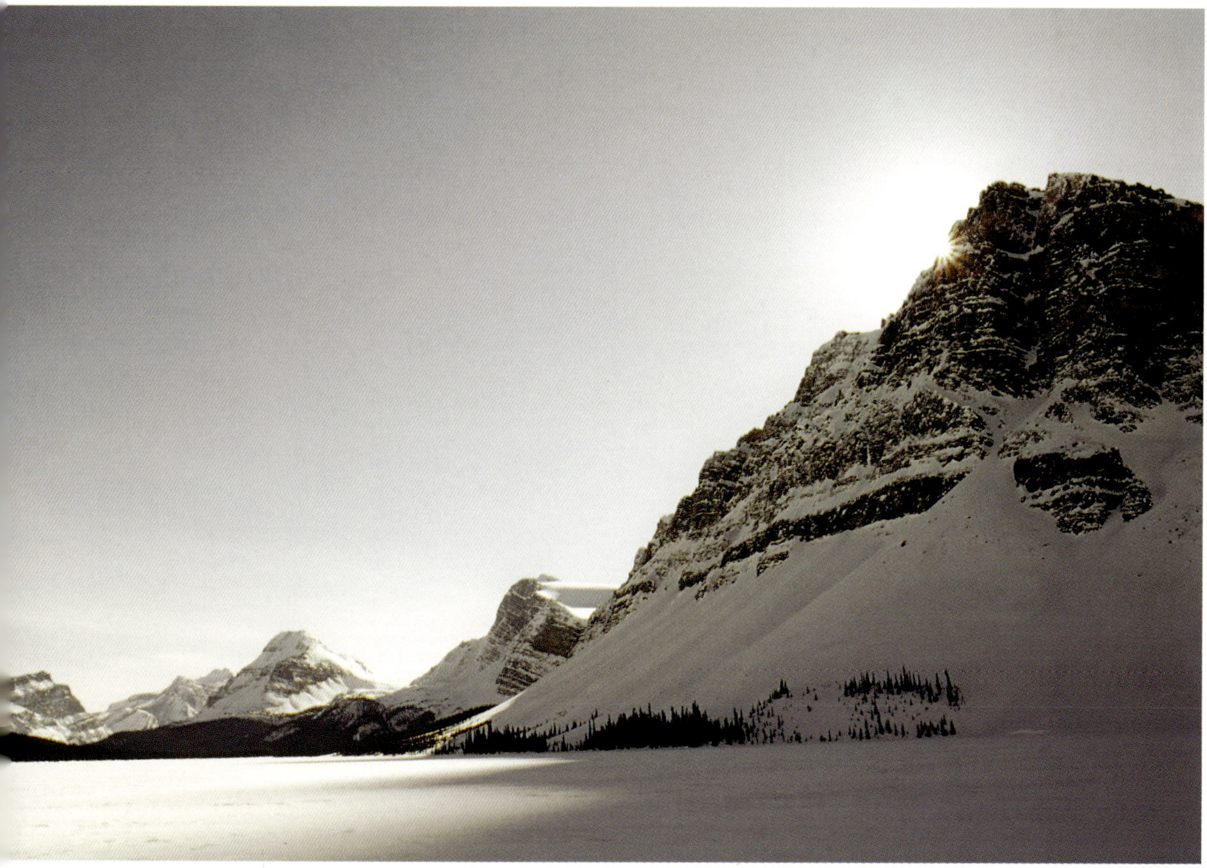

My approach to ensure an acceptable exposure for this shot—one that would both preserve detail in shadow areas while also maintaining blue sky tones—was fairly complex. It required taking readings from both a medium bright part of the sky and also directly from the right-hand shadow, and then averaging the two. Bow Lake, Canadian Rockies. Kodak E100VS, 28 mm lens.

Of course, you can change both by one stop each if you want to. In other words, with this example you'd change the aperture to f-11 and lower the shutter speed to 1/250 second.

A problem with the two-stop adjustment approach is that your composition must be almost entirely of bright snow for it to be correct. If it's not, such as when you're including a lot of sky and say just a third snow or ice, dropping two stops from your camera's exposure reading would give you overexposed shots. This would also apply to a lot of shaded snow in your shot.

The field techniques discussed in the last section, of metering off the back of your hand or from a middling part of the sky, would likely be better employed in both of these cases, and in most others. Indeed, they will generally provide the most accurate results in bright, snowy terrain most often, despite what manufacturers might say to the contrary.

Probably the safest approach of all though, if you can spare the time and film, is to snap at least one shot with each method. Try doing so in different locations and with different lighting. If you mentally note, at the time of shooting, which approach was used first, you can determine your own personal preferences for which method to use, and when.

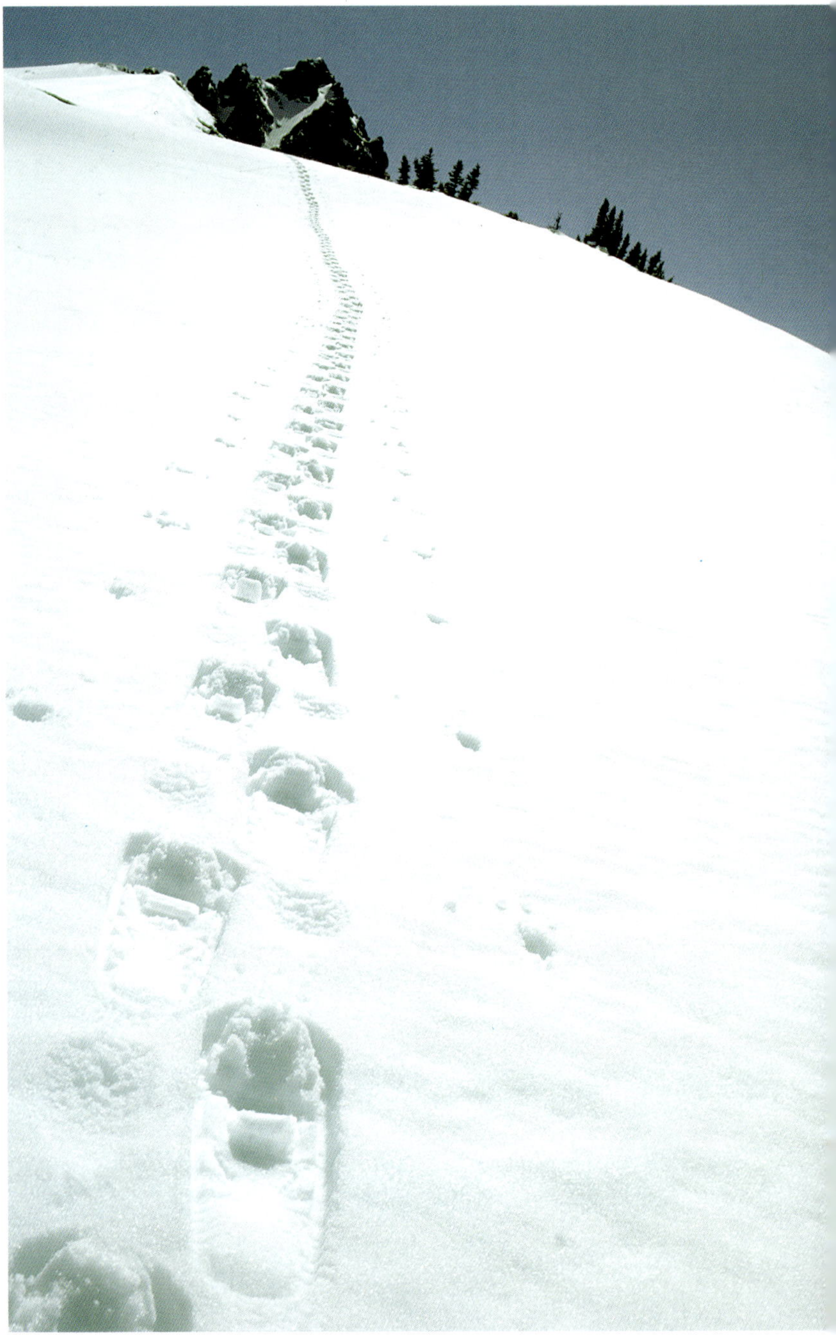

An exposure reading determined by any camera's internal meter would have rendered this shot way too dark. Since most of the frame is composed of fully lit snow, overexposing by two stops should give the right exposure. Banff National Park, Canada. Fuji Velvia, 20 mm lens.

Overexposing and Underexposing for Effect

One of the perks of really mastering your control of exposure is that you can then employ your skills to great effect in both overexposing and underexposing on purpose. Both techniques will help to change the mood of your final composition, sometimes subtly, and at other times with great impact.

Overexposure, for example, can render a surreal and almost transcendent feeling to a shot. Underexposure on the other hand, will effectively emphasize dark, brooding drama.

Your camera's meter, and even an expensive handheld incident light meter, will only give you indications of how best to emphasize mood with exposure. The rest of the process is really up to you, the photographer.

What's important is to recognize, by looking at a scene, the feeling you want to create, whether uplifting or darkly dramatic. Then it's just a matter of applying exposure fundamentals to whatever decisions you've made.

A dark storm on the horizon, for example, threatening to engulf you, the lowly mountain trekker, is a great and dramatic subject. But if you were to simply point your camera at the distant dark clouds, your camera would most likely give you an exposure reading that would treat those clouds as 18 percent gray matter, just like any other clouds. In other words, your camera would overexpose the scene and render the storm powerless.

What needs to be done, once you've recognized this limitation, is to either meter off a well-lit object or scene elsewhere—say a bright piece of sky in the opposite direction—or experiment with the manual exposure dial on your camera, by underexposing one or two stops. With any luck, and maybe in this case a little bracketing, you'll hit upon exactly the right exposure.

A light exposure gives this shot a somewhat ethereal look, and emphasizes the long shafts of light. Determining an exposure reading from sky areas would have darkened it considerably. Banff National Park, Canada. Fuji Velvia, 35 mm lens.

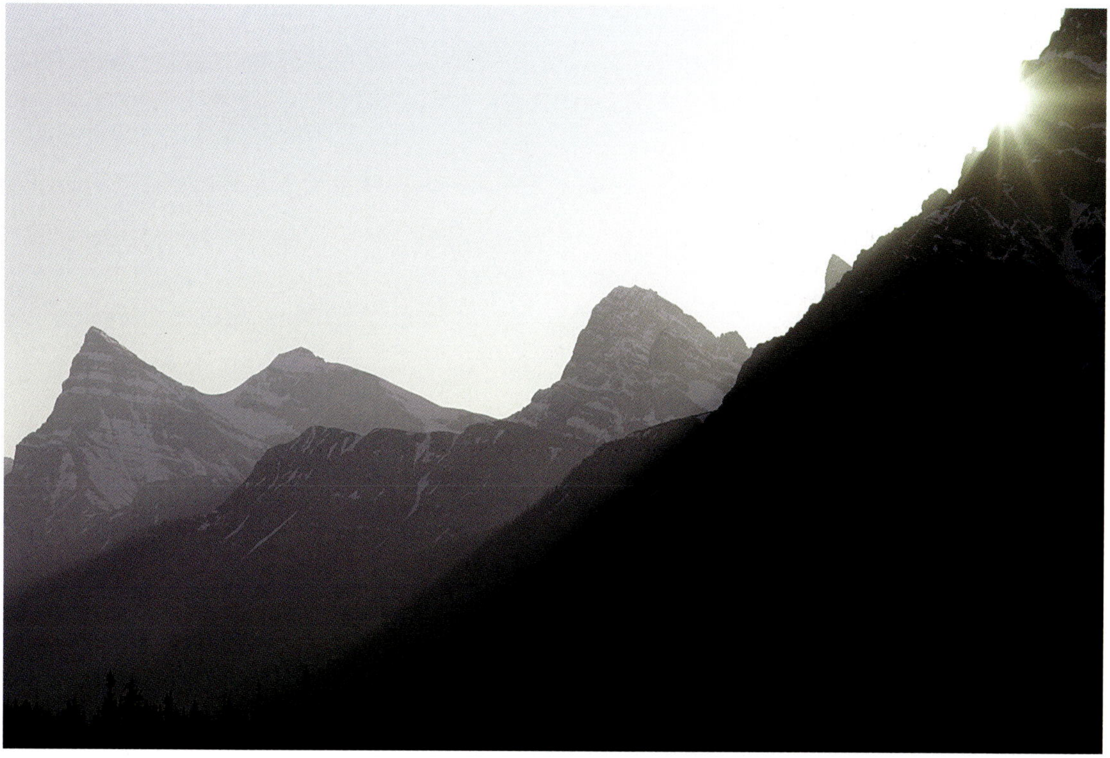

Intentional overexposure works in a similar, albeit reverse, fashion. Take the example of young kids running along a trail in an alpine meadow, with both the sun and bright mountainside behind. Your camera's meter will give you an average exposure value for the entire scene, which means the kids' faces will be dark and the mountainside fairly well exposed.

Kids, though, are great subjects to record in a light, airy, transcendent mood, and you've determined that you're not really interested in having the mountainside well exposed anyway. So the idea here would be to meter for the kids' faces and ignore everything else.

Probably the easiest way is to get close to the kids and actually point your camera directly at their skin, or take a reading from the back of your hand with the same lighting. You may even want to further brighten the scene, by a half to a full f-stop, to really heighten the airy mood.

Or, consider the cascading brook example from the last section. If you point your camera directly at the white, fast-flowing water, exposures indicated by its meter will render your final results dark and rather gray. Yet you want your cascade picture to have a surreal and uplifting feel. Metering off the back of your hand may again produce the desired result, or you may even want to overexpose beyond that by, once more, a half to a full f-stop.

With thought and a little practise, you'll find that intentional overexposure and underexposure comes naturally, almost automatically in fact.

The whole idea is to allow you to create and capture drama. And drama, probably more than anything else, is what characterizes mountain experiences and landscapes, everywhere in the world.

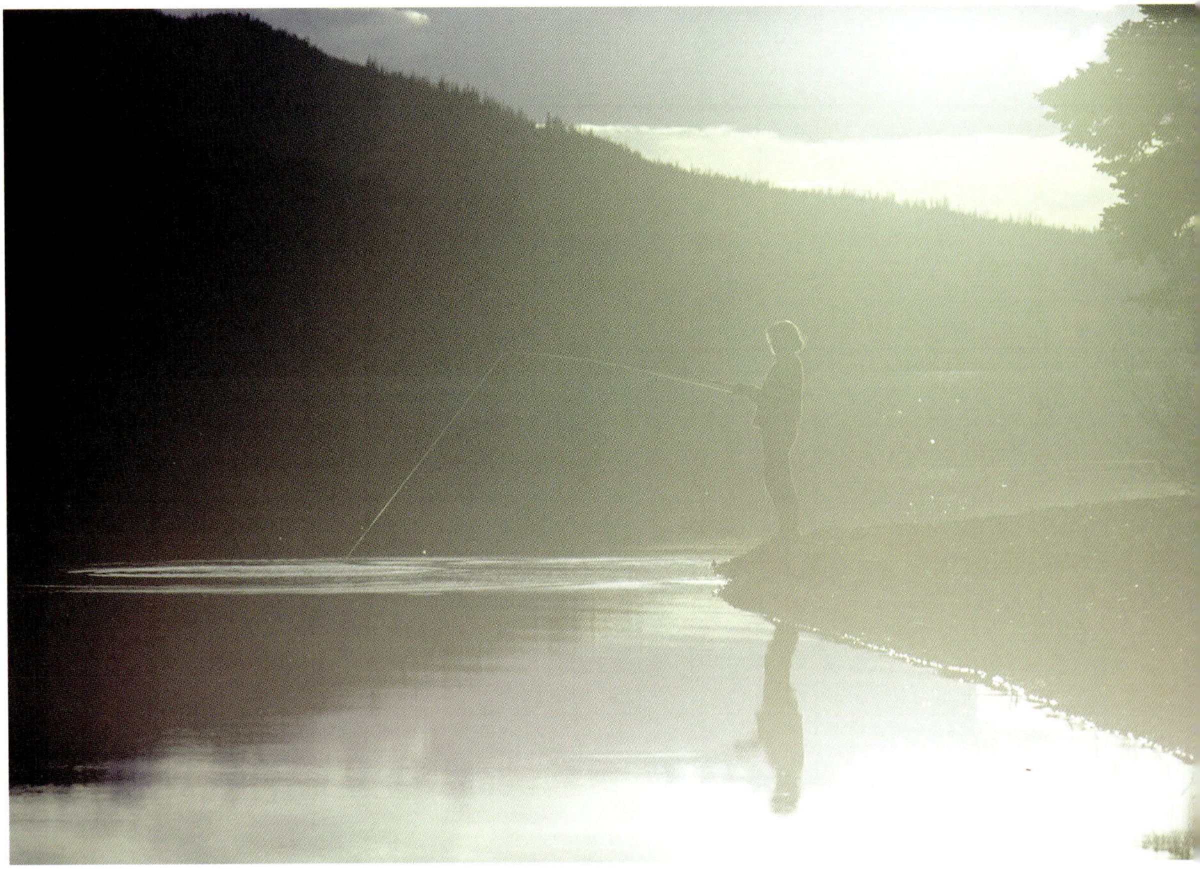

I wanted to preserve the rich evening colors in this frame, and show my subject as a rim-lit silhouette. Underexposing by a full stop from my camera's reading helped me to achieve that effect. Fox lake, Yukon. Fuji film, 70-200 mm zoom lens.

Choosing Shutter Speeds

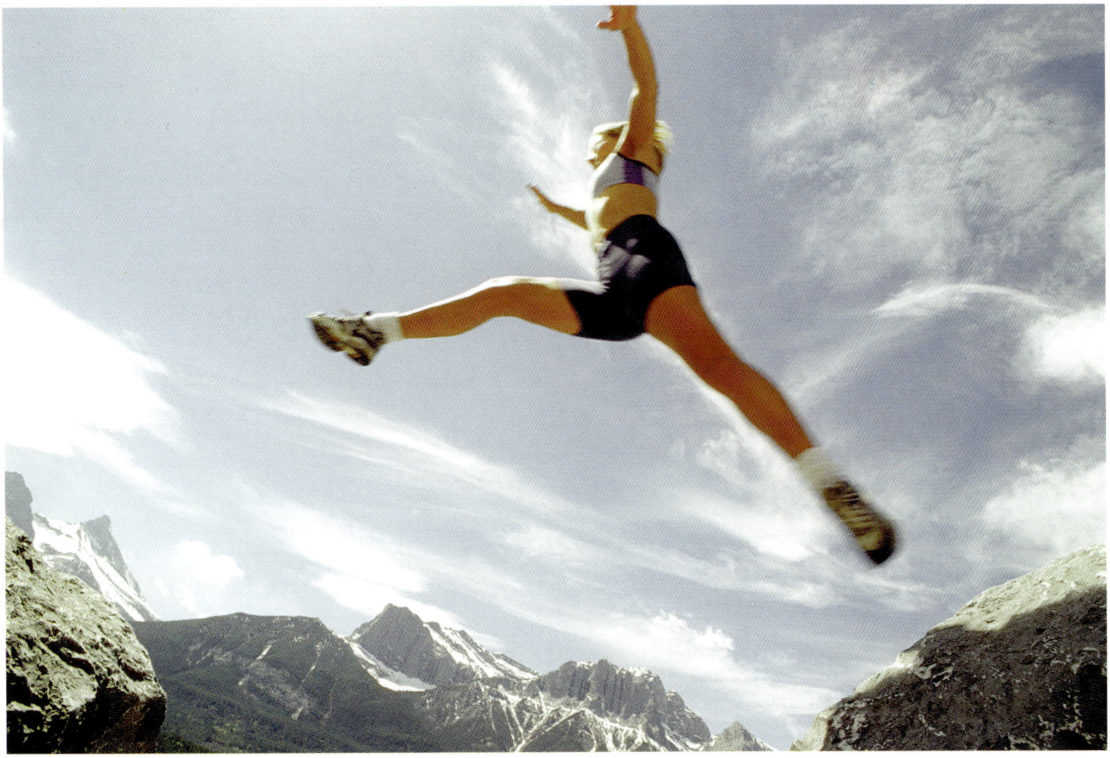

Sometimes stopping motion may not be in the best interest of your composition. Allowing for a little motion often gives a more dynamic feel, while also permitting a wider depth of field. Canadian Rockies. Kodak E100VS, 20 mm lens.

Once exposure is determined, shutter speeds and lens diaphragm opening—or f-stop—need to be chosen in a complementary fashion. With any given exposure, f-stops can be increased only at the expense of shutter speed, and vice-versa.

Depending on the particular situation and composition intended, one or the other will have to take priority (hence "shutter priority" and "aperture priority", both of which will be dealt with soon). Sometimes, though, both are nearly equally important, and then the photographer has to either use a tripod or look at different film options to overcome the dilemma of which to prioritize.

Generally, shutter speed is chosen for the following reasons: the photographer wants to either record motion as a blur, or freeze it entirely; he or she's unable to handhold the camera at a lower speed without risking camera shake and blurriness; alternatively, his or her camera—or film—poses limitations on going to higher or lower speeds.

The first point will be dealt with later, in the section entitled "Capturing and Creating Motion" page 143. The other points, of stopping motion and of limitations on handholding cameras, are addressed in the next few pages.

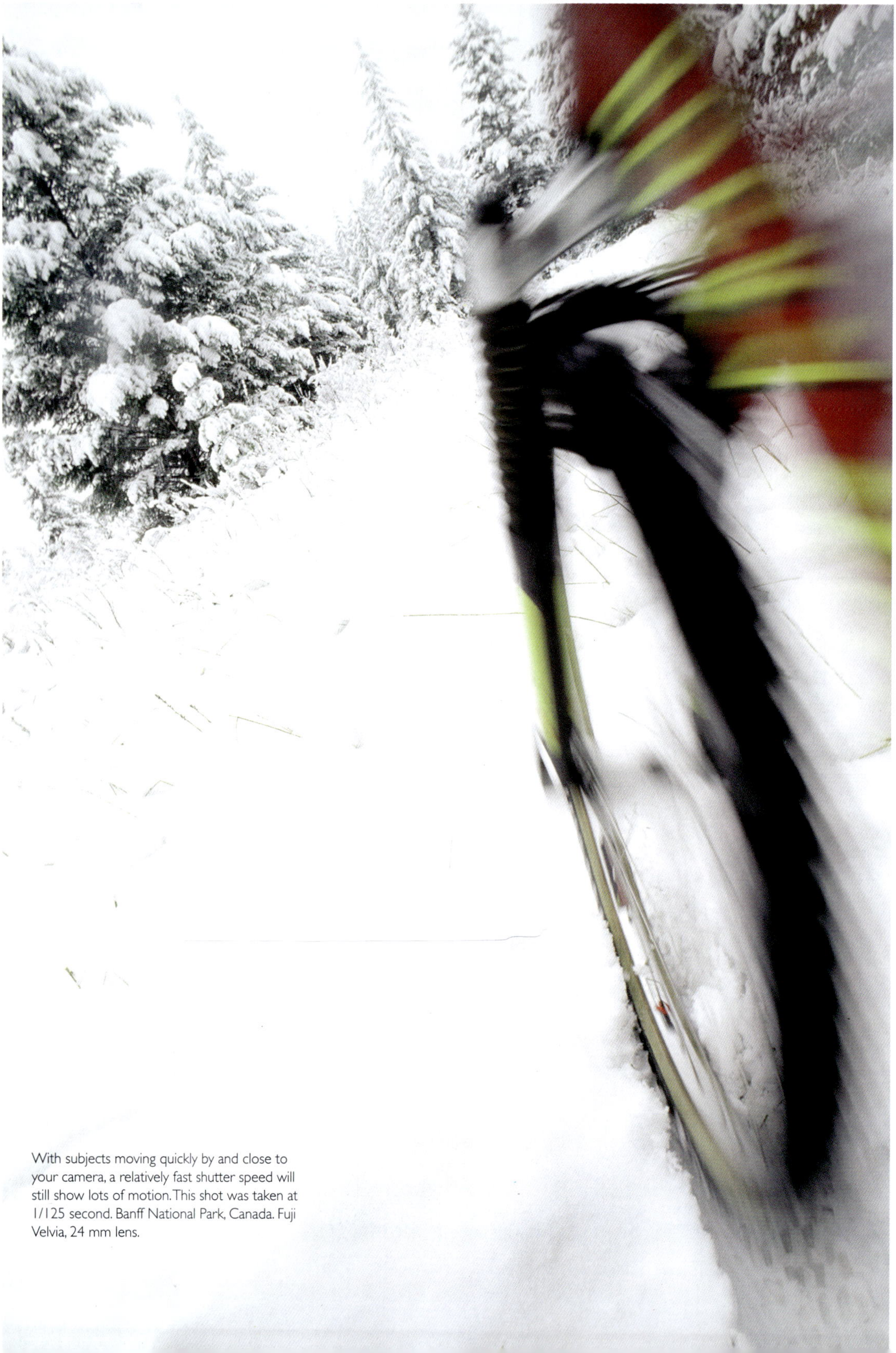

With subjects moving quickly by and close to your camera, a relatively fast shutter speed will still show lots of motion. This shot was taken at 1/125 second. Banff National Park, Canada. Fuji Velvia, 24 mm lens.

Stopping Motion Entirely

Several new camera models have been built with shutter speeds as high as, and sometimes in excess of, 1/8000 second. I don't think I've had more than a few opportunities to test this very fast speed on my Nikon F5 but, needless to say, when I have used it there is virtually no motion apparent in the resulting photos.

However, even this speed setting is probably not short enough to stop the fastest motion running perpendicular to your camera while using a really long lens. And because it's not, shows exactly how difficult it is to determine a speed that will completely freeze motion without some experimentation.

Here are the factors that will determine how fast a shutter speed you will need to stop all motion: whether that motion is perpendicular to your camera, at an oblique angle, or directly in line with the camera; the size of lens you've chosen; and the actual speed of the motion involved.

Freezing the motion of a downhill ski racer, whom may be travelling faster than 60 m/h (110 km/h), while shooting perpendicular to his path—i.e. directly across the ski run—may push beyond the highest speed limitations of your camera. This particularly holds true if you are using a lens of 300 mm or so because you are well off the slope.

On the other hand, if you are to angle your camera somewhat obliquely to the skier, say by pointing it slightly uphill, you should have less difficulty arresting his motion. This is partially why most poster or magazine views of Olympian skiers are photographed at a slightly oblique angle (the oblique viewpoint often presents a more complimentary image of the athlete as well). If you are to then point your camera directly uphill towards the skier, or downhill as he passes, even a slower shutter speed will freeze his motion.

Lens selection has an even more dramatic effect on arresting motion. Using the example above, if you were to decrease your chosen lens size to say 200 mm or 180 mm, you may be easily able to freeze the skier while shooting perpendicular to his descent.

If a wide angle lens is chosen in a different situation, say to stop the motion of a mountain biker jumping overhead at a slightly oblique angle to your camera, then a speed of 1/250 or 1/500 may be all that is required to freeze him in mid-air. This may be a useful lens choice if your intention is to expand depth of field and render the entire scene in focus as well (a technique dealt with in the next section).

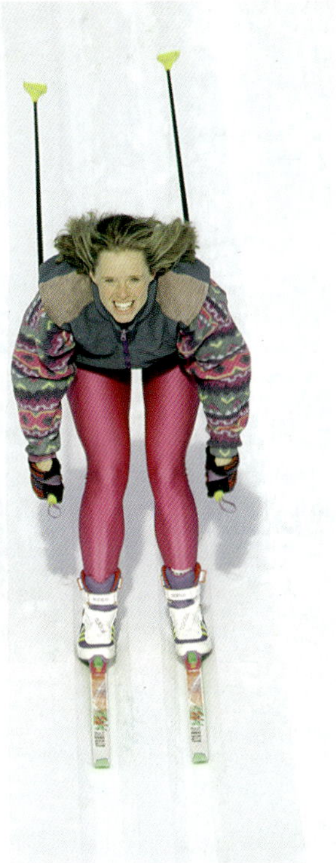

Fast moving subjects may not be that difficult to arrest if ambient light is strong. Canadian Rockies. Fuji Velvia, 105 mm lens.

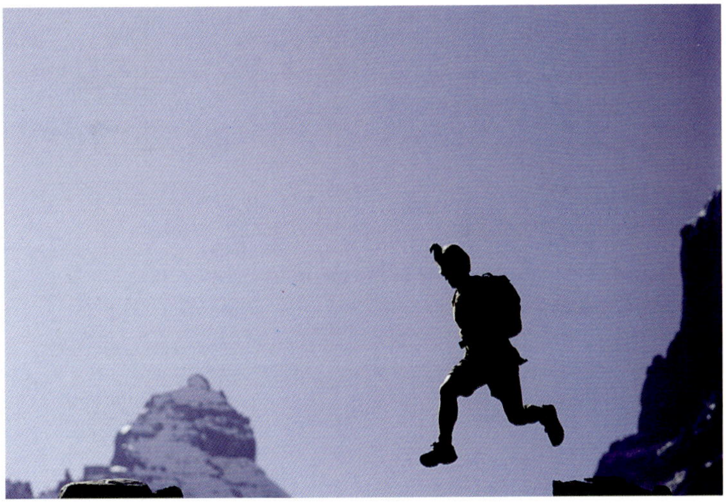

Freezing motion entirely usually means sacrificing depth of field. Sometimes this will be of benefit to your composition anyway. Banff National Park, Canada. Fuji Velvia, 180 mm lens.

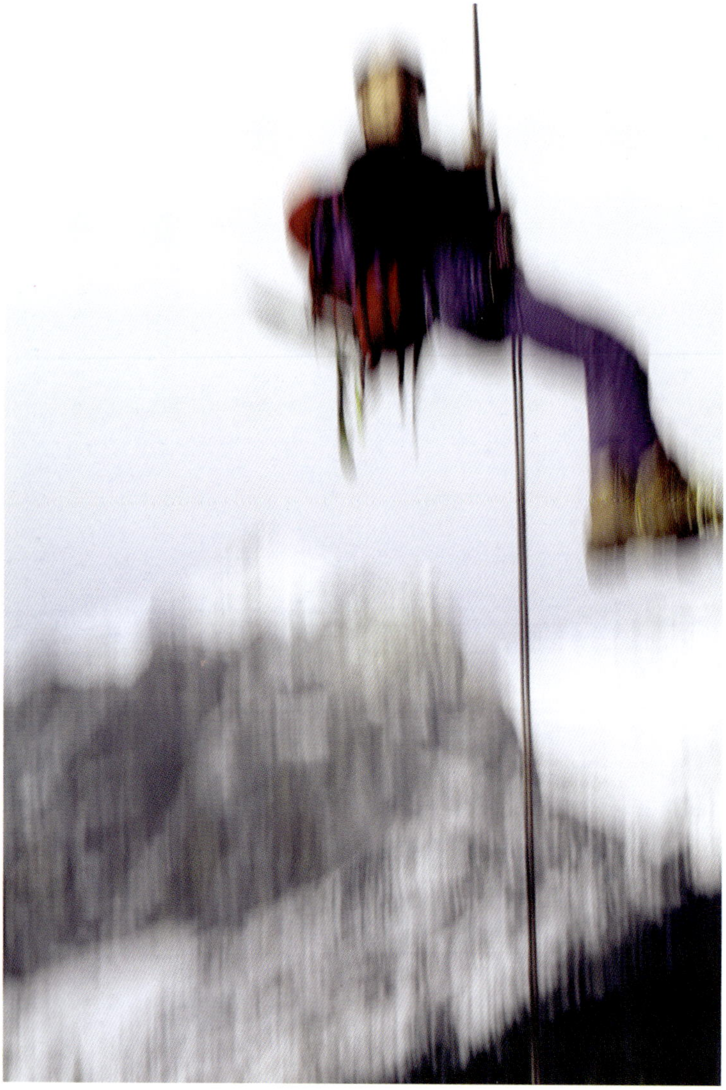

Severe camera shake, as shown here, can occur while shooting at slow speeds, especially if your shooting position is unsteady and long lenses are chosen. Canadian Rockies. Fuji Velvia, 200 mm lens.

Avoiding Camera Shake

Often shutter speed is not determined by a desire to stop motion—or alternatively, to include it—but by a limitation on your ability to hand hold the camera steadily. As a rule of thumb, all but the most seasoned photographers are unable to handhold cameras without camera shake, on a consistent basis, at values below those of a chosen lens.

In other words, shooting with a handheld camera at a speed of less than 1/125 of a second with 125 mm lens, 1/60 of a second with a 55 mm lens, or 1/30 of a second with a 28 mm lens is generally not a good idea unless your body position and your camera grip are particularly stable. If your stance is somewhat unstable, say if you're leaning out across a void or on very uneven ground, higher minimum shutter values should be chosen, perhaps 1/125 with an 85 mm lens, 1/60 second with a 35 mm lens, etc.

This being said, if you're not carrying a tripod and a situation presents itself that demands shooting at a speed slower than your chosen lens size, by all means shoot the scene.

Here's a classic example of just such an occasion. The sky has become dark and overcast, with twilight approaching, and a beautiful bull elk steps onto a prow in front of you. Your camera is loaded with slow film, perhaps Fuji Velvia with an ASA value of 50. Even at a maximum lens opening of f-2.8, your exposure meter reads 1/60 of a second.

Since you've already determined the composition demands a 125 mm lens, and you're not carrying a tripod, you need to find a particularly stable position.

Probably the best one to shoot from, if you can manage it without spooking the elk or filling your view with foreground grasses, is to lie on the ground with your elbows firmly planted. Alternatively, look for a stump or tree trunk you can support your camera on or lean against, or any other natural feature for that matter.

If you do manage to find a firm stance somehow, chances are that the resulting photo will be a success. And content yourself with the knowledge that even if you did have a tripod, the time, noise and flash of metal while setting it up may easily have been enough to frighten the elk from his lofty position.

Choosing Depth of Field

My early photography years were consumed with simply recording mountain experiences on film. I believe it was my "discovery" of depth of field that fundamentally changed my work, thanks to an investment in a camera and lens system that allowed me to manually select f-stops, along with shutter speeds.

I'm sure that many other newcomers to mountain photography might initially ignore depth of field altogether, and simply want to include everything in focus that is visible through their viewfinders. By doing so they will have, inadvertently, maximized their cameras' depth of field (a minimum depth of field, by contrast, shows very little in focus).

There are certainly many mountain situations where extending the range of focus is the appropriate measure, especially while composing grand sweeping views with a wide angle lens. However, it's always wise to first consider whether it would be best to render all components of a scene in perfect focus.

Often the trade-off in slower shutter speed is not worth mandating a wide depth of field at any rate. But determining depth of field should nearly always be the result of conscious thought and composition, not simply a default response to predetermined shutter speed.

A shallow depth of field can lend a three-dimensional effect to the finished photograph, giving it both depth and focusing the viewer's attention on select elements within the frame (this point will be expanded upon in the chapter on "The Creative Eye" on page 99). Sometimes the best choice will be to find a medium depth-of-field value, which both keeps your intended subject(s) in sharp focus but also allows certain foreground or background elements to slip out of focus.

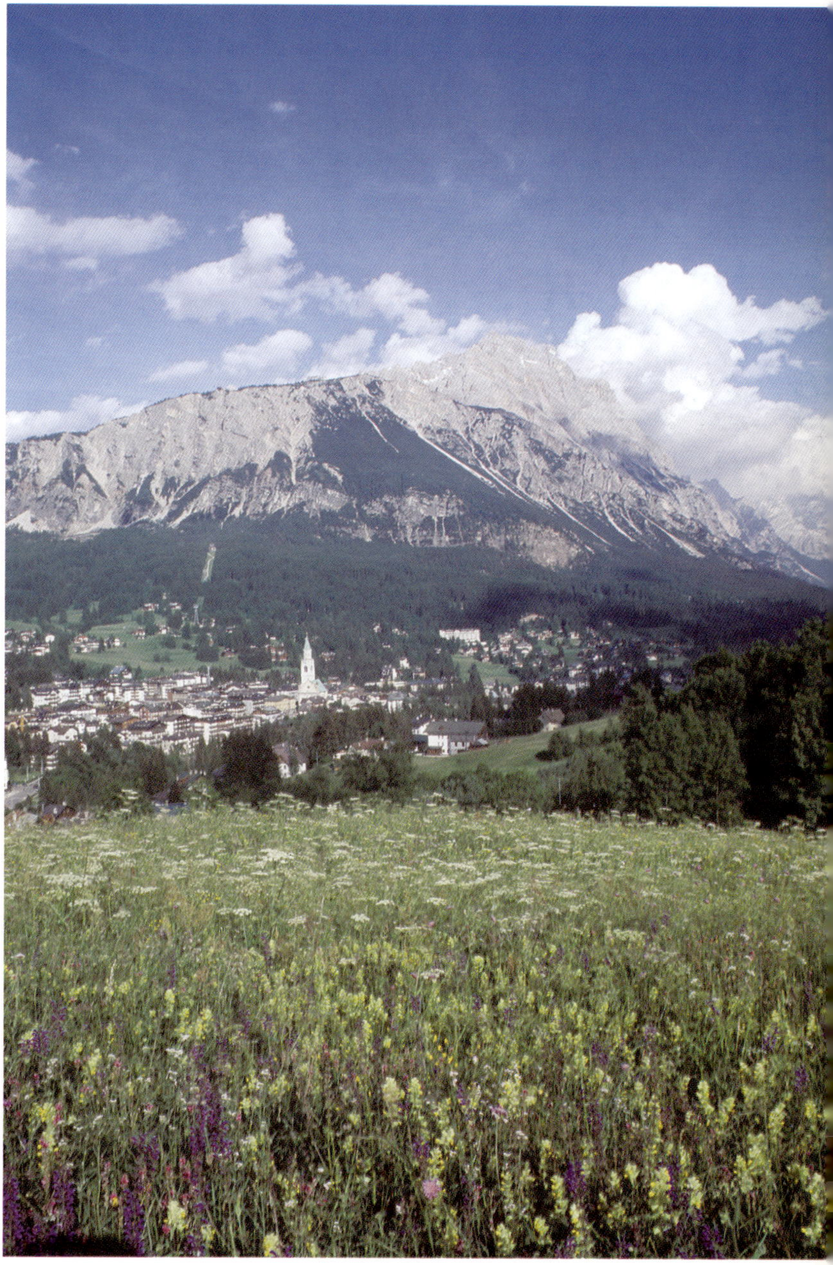

A very wide depth of field was more or less chosen by default in this shot. Foreground and background details seemed of equal importance to the overall composition. Cortina d'Ampezzo, Italy. Fuji Velvia, 28 mm zoom lens..

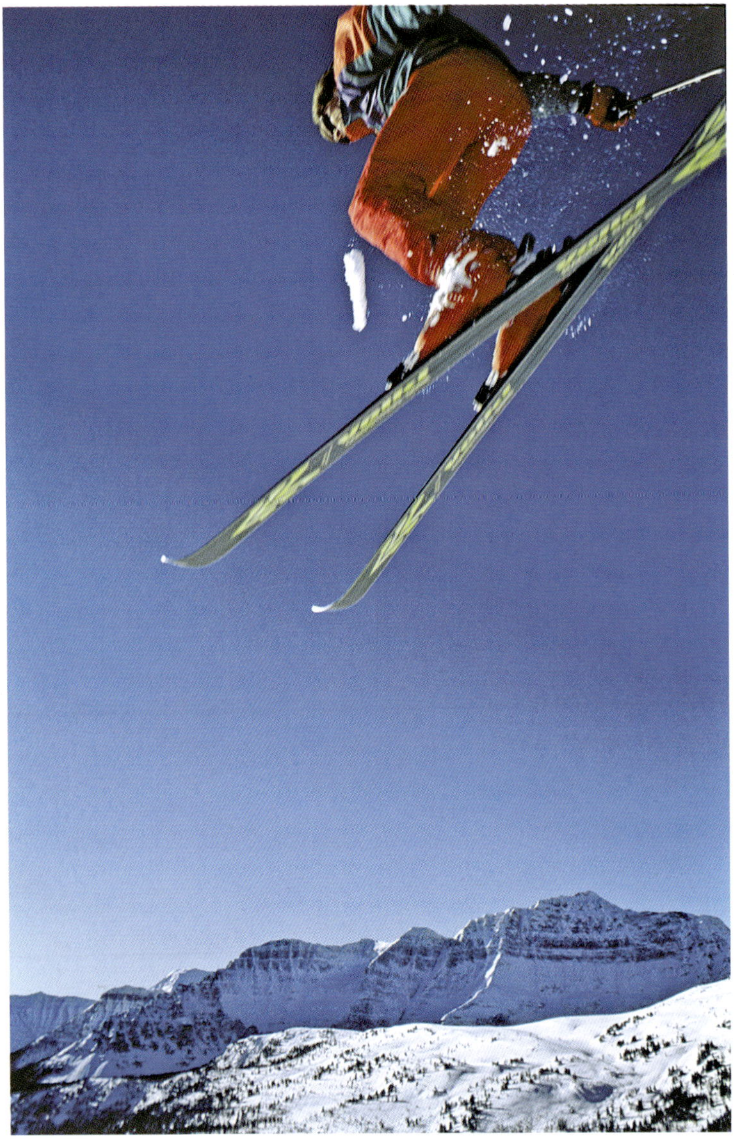

A depth of field that kept both the skier and mountains in focus struck me as being important to this shot. Because the skier was merely launching off the side of a small cliff from a standing position, little blurring resulted. Canadian Rockies. Kodak E100VS, 20 mm lens.

Maximizing Depth of Field

As mentioned in the above outline, there are times when maximizing depth of field is the appropriate choice. Imagine, as suggested earlier, you are shooting a wide mountain view with beautiful alpine flowers in the foreground and majestic peaks behind. The sun is out, fully lighting the scene, and even at the smallest lens opening (and therefore largest f-stop value, say f-22) your exposure meter reads 1/30 of a second.

This can be easily accomplished by a handheld camera. Referring back to an earlier discussion on camera shake, just ensure your chosen lens size is at least as wide as 28 mm.

Or perhaps you want to shoot down a ridge toward your climbing partner. She is your main subject, but there are also spectacular mists clinging to the distant rocky crests that you want to retain in focus.

You've determined that a 105 mm lens is needed for the composition but, because your partner is quite close to you—say eight meters (or 25 ft.) away—any lens opening larger than f-16 will be inadequate to focus on both. Thankfully, lighting conditions are very bright, and your exposure meter has give you a reading of 1/125 second at that f-stop.

Again, there is probably no need to reduce the depth of field, or worry about a tripod, in order to realize your intended composition. Just keep a solid stance.

One of my favorite wide depth-of-field compositions is less common, but arguably even more powerful. It involves the isolation of foreground details—perhaps your climbing partner's hands gripping a ledge, for example—with strong background elements, such as a glaciated range of mountains.

The only trick for successfully recording this kind of shot is to ensure that the hands will indeed remain in focus, despite having chosen the widest depth of field your camera allows. There are really two ways to accomplish this, as described next.

Depth of Field Preview

Most advanced SLR cameras have a depth-of-field preview button that allows you to check whether things in your shot, particularly foreground elements, are in proper focus. Just set your intended f-stop for the composition and then push that button.

When you do, the lens diaphragm actually closes down to the f-stop value you've chosen. By looking through the viewfinder you can see whether chosen picture elements will appear in focus or not.

A problem often arises, however, when checking depth of field at really small openings this way (such as at f-22). The viewing screen becomes very dark, since you're reducing most of the light that would otherwise reach it, and then it's really hard to tell whether anything at all is in perfect focus.

This is where the second approach is especially handy. Most camera lenses—except for some of the newer autofocus lenses for some bizarre reason—have inscribed calibrations that refer to depth of field at a given f-stop. Sometimes they are even colored, to reflect the corresponding f-stop colors on each lens (if in doubt about whether your specific camera and lens system allows for this kind of manual depth-of-field selection, check your owner's manual).

Here's the way to determine whether a given f-stop is adequate to achieve the depth of field your composition demands: arrive at maximum and minimum camera-to-subject distances, then, using the calibrations on your camera lens, match these to f-stop values. The f-stop thus arrived at should be the one you choose.

Since time was of no real consequence while shooting this view, I manually determined a minimum depth-of-field setting for the flowers, and made corresponding adjustments with my camera and lens. Banff National Park, Canada. Fuji Velvia, 20 mm lens.

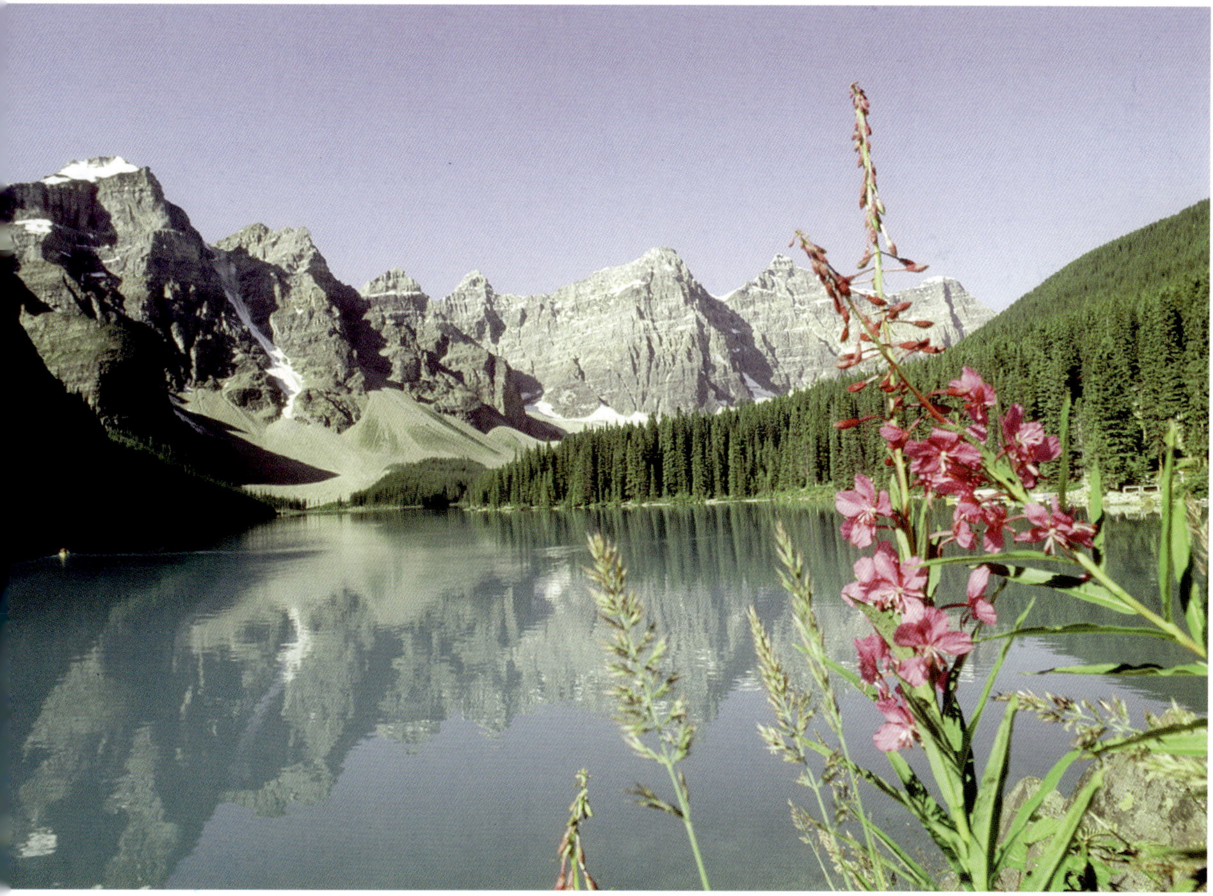

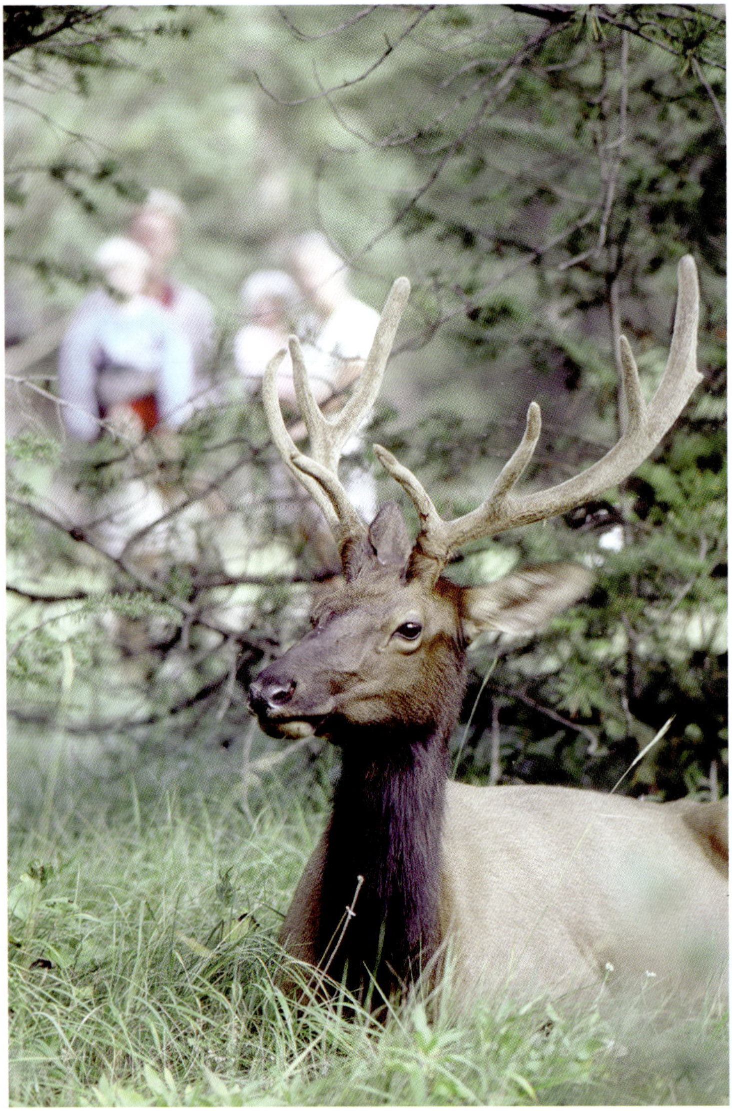

Depth-of-field preview was useful for this shot. It enabled me to arrive at an f-stop that made the distant figures discernible without having them compete with the foreground elk. Canadian Rockies. Kodak E100VS, 125 mm lens.

Finding the camera-to-subject distance extremes isn't generally that difficult. In many cases the maximum value will be at, or close to, infinity, and so it's really just determining the minimum value that requires a bit of effort.

Take, for example, the same alpine meadow as described above. Mountains are, of course, an infinite distance away, at least where any camera is concerned, and so it's the closest flowers to be kept in focus that you need to be concerned about. All that's required is to simply pre-focus on those flowers and check the numerical value on the focusing ring; this becomes your minimum setting.

The example of the climber on the ridge crest could be dealt with in a very similar manner. Maximum depth of field is again infinite, and so only the climber's distance from the camera lens—the minimum value—needs to be determined, and an appropriate f-stop chosen.

In some close-up photography situations, however, such as when an individual flower is the subject and its surroundings are intended to be mainly in focus, both maximum and minimum settings may need to be chosen. This is a somewhat onerous process that is best achieved with the camera mounted on a tripod (see "Close-up Photography" page 187).

Depth of Field Applications

As suggested earlier, depth of field should be either chosen or at least thought about for every composition. The one exception to this rule is when your intended shot is rapidly disappearing.

Take, for example, an ambling grizzly bear about to leave a well-lit meadow for dark forest. Because of the necessity to shoot fast, you'd most likely use an f-stop already established from your last shot. Alternatively, you might simply defer to the minimum f-stop on your lens to ensure a sharp picture, especially if your chosen lens is a long one.

At medium f-stop values your camera's depth-of-field preview button can be especially handy. It generally gives a good idea of what will be in focus, without showing a screen so dark it can barely be viewed.

But the manual approach for determining f-stop from a chosen field of view can also be used. The choice of which works best is really a very personal one, and often simply depends on how fast either can be implemented by you, the photographer.

Compositional reasons for choosing middle and minimum depths of field will be covered later. Practically speaking, though, there are many good reasons for settling on smallish f-stop values. The relative popularity of fast lenses owes much to these.

Here are the most obvious advantages of choosing small and medium f-stop values: as in the earlier grizzly bear example, you simply want to ensure that you get a good shot in sharp focus. A minimum—or close to minimum—f-stop, and hence depth of field, will of course allow you to shoot any scene at a higher shutter speed than if a larger f-stop value is chosen.

Here is a good example of medium depth of field. The more distant hiker needed to be recognizable, but not as much so as the one closer to my camera. Canadian Rockies. Fuji Velvia, 70-200 mm zoom lens.

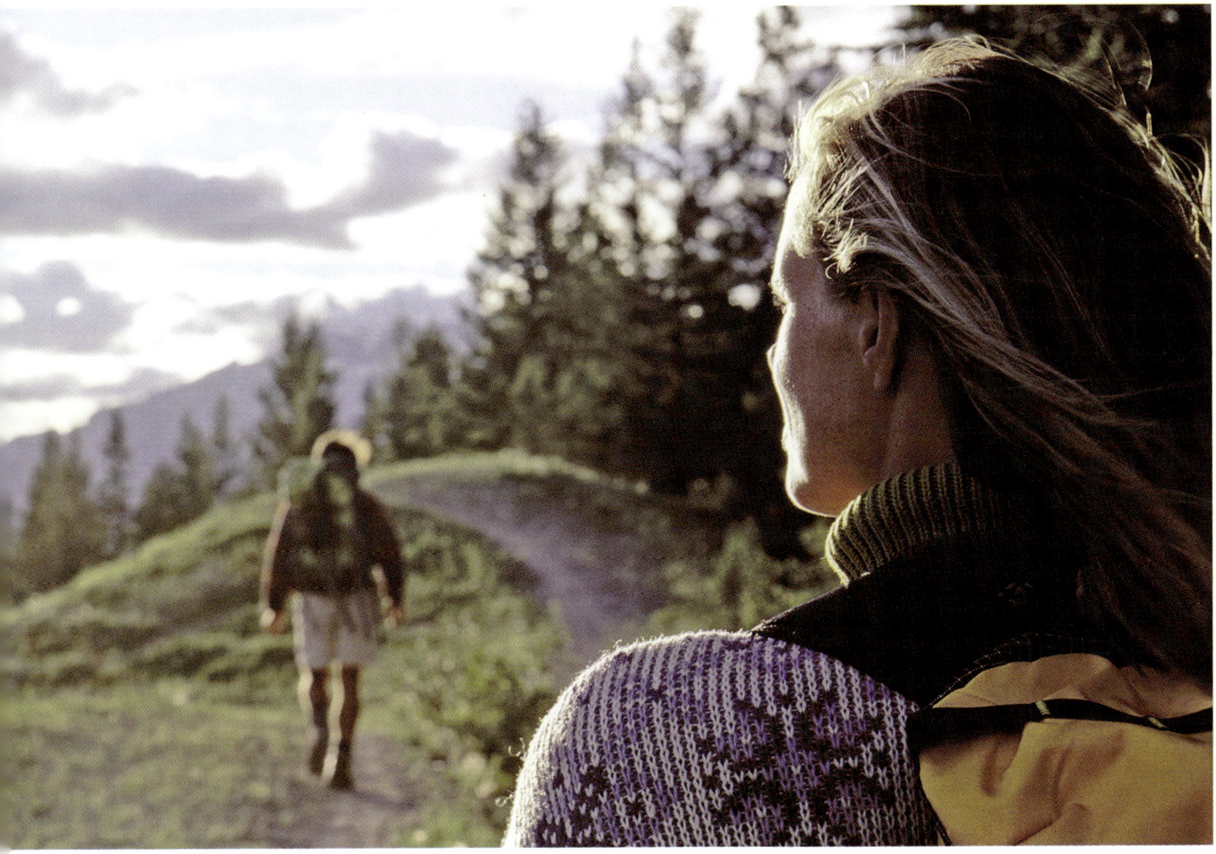

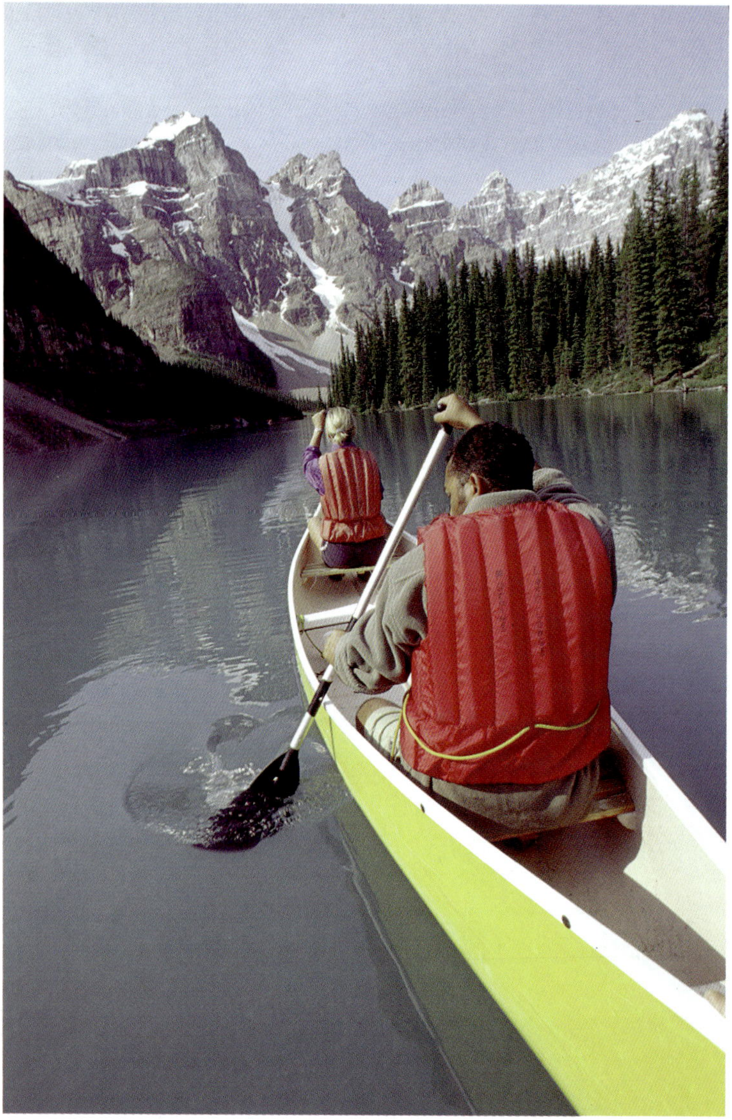

This shot maximizes depth of field. The canoe is actually not moving forward (I had a companion hold onto it) or else some blurring would be evident. Canadian Rockies. Kodak E100VS, 20 mm lens.

When a large telephoto format is needed in especially low light conditions, it's often the fastest lenses that are the most useful. This is doubly true with a fast moving subject, or if film speed is slow. Wildlife and action subjects, such as skiers, mountain bikers and energetic kids, often need to be photographed at near minimum f-stop settings when viewed through big lenses.

A medium depth of field, on the other hand, may be chosen simply to ensure that all aspects of a given subject are recorded in focus.

If your subject is oriented in line with, or at an oblique angle to, your camera, and you want to ensure that both the nearest and farthest ends of the subject are going to be focus, you will need to choose a larger f-stop than if that same subject was perpendicular to the camera. The choice of a large lens, or the reality of low light and/or slow film, may

Opposite: I used my lens' minimum setting for this shot, mainly because I wanted to isolate the young skater from background clutter. Canadian Rockies. Kodak E100VS, 105 mm lens.

constrain you from selecting a maximum depth-of-field value though. Hence, an appropriate middle one has to be chosen.

Consider another wildlife case. Say you've spotted a moose belly deep while foraging in swampy grasses, his face and body angled obliquely relative to your camera position. It's evening and you've chosen to use a large lens both for compositional reasons—you want to get a tight shot of the moose with little else showing—and because you don't want to spook the moose by getting too close physically.

You've determined, by using your depth-of-field preview button, that a minimum f-2.8 setting on your lens will record only part of what you'd like in focus. An f-8 opening will, however, render all important components in proper focus.

Although you don't have a tripod, you're confident that, at this setting but no higher because of the corresponding shutter speed, you can hold the camera steadily enough to record a sharp picture. F-8 is then, by default, the best depth-of-field compromise.

Or perhaps you have two distinct subjects, at different distances from your camera, that you want to keep in focus. Pretend that you are looking down a rope at your mountaineering companions, positioned ever so photogenically on a high ridge crest. You've asked them not to move for your composition, which you've determined needs a 135 mm lens.

Since they are oriented in a line to your camera, and at different distances away, a minimum f-stop value will show one in focus, but not both. Yet there is not enough light, and your film is too slow, to allow for a maximum setting to be chosen.

Again, some middle f-stop value that satisfies your focusing requirements while not compromising your minimum shutter speed will probably be the best one.

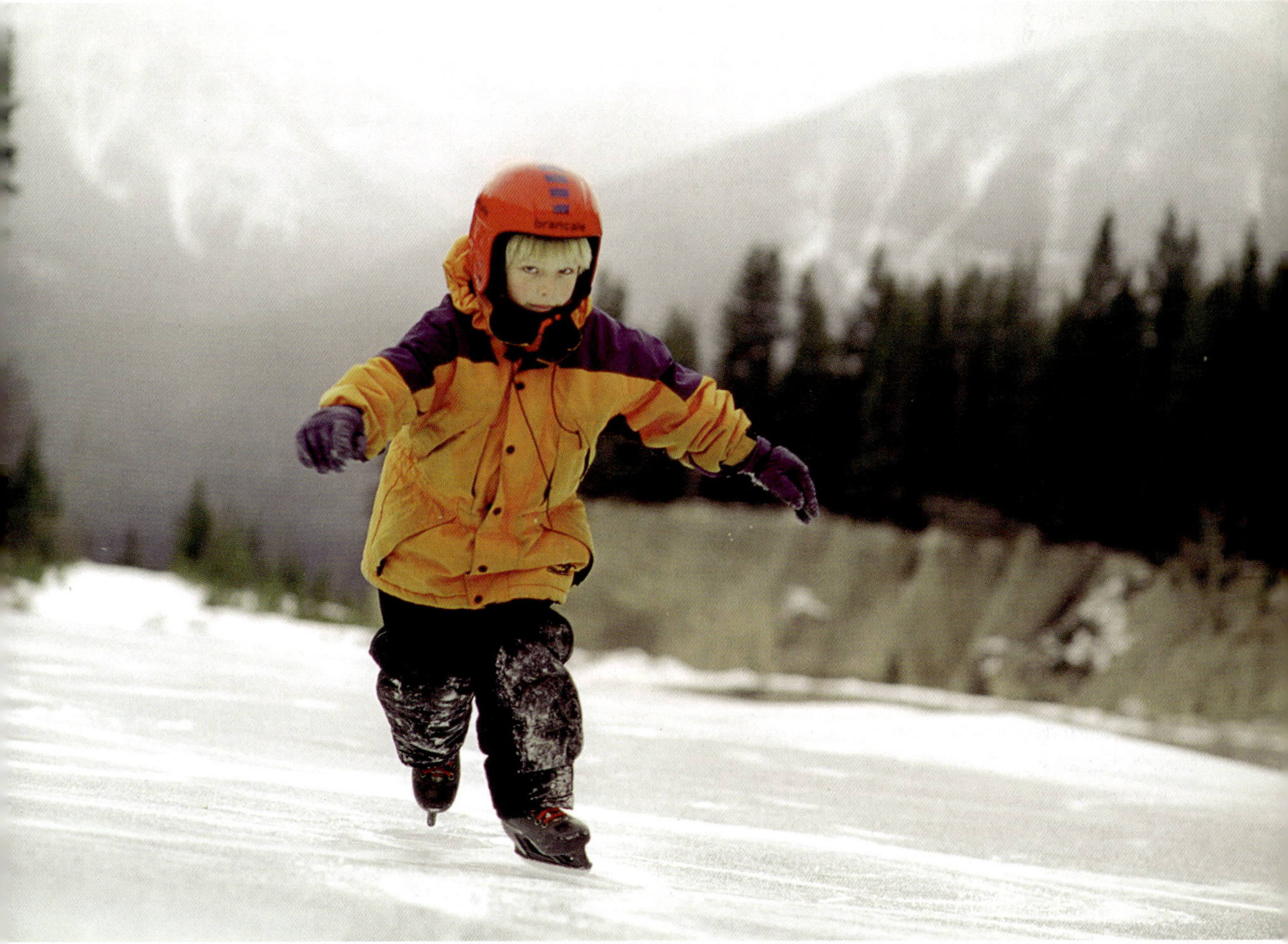

Aperture Priority

Many modern cameras allow you to either choose aperture priority, where shutter speeds are automatically selected in conjunction with exposure values determined by your camera, or shutter priority, where exactly the reverse is true.

These settings are mainly intended to facilitate automatic adjustments by your camera, when ambient light becomes brighter or dimmer. Such adjustments are then correlated to the speed or aperture settings you've predetermined.

Even if these functions don't exist on your camera, you can probably make manual adjustments that will mimic their purpose. What's most important is to think about when and why you'd most likely use either approach.

Consider the following example. You're photographing a wide mountain scene with lots of foreground detail, where a fairly wide depth of field, perhaps f-16, is needed to render all the important components in focus. If you were to choose aperture priority as per your camera's instructions, a shutter speed would be automatically selected to provide a well-exposed final result, based on your camera's internal meter reading.

Say, however, that in the midst of shooting, a cloud suddenly moves across the sun, dramatically altering the lighting on foreground flowers. To compensate for the lost light, your camera will immediately determine a slower speed for the shot. But, because you've chosen aperture priority, it won't change the f-stop. Hence, foreground flowers will remain in focus, and, as long as your camera is reading the exposure from them, they should be well exposed too.

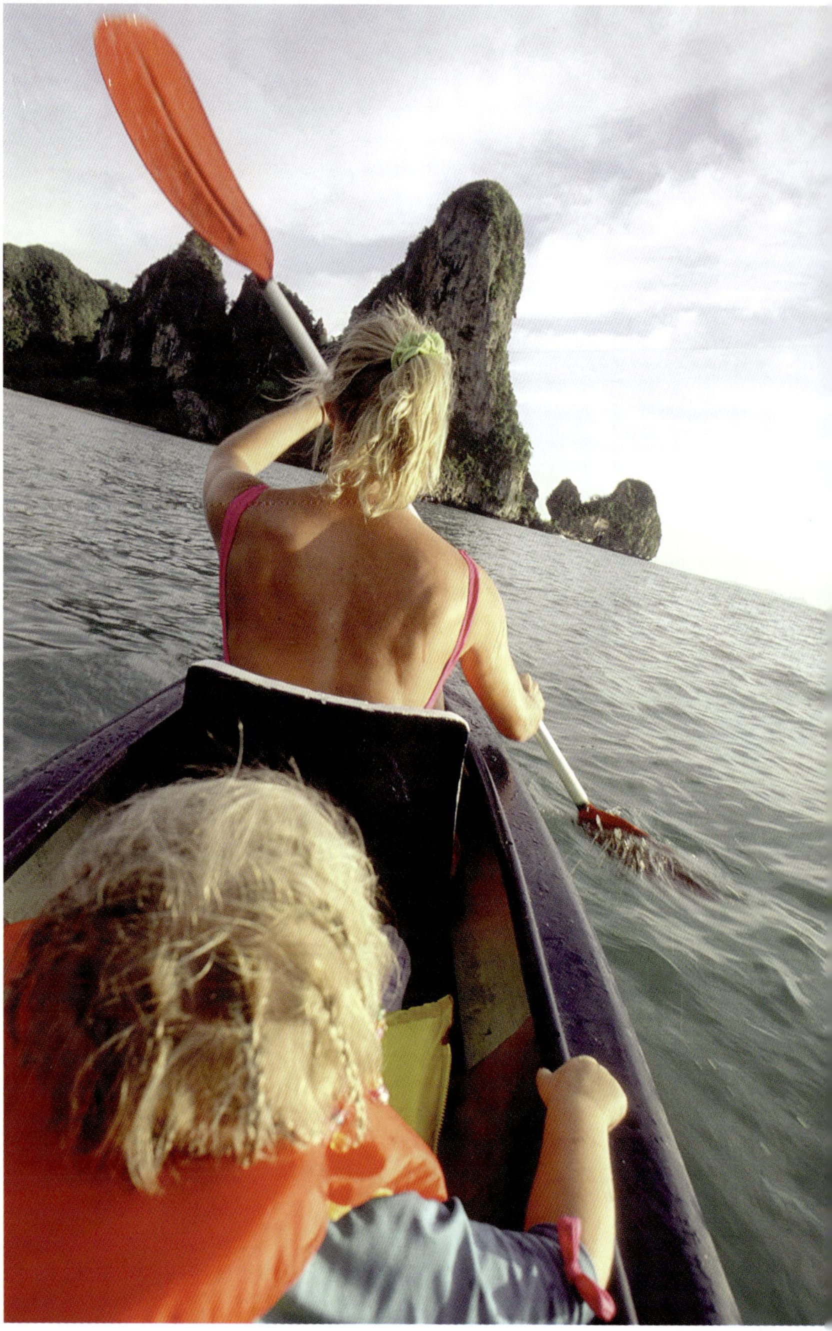

I knew I'd be unable to get a sharp result while shooting anything slower than 1/60 second because of the boat's rocking motion. Since I also wanted to widen the depth of field considerably, I used my camera's shutter priority function. Railay Bay, Thailand. Fuji Velvia, 28 mm lens.

Shutter Priority

Shutter priority allows you to pre-select speeds that are either well suited to subject motion or below what you don't think you can safely shoot without risking camera shake. It can be an especially useful function when you're quickly changing camera angles, or even your entire scene.

For example, say you're shooting downhill ski racers from the edge of a run. Your intention is shoot continuously as they enter the race course above you, then pass by and finally drop below your position.

Although your feet remain stationary, your camera swings with your upper torso as the skiers go by. As it does so, your camera's meter is invariably taking different exposure readings from the changing scene and making adjustments.

If you have chosen shutter priority and a speed of, say, 1/2000 of a second, then the skier should remain relatively sharp as you continuously snap frames. Keep in mind, however, the angle of view as it pertains to shutter speed and image sharpness (discussed in a previous section, "Stopping Motion Entirely" page 55).

What you may notice, when the results come back from the lab, is that the depth of field changes between frames in your sequence. And, unless your camera is reading exposure only from your subject, the skier may also become relatively lighter or darker between frames, depending on background brightness.

As eluded to earlier, choosing shutter priority may be a good way to avoid risking camera shake. If you're shooting scenics where you just want to maximize depth of field, but not at the risk of introducing camera shake, then a shutter priority selection will allow you to set your camera at the minimum speed you can safely handle. It will also provide assurance that the resulting depth of field will be the best one possible in view of film speed and lighting conditions.

Often, without an appropriate camera stand, this is the approach of choice when photographing wildlife in dim light. Your intention may be just to record as much of your animal subject in sharp focus as possible, without risking a soft shot because of an excessively slow shutter speed.

Generally, the tighter you approach your subject while shooting in shutter priority, the less of it will remain in focus. Face elements are particularly vulnerable to shifting out of focus. When a shallow depth of field is the best that you can manage, only the eyes, for example, or the mouth may record with absolute sharpness on film.

With this shot, my main interest was in recording as much depth of field as possible, so I used aperture priority. The blurring of the foreground foot was a hoped-for result, but I really had no idea how much would record. Canadian Rockies. Kodak E100VS, 24 mm lens.

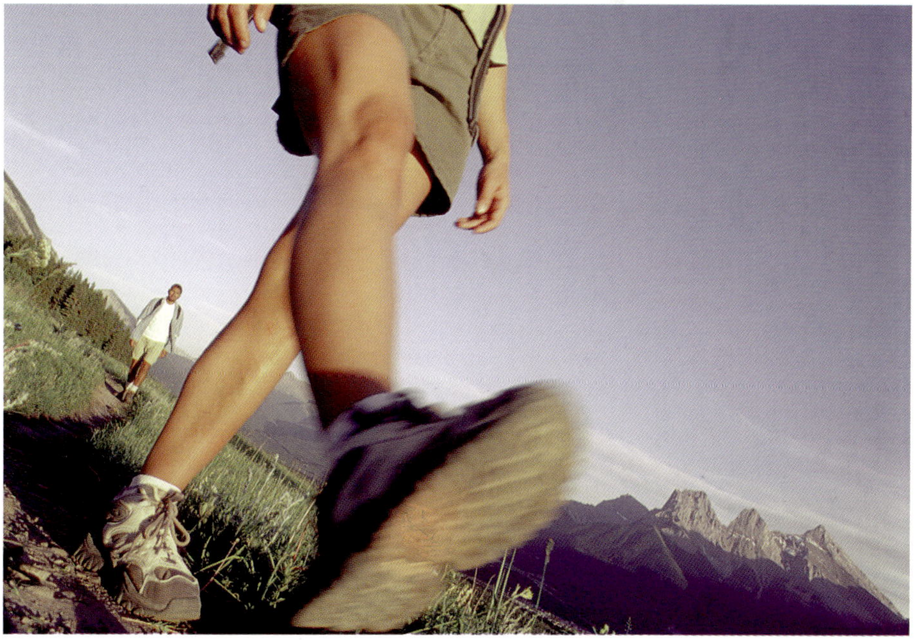

Tripods and Cable Releases

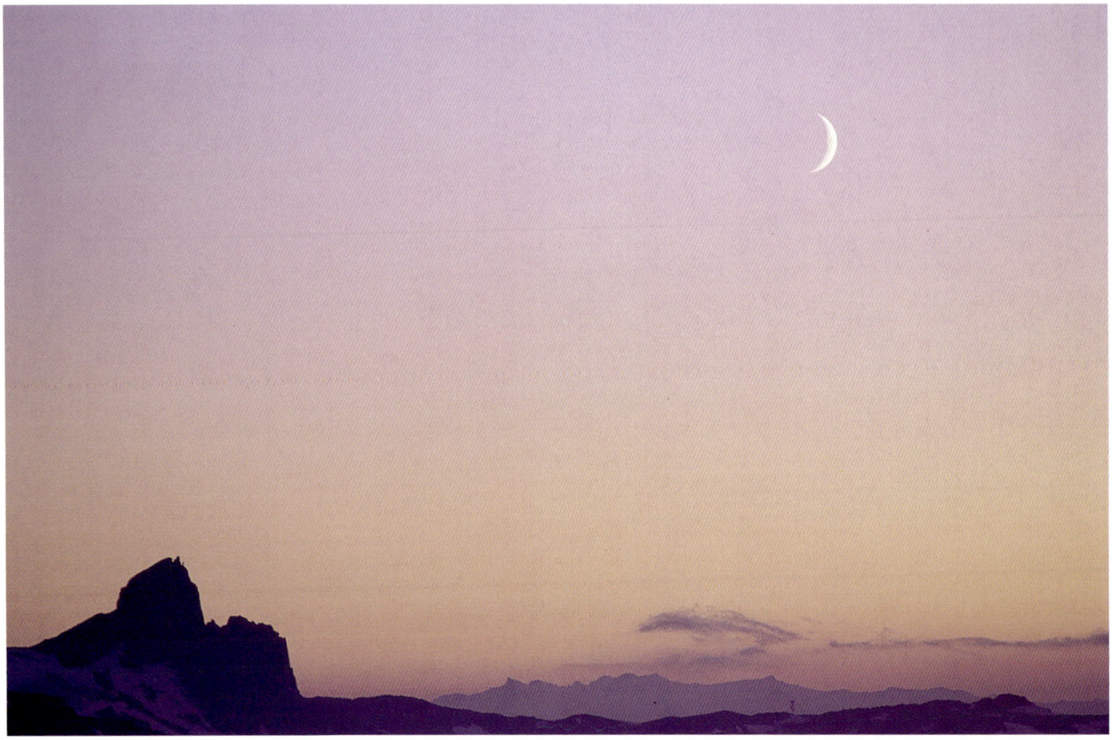

Tripods can be very useful for shots such as these, not just because they help to guarantee sharpness, but also for compositional reasons. Garibaldi Park, Canada. Fuji film, 35-70 mm zoom lens.

As pointed out earlier, a tripod—or at least some kind of camera stand—is nearly essential when photographing in very low light. It is also often needed when shooting with a really long lens and is sometimes necessary when a wide depth of field is chosen.

As a general rule, even with the steadiest body and camera position, camera stands are required when shooting at shutter speeds below the focal length of your chosen lens; for example, below 1/60 with a 55 mm lens, or 1/125 with a 125 mm lens.

Tripods are useful at higher speeds as well, providing a stable shooting platform that will often translate to greater image sharpness.

When shooting with an SLR camera, your tripod will also allow you to lock up the viewing mirror. Locking the mirror eliminates the noise of an SLR's viewing assembly flipping up and then back down, an internal movement that accounts for nearly all shutter-related sound. Since you can't see anything through your viewfinder without the mirror, shooting after lock-up is really next to impossible without a tripod.

A quiet shutter is especially relevant when wildlife photographing, since animals can be easily spooked by loud camera noises. But being able to lock the mirror up can also be useful when shooting at very slow speeds, where excessive internal vibration within your camera will make for soft, unsharp results.

Using a tripod can help vastly to improve compositions. When you're not quickly trying to compose a shot in the viewfinder because the scene or subject is about to disappear, it's worth taking the extra time to set your camera on a tripod and carefully view the scene, considering all compositional possibilities.

It may be that you want to change the horizon in your shot, or include no horizon at all. Or maybe you want to play with focus, or try different depths of

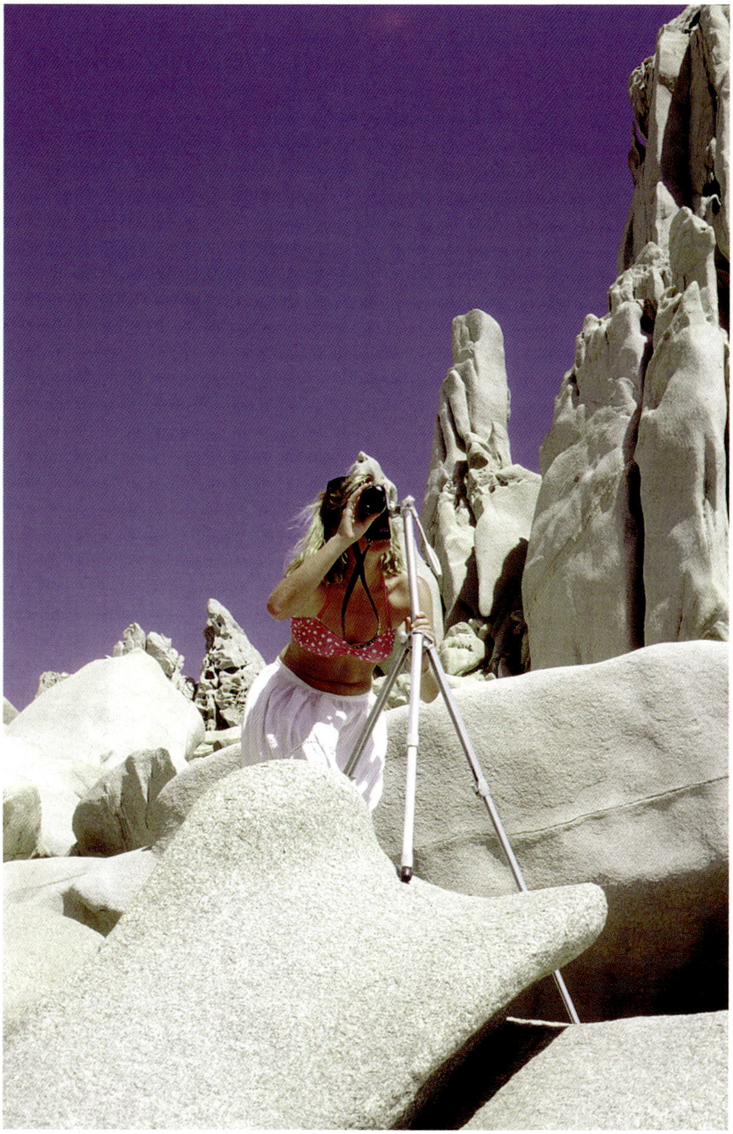

A good tripod can be set up in all kinds of terrain, allowing for the kind of shooting flexibility that a hand held camera does. Baja, Mexico. Kodachrome, 85 mm lens.

A taller tripod allowed me to shoot above the foreground ferns. My smaller, lightweight version was unable to do so. South Island, New Zealand. Fuji Velvia, 28 mm zoom lens.

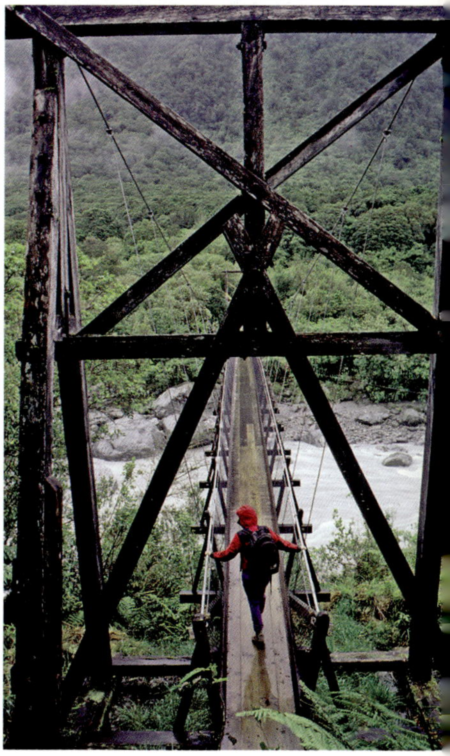

field. Or perhaps you conclude, after examining things thoroughly, that the scene is best shot vertically, even though your first impulse was to shoot it horizontally.

Many of these and other options would simply not cross your mind if a tripod weren't called into use. You won't always need one to carefully craft your compositions, especially when rocks, stumps or simply resting your camera on the ground provides an adequate and secure "stand". The tripod, however, provides a degree of flexibility that is impossible to match, and for this reason, all serious photographers sooner or later acquire at least one.

Lighter is Not Always Better

Thankfully, there are some great options when trying to choose a tripod ideal for your mountain activity. Keep in mind that lighter tripods tend to provide less stability than heavier ones. This is not to say that they are necessarily flimsy; rather, that the essential trade-off in weight may compromise how well your tripod performs in, say, high winds or with long lenses.

In addition to stability, there is also an issue of height. Many of the lightweight and more compact tripods do not extend to full viewing height, which sometimes makes it awkward to compose if you have to crunch down or squat while looking through the viewfinder.

More importantly, a low tripod extension means that you may not be able to get high enough to shoot subjects from slightly above, in a semi-aerial fashion, unless there are rocks or a hillside nearby that you can scramble up onto. This may not sound terribly relevant, but I'm always amazed how often I want a higher tripod extension when using my lightweight stand in the mountains.

So lighter may not always be better. But the important thing is to determine which size and type of tripod would best fit your particular needs. If you're planning to do lots of wildlife photography with long lenses, a heavier tripod might be a good idea, even though it'll be a significant additional weight if you're also planning long forays into the bush.

On the other hand, if your typical pursuit involves lots of alpine climbing, you may want to consider investing in an ultra lightweight tripod. It may be a little difficult to set up and record shots with on windy mountain ridges, but by using higher shutter speeds, or by placing rocks to anchor and buffer your tripod from the gusts, you should still be able to get great results.

Because of windy weather, this photo would likely not have been sharp if an ultra lightweight tripod had been used instead of a heavier one. S. Island, New Zealand. Fuji Velvia, 35-70 mm zoom lens.

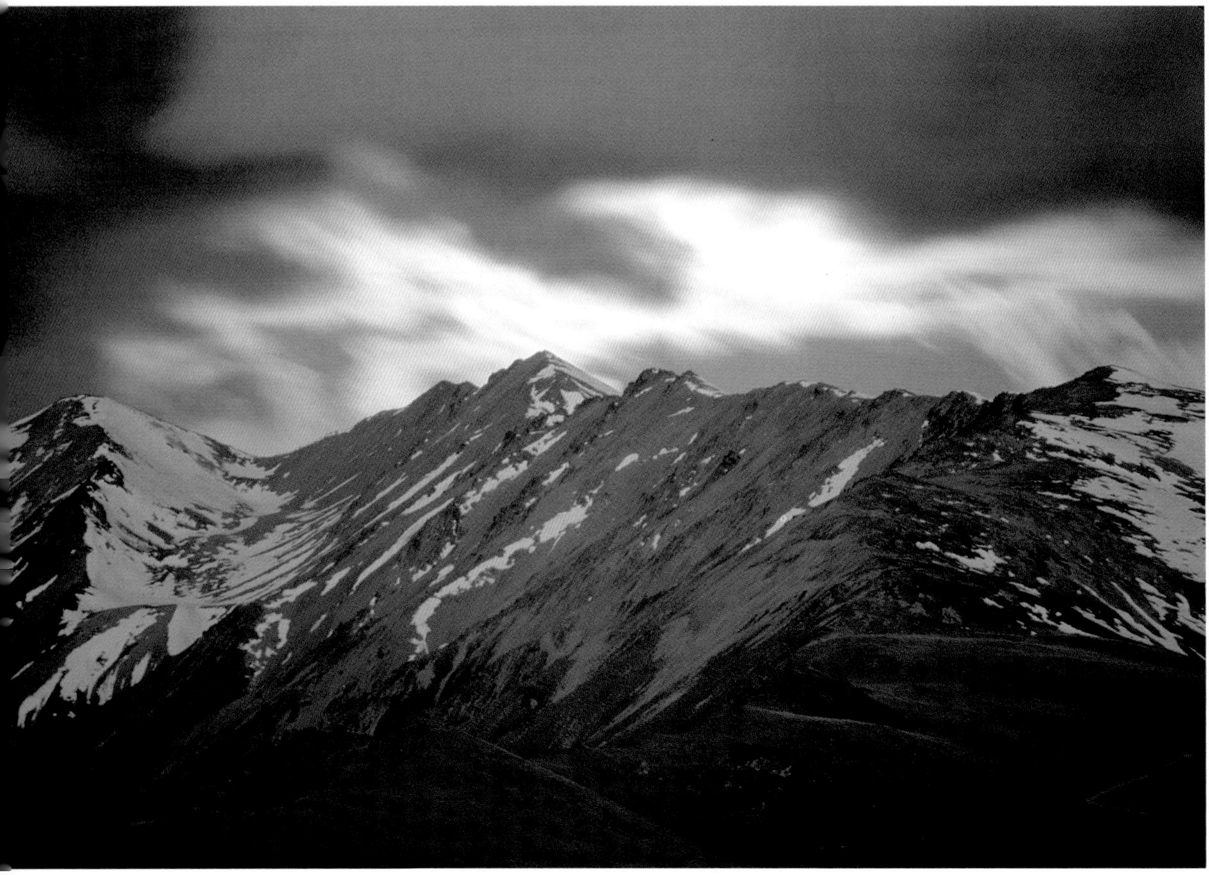

Choosing the Ideal Tripod

Often the best solution is to have a couple of tripods in your arsenal, which can be selectively chosen depending on your intended shoot or activity. Alternatively, a tripod which is neither the heaviest nor the lightest one you would normally choose may also be the best one if your photography interests range far and wide.

The essential point is that any tripod you invest in should follow with you on your outings and not be left behind because it's either too heavy to carry or too light to provide effective stability for your camera.

Price is, of course, another factor when choosing the ideal tripod. Lightweight Tiawanese tripods tend to be inexpensive, but unfortunately also break down pretty quickly under most mountain conditions. This may still be an acceptable compromise if you're either a casual photographer of if most of your mountain outings are, for example, day hikes.

But, if you need a sturdier tripod, for more aggressive outings, it's worth paying the extra cash to have a nice one. In any event, a good tripod should last you many years of regular use.

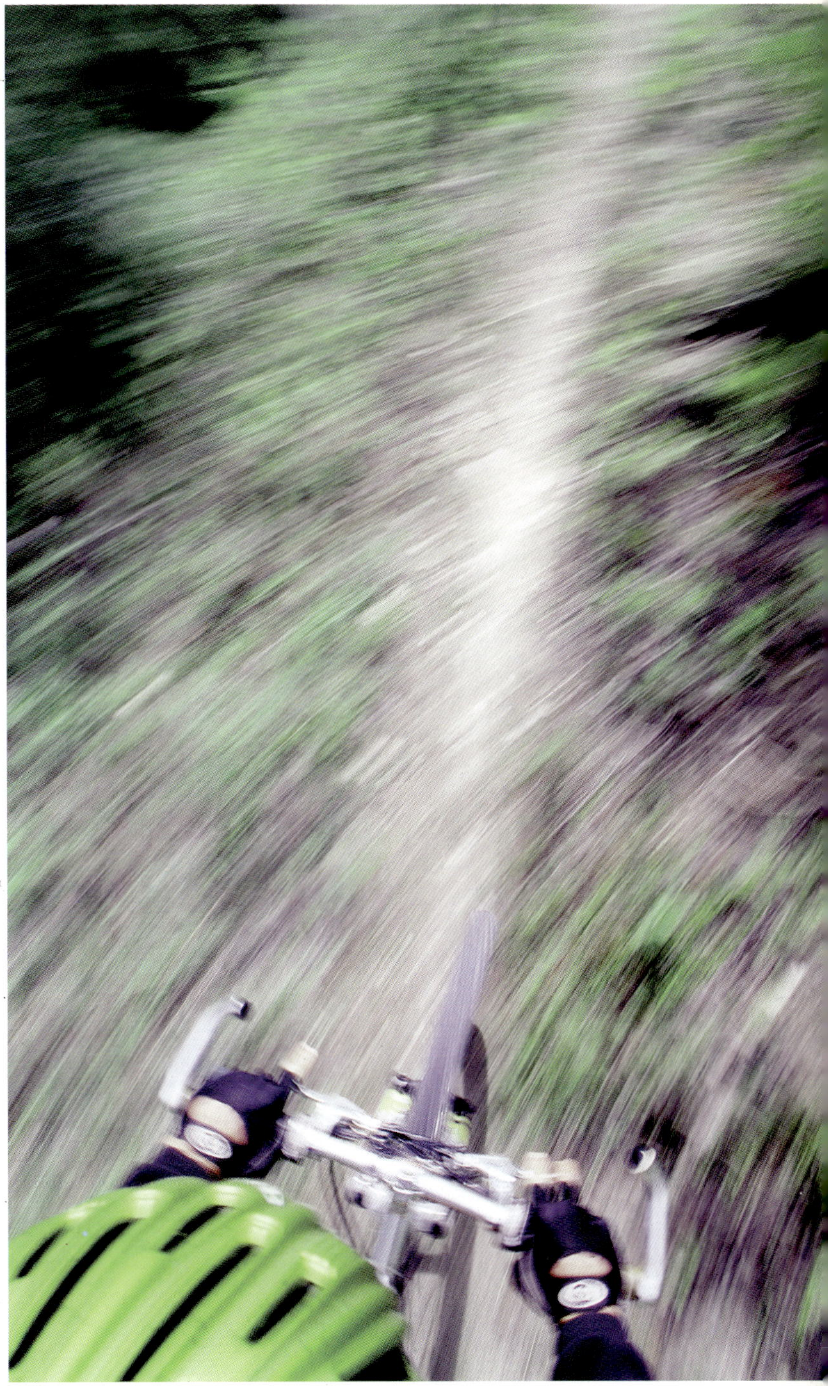

This shot was taken from a "moving" tripod, stuck inside a pack carried by the mountain biker. If it had been a heavy one, the biker would have had a hard time managing much speed. Canadian Rockies. Fuji Velvia, 24 mm lens.

Choosing a Tripod Head

Having the right tripod head for your particular photography needs is nearly as important as selecting the best stand. Again, weight is an important criteria to consider while choosing, as is bulkiness.

Tripod heads differ considerably in terms of function, but many offer more than you'll ever need. On the other hand, some offer too little, so it's important not to short-change yourself by eliminating functions or devices that might actually be useful from time to time.

Many of the tripods available at camera shops come equipped with pan heads, steered by a long handle when set up for horizontal shots. This head design was really intended for filmmakers and videographers; not still photographers. Consequently, unless you plan to do a lot of tripod-assisted pan photography—and you adamantly insist on using a handle for your pans—this type of tripod head is probably unnecessary.

Furthermore, it may even restrict your ability to shoot vertically, as many of them simply don't allow for a full range of motion. And at very least, it will weigh more, take up extra room in your pack, and the handle has a nasty habit of getting caught in things when setting up.

Consider fitting your tripod with either an RC or a ball head instead. The RC head, or 3D as they're also known, can be rapidly swivelled into position after loosening one or more screws. Most cover 360 degrees of view and therefore practically every conceivable shooting angle or requirement. They also tend to be durable and relatively lightweight.

Often the best kind of tripod head for still photography is the ball and socket type, where the camera mount rotates easily and in all directions, and can be securely tightened with just one screw to ensure absolute steadiness. They generally weigh less than any other head design, take up little space and are simple to use.

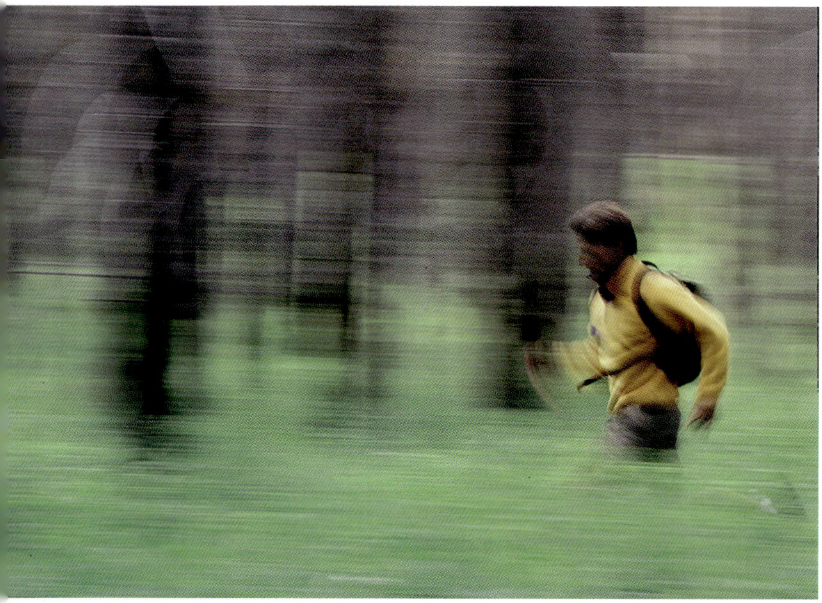

Their one shortcoming is that they can't be anchored in either a vertical or horizontal position. If you're thinking of shooting multi-image panoramas (see section entitled "Panorama Formats page 190) a RC or pan head will almost certainly be needed.

Before purchasing any tripod head, it's worth thinking about whether a plate-style mounting platform, or the more basic threaded-screw type, might be better suited to your needs.

When you need to attach a camera to your tripod quickly, as is often the case when photographing wildlife or sports-action scenes, the plate-style mount is definitely preferable. You simply slide or drop the camera into position on the tripod head, usually after pulling back its release lever. Most models automatically lock the camera into place with the spring-loaded release lever; the sliding variety generally gives you the option of tightening the camera down with a separate screw, when time permits.

If most of your intended photography is scenic or close-up work, then the simple screw-type mount works just fine. These attach directly to the threaded hole on the underside of almost any camera. They have the advantage of eliminating the requirement of mounting plates, as well as the need to re-tighten plates to your camera when they invariably loosen up.

An RC tripod head made things easier for the photographer while shooting this panned view, and probably resulted in a better composition. Canadian Rockies. Fuji Velvia, 105 mm lens.

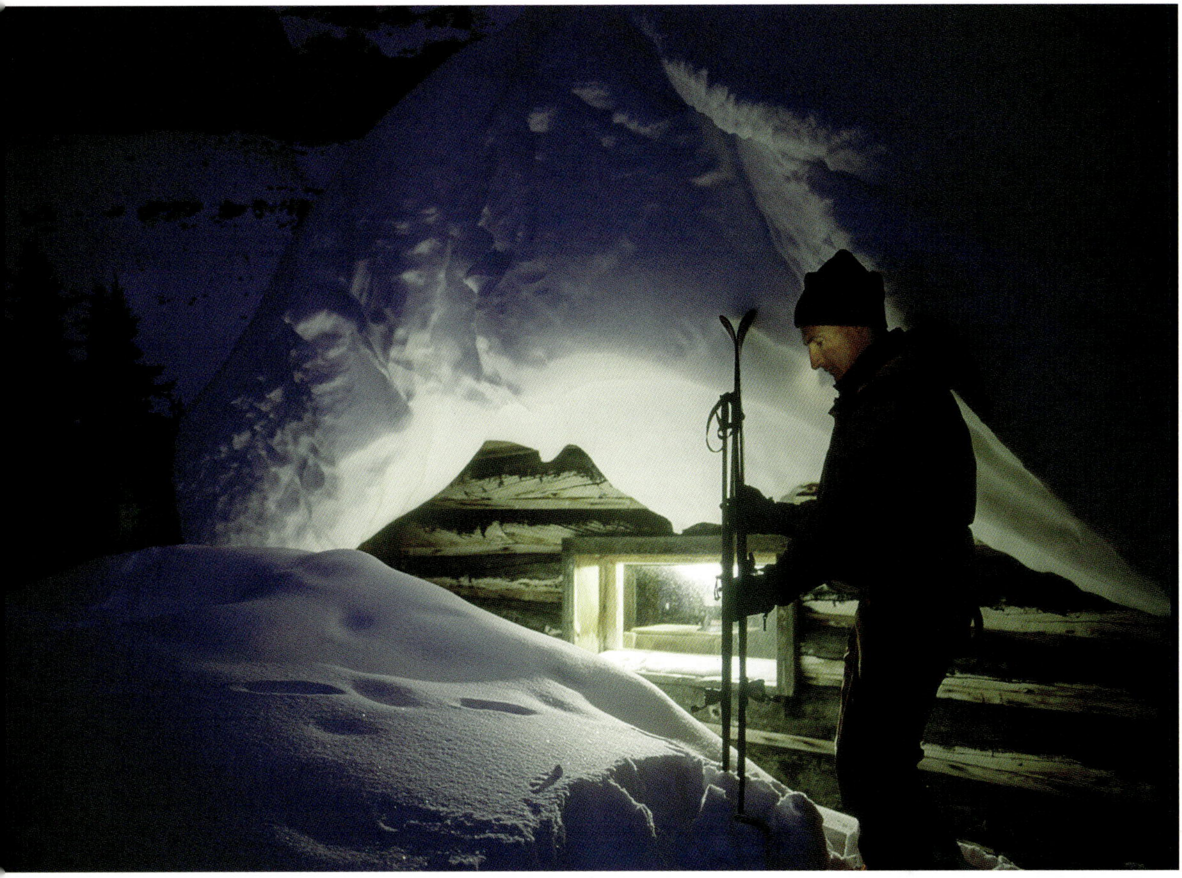

A C-clamp was attached to a ski that had been firmly planted in a snowbank to get this shot. Once I was sure the whole assembly wasn't about to tip over, I added my camera to it. Canadian Rockies. Fuji Velvia, 35-70 mm zoom lens.

C-clamp Supports

Tripods, as mentioned earlier, are almost always the preferable type of camera stand, thanks to both their inherent stability and flexibility. Alternative camera supports are sometimes worth considering for mountain travel, though, especially when weight reduction is particularly critical.

You simply may not be able to carry a tripod when you're on a hard alpine or rock climb, for example (and even if you do manage to sneak one into a haul bag, your climbing partner will likely be unimpressed when he finds it there!). A clamp-style support, which only weighs a few ounces and takes up very little room in your rucksack, might be the accessory of choice instead.

These devices are essentially the same as C-clamps used by carpenters to hold joined pieces of wood together after they're glued. They can provide a reasonably secure camera stand when mounted on the head of an ice axe—if the shaft is firmly anchored into snow, skis or even on the side of a small tree. If trying to snap a self-portrait, or perhaps capturing late evening light, and a clamp is all you have, it may also be all that you require.

Their downside is a lack of flexibility which will probably limit your compositional creativity. They are also relatively time-consuming to set up and use.

As well, clamps can be frustrating when they repeatedly slip off whatever it is that you're trying to attach them to. Probably the best advice for using them is to practise mounting the clamp to a designated support, such as an ice axe before heading out, so you know how best to utilize it and also what its limitations will likely be.

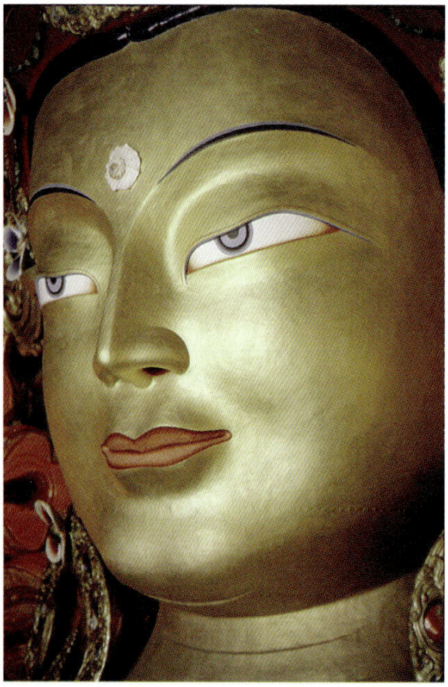

A unipod, held firmly against a railing, helped me to record this rather dimly lit interior view. A half-second exposure was required to get a wide enough depth of field. Tikse Monastery, Ladakh, India. Kodachrome, 35 mm lens.

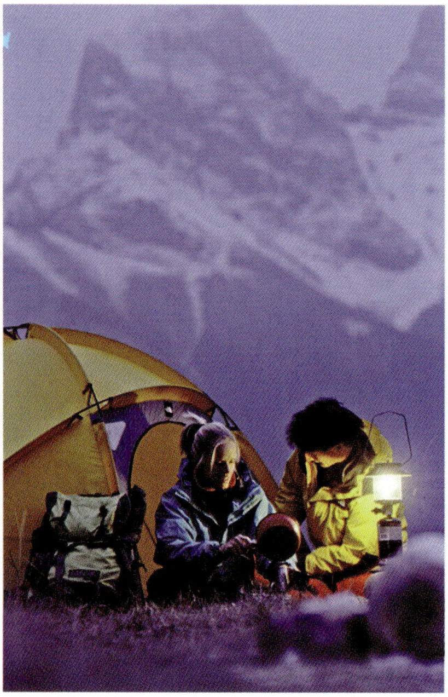

Mini-tripods are great for recording ground level views. Anything taller here would have compromised the top and bottom edges of my composition. Canadian Rockies. Fuji Velvia, 105 mm lens.

Monopods

Unlike clamps, monopods cannot support your camera on their own. They are designed only to provide greater stability for your camera, reducing most up and down and some sideways motion.

This difference, however, can allow you to shoot at much slower speeds than with a hand held camera. And because a monopod only makes contact with the ground at one point, you can rapidly alter your composition while using it, either by steering your camera in different directions, up or down, or by tilting the monopod to render a diagonal or angular framing.

Their major negative attribute is obvious: you need to keep a hand on the monopod at all times. This means that self-portraiture is virtually impossible and that time-exposures are, at very least, difficult.

Nonetheless, they can be very useful when photographing wildlife, scenics and even some sports-action work in the mountains. Additionally, most monopods are relatively compact, and—compared to tripods—fairly light. They are also quick to set up, even on the roughest of ground, and can be very rapidly moved from one spot to another.

How much slower you can shoot with a monopod than with a hand held camera without experiencing camera shake really depends on you. Again, the best advice is to experiment with yours before heading out and determine what speeds you can safely shoot at with different lens combinations.

Mini-tripods

Mini-tripods are a favorite of mine when weight is all-important and when a ground-level perspective is desirable, or at least okay. These are very lightweight stands that once compacted to only six or eight inches in length take up almost no space in your rucksack at all. Some of them can even be squeezed into a jacket or pants pocket.

They're relatively stable with wide, normal and even medium telephoto lenses. Longer lenses may work too; often the best solution to support one is to lie belly down with elbows resting on the ground, or to slide something under the lens barrel to prop it up.

Another advantage is that they can be set up on small surfaces, such as moderately sized rocks. Any such platform will have to be fairly smooth, though, and of course level.

These criteria may limit you from using a mini-tripod as often as you would like. Also, even though a ground-level perspective can be unusual and dynamic, you may want to think twice about choosing one if a lot of extraneous nearby rock is getting in the way of your composition. Ditto if you have to remove grasses, twigs and the like in order to see your subject clearly, and not behind a busy and unsightly foreground jumble.

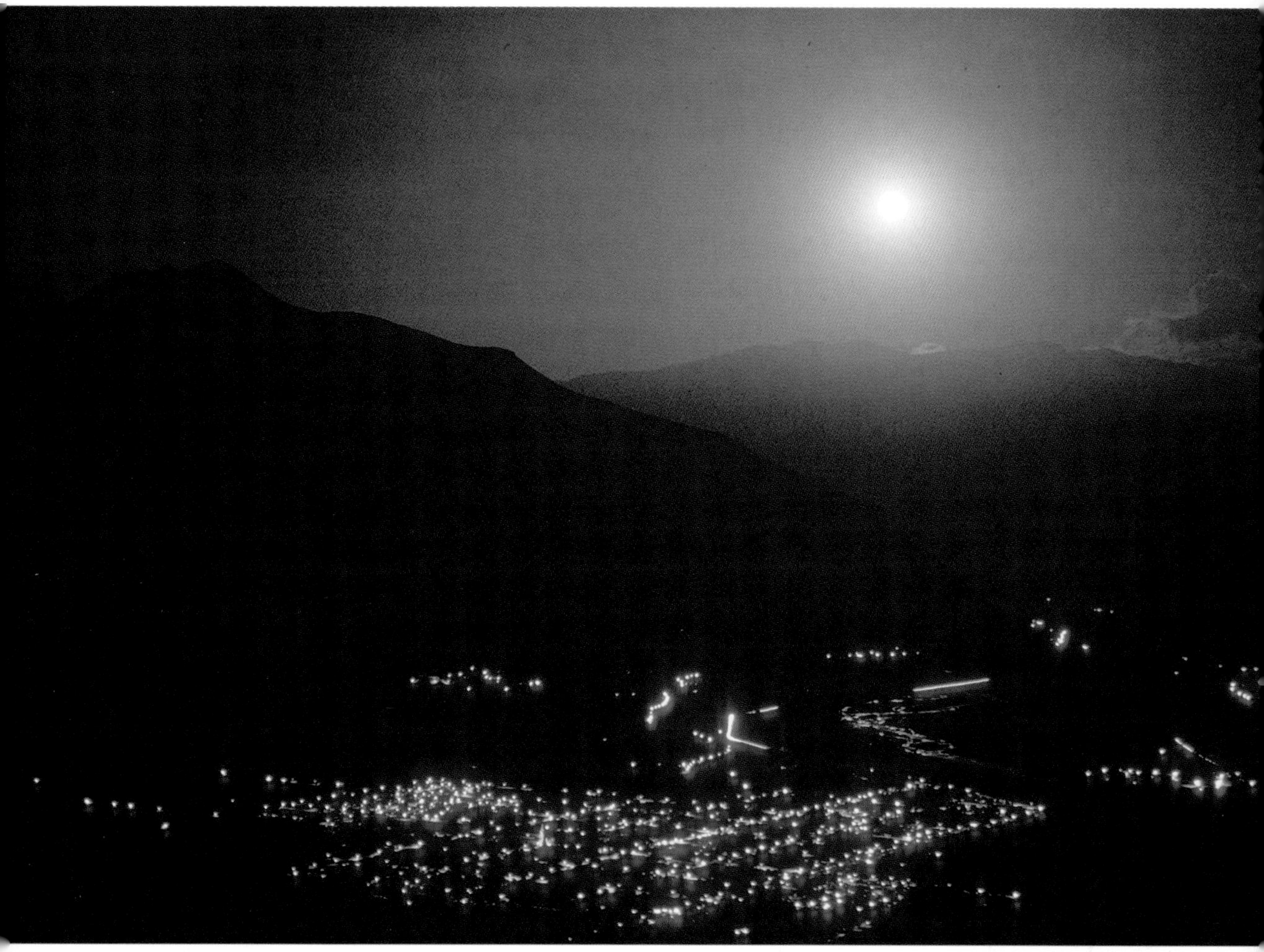

A cable release works well at nighttime, too, since most have a screw that can be locked down while you move carefully away from your camera for really long exposures. Valle de Elqui, Chile. Kodachrome, 55 mm lens.

Cable and Remote Releases

Cable releases are most commonly used, in conjunction with tripods, for shooting time-exposures. Just as locking the mirror assembly of an SLR reduces camera vibration—and hence the likelihood of unsharp pictures—a cable release makes it possible to trigger your camera's shutter without physically touching it.

When a cable release is employed together with a tripod and mirror lock-up button, all unwanted "user" movement is virtually eliminated. Note, however, that you cannot generally choose an automatic setting when your camera's mirror is locked up. Note also, that wind or earth movement, during a time-exposure, may completely undermine the use of a cable release, tripod and mirror lock-up.

Cable releases are very straightforward to use. Once one is screwed into your camera's shutter, or attached to the proper outlet if electronic, you simply need to squeeze it slowly and steadily until the shutter is released. It is best to stand slightly away from your viewfinder while doing so, although even an inch or two should be fine if your breathing is not heavy.

If you have chosen an indefinite time-exposure setting on your camera's speed dial (usually marked "B" or "T"), then you will have to hold the shutter down with the cable release until you've determined a long enough exposure. Many releases have a screw near the handheld end, with which you're able to essentially lock the shutter, and can then carefully walk away from it until the exposure is finished. Afterwards, simply unscrew the locking mechanism to release the shutter.

Another big benefit of cable releases is that they allow you to trigger the shutter while at some distance away. Say, for example, that you want to shoot a self-portrait, or join your friends for a group photo only a few meters away from your camera.

You could use your camera's self-timer of course, but a cable release allows you to trigger the shutter exactly when you want, thus improving the accuracy of your results. If your camera is equipped with a motor winder, the release will also allow you to take as many shots as you want without changing your position.

Mainly for the purpose of self-portraiture, some cable releases come with a long cord—perhaps 10 m or so—which can be wound onto a spool for easy extension when needed. Most such releases are intended for use with non-electronic cameras. They are generally powered by air, from a squeeze ball held in the hand.

As useful as they sometimes are, unfortunately they often fail to release when you want them to. On some occasions they simply fall apart. If you plan to do much shooting from a remote location, and your camera didn't come with a cable release, it may be worthwhile to invest in a battery-powered remote release.

These often have as great a range as the longest cables, require less set-up and fuss, are not as prone to failure and are more compact than long releases. They are also less likely to be seen in a self-portrait or group-portrait shot than a cable trailing from your camera.

Unfortunately, they do tend to be expensive. Check with your local camera shop, or the manufacturer, to find one that will work best with your camera.

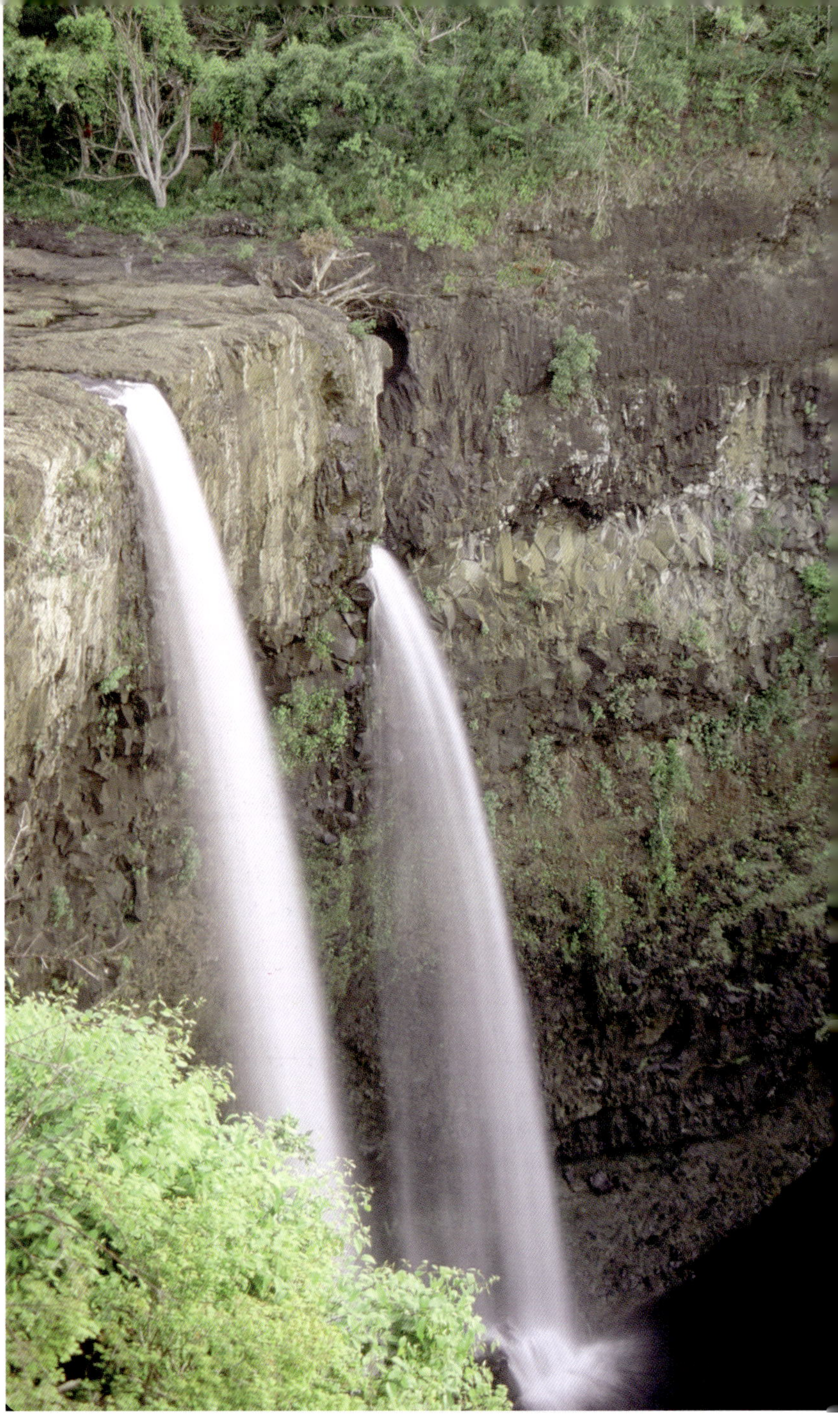

Together with any sturdy tripod, a cable release will allow you to shoot softened, time-exposed views of falling water with absolutely sharp landscape details framing it. Kauaii, Hawaii. Fuji Velvia, 35-70 mm zoom lens.

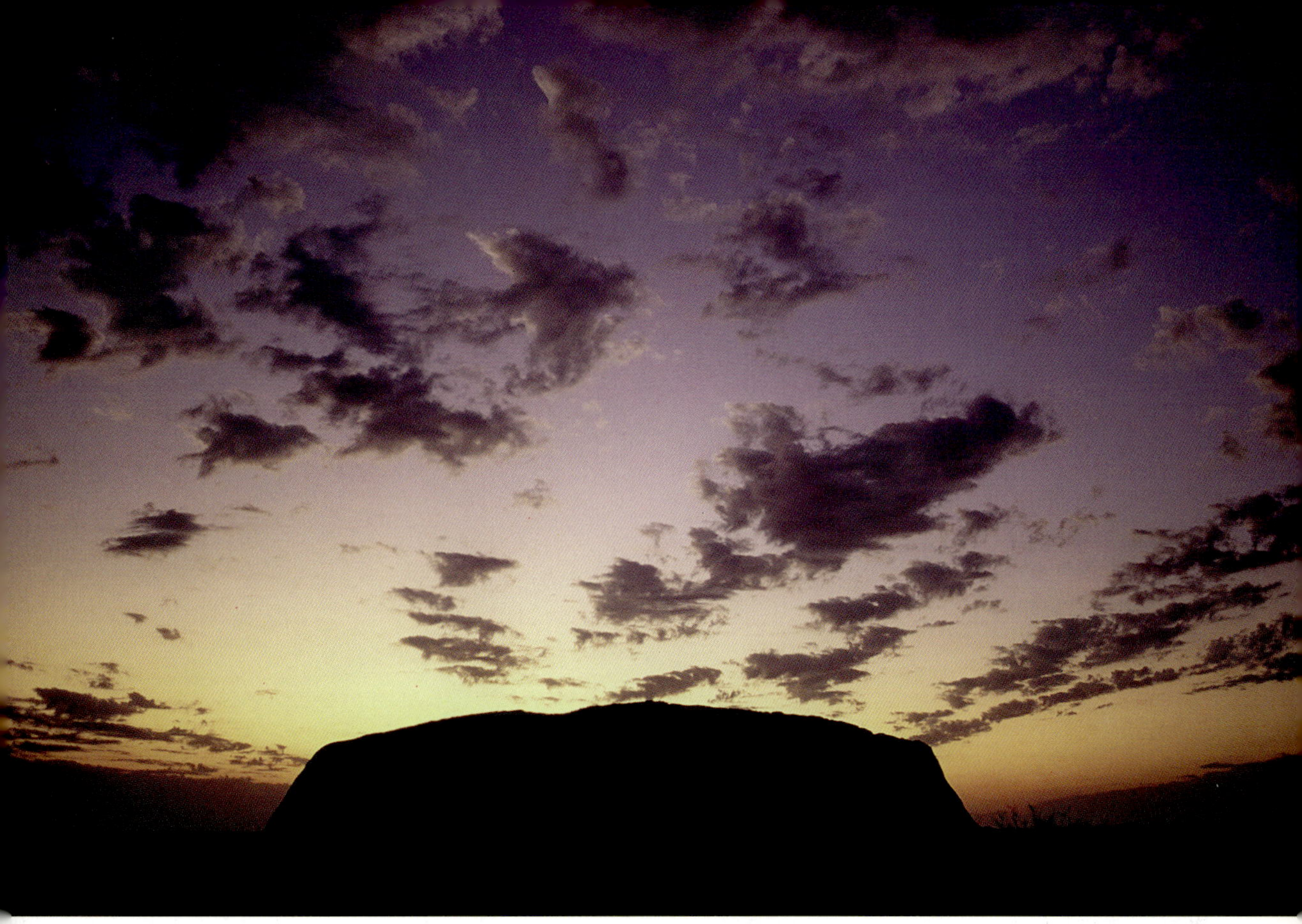

Shots like this really don't require a tripod, and you might lose the best sky colors in the time it takes you to set one up. Better to just compose carefully with a hand held camera. Uluru (Ayers Rock), Australia. Fuji Velvia, 28 mm lens.

Becoming Too Dependent on Your Tripod

The one risk in carrying a tripod on your mountain outings is that you may become overdependent on it. I would advise against employing a tripod all—or even most—of the time, unless you are mainly interested in shooting scenics. Here are some practical reasons why not.

Wildlife, as mentioned earlier, may be spooked by the noise and/or flash of metal as you set your stand up, and of course may be long gone in the time it takes to fumble with leg screws while you get your tripod oriented to the right height and position for shooting.

Your climbing partners might also not be too impressed if you continually stop them a rope-length away to set up your stand before clicking a shot. And even hiking friends might become a little impatient with what they may perceive as your excessive zeal for tripod assisted photography, if they are constantly asked to wait at trailside while you pull it out of your pack and fumble around with it.

The trick is to employ your tripod only when it's needed, or when your creativity isn't at the mercy of time constraints and other pressures. Also, to learn when it's best to keep it stowed away. This decision will be a very personal one, and it will depend as much as anything on your chosen activity, climbing or hiking partners, etc.

Even if time and friends don't discourage tripod overuse, though, here are some other things that might. When you're unable to set up a tripod on really uneven or unstable ground, for example, you want to have the flexibility, as well as capability, to still shoot your intended scene with a hand held camera.
Likewise, when it is difficult, even with the most adjustable tripod head, to orient your camera in the way that

you'd like—say obliquely upwards from very close to the ground—it's good to know that with a simple hand held position you might be easily able to get the shot.

Consider a perspective looking straight down a cliff to your climbing partner. If, as is often the case, you have to lean out somewhat from the cliff's edge to get the best view, it will be virtually impossible to record the scene with a tripod, but fairly easy with a handheld camera.

There are also many good creative reasons for not becoming too dependent on your tripod, which will be examined more thoroughly in the next chapters. Here, briefly though, is the most important of them.

Sometimes it's worth having your camera move in a shot. Your tripod, which really encourages establishing a stable, but static, camera position, will discourage this kind of movement (that is, unless the camera is attached to a tripod as part of a moving system, in which case the tripod becomes a dynamic, not static, tool).

Assume, for example, you want to follow the motion of kids running down a trail directly into your camera. By running backwards with your camera low to the ground, and with a wide-angle lens and fairly slow shutter speed, you should be able to record the kids in relatively sharp focus while creating a sense of motion as grasses alongside the trail blur.

These reservations having been stated, your tripod will still likely become one of your favorite shooting tools in the mountains. And in conjunction with a cable release, it can allow you to explore photography options you may never have thought possible before using one.

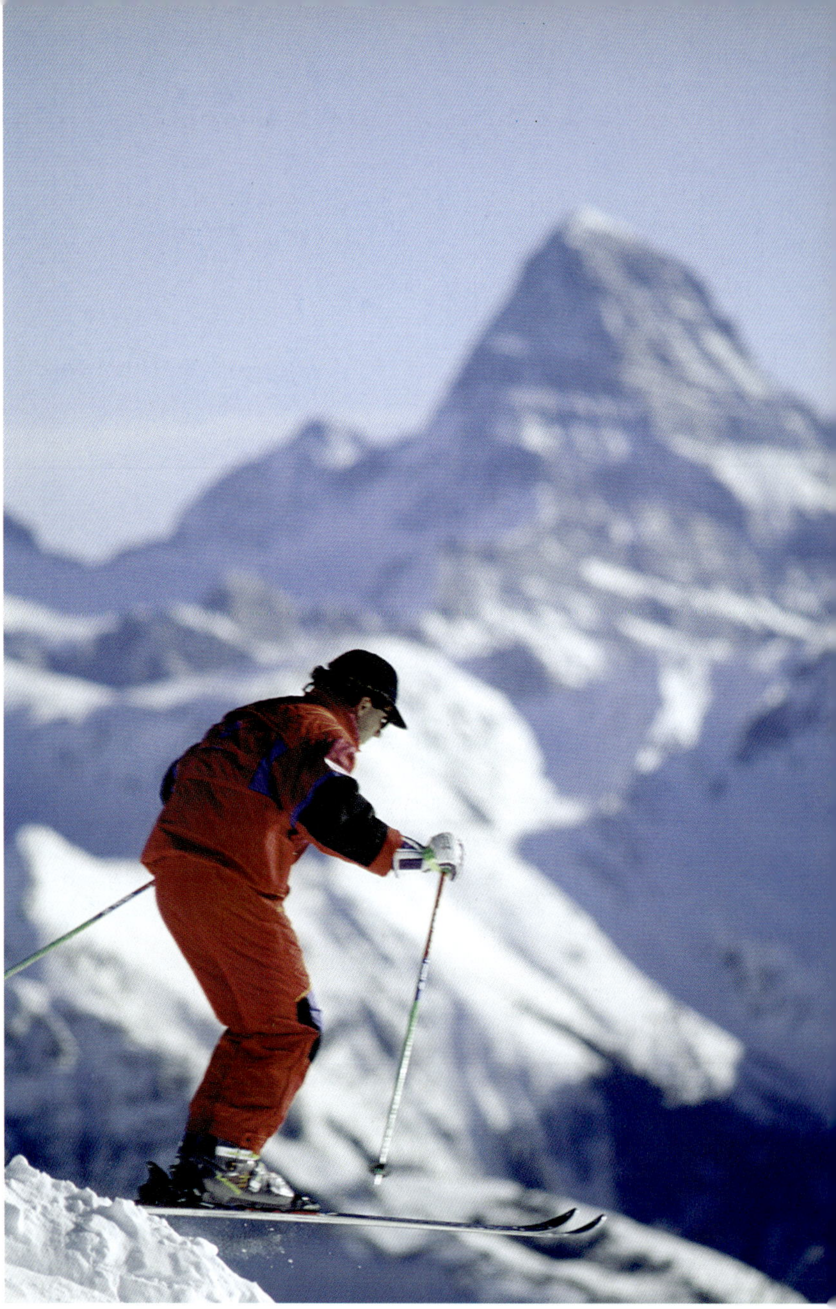

Even with really long lenses you can make do without a tripod if you have to. The best approach is to lie on the ground with your elbows steadying the camera. Canadian Rockies. Kodak E100VS, 300 mm lens.

Tripods, Releases and Mountain Safety

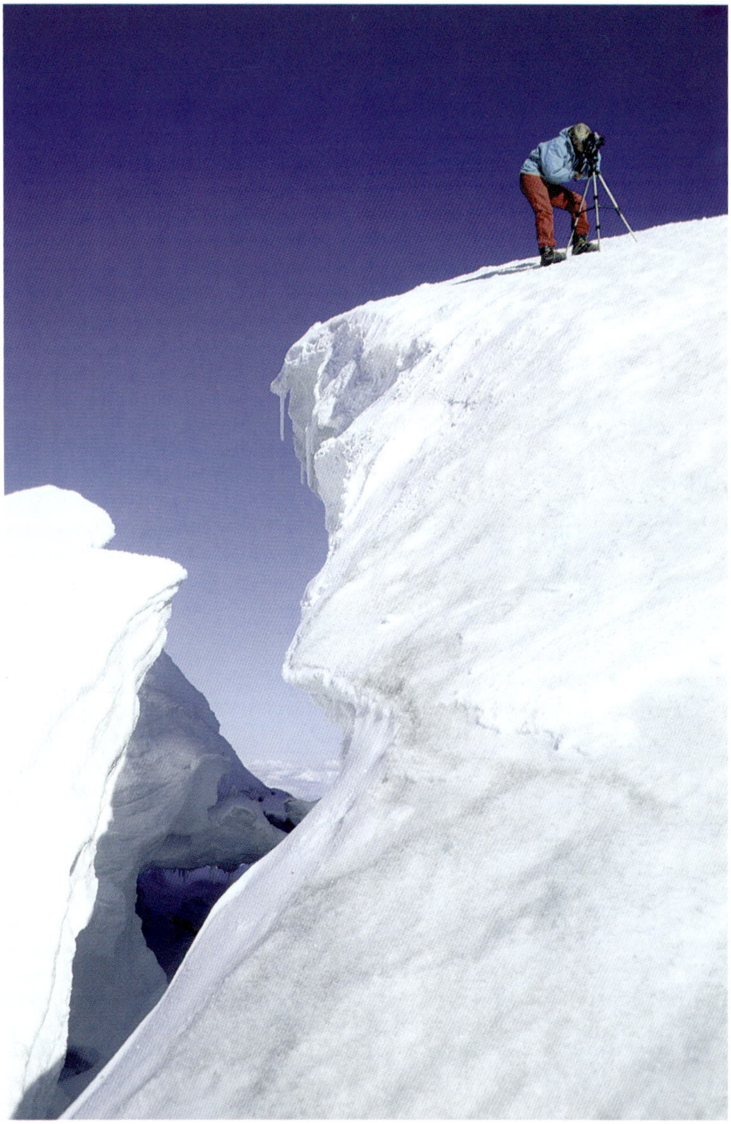

When shooting close to objective hazards such as this, a tripod can enhance safety by making one stay put.. Canadian Rockies. Kodak E100VS, 105 mm lens.

Believe it or not, proper use of tripods and releases can actually make photography safer in the mountains. Improper or careless use, on the other hand, can make things scarier.

To avoid accidents resulting from the dangerous use of these or other accessory items—and even of cameras themselves—it's perhaps worth taking a moment to consider safety issues unique to mountain photography.

The most obvious hazard posed by tripods, especially on high alpine ridges, is that they attract lightening. In fact, a tripod and camera assembly offers an almost perfect lightening rod, and a number of mountain accidents have been either directly, or indirectly, attributable to them.

While photographing a distant storm from a lofty position it is very easy, for example, to get swept up in the moment and to forget, or neglect to think about, how hazardous the incoming cloud mass may be. If your attention is fully directed towards what you see through the viewfinder, you might suddenly find yourself within striking distance.

I remember watching a TV show some years back where a photographer was both videotaping and photographing a storm moving across a mountain landscape in the southwestern U.S. His two cameras were mounted on tripods roughly 20 feet apart, with the photographer standing just back from the still camera.

Quite suddenly the storm moved right overhead, into the danger zone for those below. A still photograph taken shortly after shows a lightening bolt striking and destroying the nearby video camera. Fortunately the photographer was okay, just a little shaken, but no doubt careful to stand some distance away from any tripod while shooting electrical storms from that point on.

Tripods can also help to avoid accidents, though, principally by forcing a photographer to seek out, or create, a static shooting platform. In short, viewing through a tripod-mounted camera forces you to stay put.

While photographing, it's incredibly easy to get swept up in the creative moment and to forget all about mountain hazards. All too often mountain shooters have fallen over cliffs and even into crevasses, usually while composing through their viewfinders and walking forwards, or backwards.

Always make sure, however, that your tripod set-up is stable enough to survive sudden gusts of wind. This point is especially relevant when erecting a tripod on a ridge crest.

If you happen to be doing so, and say you then move away with a cable release or remote trigger in hand, there is probably no way to save your camera and tripod if they were to suddenly be knocked over the edge by a big wind gust. And, if this scenario wasn't already bad enough, it's possible that you could also lose your footing and fall in the ensuing panic to save your camera.

Cable releases, like tripods used carefully, may help to prevent accidents too. For self-or group-portrait photography, they eliminate the need for you to set a self-timer and then run into your intended scene.

I recall tripping badly while racing into a self-timed shot years ago. Because my chosen lens was a 105 mm and I intended to be quite small in the shot, I had a long distance to travel in the short—10 second—duration of my camera's self-timer. Although my stumble didn't result in serious injury, it could have, as I was on a knife-edged ridge with hundreds of feet of sheer exposure below.

Note that all high-mountain, and high-angle, photography is inherently dangerous. Whenever possible, climbing situations should be rigged carefully before shooting, and only when you're thoroughly satisfied that you've addressed all possible hazards and potential problems should you then turn your mind toward photography.

Rigging, and associated safety issues, will be dealt with in detail in a later chapter. The central message of this section is that a patient, methodical approach to high-mountain shooting—and the appropriate use of equipment—will likely reward you with a longer life, as well as better photographs.

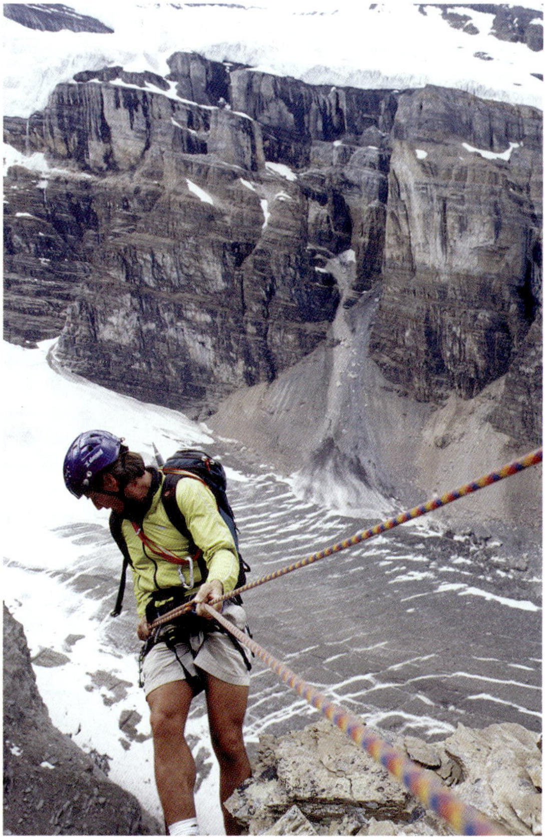

For direct overhead shooting such as this, a tripod is often more of a hazard than a help. It is better to just find a secure stance to shoot from, ideally sitting or kneeling. Canadian Rockies, Kodak E100GX.

Color, Black & White Or...?

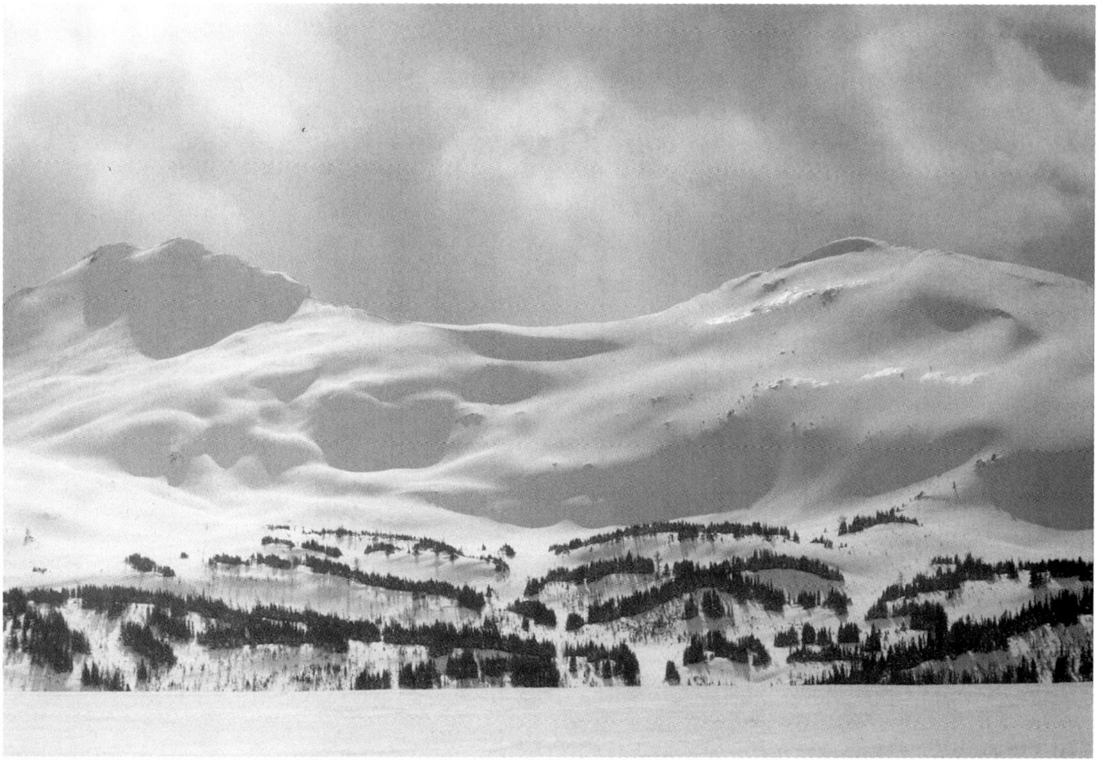

The black & white medium is great with monochromatic subject matter, and also for recording contrasts in texture and lighting. Canadian Rockies. Agfa Scala, 105 mm lens.

If digital is your chosen photography medium, many of the comments below may not seem terribly relevant. In fact, they are: most digital cameras still allow the user flexibility to choose color, black & white, or something else when outputting. A better understanding of analog options will almost certainly advance your creative abilities while shooting digital.

Choosing exactly the right film for a given mountain shoot is, in many ways, more complicated than ever before. Or, looked at another way, the options have increased exponentially. More latitude exists now for creativity with film than at anytime in the past.

However you look at it, there is certainly an unparalleled diversity of film types on the market these days. Similarly, alternative methods for exposing film have experienced a surge of interest lately.

Many of these were seldom, if ever, called into use as recently as 10 years ago. Cross processing—whereby transparency film is processed as though it were print film, and vice versa—has fully entered the photography mainstream. So has push processing to exaggerate grain size.

There has also been a recent rekindling of interest in century-old photography techniques. Hand-coloring black & white prints has become fairly commonplace, as has sepia toning. In many cases, professional photographers will set out to actually replicate old styles, whether to create a sense of nostalgia or to simply carve a creative niche for themselves.

The good news, at least to those of us who are constantly trying to push the creative limits of photography, is a trend towards greater tolerance and even the approval of alternative film usage. Film selection and processing, in other words, is no longer necessarily approached with a mandate to

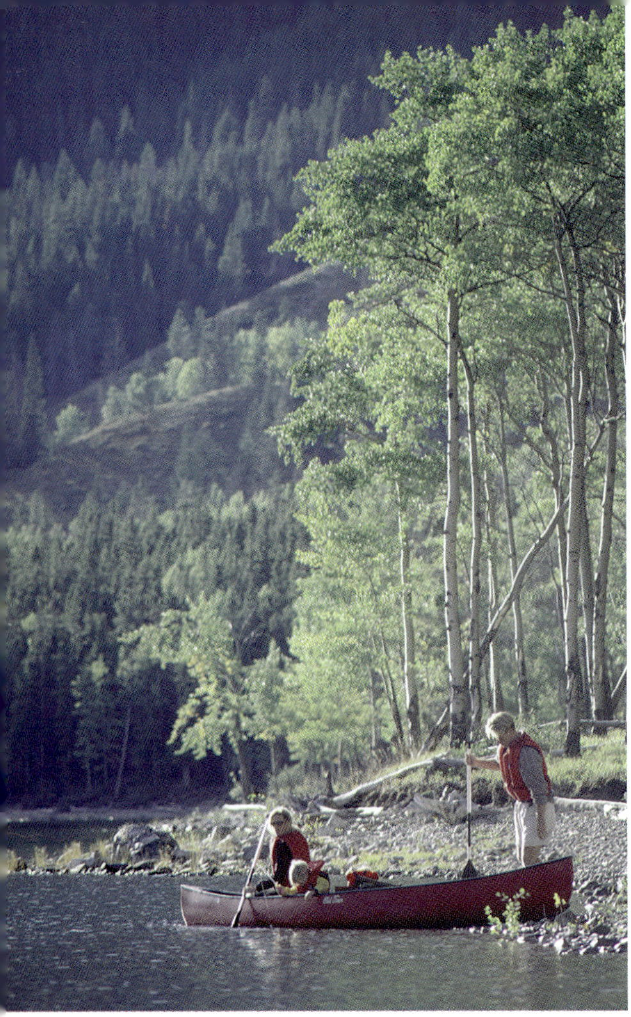

There are a huge number of color films on the market these days, some certainly better at recording subtleties in tones and shades than others. Canadian Rockies. Fuji Velvia, 180 mm lens.

simply reproduce reality, or to depict things only as visualized through a viewfinder.

Nonetheless, most photographers will be mainly interested in recording subjects and places within the creative bounds of reality. There is good reason for this, especially in the mountains.

For one thing, most mountain experiences are already diverse and of significant interest in themselves. Why stretch them outrageously? For another, much alternative film usage and processing technique is quite experimental. Needless to say, there's nothing worse than botching a photographic record of great mountain experiences by choosing the wrong film or lab technique.

I'm not really a proponent of either approach—both are perfectly viable. Often I will take two cameras on a trip, one loaded with slow speed color film and another with something else. This way I can record the shots I'm after and also experiment a little.

Whether color, black & white or something else is best to shoot with depends on a wide variety of technical and compositional factors, which will be addressed in this section. The choice will also always depend on your personal preference.

What I would encourage, above anything else, is to carefully consider the mood and central point of any shot before deciding what to shoot it with. As your experience increases, you might find you can pre-visualize a scene in different film formats, and thereby choose the one best suited to it, or the one that you like the most.

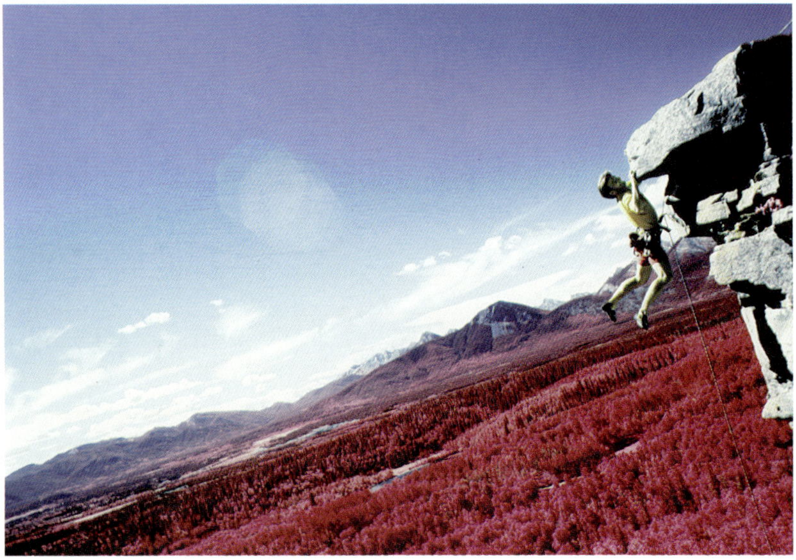

To create an edgy or radically different look, try shooting on infrared film. It doesn't always work well, but it does sometimes give compositions a vibrancy that might otherwise be lacking. Canadian Rockies. Kodak EIR, 28 mm lens, yellow 15 filter.

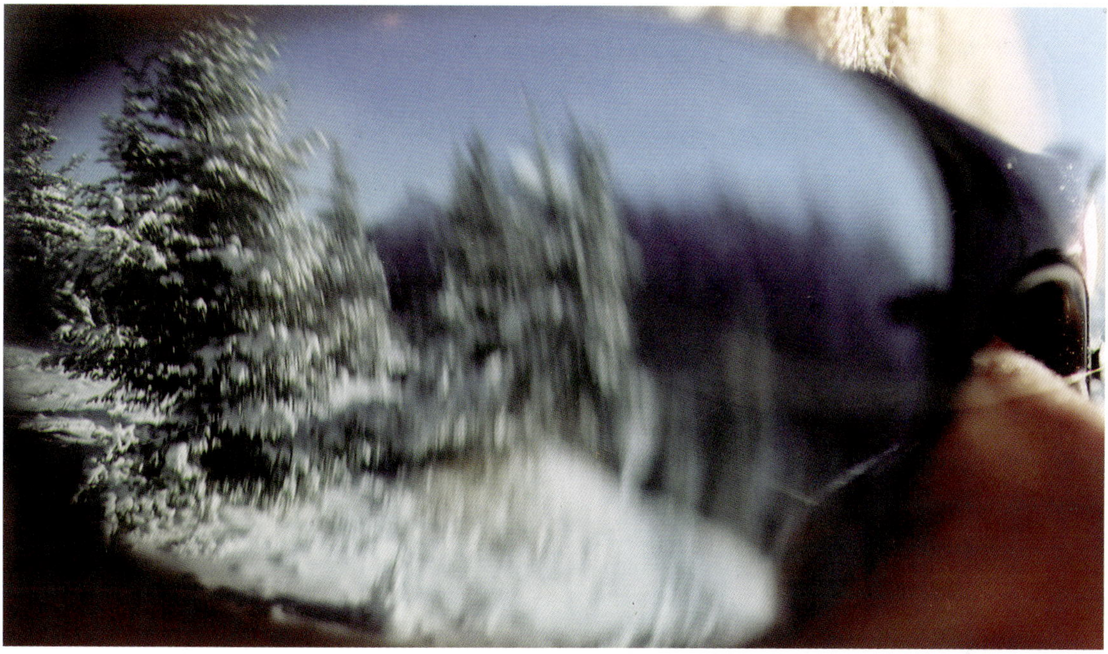

Photographing with print film offers some advantages over shooting transparencies. Both this print and the print on the next page were cropped from their originals to "tighten" them by eliminating extraneous detail. Canadian Rockies. Kodak 160VC and Tri-X pan, 105 mm macro lens.

Shooting Slides vs. Prints

For years I've been asked by friends and others keen to explore the mountains with their cameras about the relative merits of shooting with transparency versus print film. And my response has always been the same: which of the two mediums do you prefer?

They are, after all, birds of a completely different feather. Whether one works better than the other really boils down to personal choice, and habit. Would you rather show photos to others mounted in an album or projected onto a screen? Do you have a light box and loupe to help edit your best transparencies with? Or is it far easier for you to simply leaf through prints?

There are, though, some exceptions to this way of thinking that are perhaps worth noting. At least one of them has particular relevance to mountain photography.

This, in short, is that it's obviously far easier to show your work to groups of people projected onto a screen than in a photo album. Most mountain people I've met do, sooner or later, want to share their adventures with groups of like-minded people. It might be just for fun, or to elicit interest in embarking on similar mountain travels together.

Alternatively, perhaps you'll want to put on a show for groups of non-mountain people. Your intent might be to convince them of the inherent rewards of mountain experiences, or simply to scare the be-jaggers out of them with some really hair-raising shots.

If either of these scenarios sounds familiar, you'll probably want to stick with transparencies. It's very difficult to produce quality slides from prints. On the other hand, it's rather easy, and inexpensive, to produce excellent prints from slides.

Here are some other advantages of shooting transparencies. They will always be of slightly better quality than prints, since they are a first-generation product (prints have to be created from negatives, and so are a step removed from original processing). They are generally preferred by publishers and advertisers, in the event you have plans to sell or show your photography down the road. And they ship better, whether to friends or to clients.

Be careful, however, not to project your best original slides over and over again. Repeated and lengthy exposure to the projection lamp will deteriorate them. It's best to have duplicate slides made up to avoid having favorite work fade prematurely (most good transparency films have a life of 30 years or more before natural deterioration begins).

This cautionary note does point to one of the benefits of print film. Negatives can always be put away for safekeeping, meaning your best original material is never compromised while on display.

Another point to be made in deference to print films is that you have the ability, while printing, to make custom adjustments. "Burning" in dark areas to make them brighter, "dodging" for the opposite reason, and enhancing or reducing color are a few of the things that any lab technician can do for you. Slide films allow for no such adjustments.

With prints you can always crop out bits that are uncomplimentary to your composition too. This can either be done during the printing process, by providing your lab technician with marks indicating an intended crop, or afterwards, using a sharp knife or pair of scissors to simply chop unwanted segments.

Also, if your main interest is black & white photography, you'll probably find that you gravitate mainly toward print films. There is an excellent black & white slide film available called SCALA (from Agfa), but its processing options are rather limited at the moment. Black & white print films, on the other hand, are widely diverse in features and are also easy to find and process.

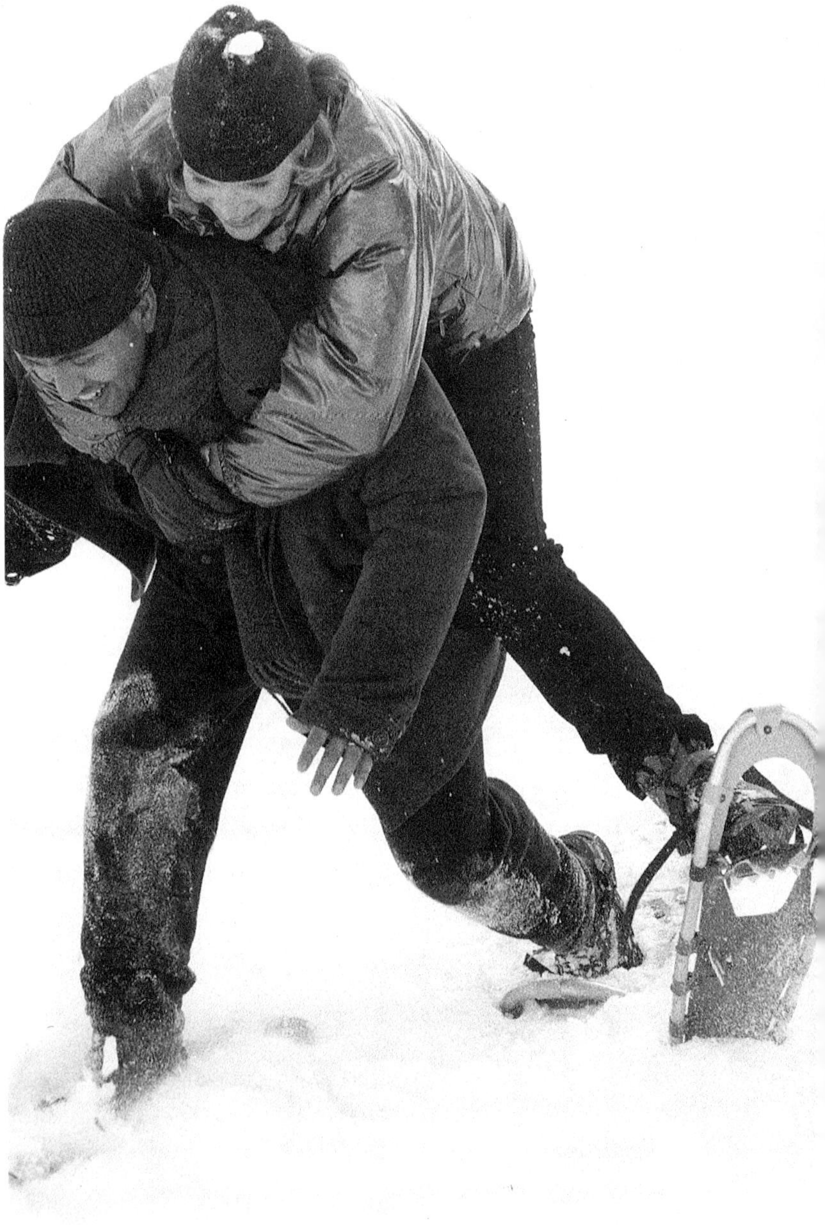

Fine-grained black and white films often record details beautifully, especially in monochromatic light. Canadian Rockies, Ilford 100 film.

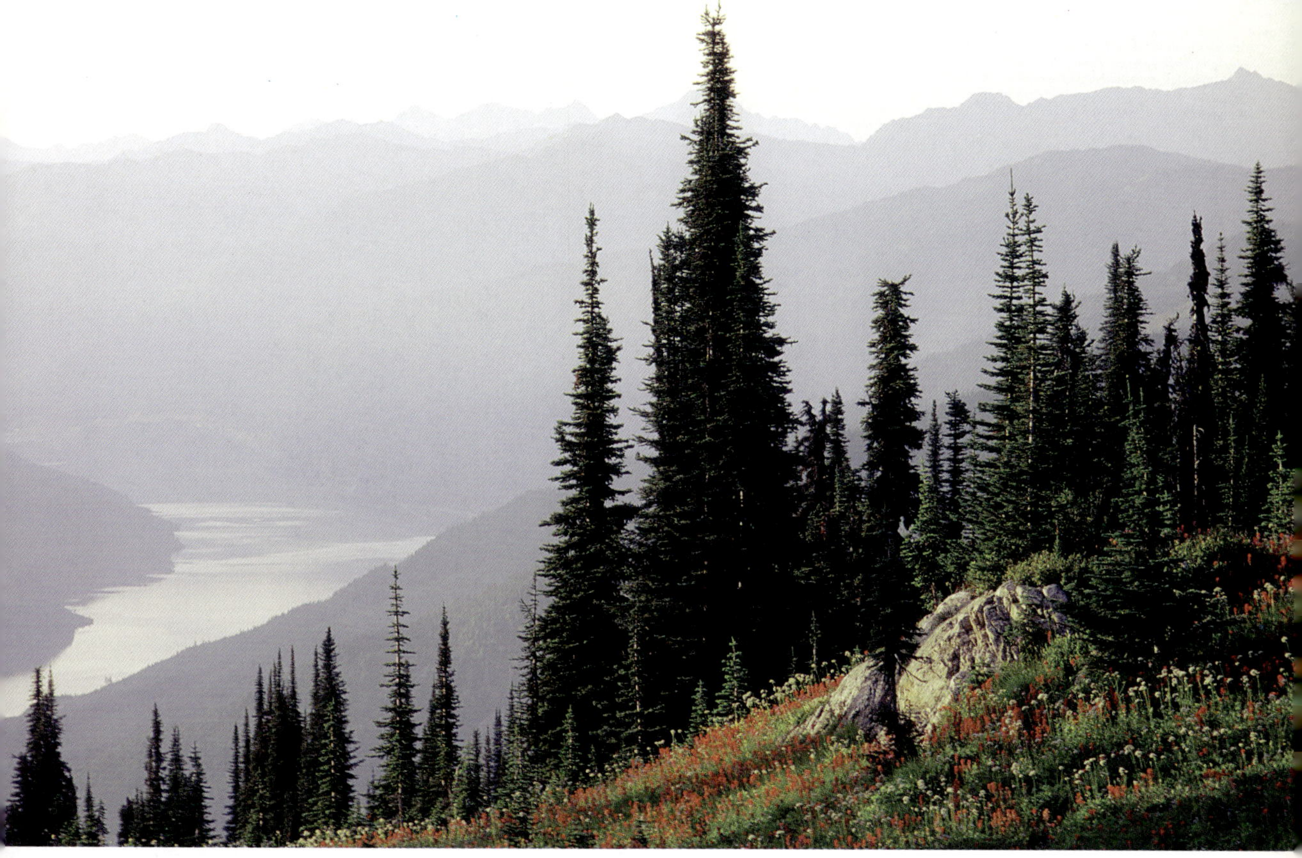

A slow film will deliver much better reproduction of minute details than a fast one, because of its finer grain composition. Selkirk Mountains, Canada. Fuji Velvia, 28 mm lens.

Slow Films vs. Fast Films

Slow films could probably best be identified as ones having an ASA value of 100 or less; medium-speed films at between 50 and 400 ASA; and high-speed films are ones with higher ASA values than 400.

The main advantage of slower films is that they will always render the sharpest results. Emulsion grain size becomes incrementally smaller with each lower ASA value. This has particular impact under magnification, when your images are projected onto a screen, for example, or blown up into large size prints. At the slowest speeds, 35 mm grain is virtually impossible to detect, unless your image is blown up into poster or billboard size.

The other advantage of slow-and medium-speed films is that there is a greater variety of them available, particularly in transparency format. Your options are therefore not as limited when shopping around for the right ones.

The significant disadvantage of slower films is that they make camera operation more difficult in dim light. If you use my guide, suggested in a previous section, concerning shutter speed selection, then you'll likely try to avoid handheld shooting at speeds lower than the focal length of a chosen lens. That is, at nothing slower than 1/125 second with a 125 mm lens, 1/30 second with a 28 mm lens, and so on.

This limitation can be onerous at times. If a higher speed is needed to record action, or a greater depth of field is required than allowed by your minimum speed selection, then you might just be out of luck. Of course, the use of a tripod can often remedy the situation, especially when scenery or compliant human subjects are your main focus. But not always.

For example, think about shooting past nearby alpine flowers to a colorful slope and mountain backdrop. With a tripod, a slow film might be adequate to

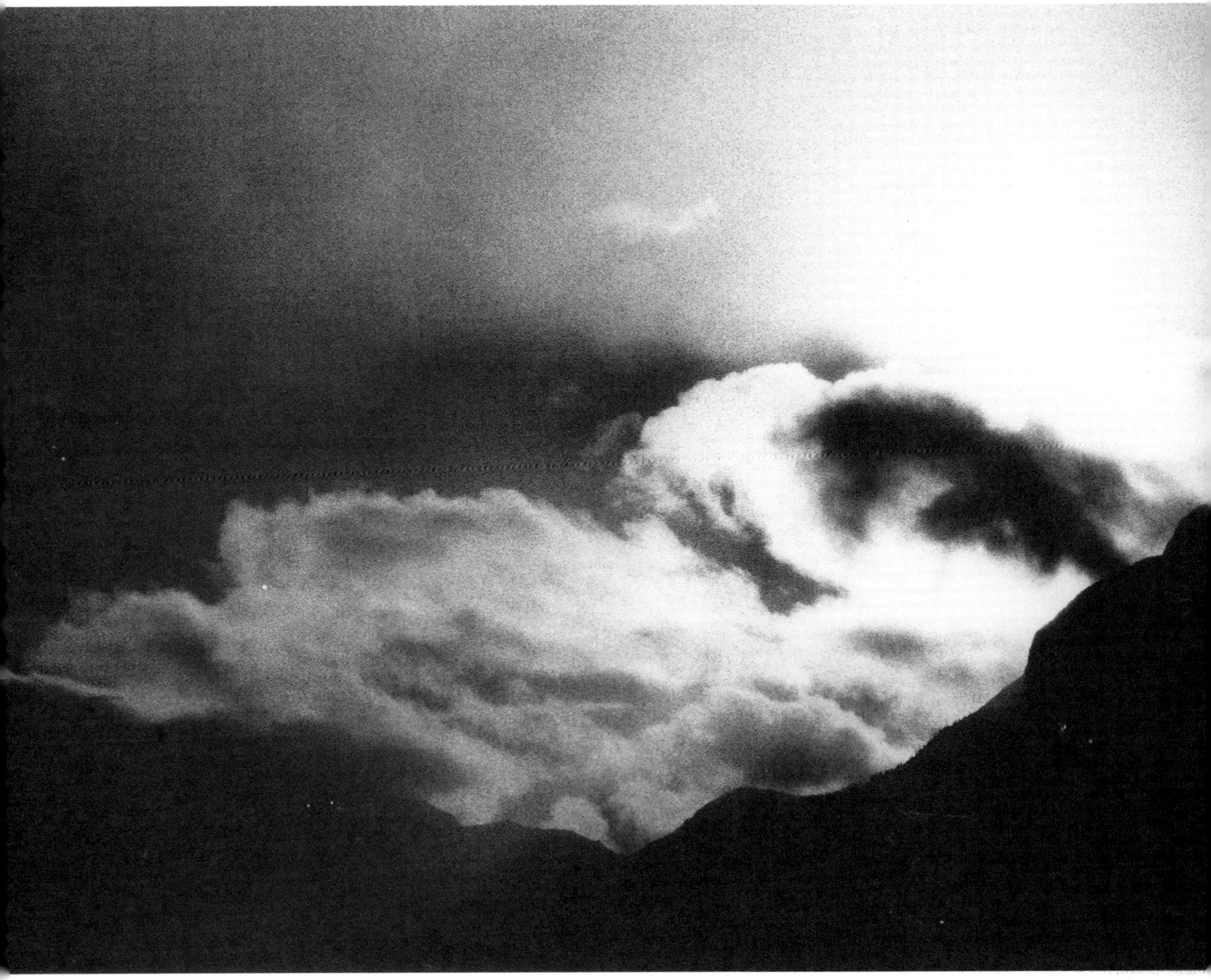

High-speed films can produce a striking grain effect with some subject matter. The trick is usually to simplify your composition while shooting with them. Canadian Rockies. Kodak 3200, 105 mm lens.

everything in focus. But it probably wouldn't do if a breeze came up.

Or consider an even more likely scenario. Say you're trying to photograph a bear moving along through forest glades after the sun's intensity has begun to fade. Even if you're using a tripod, there is probably no way to register him sharply with slow film. The same would hold true while trying to photograph a mountain biker cruising past after the sun has set.

So faster films might sometimes be preferable when shooting fast moving subjects in dim light, or to include a wide depth of field. Remember though, that if the film you choose is too fast, you may just lose to reduced film sharpness any gains you made to improved subject sharpness.

This might not always be a bad thing. Some photographers, in fact, choose fast films—or use push processing—simply to enhance grain size. This serves primarily an artistic purpose. If you choose to follow suit, first ensure that your subject matter and mood are suitable to a grainy rendering. Otherwise, try to stick with slower films.

Color Films

The color film market, both transparency and print, has especially taken off in recent years. There is now a plethora of types available through most camera stores. They range in speed from a very slow 25 ASA to 4000 ASA or even higher. They also come in a variety of color saturation, from neutral to very saturated.

Saturated films are ones in which colors are most vibrant, particularly the reds, yellows and greens. Their appeal is fairly universal, probably because they often render things slightly more colorful than they actually are. Disney, to cite one example, has been very successful in its promotion of saturated colors on the movie screen.

Their strongest feature is also their downfall. Because they are prone to enhancing color somewhat, they will tend to redden faces and other areas of skin, sometimes unacceptably. They also tend to exaggerate contrast somewhat, both between colors and also between light and dark areas.

Neutral or unsaturated films, on the other hand, will faithfully record skin tones, but may render vistas and colorful foregrounds somewhat lackluster. Films somewhere in the middle strive to compromise between the two. Sometimes, in practise, they work well. At other times they don't.

So, to ask the question again, with all the options available, what are the best choices? Consider, first, your expectations.

If you're out to simply record dramatic mountain scenery, perhaps with distant human subjects, the best films will likely be slower and more saturated. Ditto if you're more interested in heightening drama than in reproducing colors perfectly. Look for an ASA rating of 100 or lower and a high saturation rating (if none is visible on the label, ask a qualified salesperson for his/her opinion).

If, on the other hand, your human and wildlife subjects are close at hand or prominent in your frame, you might want to choose a less saturated variety. This may not mean selecting the least saturated film available though. Perhaps a middling one would be best, especially if you want to preserve or heighten the drama of a mountain setting.

Of course, as mentioned in the last section, the quantity of available light will play a big part in determining how slow or fast a film speed you choose. So will your subject matter, whether fast moving, slow moving or stationary. There tends not to be as much variation between saturated and unsaturated high-speed films as lower speed ones, but inherent subtleties still make it advisable to try out different ones.

On a typical mountain outing, I'll pack a roll or two of relatively high-speed film (400 ASA or higher) with a moderate saturation rating. As often as not, they'll sit in the bottom of my camera bag. Sometimes, though, especially in fading light, their merits become very useful, whether to allow a sharp snap of fleeting wildlife or to give me the subject-to-infinity depth of field I'm after.

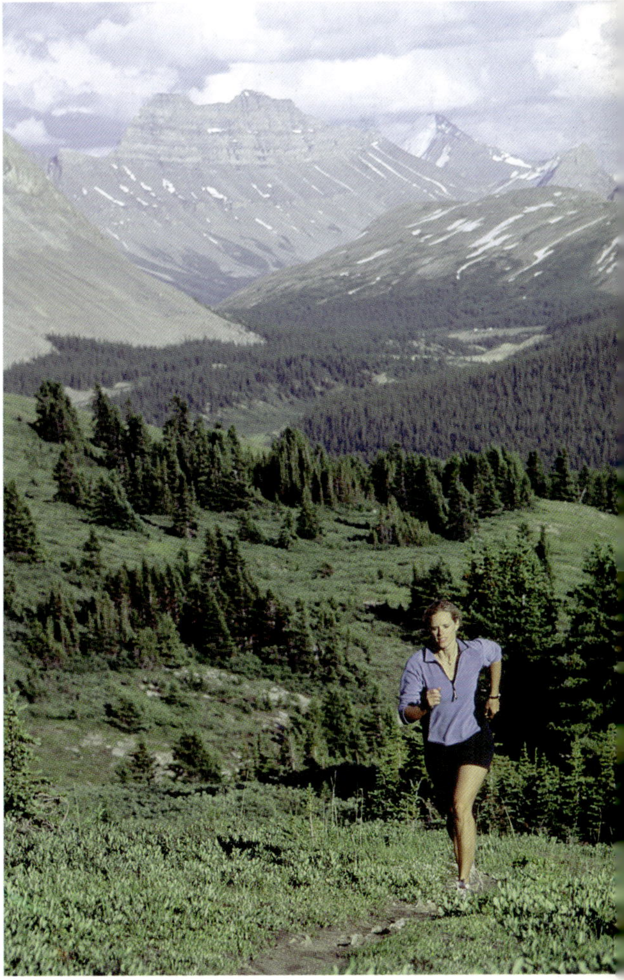

I needed a slightly faster film for this shot to arrest my subject's motion while also rendering landscape details in a recognizable fashion. Canadian Rockies. Ektachrome 200, 85 mm lens.

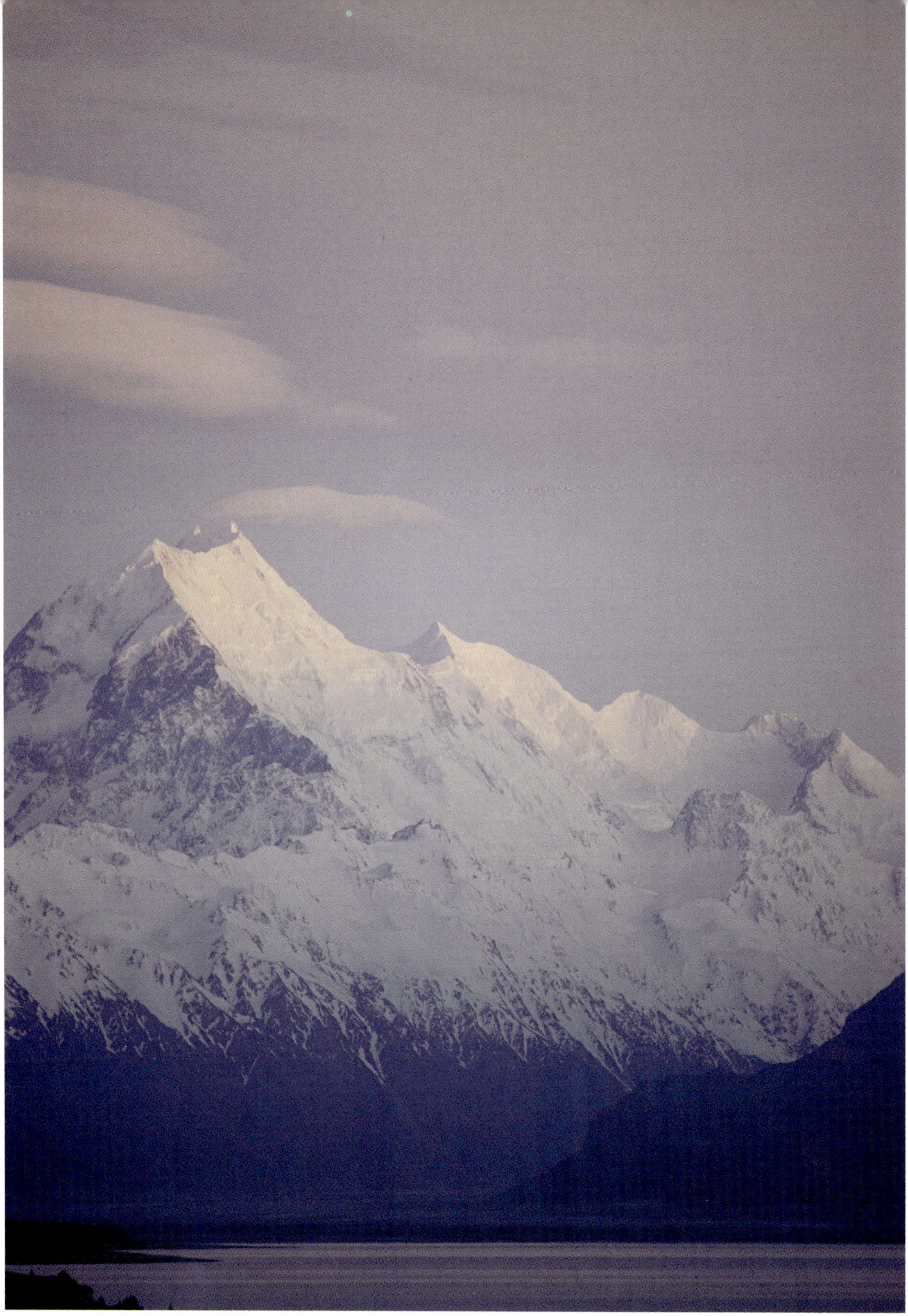

This view was shot on slow, saturated film with my camera mounted on a tripod. You really can't beat slow films in terms of both color reproduction and resolution, with such subject matter. Mount Cook, New Zealand. Fuji Velvia, 200 mm lens.

Harmonious and Complimentary Colors

As any fashion guru will tell you, some colors work well together and some don't. When viewing nature on its own, of course, this is not really an issue. Natural colors are always in balance and are accepted as being so. And, with certainty, colors in the mountain environment are partly what makes it so striking and compelling to photograph.

However, the introduction of artificial color changes this balance. Whether it be the garments your companions are wearing when you want to include them in your shots, or their sports and camping gear, the colors and relative prominence of subjects may well determine the overall effect of a shot. Sometimes for better, and sometimes for worse.

Needless to say, bright primary colors, especially reds and yellows, are particularly striking in a mountain context, where the predominant colors are blues and earth tones. Subdued oranges and purples are less so, and colors like evergreen, navy and dark browns are often passive to a point beyond sublimity.

Ten or 15 years ago, a good action photograph couldn't contain enough reds and yellows. Or so it seemed. Most manufacturers of mountain garments and gear rode that trend to a large extent. At one point it was nearly impossible to find anything but either a bright primary color, or a very dingy one, for those who bucked the trend altogether.

Then came the 1990s, and a partial return to earth tones established decades earlier. Primary colors retreated from mountain fashion somewhat, although not completely. Today, there's quite a color range available to anyone purchasing new mountain gear, with plenty of vibrant oranges, greens, purples and subdued yellows and reds on the shelves.

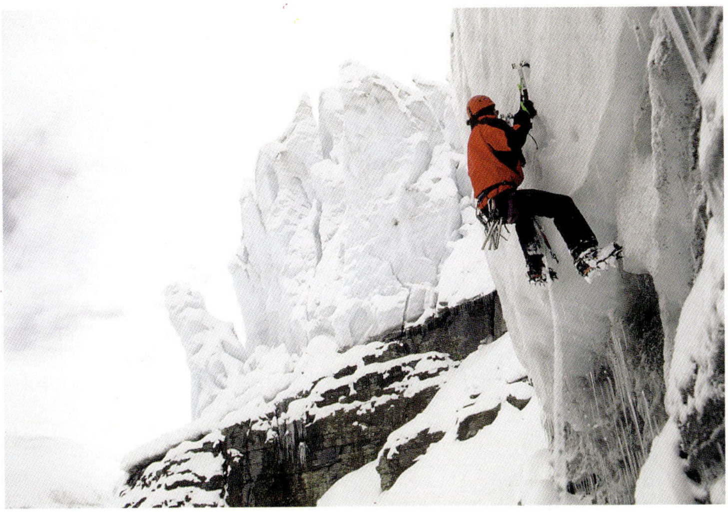

Perhaps too bright in other circumstances, the climber's red coat and helmet work well in the context of this relatively drab setting. Canadian Rockies. Fuji Velvia, 28 mm lens.

These are the "artificial" colors I most prefer to work with, at least while shooting color film. If I have the option of steering my mountain companions toward articles of clothing or gear before heading out, I tend to choose ones sporting vibrant, but not brilliant, shades. If I don't, and I intend to include them in some shots, I'll sometimes take along some appropriate items for my subjects to wear or use within this color scheme.

Why? Most films reproduce these colors well, and though they stand in contrast to the mountain landscape, they don't do so in a particularly loud way.

Deep earth tones such as navy, evergreen and chocolate brown are not as well rendered on film. Also, they often "clash" with natural colors, since they're close to many of these, but not close enough. Really bright reds and yellows are often overpowering, sometimes outrageously so.

There are no hard and fast rules here though. Color coordination is an intricate science, a professional occupation, in fact, for some people. The brightest reds or yellows on earth may look great when shooting a distant climber against a backdrop of blue and white mountains. And neutral colors, perhaps even earthy browns, might work just as well while shooting a hiking companion in a dark evergreen forest.

When in doubt, consider whether the colors your subjects are wearing harmonize with the scene or not. Do they complement the existing natural color, are they too loud or, alternatively, are they too dull and uninteresting?

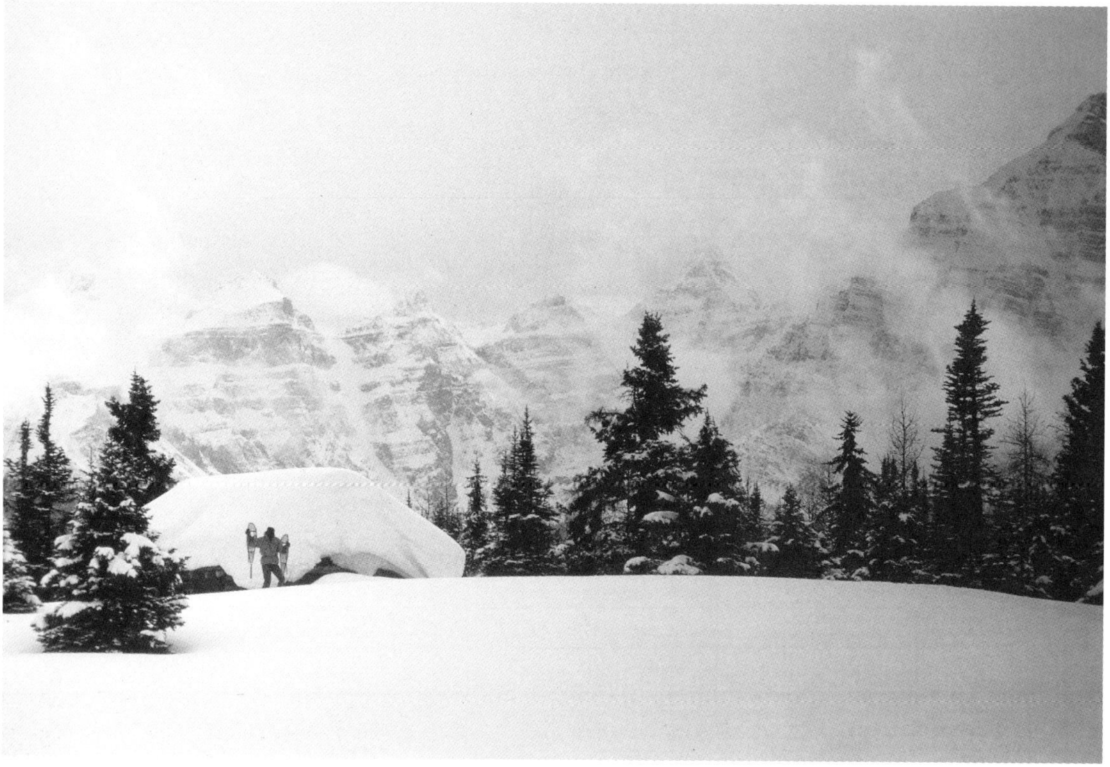

My endeavour was to create a nostalgic look with this shot. The monochromatic light and setting suit a black & white approach too. Canadian Rockies. Agfa SCALA, 180 mm lens.

Black & White Films

Pure black and white shades can be particularly tricky to work with while shooting color film. This in no way offers a rationalization for black & white photography. But it does point to a fundamental quality about it.

Black & white photos help to create a simplicity, and an attention to detail, that is often lacking in color photography. They have the power to render fairly dull, monochromatic scenes into something more lively, more interesting. They often convey a sense of nostalgia for earlier times, before the existence of color film. And, most of all, they capture mood in a way that color photography is often unable to.

Their downside is, of course, primarily that they can't express color. And since most of us are so accustomed to seeing in color, the adjustment to colorless imagery is often difficult.

The less important disadvantage of black & white films is that almost all of them are oriented towards prints, not transparencies (there is one notable exception to this generalization, as noted earlier: a black & white slide film called SCALA, from Agfa. At 200 ASA, SCALA has a reasonably fast speed and is beautifully fine-grained at that. Its only serious downside is that, once exposed, it has to been sent away to one of very few labs for special processing, a somewhat onerous requirement for those of us who don't live in the largest city centres).

Note that not everything photographs well using black & white film though. Some subject matter is much better geared toward it than others, especially when colors are not pronounced but textures are rich.

Take, for example, a mid-winter scene showing a snow-covered mountain hut with snow-laden trees or mountains behind. This scene might be completely monochromatic if it's overcast or snowing. It would thus be excellent subject matter for black & white film. The inclusion of old snowshoes, say, or a companion dressed in traditional garb, might strike a nostalgic chord, making it possibly even better in black & white.

Or consider a scene showing a climber against a complex backdrop of rocky cliffs. By using black & white film, and even a wide depth of field to keep everything in focus, the complex backdrop will likely appear simplified owing to the elimination of color. Details, both in the cliff and of the climber, will look less busy, and likely more intriguing.

When there are mists swirling around mountain peaks, the inherent mood may also be best caught on black & white film. Again, this is particularly true if there's not a lot of interesting color to be seen, perhaps on overcast days or in harsh, mid-day light. Downward-angled views toward clouds enveloping glaciers, or crags of rock and ice, can be especially good black & white subjects.

Even if black & white is not especially your thing, experimenting with it might teach you a lot about photography in general. It forces one to simplify, pay attention to detail and look for tonal range and contrast. For this reason, it's a great medium for any enthusiastic photographer to try out.

Filtering is somewhat more complex, yet arguably more important, with black & white film than with color. Check an earlier section on black & white filters before buying and using any. Alternatively, find a guide or consult specific reference sources if you want more information (see reference section page 219 for some pointers).

The runner was wearing brightly colored garments that clashed with, and drew attention away from, background details. Black & white film helped to create the compositional balance I was after. Canadian Rockies. Agfa SCALA, 20 mm lens.

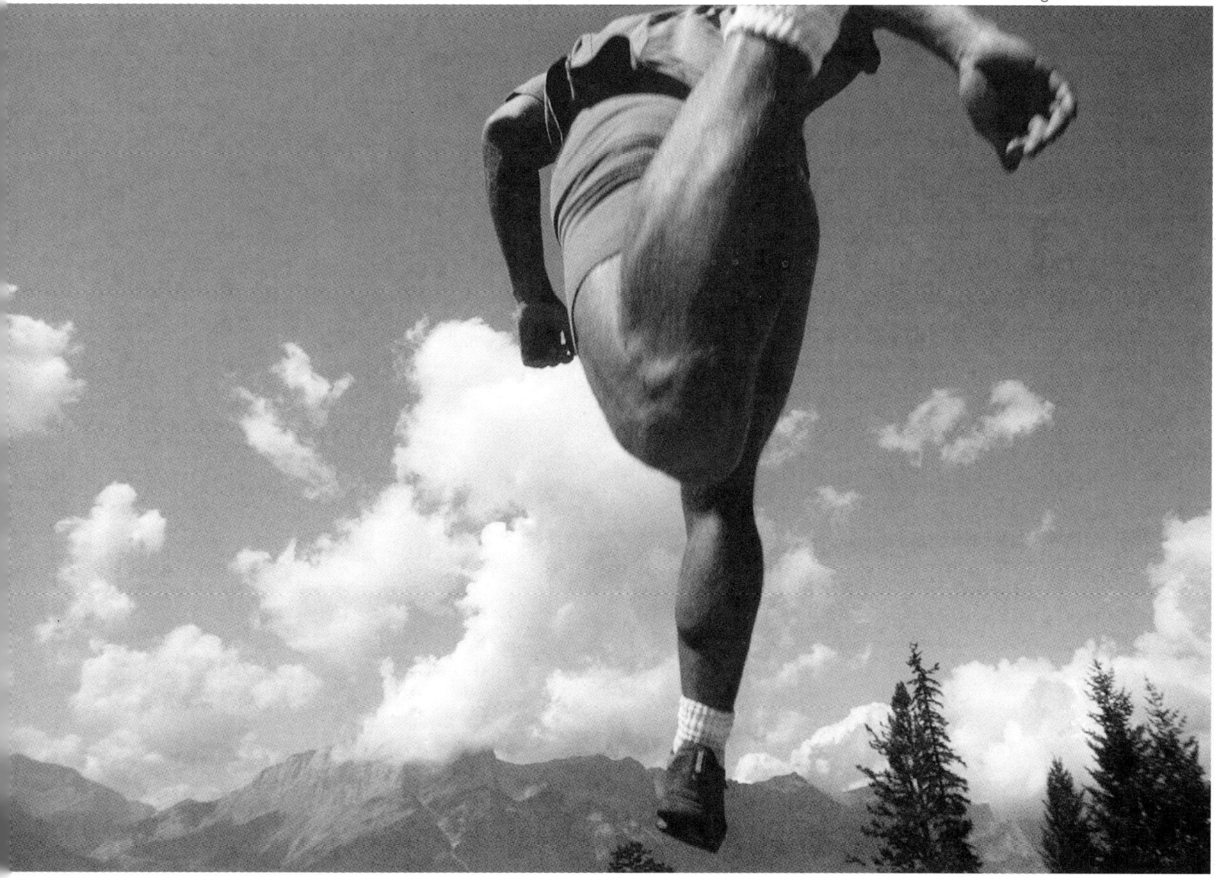

Black & White Graduated Tones and Contrast

One of the most aesthetically pleasing aspects of black & white films is their tonal range. Every shade of color has a unique tone when transferred to this format, meaning that any given black & white shot can boast a nearly infinite range of grays.

While this tonal range can be put to great use, some tones and shades work better together than others. In general, the best combinations either communicate the inherent subtlety of a scene, or strive to set apart—perhaps exaggeratedly so—contrasting elements.

Conversely, the absence of either subtlety or contrast will often render a black & white shot impotent. At such times it might be best to shoot in color.

Recognizing subtlety requires a watchful eye. High contrast is more typical in mountain environments, both in terms of features and lighting. A subject's subtle tonal range will likely not jump out at you as obviously as, say, the contrast between glittering ice and a blue-black sky. Yet with careful study there are just as many possibilities for capturing graduated tones as very contrasty ones.

Overcast lighting is especially good for shooting within a subtle range. Facial or other skin tones will often offer an especially beautiful and seamless gradation of tones when caught on black & white film in this light. So will a luxurious forest of conifers, particularly if mists are swirling around tree trunks, or when bark, tree boughs and ground vegetation are all nearly the same brightness.

Water can also be a great medium for subtle black & white photography. On a calm, overcast day, a faintly textured lake or pond surface may again record seamlessly, boasting a nearly endless gradation of tones. A bright or windy day will probably show exactly the opposite, by comparison. Shooting towards the sun and across a lake surface in windy weather may actually push beyond the contrast latitude of your film, such that peaks and troughs of every little wave might

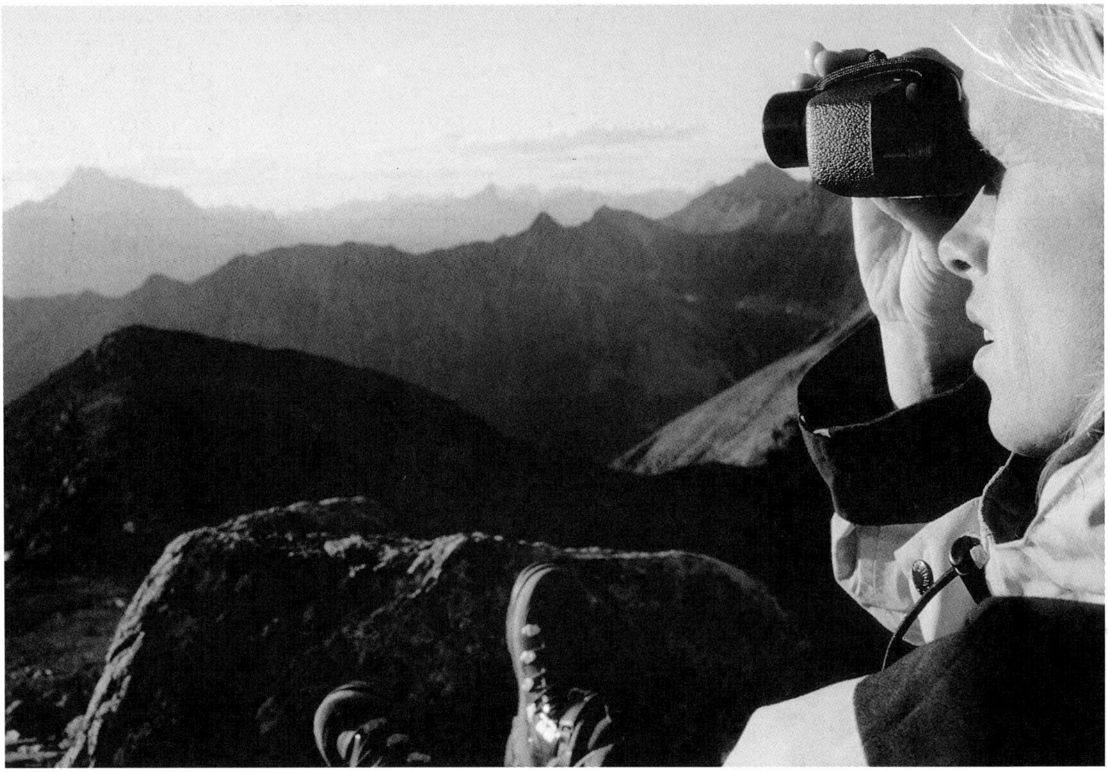

Black & white films often record contrast beautifully. Some of the detail preserved in this scene would likely have been lost if shot on color film. Canadian Rockies. Agfa SCALA, 28 mm lens.

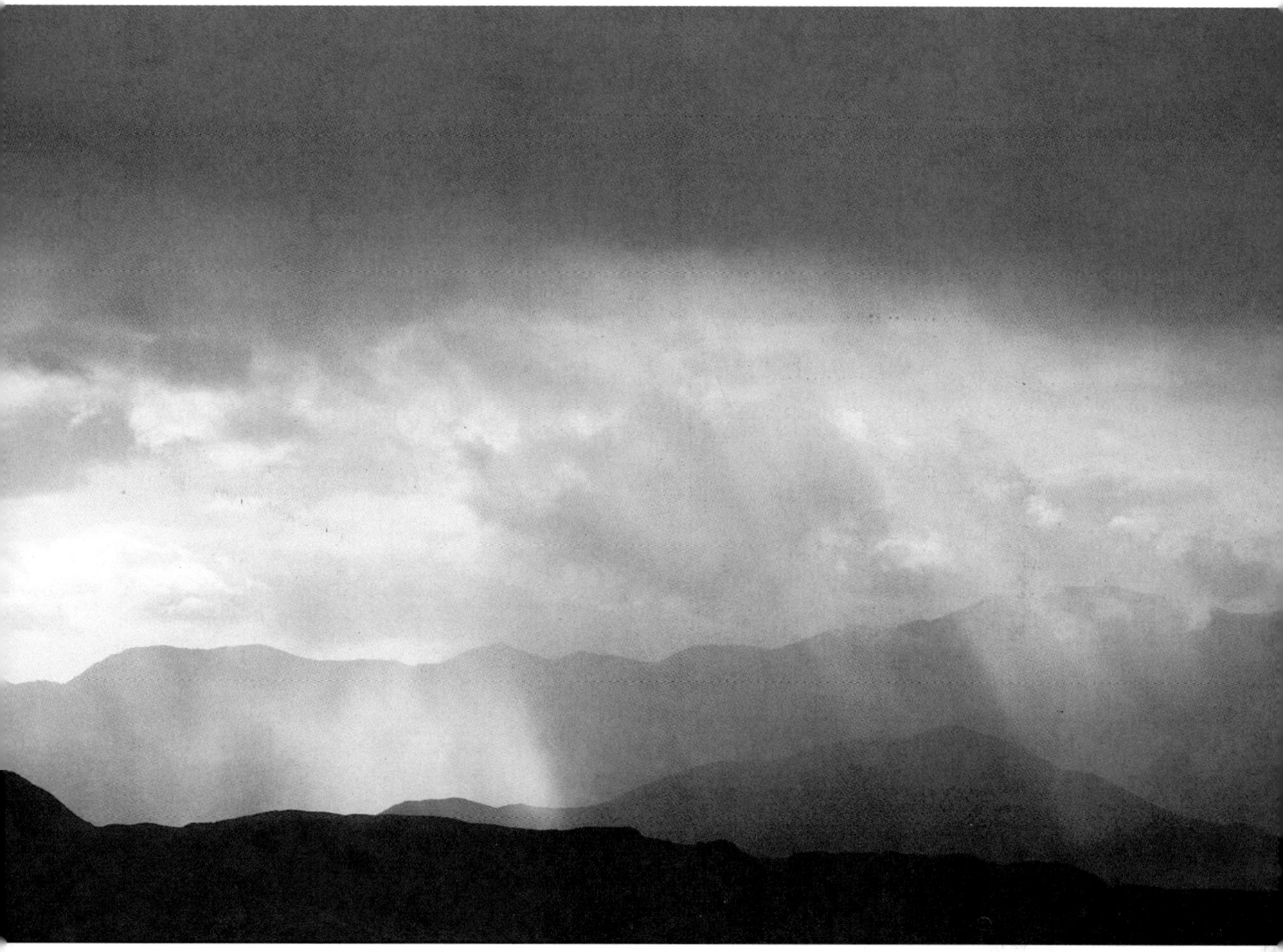

The graduated tones in this stormy view are perhaps its most dominant feature, owing to the absence of color. Death Valley, California. Agfa SCALA, 105 mm lens.

appear almost perfectly white and black. This kind of contrast can be ever so effective to set elements of a scene apart.

An icefield never conveys as much purity as when contrasted against deep, high-altitude skies on black & white film. Similarly, storm-laden dark clouds might look even more ominous in black & white than color if the snow-capped foreground mountains are brightly lit.

Capturing high contrast on black & white film should never be limited to scenics either. While sidelighting a subject's face (see "Sidelighting" section page 156), contrast can be strikingly effective, particularly if your subject has a strong, well-chiselled face.

In the same way, subjects with radically different skin tones, such as white and very dark, can be included together yet set apart in an interesting juxtaposition. Ditto when shooting with subjects that occupy shaded and sunny areas of a composition, as a belayer and climber might be on a partly shaded cliff face.

The point, as illustrated in all of the above examples, is to capture the right degree of contrast for the mood and subject matter of any black & white shot. Subtle tones aren't generally a salient feature of high mountain experiences; nor are very contrasty ones in the context of deep forest exploration. Consider your intended effect carefully, and also always consider whether it will even suit the black & white medium.

Sepia Printing and Hand Coloring

Sepia toning and hand coloring are techniques applied to existing black & white negatives, prints or, rarely, transparencies. Neither process really has to be considered until after shots are taken and processed normally. Both are intended to add impact in a final rendering, but without losing any integrity of the original negative, print or transparency.

Created from negatives, sepia prints are rendered with brown and amber tones, rather than with the blacks and grays that typify black & white prints. Most photofinishing labs will print your black & white negatives in sepia if you request them to do so. Often there is no additional charge over the cost of simply producing black & white prints.

Many digital cameras will allow you to change a captured image to sepia, and print it out that way if you like. This may be the best, and cheapest, way to experiment with sepia, since if you don't like the final look, you can simply refer back to the original photo.

Sepia, even more than most black & white treatments, often has a nostalgic appearance. Its brown and amber shades may look faded, even deteriorated, if toning is well carried out. Hence, it may be an effective choice when you want to emphasize, or exaggerate, antiquity in a shot.

The idea behind hand coloring is very different. When it is used selectively—that is, when only certain parts of a print are colored and the rest left as black and white—the effect is to make a subject really "pop" out.

For example, say you have a particularly strong black & white shot of a climber jumping a crevasse. If you were to hand color only the climber and possibly a piece of trailing rope, his jump might seem to practically lift right off the print surface. It would certainly be a more effective look than if the print were left in an entirely black & white form, and probably more so than if originally shot in color too.

When an entire print is hand colored, on the other hand, it generally takes on an appearance that sets it intriguingly apart from a color photo of the same thing. Hand coloring is almost never used to simply reproduce true color, except in the rare circumstance the colorist is trying to render an old black & white print with a modern feel. After all, what would be the point of going to all that work when color film could be so easily employed?

Note that almost all hand colorists will start with large black & white prints, at least of an 8x10 size. Masking is required if some areas are to be left uncolored, and the rest is accomplished with dyes and a bleaching solution.

A detailed discussion of hand coloring is beyond the scope of this book (see reference section page 219 for tips on where to find more information). It is an art form in its own right, at least if practiced well.

Sepia toning is generally accomplished at the time of printing, upon request and usually with little or no additional cost beyond normal printing. This print shows a fairly subtle sepia effect. Canadian Rockies. Kodak Tri-X, 180 mm lens.

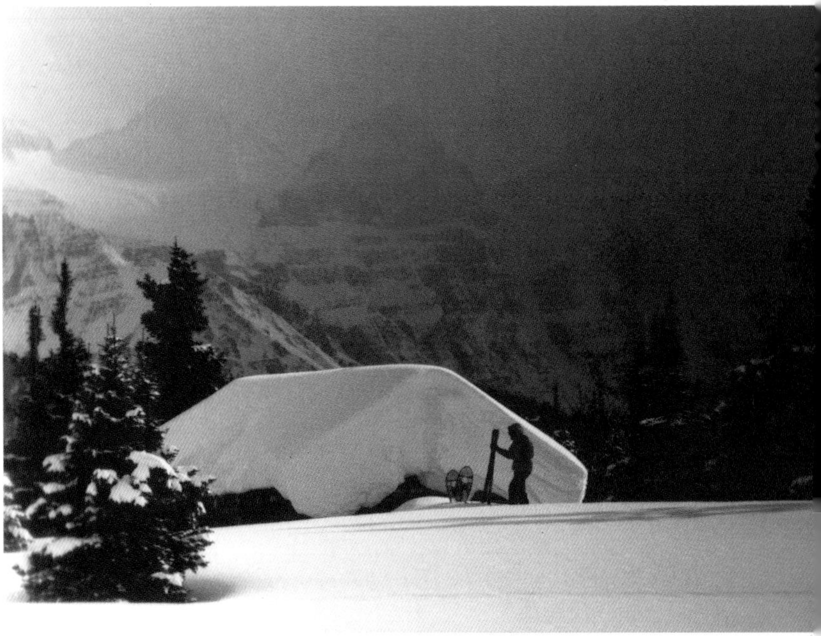

Alternative Film Treatments

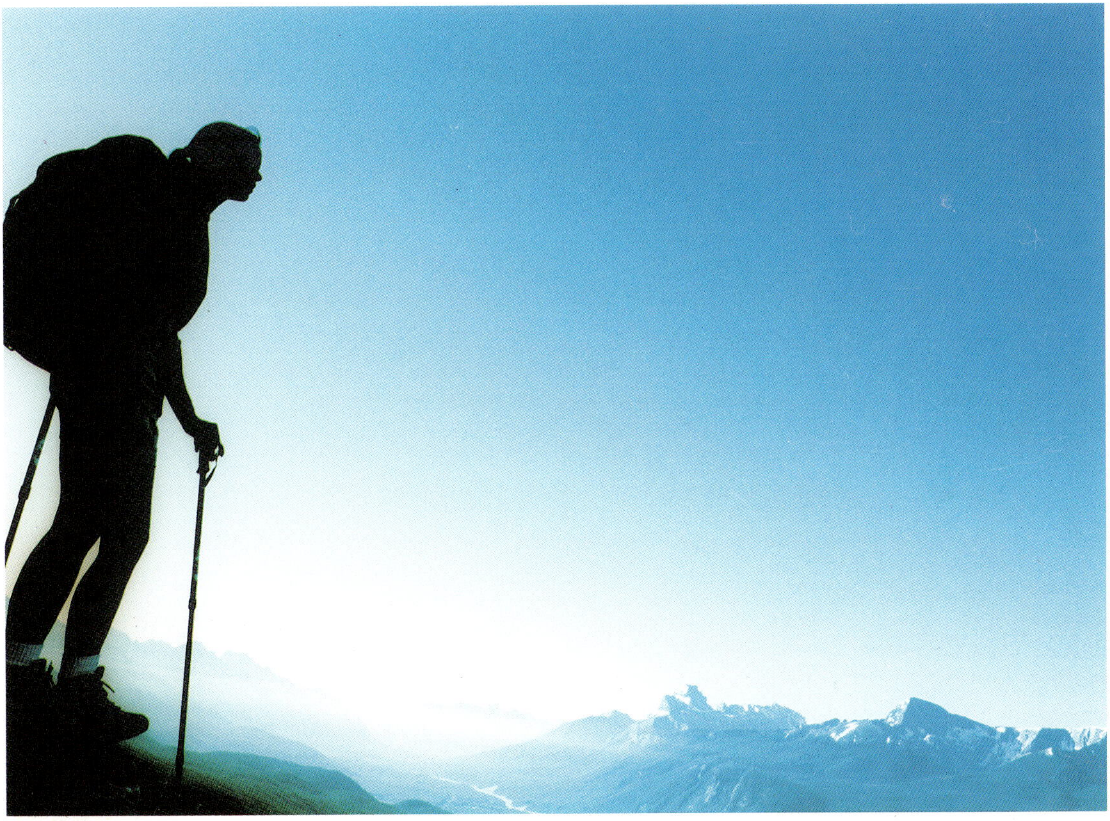

This shot was recorded on E-6 film, cross-processed in a C-41 bath and then printed normally. Often cross-processed silhouettes will "bleed" into surrounding areas, although this one doesn't do so to any significant degree. Canadian Rockies. Kodak E100VS, 28 mm lens.

Cross-Processing Color Film

Cross-processing is literally what its name implies. E-6, or slide film, is either treated as though it were C-41 print film and processed in a C-41 chemical bath, or print film is subjected to an E-6 chemical bath. Then the resulting negatives are made into prints by custom or mechanical processes, to practically any size or shape.

The point of this chemistry reversal is to change the look of the subject matter, but not outrageously so. Cross-processing tends to heighten contrast across any given scene, often "blowing out" light areas, while deepening shadows. It will also alter colors, sometimes in interesting ways, but as often in unacceptable ones. Greens usually are especially effected, and sometimes unknowingly introduced.

The cross-processed "look" has gained a great deal of momentum in the last decade or so (its popularity has, however, begun to fade recently). You may have seen it in use, on TV commercials or magazine ads, without even being aware of the particular treatment involved. Often a photographer—usually directed by an ad firm in cases such as these—sets out with the intention of creating an "alternative" reality on film, something eye-catching but not too crazy.

Cross-processing can sometimes work well in a mountain context. Here's an example that might help to illustrate where and when.

Assume you have a climber subject perched fairly close by on a high mountain ridge. Subtle evening sunlight illuminates both climber and the distant landscape, nearly eliminating shadow areas completely.

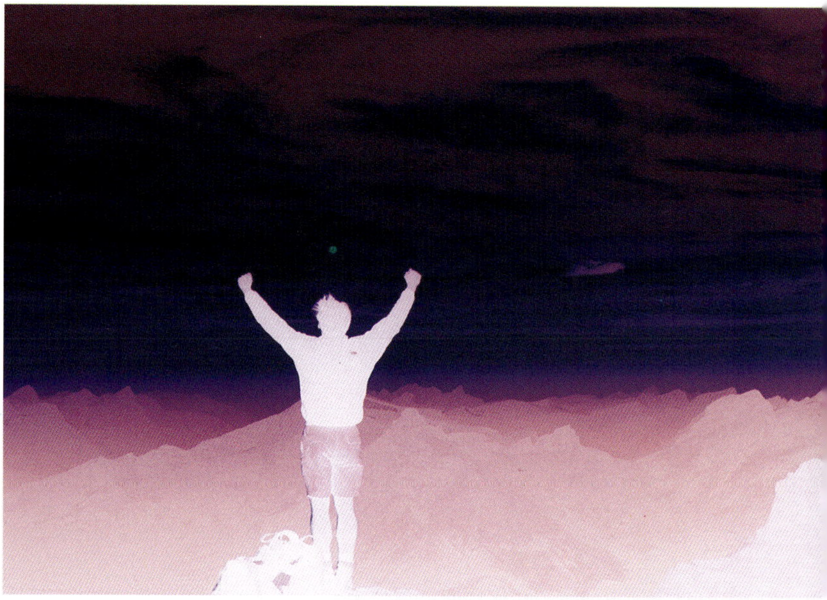

Sometimes a cross-processed negative will be of such interest that it might not even need to be printed. This view was shot on E-6 film and processed in a C-41 bath. Canadian Rockies. Fuji Velvia, 35-70 mm zoom lens.

Recording this view on color film and processing it normally would probably be worthwhile. Doing so certainly constitutes a reasonable creative choice. Cross-processing the exposed roll might just be a more intriguing way for you to go though. Thanks to the uniform lighting, almost any cross-processed version should remain within acceptable parameters of reality. Yet the visual alteration created could be quite exciting.

Note that cross-processing is not for everyone. Getting exactly the right effect usually requires a lot of experimentation, especially with film types and filters. Printing the cross-processed negatives requires a fair bit of finesse and an eye for detail. It's a complex science and, as such, a thorough exploration of the myriad possibilities and effects achievable is well beyond the scope of this book (check the reference section page 219 for places to find more information).

Your favorite lab might also refuse to cross-process film, as the mixing of films with solutions can alter bath chemistry to the point where the resulting slurry is unusable for regular processing.

If you do like the look of cross-processing, though, or you feel the desire for a little experimentation, try the following approach. Take a roll of either Fuji Vevia or Kodak E100VS film (both cross-process rather well). Shoot a variety of scenes with it, some brightly lit, some dimly, and of different subject matter, with and without people. Then ask your lab—or look for an accommodating one—to cross-process this film (it should be developed as C-41, since both of these films are E-6).

Finally, produce a set of prints from the best-looking negatives or a contact sheet from the whole filmstrip. Analyze it carefully, to see specifically which lighting angles and conditions look best and worst, as well as subject matter and composition. Make mental or, better still, written notes about what to pay attention to next time around, and what to avoid.

Remember to shoot, and process, any particularly unique or unrepeatable scene in your tried-and-true way as well. This will have to be done with a second camera or on another roll, since it's not really feasible to cross-process only part of a filmstrip.

However you do it, be sure to mark the roll for cross-processing clearly, preferably with a label that won't peel off, or with indelible ink. Otherwise it could be confused with rolls you've determined should be processed normally!

Tungsten Film

Tungsten and infrared films offer yet more opportunity for experimentation. Like cross-processed color film, both can be used to highlight, and even complement, certain subject matter or light conditions. Used without thought though, they can just as easily produce unsatisfactory results, at times weakening the value of a given scene.

Tungsten films were initially developed to produce "normal"-looking results while shooting with tungsten lamps, either in a studio or other indoor settings. Unlike daylight films, they were never really intended for outdoor use.

That being said, when shot outside—and especially in the mountains—they can provide striking results, given the right ambient lighting conditions.

Tungsten light sources produce a very amber quality of light (they are typically rated at 3200-3400 degrees K, compared to 5000 degrees K of bright sunlight). When reproduced on tungsten film, these amber tones are unnoticeable, having been fully compensated for.

Full daylight conditions, however, lack any sort of amber or yellow cast, and are, if anything, blue by nature. Since the compensating color used in tungsten films is also blue, any shots taken while shooting with tungsten film out-of-doors will sport a very blue look.

This blue will invariably be cold in effect, lacking any of the warmth of, say, tropical blue shades. It's a color that communicates hardness and stark realism. You might have noticed the application of tungsten blue casts in magazine advertisements for business, where the prevailing undercurrent is one of cool calculation.

Of course, some aspects of mountain adventure suit the "cool" look too. Take, for example, an ice climber scaling a vertical wall on a frosty day. Whether your climber is in the shade or under an overcast sky, regular color film will likely record him against a backdrop of gray colors. Why not cast the scene in blues instead? Not only will this look likely be more visually appealing,

Tungsten film deepened the twilight blues of this mountain scene, but recorded fairly normal skin colors. A lantern was placed in the lower left corner of the frame to provide warm lighting. Canadian Rockies. Kodak 64T, 85 mm lens.

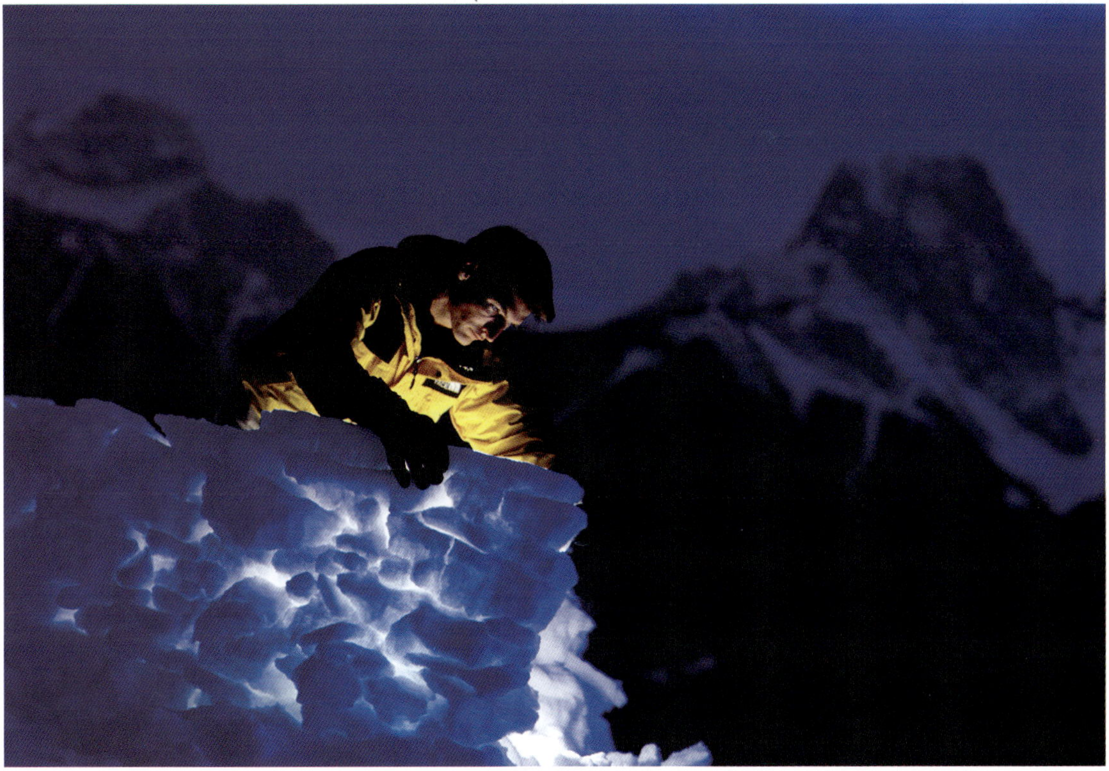

but there is also probably no better way to emphasize the icy surroundings.

There are two things to note carefully while using tungsten film though. One is that skin tones will be rendered with a blue distortion. This isn't necessarily an issue while shooting in the shade, or on an overcast day. When sunlight is falling on some part of your subject's face though, the look can be very unattractive; illuminated areas usually appear an anaemic pinkish-blue in color.

The other thing to be aware of is that objects that are assumed to be of a particular color aren't included in your tungsten shots. Take trees, for instance. We all know they look green, at least when viewed in daylight. If shot on tungsten film, or even included in peripheral areas of a shot, the resulting bluish look is rather odd, and almost never complementary.

For these reasons I usually limit my tungsten shooting to high mountain areas, or those bereft of vegetation (such as an ice climber's surroundings), and/or to twilight times of the day, when the deep blues of the early morning or late evening change our perception of the way our mountain environment looks. At these times of day, tungsten film will often serve to actually deepen and enhance the ambient blue cast.

Most of all, I almost always intend to show coldness while shooting with this film. The only exceptions that come to mind are when I want to record a subject's face illuminated by the ambient glow of a dim lamp or campfire. Regular color film may render overly reddish skin tones in both of these cases. Tungsten film, on the other hand, will likely preserve a warmish feel, while also producing acceptable skin tones.

Like regular color film, tungsten film comes in a variety of speeds (Kodak, for example, produces tungsten films—marked with a "T" following the ASA value—in 64, 160 and 320 speeds). Choose it in the same way you would choose any film.

If your endeavour is to record beautiful twilight scenery with a tripod-mounted camera, the slower, finer-grained film will likely yield the best results. If photographing faces around a campfire, on the other hand, one of the faster films might be necessary to prevent subject blur.

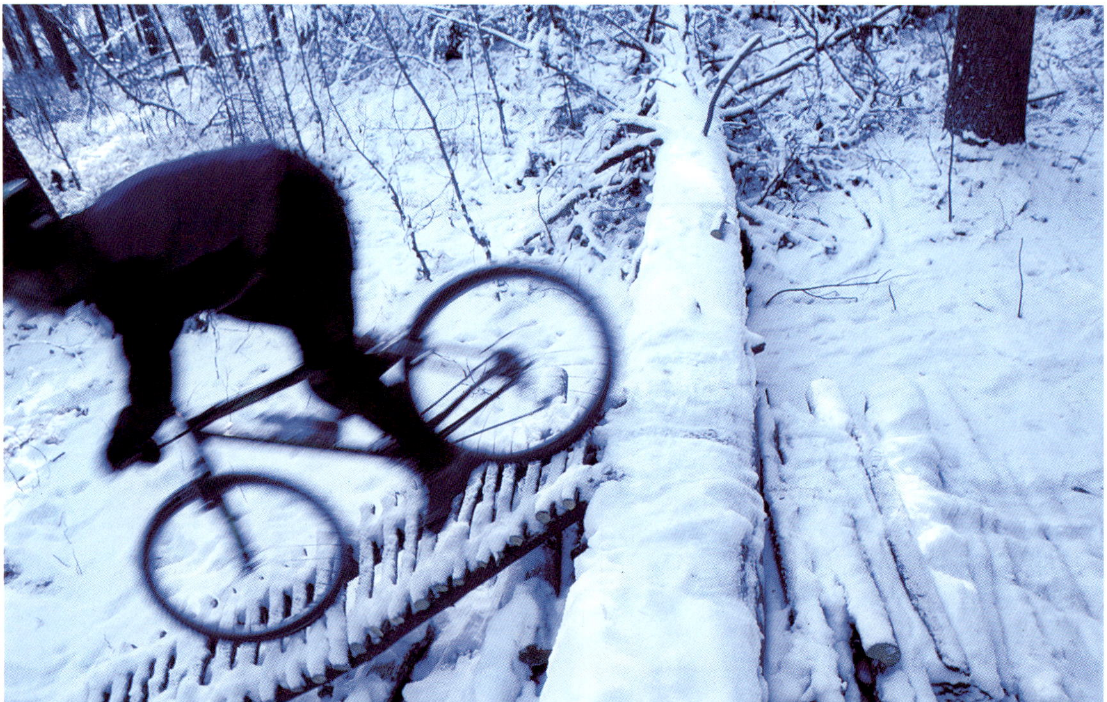

I used tungsten film in this shot to intensify the cold ambient light. Even though the sun strikes small areas of the scene, they appear to lack any warmth. Canadian Rockies. Kodak 64T, 28 mm lens.

Color Infrared Film

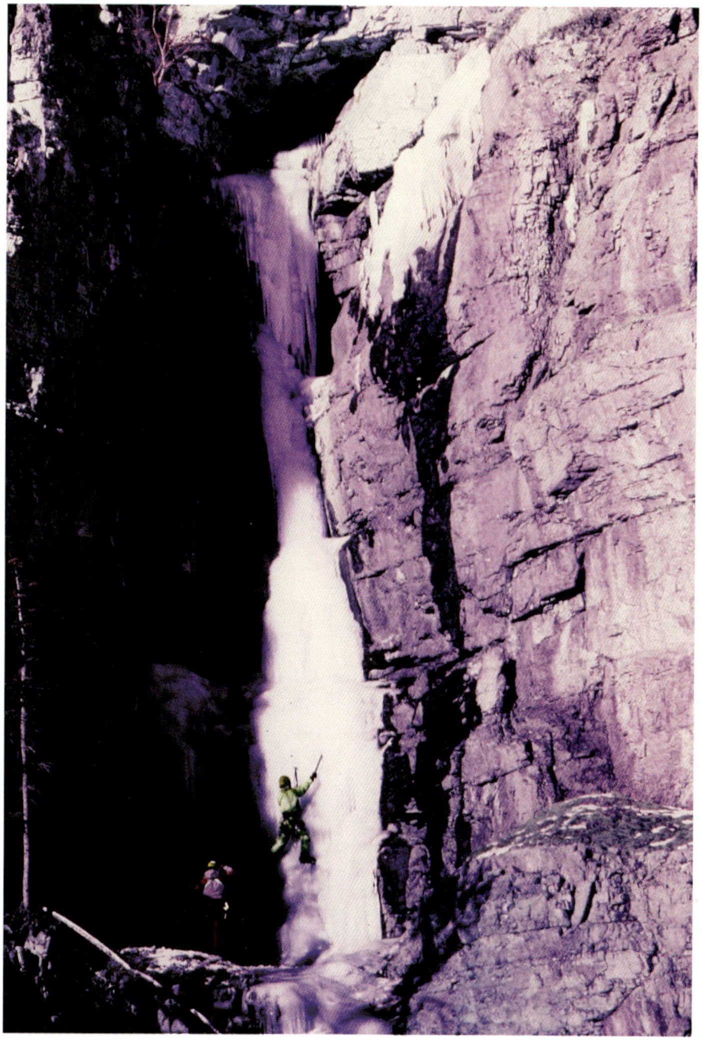

Unfiltered infrared film imparts a pinkish cast to most scenes. The lead climber's suit-color was actually mango; infrared turned it lime green. Canadian Rockies. Kodak EIR, 35-70 mm zoom lens.

Color infrared film will alter the look of a scene or subject in a totally different way than tungsten film. Used unfiltered, a pinkish cast is sure to dominate. With strong yellow or orange filtration (either of which I would recommend), colors will range from interesting to downright amazing.

In almost every case, though, the overriding feeling is light, fun and generally positive. A clear sky will appear an absolutely surreal but lively shade of blue when filtered and properly exposed on color infrared film. Other colors change even more dramatically. Anything that absorbs lots of infrared light, such as vegetation or blue garments, take on shades of red that range from subdued to brilliant. Red things tend towards yellow, orange things towards green and so on.

Infrared films are particularly exposure sensitive. A full f-stop up or down might make or break a shot. Even half a stop will make a huge difference in results. Bracketing is therefore not a bad idea.

Contrasts are also very dramatic. Lighter areas of a shot tend to burn out, while dark areas darken further, if anything. This can be particularly problematic, or creatively interesting, with skin tones that are well lit by comparison to background areas. Directly illuminated skin, particularly if it's light colored, will often bleach out completely.

The resulting look might actually be complementary to your subjects. Under-exposed skin, on the other hand, which tends towards a rather sick color of yellow-green, is almost never attractive. For this reason it's quite important to reflect a lot of light onto the face of a backlit subject, or at least to meter exposure directly from that subject's face.

As with cross-processing, the only way to really know what is going to happen while shooting with color infrared film is to experiment repeatedly, making mental or written notes as you do. Once you've got a reasonably good feeling for the effects it produces, you'll be able to determine how best to capture a particular scene in infrared, or whether to even bother doing so. There is no conventional wisdom governing such choices—they're very personal. What's acceptable to one person may not be to another.

For example, I'm not generally keen on recording vegetation with reddish tones. So I'll either choose a setting, or camera angle, that minimizes a view of trees or grasses. Rock, ice, sky and water (which, like sky, changes only slightly when shot on infrared) are my preferred backdrops. Other photographers might prefer a more abstract approach and include more vegetation in their shots.

A couple of important technical observations need to be considered while using infrared film. It is so sensitive to light that even small amounts of ambient brightness can destroy several frames, particularly at the ends of a poorly handled roll.

First then, always load and unload it in absolute darkness. This can be a little tricky in practise, especially if you're caught up on an icefield in mid-day at the end of a roll. If you are, try to shelter the camera and film completely by building a tent with dark-colored garments. Ask a companion to help you do so if possible, and note that you'll need to guard against light from below as well as from the sides and above.

Absolute darkness means you won't be able to watch the film tail engage with your camera's take-up spool. It takes awhile to learn to load film with your fingers only (especially for those of us without auto-loading cameras), but with a little experience it's not too hard. Just remember to check that your film has loaded properly when you shoot the first frame or two.

The other thing that is important to guard against is pointing your camera directly at the sun, or even to have the sun occupy a corner of your viewfinder. The resulting shot, if taken, would not just be completely destroyed by light, it's likely that adjacent ones will be damaged as well.

Keeping these considerations in mind, go out and have some fun with it! Kodak makes a great product, known as EIR (note that Kodak also makes black & white infrared films which, although often providing beautifully subtle results, can't match the intense dramatism achievable with color infrared). I'd recommend choosing the E-6 processing option and calibrate your exposure meter to the setting thus indicated on the film package.

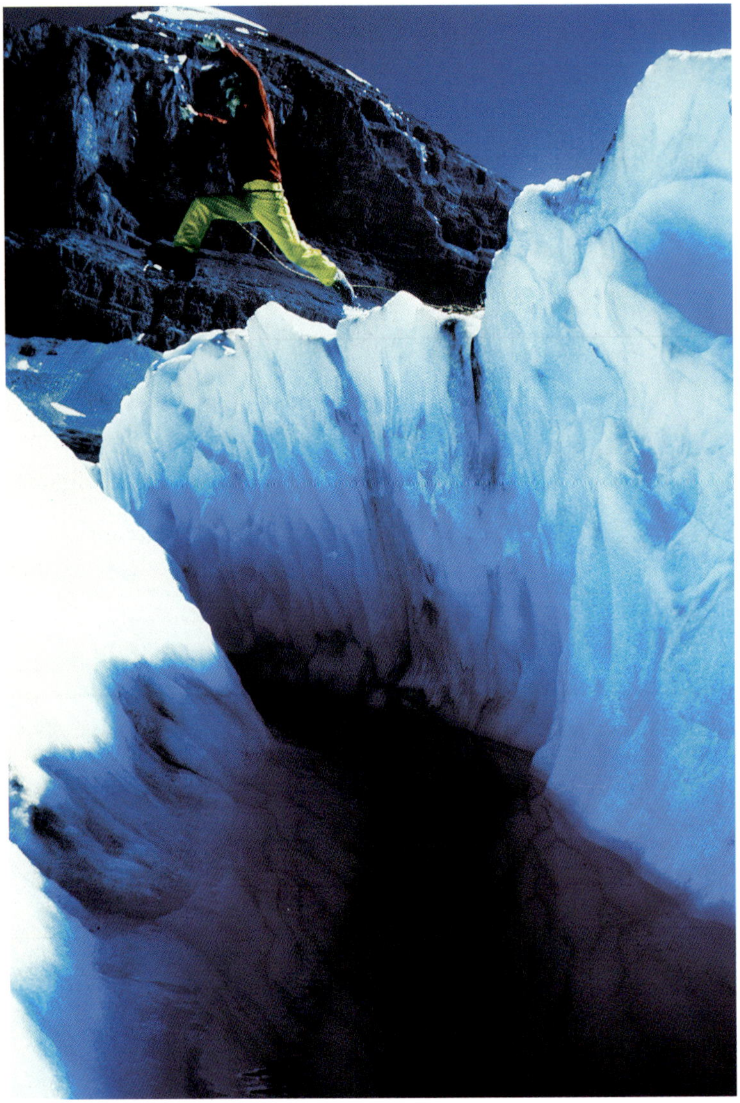

With infrared film and strong yellow filtration, ice and sky blues will generally intensify. Reds, such as the climber's leggings, turn yellow. Yellow and blue garments tend to go red. Columbia Icefields, Canada. Kodak EIR, 24 mm lens, yellow 15 filter.

Try attaching a yellow 15 filter, or even something with deeper, more orange tones to your camera lens while shooting infrared film. If your camera is an SLR model, its internal light meter will compensate for the loss of light due to filtration; if a rangefinder, be sure to follow the adjustment instructions that come with each filter.

The Creative Eye

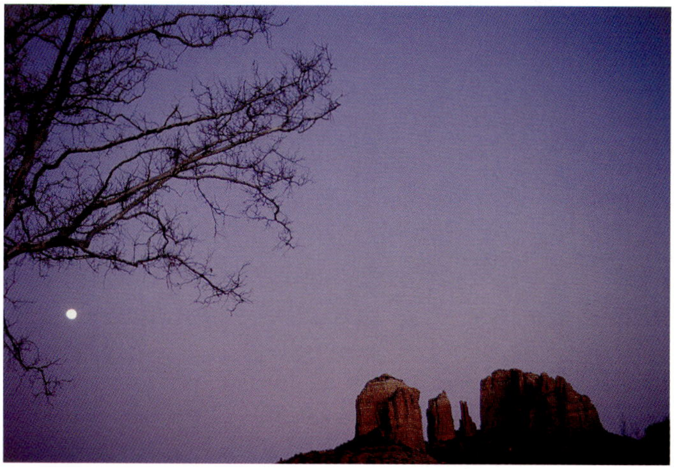

Sometimes very different elements of a scene work together in a complementary fashion, helping to build a strong composition. At other times they compete and erode each other completely. Oak Creek Canyon, Arizona. Fuji film, 28 mm lens.

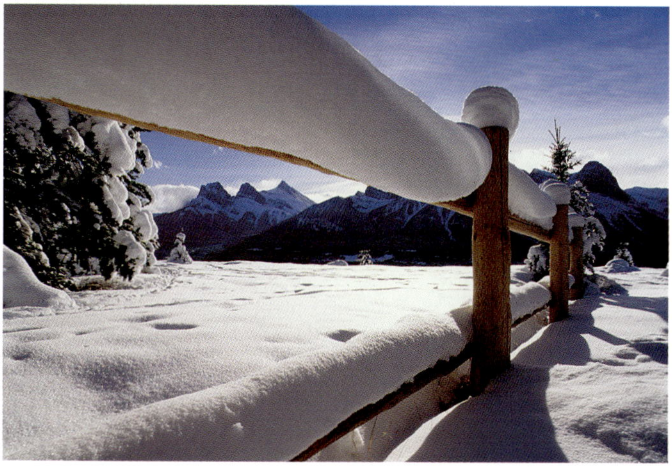

Strong lines are often pleasing compositionally, particularly when they draw a viewer's attention into a scene. Canadian Rockies. Fuji Velvia, 24 mm lens.

Composition, more than anything else, determines the quality of any finished photograph; one's ability to compose well will underscore the difference between a good shot, and a dull, uninteresting one.

That being said, there is no hard science by which to judge compositional finesse. Compositional "rules" can often provide a good framework for shooting, but by no means should one consider them an absolute authority on the subject. Exciting results can be achieved by breaking the rigid conventions on composition almost as often as sticking by them religiously.

Nonetheless, such rules establish a useful starting point in any compositional discussion. They provide structure and a sort of visual framework, which can be very useful while looking through your camera's viewfinder. Furthermore, in order to break ways with strict compositional bias, it's important to first have a firm grasp on the fundamentals of "proper" composition.

This section will examine some of the basic compositional principles, stretch them a bit, and then throw them out altogether in an effort to illustrate the myriad possibilities in photographing any scene or mountain activity well.

Don't feel daunted by the complexity inherent in the following compositional discussions. As with exposure control, the most important thing—as least while expanding your photography horizons—is to simply think about what statement, mood, or effect you want your photograph to communicate. Experiment lots and focus on creating exciting shots, not just on producing "good" photographs in any conventional sense of the word.

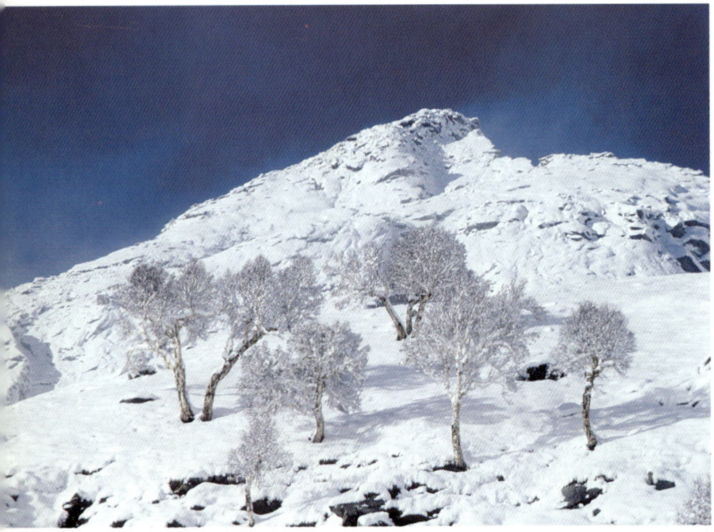

An otherwise nondescript grouping of birch trees looked absolutely magical after a snowstorm. Isolating them from surrounding areas made the most pleasing composition. Himachal Pradesh, India. Kodachrome, 85 mm lens.

This waterfall wasn't particularly striking at first glance, but its highlights were nonetheless captivating somehow. Underexposing the entire scene seemed an obvious way to best capture it. Canadian Rockies. Kodak E100VS, 28 mm lens.

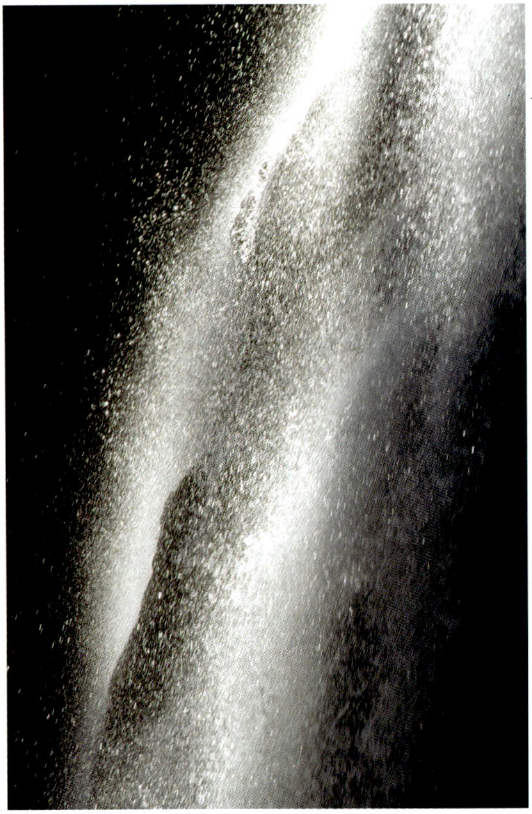

The Art of Seeing...

A well-known Canadian photographer, Freeman Patterson, wrote an excellent and insightful photography book years ago entitled *The Art of Seeing*. Within its beautifully illustrated and well-written pages, Patterson drew attention to the basic, but essential, starting point of good photography that so many authors of previous books had neglected.

Seeing clearly and artistically is truly the first stage in composing well. Much of the world's great photography shows the inherent ability of the artist to simply open their eyes to the environment or human activity surrounding them.

Often the trick is in simplifying, at a glance or through careful study, your chosen subject so that surroundings do not overwhelm and render your final composition "busy" or visually distracting. This is especially true when photographing in the mountains, where subject matter can be particularly complex and the need to simplify is therefore greater.

Patterson argues persuasively in his book that in order to fully develop your personal "art of seeing", you first have to free your mind and approach any subject without convention or constraint. In other words, you must learn to abandon all mental clutter and allow your eyes and mind to really "see". For anyone with knowledge or experience of Zen, this process should seem easy to grasp.

And like other Zen principles, the methodology of setting the mind free is universal. It really applies regardless of your photography experience or knowledge base.

The art of seeing is not only about appreciating the serene beauty of nature; it can just as easily mean seeing something tremendously photo-worthy in action, such as a climber's deft movement or skier's wipeout. Even facial expressions can offer a sort of rapidly changing beauty worth paying attention to. Your companion's tight grimace while waiting out an unexpected snowstorm might be one, for example, or the look of summit exultation in their eyes.

...and Being Flexible

I often find that when I approach a shoot with a bunch of preconceptions or an exact plan of my intended outcome, other possibilities are simply blocked from view. On the other hand, when I take a looser, less-formulated approach, a whole variety of interesting subjects often present themselves.

Not that having specific ideas or an overall shoot plan is a bad thing. But, put in the crudest pseudo-psychological terms, try to keep those ideas tucked in the back of your mind or even on paper, and allow your eyes and mind to roam freely, exploring and composing as they do so.

Here is an example to illustrate this point. Say you set off to shoot in a beautiful mountain meadow in soft evening light, and the weather turned foul unexpectedly. You might not pay attention to pearls of rain gathering on the leaves and blossoms of wildflowers in that meadow unless you were really prepared to "see" this picturesque development. Chances are that you may have packed up and gone back to camp with the first drops of rain, as I used to on a regular basis.

This illustration draws attention to another issue that will be discussed in more detail later, but is also really all about "seeing": photography on a micro versus a macro scale. Mountain environments are commonly typified in terms like "grand", or "sweeping". Often, however, the alpine microcosm is completely overlooked; that is, until weather or something else forces a more intimate view.

In the end, having the flexibility and openness of mind to adapt to new or unexpected conditions will reward you with more great imagery and a more diverse variety of photos as well.

Mental flexibility of this kind is generally more difficult to come by when you are not alone. If you were to enlist others to help with a shoot—perhaps climbing partners that have agreed to "model" for you—new photography angles or possibilities may simply not be imagined, either because you are distracted by your models, or owing to the pressure of having them wait your instructions.

It may be even harder to stretch your mind if you've already discussed your shooting intentions with them. To abruptly change things because they didn't work out quite how you imagined or because time constraints limit your ability to do as you intended, demands an inordinate amount of mental freedom. Many of us, at some unconscious level, will feel too constrained to do any such quick about-faces, which means our ability to experiment may be severely limited when things don't work out as we plan.

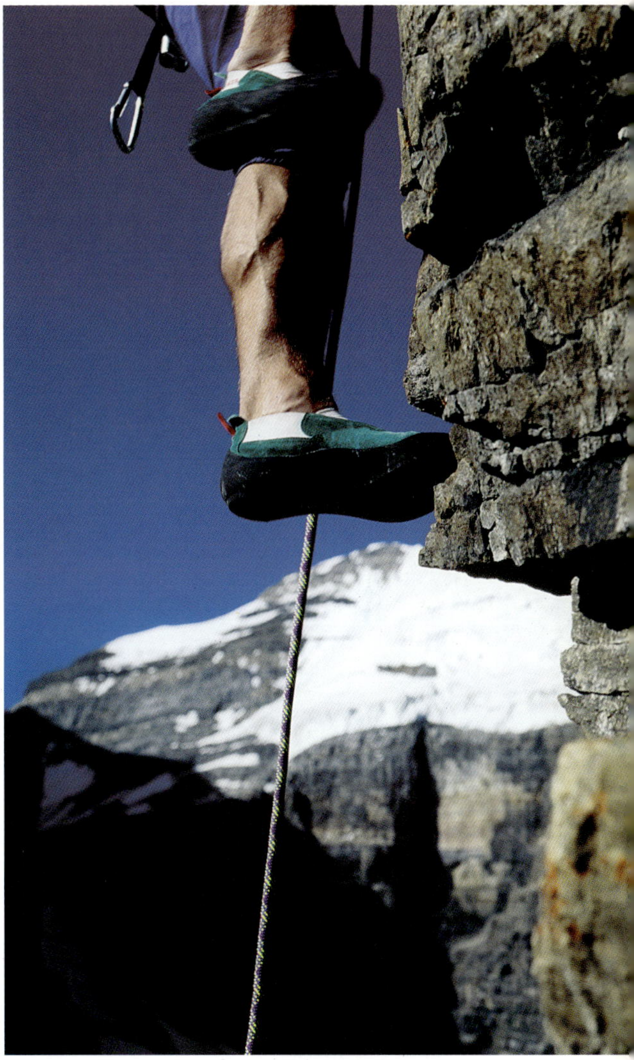

This scene wasn't as dramatic as I was hoping it to be, at least not for a full body–shot of a climber. Focusing on details instead gave me the drama I was after. Canadian Rockies. Fuji Velvia, 105 mm lens.

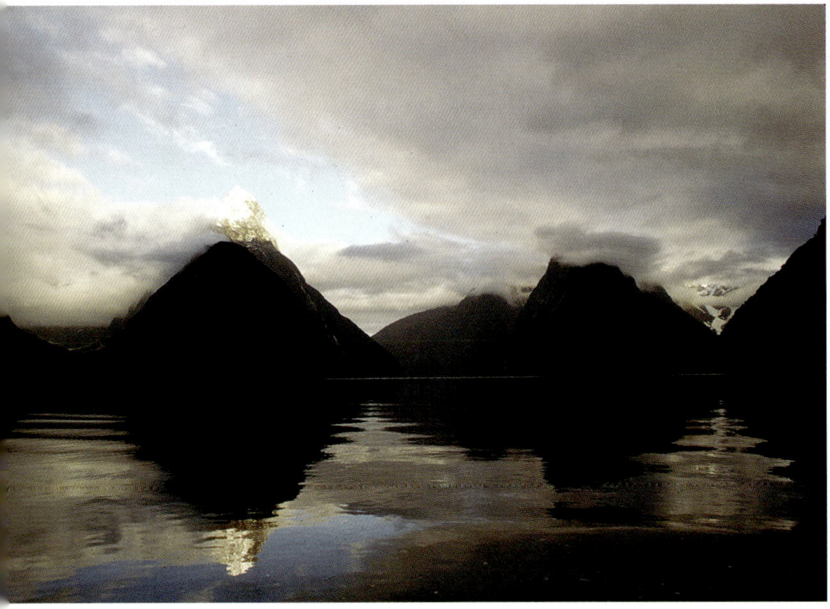

I thought I would be completely out of luck one morning when I got up to shoot this scene. Only one small patch of blue was visible anywhere in the sky. By waiting and watching over the course of an hour or two, though, this patch moved into an ideal position for the shot to be taken. Milford Sound, New Zealand. Fuji Velvia, 35-70 mm zoom lens.

To the Craft of Visual Communication

The popular adage "a picture is worth a thousand words" is, in my mind, truer in the mountain context than in almost any other. Showing your family and friends exciting and well-composed shots from your last mountain outing will generally captivate their interest more than the most inspired monologues. I've often found that a tightly-edited slide show can weave spells of fascination with an audience that isn't pre-disposed to mountain experiences or places at all.

Photography, even when it's not strictly artistic, can be one of the most powerful mediums of visual communication. And, as with all art forms, what underlies the success of any photograph to communicate powerfully is a combination of content and composition. Lighting and film choice, while important, take a back seat to good compositional craftsmanship.

Communicating well means knowing first what it is you want to communicate. If your climbing partner is pulling himself over a difficult overhang, for example, it may be best to close in tightly with a long lens to show facial expressions, or arm muscles bulging while knuckles turn white under the strain involved.

On the other hand, if the background scene is really majestic, it may be best to use a wide lens to show your partner, and his exertion, in the context of a grand mountain experience.

In situations like these, and many others, making a firm decision to communicate a central point will make all the difference to what is interpreted by your viewers. It may not be a "message" that you want to communicate either, but rather a mood or feeling. No matter: the finished photograph, if shot well and with interesting content, becomes a fantastic "tool" of communication.

This photograph communicates more, to me, than just setting and activity. It also speaks of the child's carefree and adventuresome attitude. Bugaboos, Canada. Kodak E100VS, 28 mm lens.

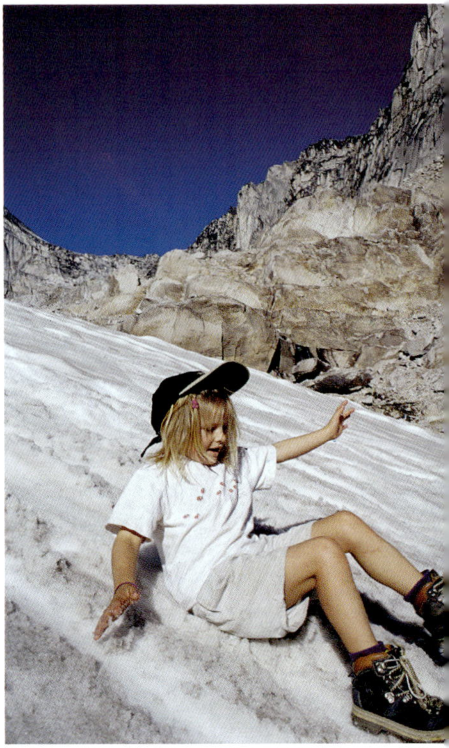

Lines, Shapes and Patterns

Mountain environments are inherently rich in lines, shapes and patterns. These can provide the observant mountain photographer with a powerful compositional framework or, at very least, will help to focus attention on a chosen subject or scene.

Rock and glacial ice, for example, is often layered or stratified in strongly visual ways. In some cases, these formations might in themselves provide an interesting photographic study, or they might converge aesthetically towards, say, a distant climber or skier.

Ice that forms at night over a mountain creek often shows patterns of great complexity and beauty. This also may be worth photographing in its own right, or as a backdrop, perhaps, for a beautiful bird that has alighted on a foreground twig.

On a macro scale, patterns can be awe-inspiring. A range of mountains, for example, seen from a distant summit or even from an airplane, is one of the most richly textured patterns observed anywhere. Likewise, a heavily crevassed glacier, seen from above or obliquely from the side, can provide an exhilarating backdrop of lines and shapes.

The important first step, for even those of us who have spent a great deal of time photographing in the mountains, is to recognize the inherently beautiful patterns in any alpine environment. These may elude observation altogether if your eyes roam across a mountain scene, taking the surroundings for granted, and not pin-pointing anything in particular.

Cloud patterns are sometimes intriguing subjects on their own. In this shot they complement the nearly perfect pyramidal shape of a low–lying mountain. Innsbruck, Austria. Fuji Velvia, 85 mm lens.

Similarly, an awareness needs to be well-honed to appreciate lines or patterns you, your subjects, or some man-made construct might contribute to a scene. For example, skis or a rope can provide great compositional lines to draw your viewer into a scene. Tents pitched in a meadow, if viewed from above, might prove to be arranged in a visually exciting pattern. Silhouetted climbers on a distant nub may provide the shapes your photo needs.

Alternatively, instead of simply trying to observe lines, shapes and patterns, which can be a haphazard exercise at times, you may actually want to create some. Consider the example of a rope leading into a climbing scene. If you really want to dramatize the compositional line created by this rope, try bringing the end nearest you right up beside the camera lens. The closest bit of rope will likely be out of focus if your climbing subjects are in focus, but this will simply add depth to the strong line created.

The silhouetted climbers cited above might merely need to be rearranged, maybe on the basis of height or profile, to record them as an interesting shape in your composition. On the other hand, perhaps simply altering your shooting position, or asking them to move slightly, may make all the difference.

With tents seen from above, a pleasing pattern could easily be created while setting up camp. It might take a little longer to do so, but the effort could reward you with some great pictures.

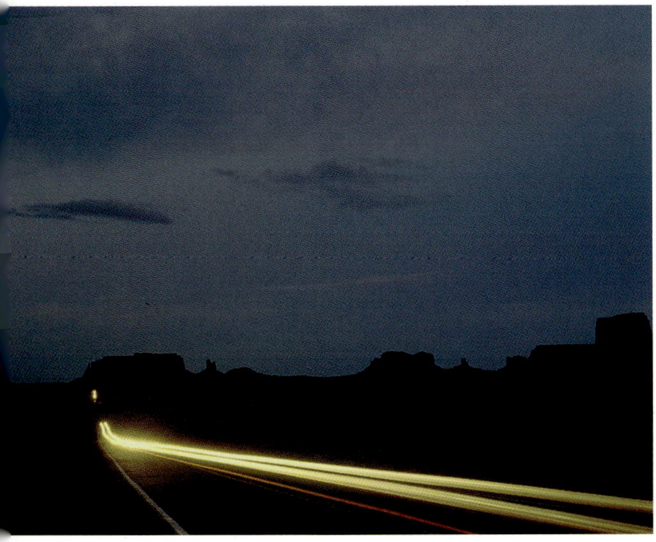

Lines and patterns need not be natural to be interesting. Here a long exposure of car headlights creates lines that draw attention toward the twilit backdrop. Monument Valley, Arizona. Fuji film, 35-70 mm zoom lens.

Texture, Tone and Contrast

The mountain environment also contains some of the richest and most diverse textures, tones and contrasts found anywhere. And just as with lines, shapes and patterns, the trick is first to spot exciting combinations and then to use them as best as you can.

Texture, from a photographic standpoint, relates to the surface quality of some object or scene. Rapidly flowing creek water has a certain texture, for example; calm, serene pond water has quite another. Snow and rock surfaces also vary greatly in texture, as do vegetated landscapes seen from afar. Even man-made objects, such as garments, climbing hardware and other mountain gear, present a tremendous variety of textures.

Tones are graduated through the color spectrum from bright yellows to deep purples. With black & white photography, tone relates mainly to shades of gray, the range of which is quite infinite. A perfectly clear mountain sky is a great study in tone: deep blues and, sometimes, even purples give way to steadily lighter shades nearer to the horizon.

Mountain contrasts, as mentioned earlier, are unparalleled in scope. Consider taking a quick trip from a deep mountain canyon, which may be rarely, if ever, penetrated by sunlight, to a glittering icefield above. The contrast in light could hardly be greater—if you consulted a light meter for settings in the two locations, you'd probably find there was 100 times more light on top than down below.

Anyone with a natural eye for photography probably feels an instinctive pull towards aesthetic combinations of either texture, tone and contrast. If you're one of these lucky people, you'll probably record such combinations without even thinking about them.

Even so, you might find it helpful to try evaluating any scene that appeals to you on the basis of its inherent texture, tone and contrast. New possibilities may occur to you that wouldn't come by intuitively.

Contrast, in this shot, comes from sunlight striking a distant body of water. Unusual atmospheric conditions and foreground details help to create interesting tones throughout. Coast Mountains, Canada. Fuji film, 70-200 mm zoom lens.

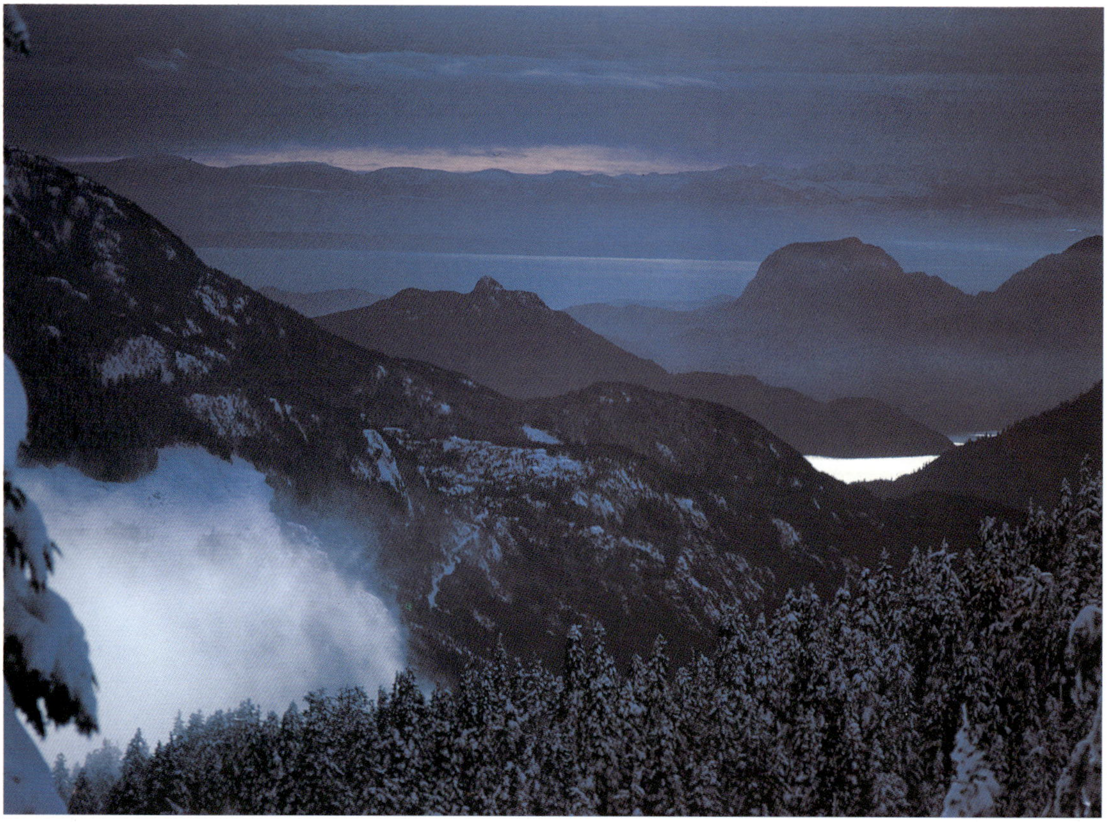

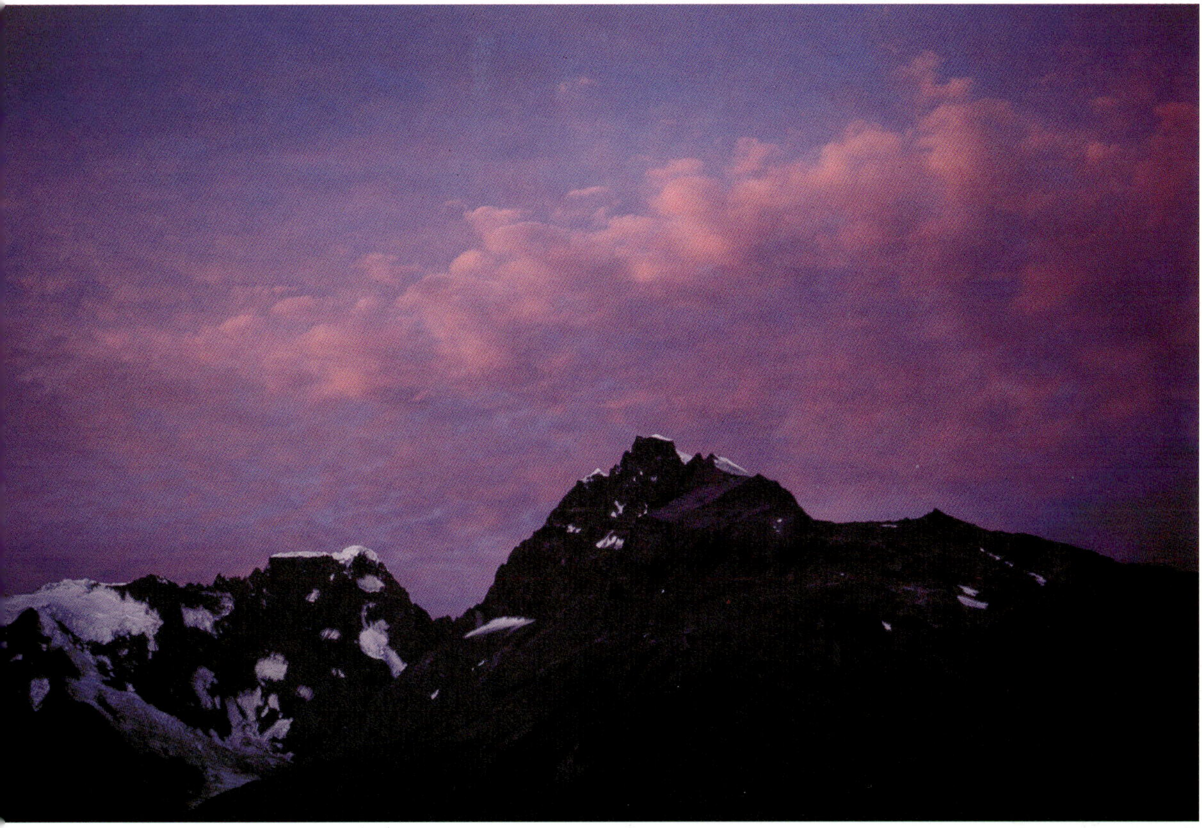

Cloud patterns have contributed a rich texture to this photograph. Ambient lighting was strong enough that mountain details also do so. Upsala, Argentina. Kodachrome, 85 mm lens.

For the rest of us, examining the intended scene, or even an unintended one, from the standpoint of these variables will make a huge difference in results. Once you've spotted textures that are interesting, try to combine them in exciting ways, perhaps by matching some and contrasting others.

Look for tonal gradation in water, snow and rock surfaces, as well as skies. Keep in mind that skin will vary in tone as well, especially when exposed to different light sources and shading.

Contrast can be technically difficult to work with at times. As already mentioned, some film types are better suited to high contrast situations than others, or, put another way, some films deliver more contrast than others.

Bear in mind that high–contrast is not necessarily a bad thing. If worked with knowingly, it can be effectively used to heighten drama. The point is to acknowledge its presence whenever possible, and then determine how it might be used to improve your compositions.

The "Rule of Thirds"

Probably a more widely recognized compositional rule than any other, the "rule of thirds" relates to the positioning of your subjects roughly a third of the way across, or up or down, your frame of view.

Consider, for a moment, your camera's viewfinder as a painter's canvas. If you were to draw two imaginary lines across this canvas, neatly dividing it into three equal horizontal segments, and then two vertical lines to create three equal vertical planes, the point at which the lines intersect become "centres of thirds," where your subject would be best placed.

Why thirds? For one thing, this kind of positioning is pleasing to the eye. Somehow, weighting your subject in one third of the frame balances the rest of the scene, without diminishing either aspect.

For this reason, above all others, most great painters, photographers and other visual artists have generally followed—and continue to heed—the rule of compositional thirds. You'll notice the application of it almost everywhere if you're looking, even on the TV set or in Hollywood films.

But the rule of thirds does not only satisfy a strictly pleasing or artistic compositional purpose, it also provides a certain dynamism that generally doesn't exist if you, say, place your subject dead centre in your photographs. The two-thirds of a frame that remains to either side of your subject, or above or below it, is space that your subject can, and probably will, move into and perhaps across. Hence, your viewers are given the sense of a continuum of movement onward from where you stopped action in your still frame.

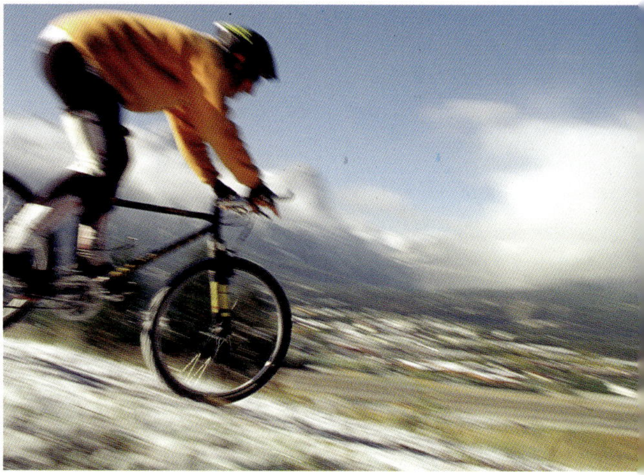

The biker's main features—his hands and head—have travelled about 1/3 of the way into this photograph. It's clear to any viewer where he'll be going next. Canadian Rockies. Fuji Velvia, 28 mm lens.

Say you are photographing your backcountry skier friends, who are fairly close together and relatively distant from your position. You've chosen a wide lens to include the mountain backdrop, and you've positioned the skiers on the bottom horizontal third of your frame. If you were to then centre them at roughly where the left-hand vertical third intersects this horizontal third, facing right, you would create a subtle sense of movement into the empty two thirds of your frame.

In effect you would be articulating the skiers' motion to your viewers. The same principle applies with up and down movement as well; if these skiers were to descend a steep slope you'd want to position them in the appropriate centre of thirds to suggest where they are headed. Even without creating a series of images showing their actual descent, you should, with this approach, capture a strong sense of their movement.

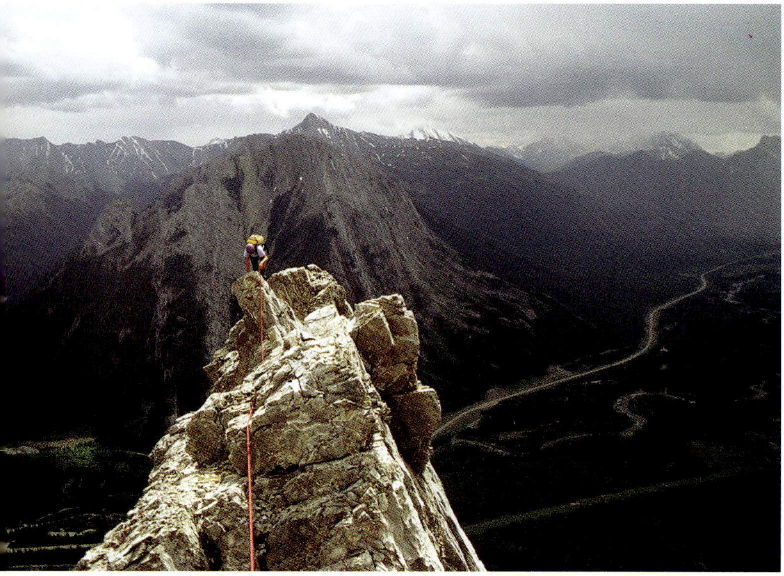

This is a classic "rule of thirds" shot. The climber is almost exactly a third of the way across, and a third of the way down, from the frame edges. Canadian Rockies. Fuji Velvia, 24 mm lens.

Variations of The Rule of Thirds

Not as commonly seen in photographs, but really just a variation of this rule, is the placement of subjects facing away from the remaining two-thirds of the frame; or, in other words, towards the closest edge of the frame.

This can be a very effective way to describe really fast action to your viewers. If you were photographing a mountain biker zooming through your frame, and fairly large in the context of the overall scene, then showing the biker on the verge of leaving your shot would amplify the apparent speed.

Ditto for a downhill skier in fast descent. Even if the action isn't all that fast—a runner on a mountain trail for example—showing him about to leave the frame could easily exaggerate his actual pace.

Alternatively, this kind of positioning can be a great way to depict how high, or low, your subjects have travelled. To really dramatize a mountaineer nearing the summit of a peak, for example, it might be best to place the climber in the upper third of the shot, continuing the ascent. The obstacles that have been overcome, and the surrounding mountains, could then be shown below.

Rappeling downward from a high position, on the other hand, might be shot either way: you may want to communicate how far below the anchors the climber has rappeled, or the huge distance he has yet to go.

In fact, in a lot of situations both approaches may be perfectly viable, and might just communicate slightly different things. When this is the case you can't go wrong by shooting them both ways. You can, after all, choose your favorite view over your light box or print folder later.

The other significant variation of the rule of thirds involves subject placement 1/3 or 2/3 up the frame, but perfectly centered across it. This framing tends to heighten drama. For example, if you were to centre your climbing companion 1/3 of the way up your frame, and quite small relative to the entire scene, you would give a very strong sense of his solitude or isolation.

On the other hand, framing the same subject 1/3 of the way across but halfway up the frame would likely magnify the vertical space the climber occupies, increasingly so as his size diminishes relative to the background. If he were half way up a vertical cliff and quite distant, for example, the mountain walls both above and below him would appear vast, and his position insignificant by comparison.

These are just a few different takes on the rule of thirds, not an exhaustive list of variations. Nonetheless, the examples cited should at least give you an idea of the numerous possibilities available.

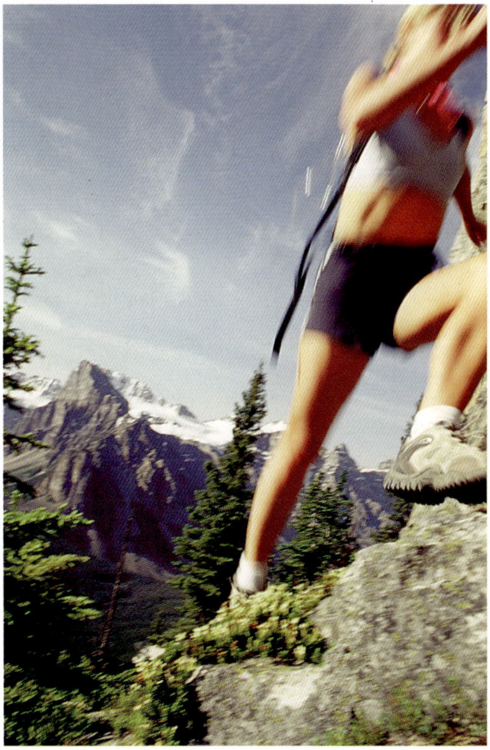

Here is another view of a subject about to exit the frame. The dynamic effect of the shot results partly from this as well as from camera and subject motion. Canadian Rockies. Kodak E100VS, 28 mm lens.

The biker in this shot is 1/3 of the way across this scene—but facing away from it. His positioning leaves the viewer wondering where he is going, which was actually the photographer's intent. Columbia Icefields, Canada. Fuji Velvia, 24 mm lens.

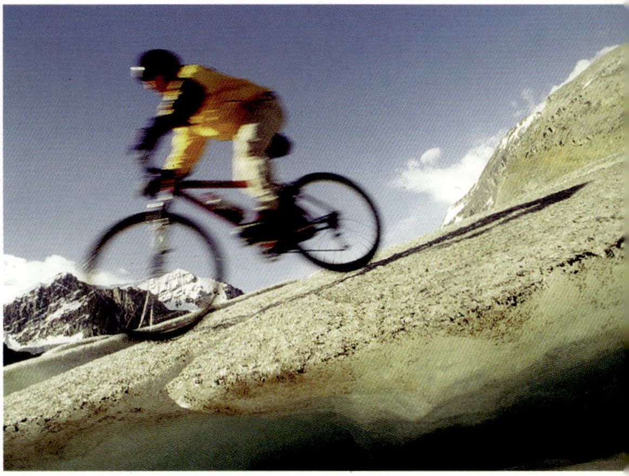

Disregarding the Rule of Thirds

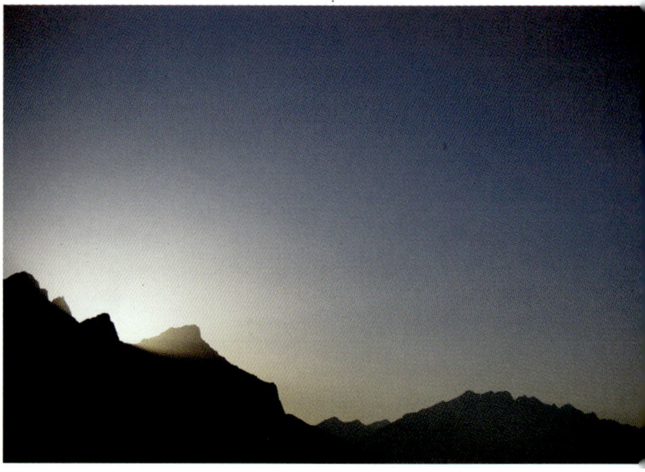

This shot's framing, with the mountain horizon less than 1/3 up on average, amplifies the evening sky. Often composing in such a way will give photographs a transcendent feeling. Banff, Canada. Fuji Velvia, 35-70 mm zoom lens.

The rule of thirds, despite its historical prominence (and continued relevance), became one of the first of the compositional "rules" to be abandoned in the modern era of more experimental photographic technique.

By no means has this disregard always been successful; some subject placements just look horrible when a particular fashion begins to fade. But it is certainly possible to create some stellar results that deviate from the rule of thirds. Mountain environments, with their various activities, offer some unique opportunities to experiment with other subject placements.

Probably the simplest alternative placement might be best described as the "positioning of sixths". As this name would imply, subjects are centered at points defined by dividing your viewer "canvas" into sixths, not thirds.

Usually the idea is to have them near the edges of the frame. In other words, centre them roughly at the final sixth in either the horizontal or vertical plane (but probably not both. A fairly common framing of this sort has the subject 1/6 across, and 1/3 or even halfway up or down in the vertical plane).

This kind of positioning can create a very dramatic sense of space. If a hiker subject, for example, was standing on top of a high promontory with mountains below, the 1/6 framing might work especially well. The hiker could be positioned to look out across the field of view—fully 5/6 of the total–rendering a seeming vastness to the mountain backdrop. If the hiker was quite small in your composition the sense of space would increase further.

In this example a 1/6 framing in both horizontal and vertical planes might also work. Assume your subject was high above the distant mountains. By placing the subject in the upper and left-hand sixths, facing to the right, you would probably give the composition a great sense of airiness, as well as space.

Note that "sixths" are by no means an important fraction to keep in mind. Quarters and fifths can also work well, and even eighths and ninths in some cases. You be the judge; chances are that if you think and intuitively feel that it makes sense and might work, it probably will.

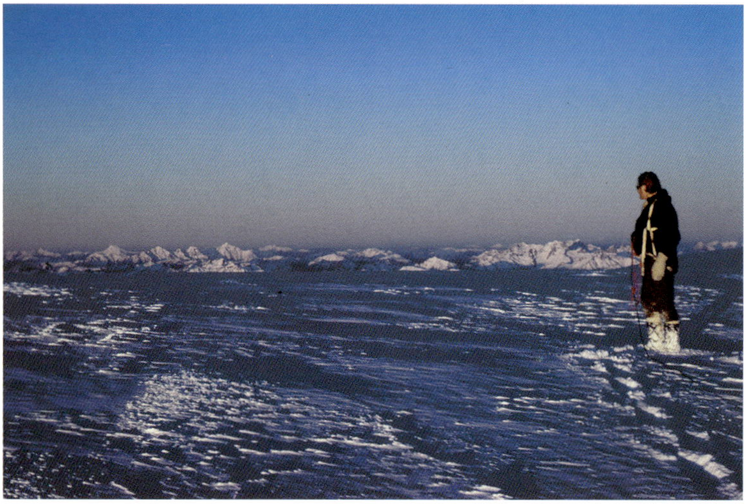

I kept the climber close to the frame edge in an effort to amplify the summit vista. The 1/2 vertical framing would probably not have worked at all if I hadn't done so. Mount Baker, Washington. Kodachrome, 35 mm lens.

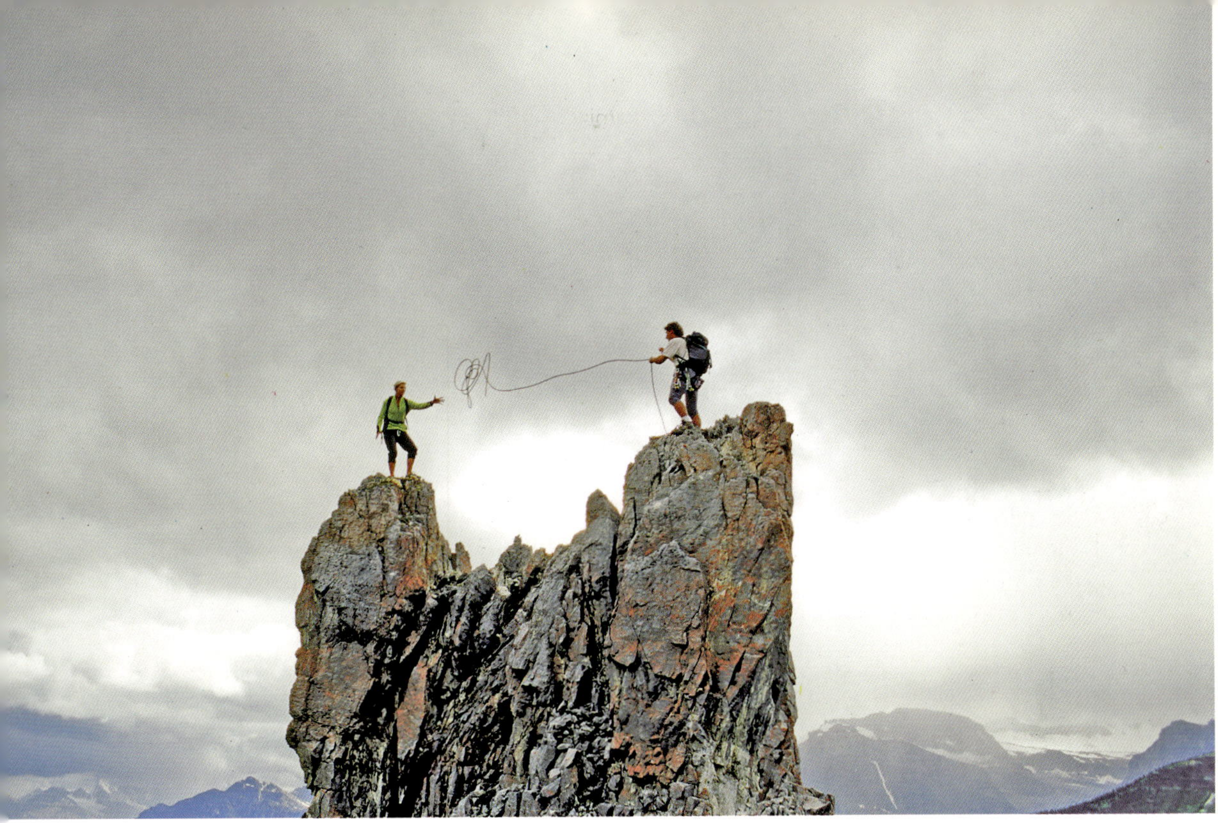

Here the climbers occupy the frame's dead centre. Such framing works, in this case, because it draws attention to what they are doing. Canadian Rockies. Kodak E100VS, 28 mm lens.

Dead Centre Positioning: Static Shooting

Again at odds with the rule of thirds are some great opportunities for positioning your subjects in the absolute centre of your picture frame.

In most of these cases your subject will be quite large relative to other components of your composition. Also, in many circumstances, motion will be an important factor, and often the primary determinant of a shot. A detailed discussion concerning the use of motion while shooting mountain activities is yet to come. What I'll focus on below is how centre-weighted framing can be effective with "moving" still images.

But, first, let's consider some rather static dead centre examples. A fun portrait technique, usually involving a wide-angle lens, is to shoot obliquely and slightly downwards into your subject's face, generally from only a few feet away. In most cases, your subject's face is positioned in the very middle of the frame. Any distortion that occurs, because of the wide lens, will only add to the fun and carefree nature of this kind of framing.

Where might you use this technique? A mountain summit can be a great place, for one. If you were to choose a 20 mm lens or wider, and stand just a little taller than your mountaineering companion—say on a mid-sized rock or small snow slope—you could snap a great portrait while capturing the mountains below at the sides of your frame, thus really emphasizing the summit "experience".

This style of shooting is very hip at the moment, and incredibly easy in practice. Generally it works best in the horizontal format. Note that absolute centre weighting is not critical to the success of the outcome, but distortion with very wide lenses may be more objectionable with your subject positioned to either side of centre. It's easy to judge the preferred centering in any event, since whatever you see through your viewfinder is more or less what you will get on film. The point-of-view perspective offers some great possibilities for a centre subject placement. This term literally means what it suggests: the point-of-view of the photographer is what's depicted on film. More will be said about point of view shooting later. Here, though, are some examples of where this technique is applied to "centre" subjects.

If you are travelling alone in the mountains and you want to capture a scene with human elements somehow, you really have only two choices. You can either mount your camera on a tripod and snap a self-portrait, or shoot some body part from where you sit or stand. These could include your boot-clad feet, a hand, or—if you can hold your camera steadily with one hand outstretched in front of you—your portrait in the fashion described above, with a wide-angle lens.

You don't, of course, have to be alone either. When your friends are ahead of you, off to the sides, or even behind when you're shooting a one-handed self-portrait, you can easily record them in the background.

In any event, chances are that you will want to place immediate body elements—for instance your principal subjects—in the centre of view. Why? This framing creates a pleasing symmetry, especially when you shoot down your arms or legs, where diagonal "lines" are created through distortion by your wide-angle lens, leading inwards toward the centre.

The climber's dead centre framing is "explained" by the rope leading towards him. Rather than looking static, the whole composition has taken on a dynamic flow. Canadian Rockies. Fuji Velvia, 35-70 mm zoom lens.

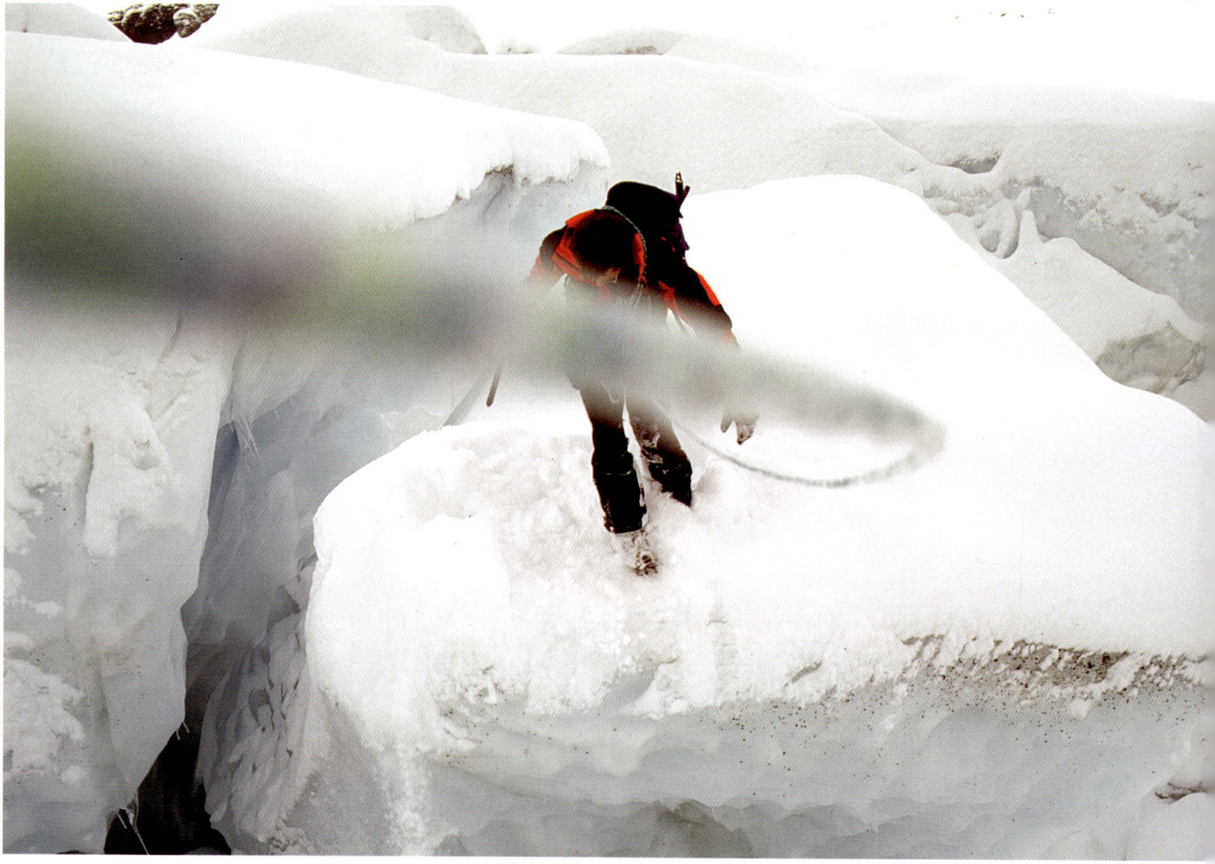

Dead Centre Positioning: Motion

Probably the best example of an in-motion centre framing is also the point-of-view shot. If you want to suggest your presence in some mountain activity, whether on your own or with companions, a point-of-view perspective can be especially graphic.

Say you are skiing down a picturesque backcountry glade. While looking down, you catch a glance of powder billowing out as your ski tips glide forwards. Since you are momentarily alone, trying to capture others enjoying the same experience is not possible. So why not try to shoot the scene exactly as you see it?

An effective shot of this scene might require a few gymnastics—and risk a possible spill—in order to see scenery sweeping by and not just your feet and snow. However, if you've ever succeeded at squatting on the backs of your skis, it probably won't be that difficult to pull off. Owing to the straight line that could be drawn forward from your camera position, the advancing ski tips will probably be best kept close to the centre of your composition.

The same approach could be used while riding a mountain bike, Nordic skiing with set tracks, parasailing, horseback riding and, with a little more difficulty, even hiking or climbing. It's a great technique to experiment with because, for one thing, you'll never know exactly what you've recorded until results return from the lab (or until you play them back on your digital camera).

One other technique that implies motion, although doesn't usually record it, also demands a subject framed at essentially dead centre. It is an even more experimental technique than the ones described above; in fact, I don't think I've ever seen an example of it in print or at anyones slide show.

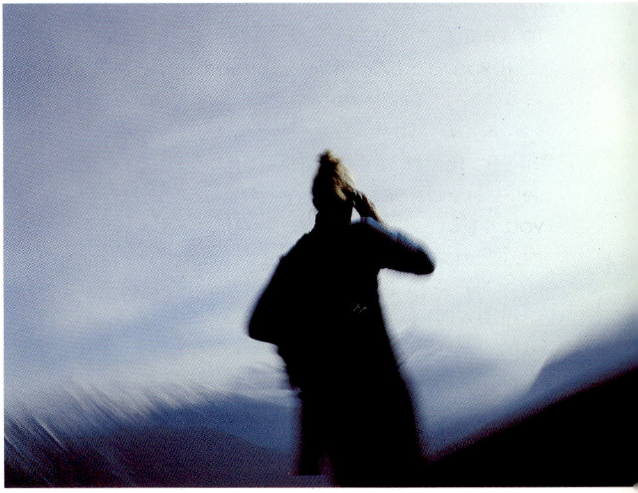

This shot shows what I call "circular panning". Once you've centered the part of your composition that you want to keep in focus, you merely twist and shoot. The trick is to use the right shutter speed and not lose sharpness at the centre. Canadian Rockies. Fuji Velvia, 35 mm lens.

The circular pan technique, as I call it, involves pivoting your camera in a circular direction with generally a wide lens. As long as your subjects are positioned in the absolute centre of the frame, they will remain fairly sharp—as long as they're not moving much—while the four sides of the frame blur in concentric patterns. A detailed discussion of this technique, and the best time to use it, will follow in a later section on panning. Suffice to say, though, for the time being, that it can render some very eye-popping results with the appropriate choice of background.

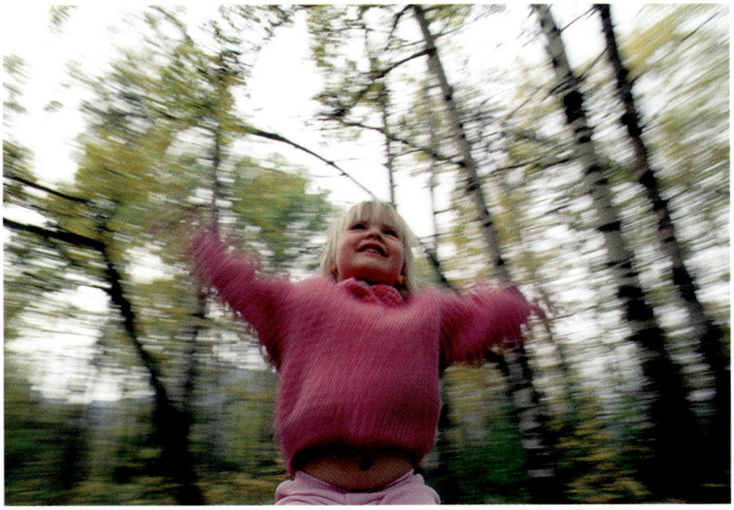

I had my young subject sit on a swivel chair for this composition. I then attached a partially extended tripod to the chair, and asked her to open her arms while I swivelled the chair and clicked off the shutter. Canadian Rockies. Fuji Velvia, 28 mm lens.

Cropping Your Subject

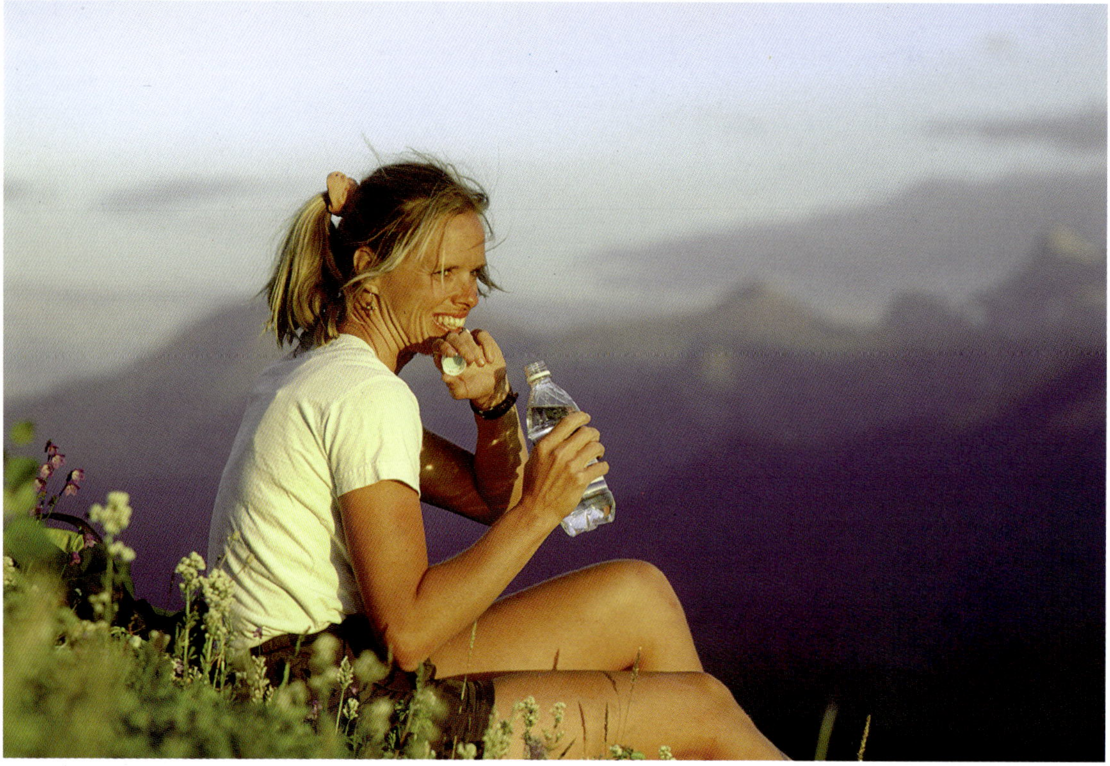

A medium crop was used in this composition. Most of the subject's body is visible, but it also occupies the majority of space within the frame. Canadian Rockies. Fuji Velvia, 105 mm lens.

As with the rule of thirds, ideas about cropping range from classic and traditional to the experimental and occasionally outrageous. And, just as mastering good subject placements in a conventional sense are important before deviating far from them, so too is learning good cropping fundamentals before attempting any of the bizarre crops that only sometimes work.

Cropping refers to how much of your subject will be kept in the frame and how much will be left out. A "tight" crop means getting close to your subject and, usually, filling most of the frame with it. Portraits fit into this category, as do close-up shots of hands, feet, flowers, or...grizzly jaws. "Looser" cropping means that you've pulled back from your subject to include full body profiles, as well as background scenery.

Most mountain photographers will shoot primarily in the latter, looser mode. This probably has mainly to do with the magnitude of mountain environments and the corresponding smallness of human subjects within them. Tight crops, however, especially juxtaposed against loose crops, can be very effective. In a slide show or other presentation of your work they will often help to break up the monotony of same-looking scenes.

Traditional cropping parameters for human subjects, arranged from tight to loose, are more or less as follows: head and shoulders only (portrait crop); waist up; mid-thigh upwards; full body profile; and then a progressively smaller profile relative to the scene (see photos). Cropping your subject at or below the knees (i.e. cutting out the feet), or at mid-chest height is generally not endorsed within the classic mind-set.

Yet today a lot of photography is shot and marketed commercially with exactly these crops. Much of it includes action and gives the impression that it was shot "on the fly", which indeed it may have been. Sometimes, as mentioned earlier, these crops work. Almost as often they don't, even at times in pictures created on big advertising budgets.

As with other compositional techniques, a little thought has to be spared for exactly why a particular crop is chosen over any other. Often the mental process involved needs to be a quick one; if you are shooting a grizzly from relatively close by—and from a safe position!—it might be worth trying to get a tight, head-and-shoulders crop. On the other hand, even if you could get a tight crop, this may be a poor choice if the bear was picturesquely positioned in a mountain setting.

Or, going back to an earlier example of a climber surmounting an overhang, you may have to decide whether the facial expression or the greater mountain experience is more important to your composition. For your photos to communicate as effectively as possible, cropping decisions need to derive either from rational thought or inspired vision.

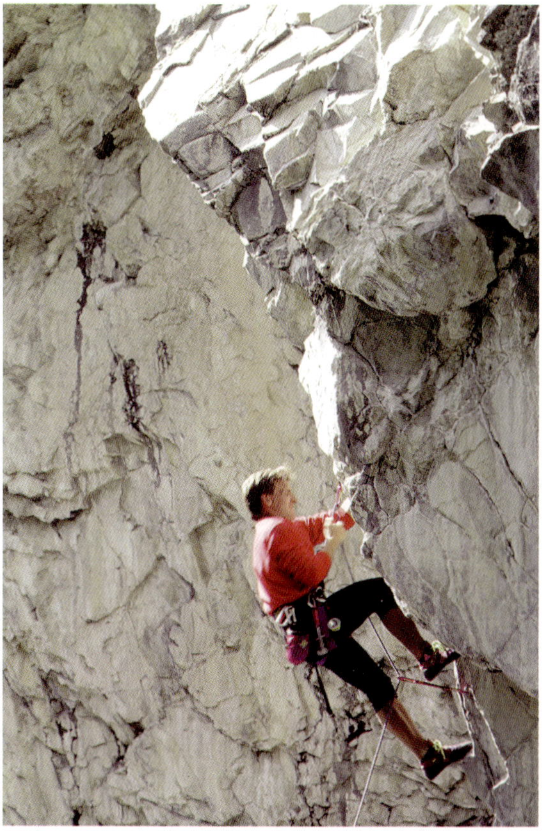

This is an example of looser framing that often works well when you want to show a little more surrounding environment than in the previous example. Canadian Rockies. Fuji Velvia, 70-200 mm zoom lens.

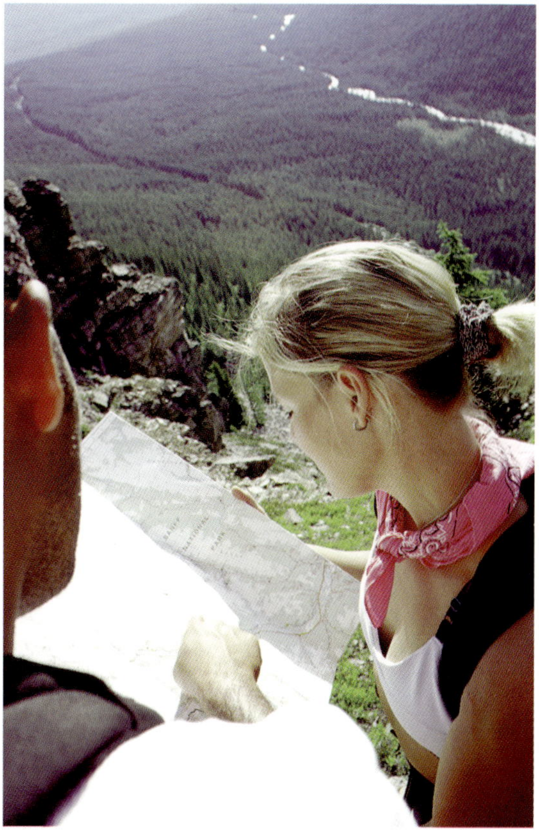

This photo shows a tight, almost intimate, cropping. The creative idea was to essentially peer in on the dialogue taking place between these two subjects over routefinding. Canadian Rockies. Kodak E100VS, 24 mm lens.

Very Tight Crops

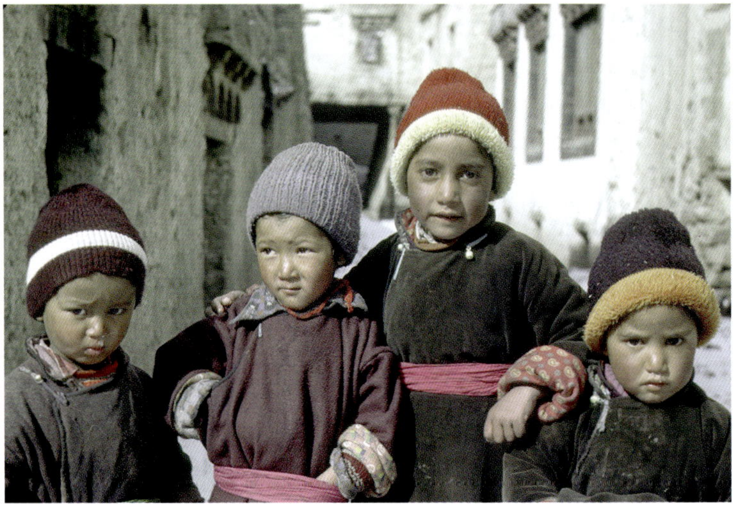

This photo shows standard portrait framing. Since four kids had to be squeezed into the shot, framing is not particularly tight on any one of them, but it is on the group as a whole. Manali, Nepal. Kodachrome, 85 mm lens.

Cropping more tightly than for a conventional head-and-shoulders portrait can be especially graphic. Just ensure that it makes sense to do so.

If you're fortunate enough to approach some mountain mammal at close range, it might be worth trying to snap a really tight shot of just eyes, nose and mouth. But be careful! Most "open jaw" views of animals such as grizzlies are captured behind the safe bars or screening of a zoo, not in open terrain.

Human subjects can offer great opportunities for ultra tight cropping. The climber's facial expression mentioned above might be best depicted with only eyes, mouth and an ear showing, for example, perhaps near one edge of a horizontal frame.

By cropping at mid-forehead and just below the chin, you will really draw attention to your subject's exertion. If you include a hand on the other side of the frame, perhaps grabbing an overhanging knob, the shot will likely be more powerful yet.

Even tighter framing might be warranted. Just a hand placing a cam, or an ice screw, can make a great shot, particularly if it leads upwards toward your route, or back downwards toward your out-of-focus climbing partner.

To do justice to this kind of scene you will most likely need a wide-angle lens; sometimes the wider the lens the better. The trick is in using your lens to its fullest ability without distorting foreground or background to an extent where either subject details look unnatural or the impact of the scene is lost.

On the other hand, when shooting really tight framing from a distance, or when details are all you want to include in a shot, a telephoto lens is usually best. At times—especially with wildlife subjects, or companions a long way away—the longer the telephoto lens you use the better.

Several photos in this book show one or the other approach. Probably the best way to distinguish between them is to think in terms of shooting straight at your subject (telephoto), or into and then past it (wide angle). A little practise is all that's required to get a good handle on which technique is most effectively applied when.

One last consideration. Because foreground detail is so dominant in a tightly cropped scene, fine adjustments may make all the difference between a successful composition or not. Pay close attention to subtle variations in subject placement and angle. Watch also for unwanted bits of dirt or blemishes on your subjects; but ensure, on the other hand, that those that should be visible do show up.

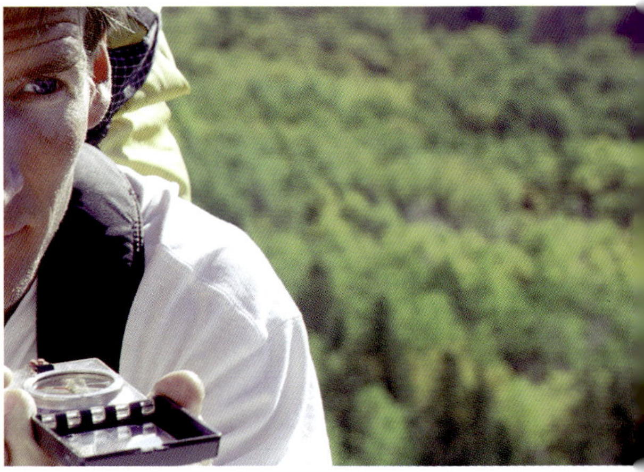

Here is a composition that is very tight, but also manages to show much of the background landscape. "Split" framing like this is a useful device for achieving both of these aims. Canadian Rockies. Kodak E100VS, 105 mm lens.

Small Man-Big Environment

The small man-big environment view might be best thought of as an ultra loose cropping. Mountain environments are especially well suited to this kind of framing for two main reasons. As mentioned earlier, mountains are huge when compared to humans, and the juxtaposition created when human subjects are kept small in a vast alpine realm delivers a very poignant statement about our relative frailty and vulnerability.

The other reason is artistic. Often, mountain environments are graphically simple; rock, ice and snow, along with sky, pretty much summarizes most high alpine areas. Even lower down, where inherent complexity is somewhat stronger, it is relatively easy to create compositions that suit smallish human subjects.

A lot of novice photographers will, without ever thinking about it, shoot their friends very small in any scene. Sometimes these compositions work, which is perhaps the best testament to how good smallish subjects look in the mountains.

More often, however, they look as amateurish as they were shot. In fact, when I'm asked to dispense with photography advice for mountain friends, almost invariably I tell them first to get tighter on their subjects.

The point is that, as with all other aspects of good composition, both a scene and purpose need to be first fully recognized before a small man-big environment cropping will work.

For example, consider a group of ski mountaineers roped together crossing an icefield, with glaciers clinging to surrounding peaks and the sky a deep blue above. Even after compensating for underexposure on snow and ice (see Exposing Correctly on Snow and Ice page 49), your subjects will appear very dark relative to the brilliance of the scene. Consequently, they could potentially provide you with simple, yet graphic and nearly silhouetted, small subjects when seen from a distance.

Keeping safety concerns in mind will of course dictate whether you can pull far enough away to shoot your companions in this manner or not. If so, this may prove to be an especially effective small man-big environment cropping, as a group rendered tiny suggests even more mountain vastness than if only one individual was made small.

Little figures on a distant mountain summit can also render an exciting composition, particularly with late evening or early morning lighting. The summit experience, as well as a sense of partnership or camaraderie, is often better depicted in this fashion than in any other. A single figure will also work well in this setting, conveying to the viewer a strong feeling of solitude as well as summit elation.

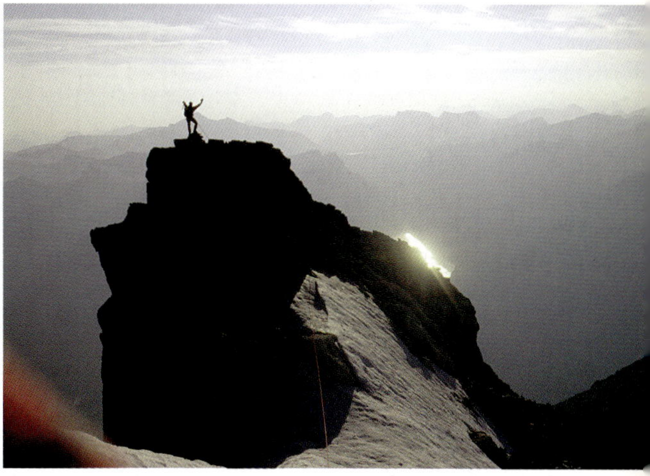

A classic small man-big environment crop. The distant figure is clearly etched against background mountains and sky. Except for a connecting rope detail in the foreground, this view is also a fairly simple one. Canadian Rockies. Kodak E100VS, 28 mm lens.

The strong, hazy backlighting allowed my subject to stand well apart from background mountains. An uncluttered simplicity of foreground and background elements was again important to the composition's success. Canadian Rockies. Fuji Velvia, 180 mm lens.

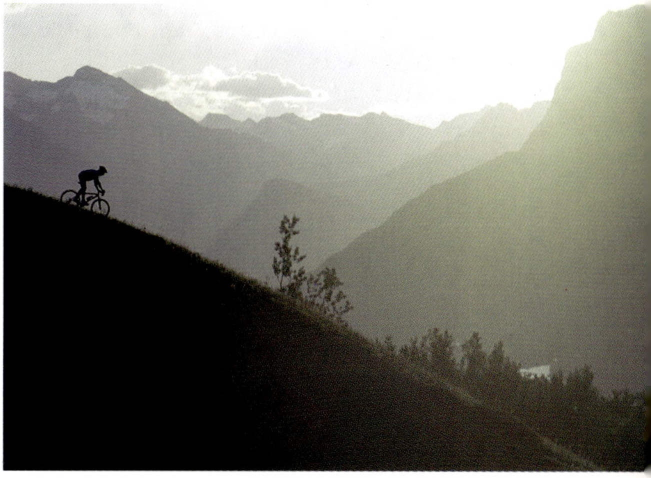

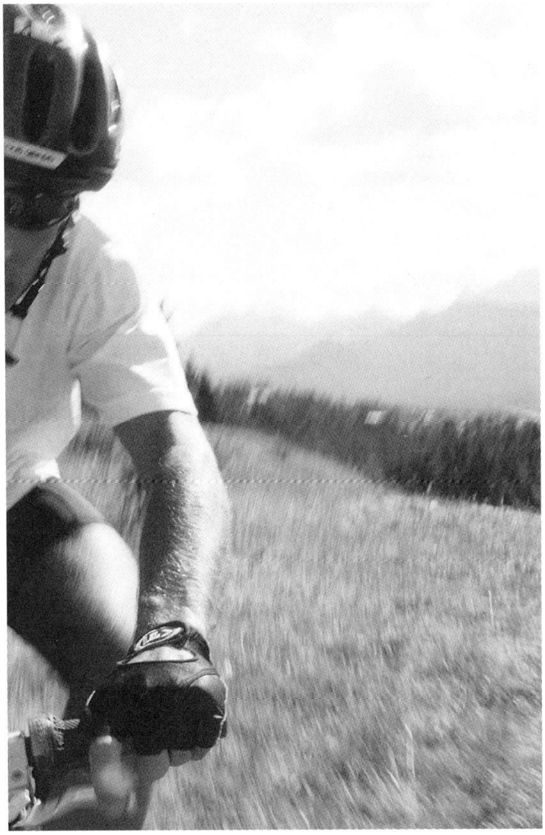

Radical crops often suit high-speed subjects well. Here the subject's body has been effectively bisected, and the whole shot races forward along with the biker. Canadian Rockies. Agfa SCALA, 28 mm lens.

Radical Cropping

Experimental crops are a lot of fun to shoot, and if you're willing to waste a bit of film to get the occasional great result, I'd highly recommend trying some. Of course, if your camera happens to be a digital one, so much the better!

One that isn't particularly radical, or wasteful, is both easy in practise and actually fairly common. It involves cropping slightly above the knees. Unlike a standard mid-thigh crop, however, only feet and lower legs are kept in the frame—no other body parts.

This is a particularly effective crop to illustrate hiking, as it really focuses in on the activity, and also the trail or terrain your subjects are hiking across. If you're with two companions, shooting past the moving legs and feet of one companion to the other in full profile ahead often makes an especially striking and very dynamic composition.

With this composition, and in most others showing a lower leg crop, the photographer needs to shoot from near ground level, usually holding the camera level or angling it slightly upwards. I find that actually lying on the ground generally offers the best perspective. Then, depending on whether you want grasses or flowers in the extreme foreground or not, either rest your camera on the ground, or rest your elbows on the ground while holding your camera.

When cropping more radically, it's often important to capture subject movement. If a mountain biker were to come zooming down a trail towards you, for example, you could potentially record an excellent shot of him at the point he leaves your frame. The biker himself needn't be visible in the final composition; a wheel, foot on a pedal, and perhaps his hands clutching handlebars would be ample.

Note that the biker's motion needs to be communicated for this to really work. Choose a speed that makes sense in view of your lens selection, depth of field requirement and the biker's speed. I would recommend 1/30 of a second with a 24 mm lens and a moderately fast biker, but the best way is to experiment with a variety of different lens and speed combinations.

Again, you won't know what you've recorded until results return from the lab (unless, of course, you're shooting with a digital camera), but this is, after all, part of the thrill while shooting experimentally.

Other even more radical crops can also look great, especially from overhead or ground-level perspectives, looking straight up or down. Shooting upwards from inside a crevasse towards a climber leaping across it, and directly above your camera, may reward you with an exciting shot showing just legs and lower torso, as well as the icy sides of the crevasse.

On the other hand, shooting straight down onto a Nordic skier double-polling along a track—perhaps showing just the forward half of his face, hands gripping poles and the track stretching ahead—could be a really effective crop.

Perhaps the best advice to give is, if you think it might work, and there's no risk in trying it, give it a go! Film, after all, is relatively cheap, and the prospect of shooting a truly original and compositionally sound shot or two makes wasting even rolls of film worthwhile.

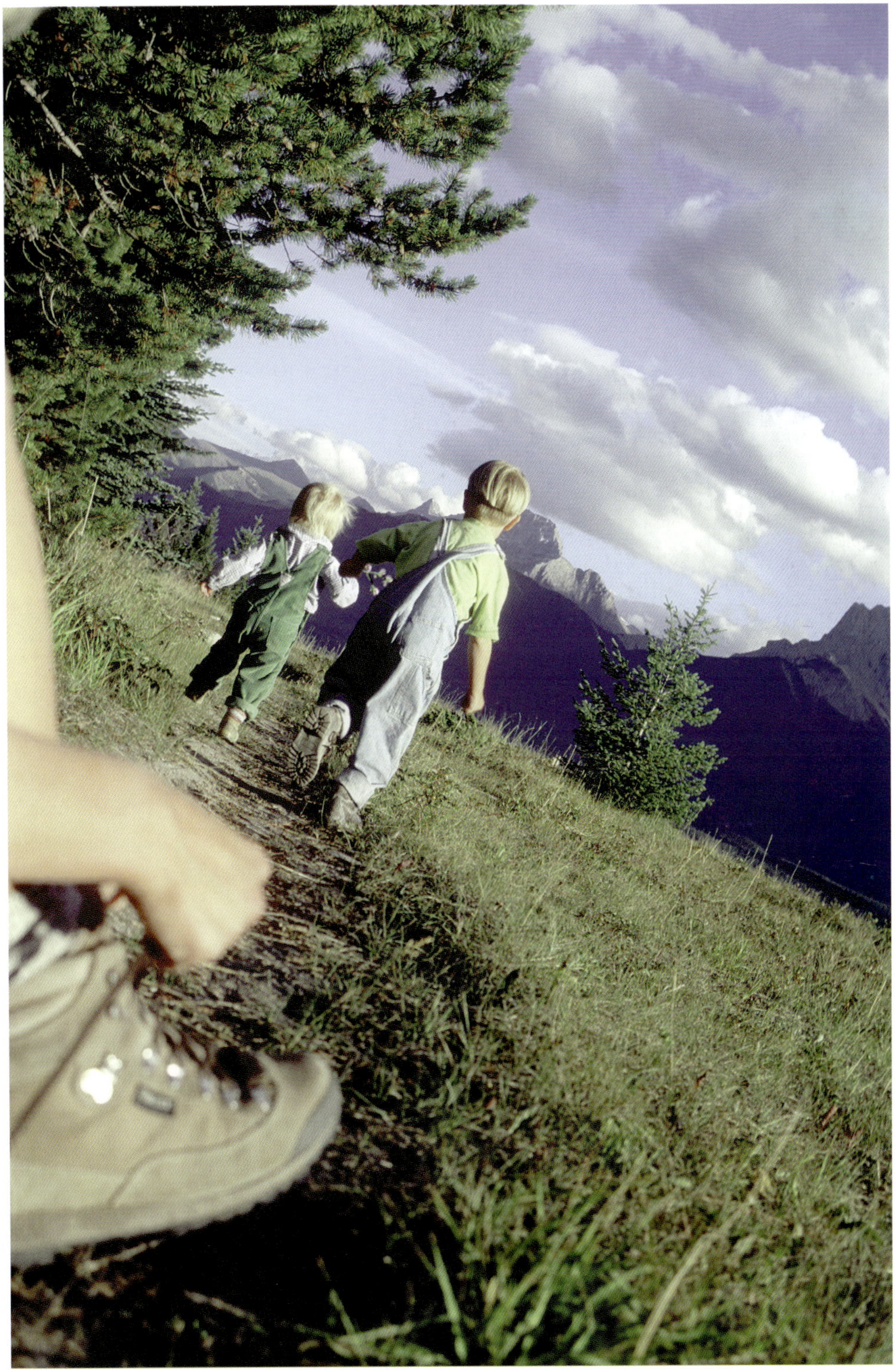

A radical crop of the foreground subject draws attention to, and makes sense in terms of, the kids running ahead. On its own it would look contrived and probably indecipherable. Canadian Rockies. Fuji Velvia, 24 mm lens.

Horizontal Framing

Most photographs are shot horizontally. Not just by novices either; according to bulletins from several big photo agencies, almost 70 percent of all the images received from thousands of professionals operating around the world are horizontal.

Probably the best explanation for this phenomenon is that our cameras are most easily held horizontally. Whenever I pull mine from my camera bag I almost automatically first position it in that fashion, and only after stopping to think for a moment will I perhaps change to another.

Another good reason is that our eyes tend to see things horizontally, rather than vertically. It's far more natural to pivot eyes from side to side, and far easier to swing your head in the same fashion, than to move your head or eyes in an up and down fashion.

And, finally, there is the issue of speed. If a scene is about to disappear, most photographers invariably reach for their cameras and promptly position them horizontally. Wildlife photographers, I'm sure, have a particular bias for horizontal framing. The additional second, or even a fraction of a second, that it takes to position a camera vertically may make all the difference between snapping a vanishing subject, or not.

But there are also many good compositional reasons for framing in this manner. A horizontal framing can create a feeling of wide expanse that suits the mountain environment well. This feeling may be further exaggerated by placing a small subject at an edge of the

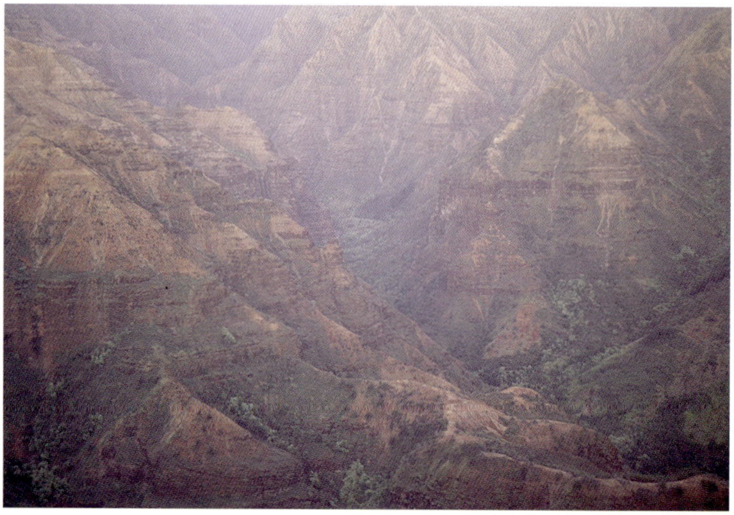

This scene looked great in both horizontal and vertical formats. I couldn't decide which I liked better so I shot it both ways (see the vertical version on the next page). Waimea Canyon, Kauaii, Hawaii. 70-200 mm zoom lens.

Horizontal framing works very well with this shot because I didn't want to include any more leg than is shown, and also because I wanted to give a sense of where the hiker had come from. Canadian Rockies. Fuji Velvia, 28 mm lens.

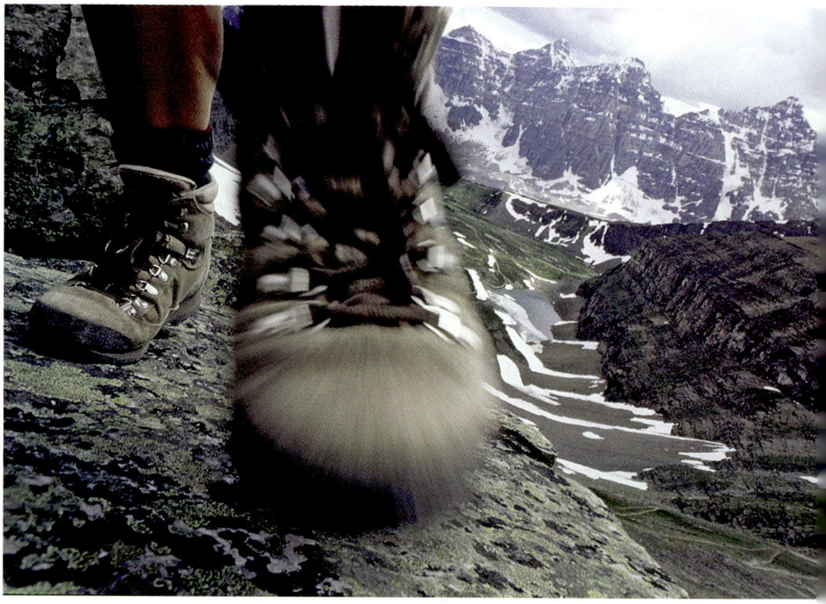

frame, as mentioned in the last section on cropping.

Also, if enough horizontal shots are linked together, it's possible to create a 360 degree "panorama" of views from a single position. Mountain summits are particularly good places to attempt this endeavour. In a later section (see "Panorama Formats page 190) I discuss how such summit views can be spliced together afterwards into a single long print. With the help of modern digital technology this could probably be achieved seamlessly, if desired.

Eyes readily adjust to horizontal framing; those of your viewers' every bit as much as your own when peering through a camera. And we are all habituated to the horizontal format. Our TV sets and movie screens are probably the best testament to that; not to mention computer monitors, billboards and other media surrounding us.

But again, as with all other compositional components, choosing a horizontal framing should—at least as often as possible—involve creative thought and planning. Even if speed dictates a very fast framing, try to quickly consider all framing possibilities while adjusting focus or setting the f-stop.

Vertical Framing

Once you've become as comfortable hand-holding your camera vertically as horizontally, and positioning it that way on your tripod, you'll likely feel your creative parameters widen tremendously. Mountain activities often beg to be photographed vertically; climbing and skiing particularly can look more exciting when oriented that way in your camera's viewfinder.

Vertical compositions suggest a certain dynamic flow that is often absent in horizontal views. A climber throwing his rope for rappel is a good example. If shot vertically, the photograph will record his height relative to surroundings and show where he's going. If shot horizontally, neither of these things will be well-communicated.

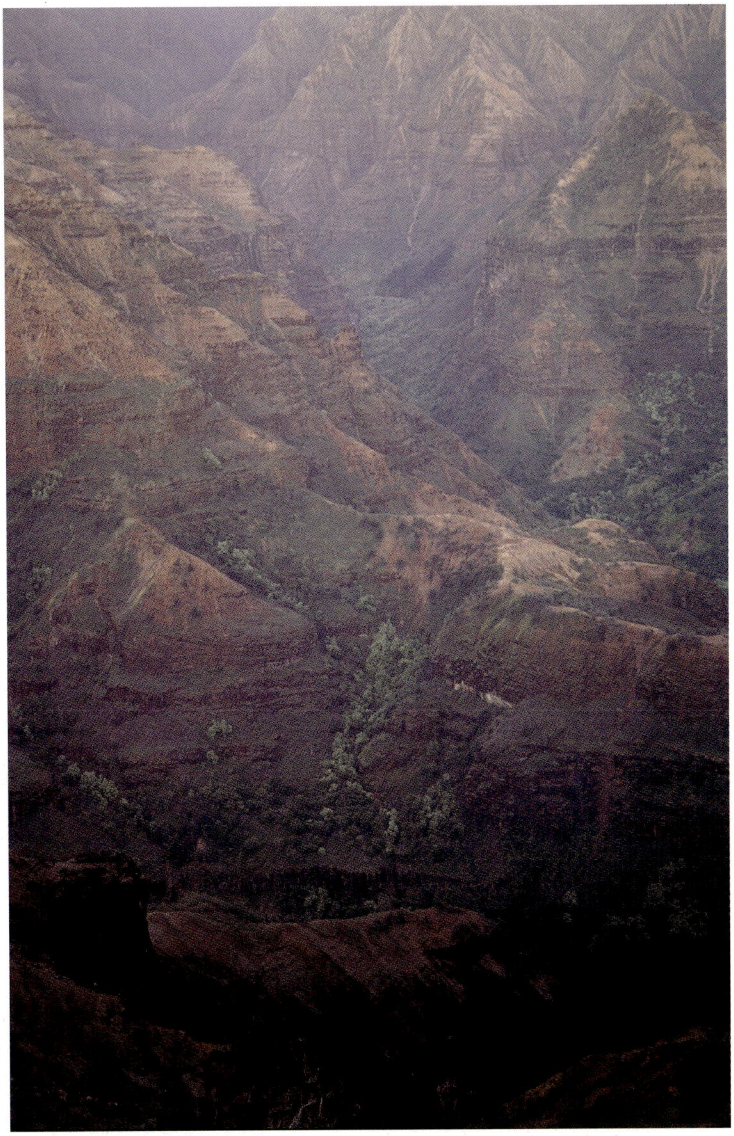

Here is a vertical "take" of the same scene shown horizontally on the previous page. It gives a better feeling of the canyon's depth, but a weaker idea of its breadth. Waimea Canyon, Kauaii, Hawaii. 70-200 mm zoom lens.

Mountain wildlife scenes will likewise often be better recorded vertically. When your intent is to capture animals in the context of their surroundings, then it's these surroundings that should dictate the best framing orientation. If your subject happens to be a mountain sheep below a craggy ridgeline, chances are that you'll want to shoot it vertically.

Many of the mountain scenics you'll want to record will also have an overriding vertical bias. This tends to be true regardless of the lens you choose for a given composition. Wide lenses dramatize interesting foreground elements and mountainous backgrounds when held vertically. And telephoto lenses, because they "draw" the viewer further towards a backdrop than with normal or wide lenses, often demand a vertical composition, especially in more rugged alpine areas.

Finally, if you're thinking of ever selling your pictures to magazines, either alongside text or on their own, then vertical framing becomes even more important to master. Most magazines prefer to see photo selections more heavily weighted towards vertical shots, so that full page or cover uses can be rendered easily.

The best way to become really proficient at hand-holding your camera vertically is to simply practise a lot. Choose a faster speed setting than you would normally use with a horizontal shot to overcome additional camera "jitters" that might occur, at least to begin with. Watch your horizons carefully if you want to record them truthfully; it's easy to overlook tilted angles while focusing attention on other elements of the picture if you're not careful. Tilted or diagonal framing, which will be dealt with in the next section, should in most cases be planned, not the result of sloppy framing.

Positioning your camera vertically on your tripod can sometimes be a bit of a trick, depending on your particular tripod and other factors. Be careful not to imbalance the tripod if your camera and lens combination is heavy. Raising the tripod leg closest to your camera will usually prevent it from tipping over on that side. Watch for sudden gusts of wind especially; I've had more than one vertically mounted camera tip over in windy weather, thankfully always on relatively soft ground.

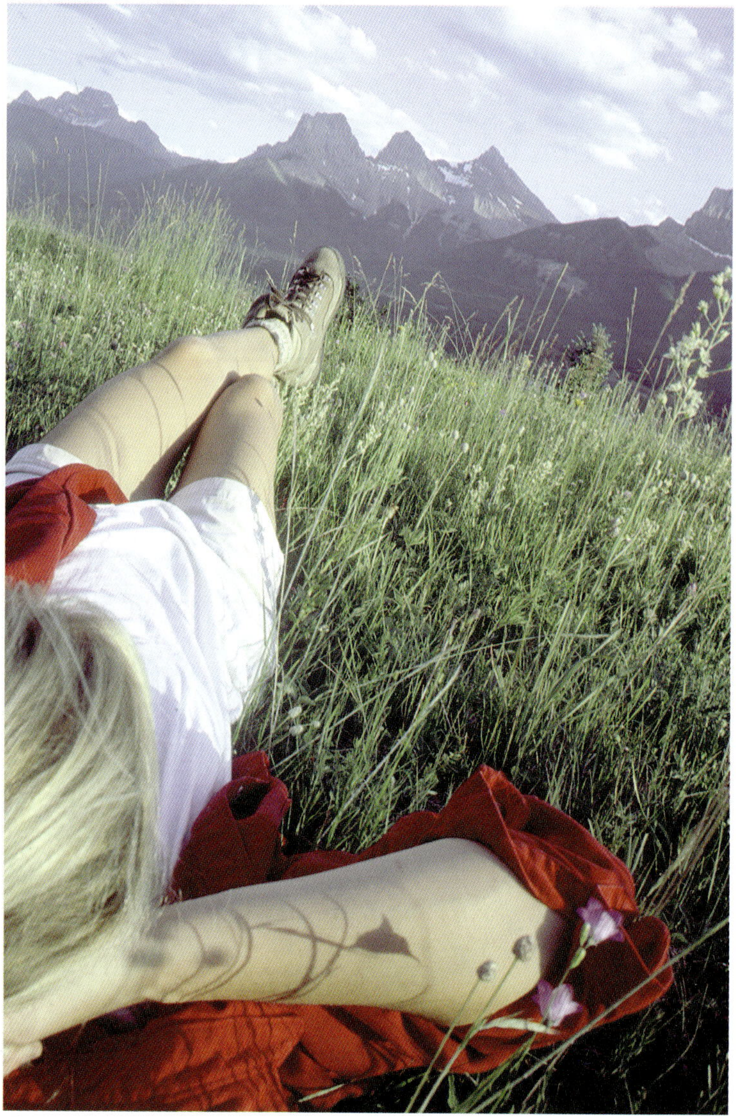

Wide-angle lenses suit vertical formats particularly well. In the mountains they will often dramatize, and sometimes exaggerate, vertical dimensions. Canadian Rockies. Fuji Velvia, 20 mm lens.

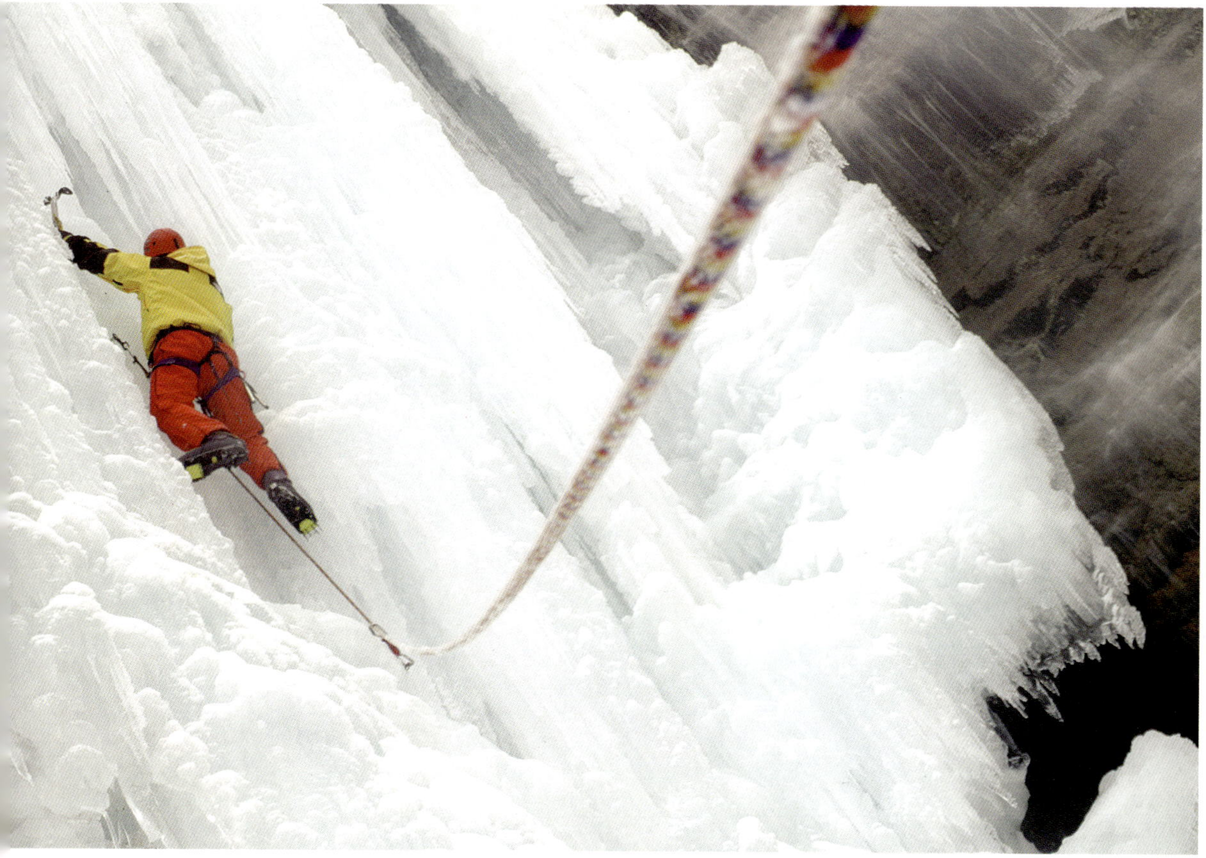

Although this tilted framing makes the climb appear less steep, it nonetheless makes it look more formidable somehow. Falling water on the right side would certainly convince any skeptical viewer of the climb's steepness. Canadian Rockies. Fuji Velvia, 28 mm lens.

Tilted Framing

Tilting your camera on purpose runs, again, counter to classic conventions on composition. As with radical cropping, discussed in the previous section, the idea is usually to record a sense of compositional abandon, or spontaneity.

Although mountain scenics and wildlife shots should rarely, if ever, be recorded in such a manner, tilting can render great effects with your human subjects. Showing one of your companions wiping out on skis is a perfect instance, particularly if you come in fairly close and show the moment of impact. Another is photographing a mountain biker coming towards you at full throttle on a mountain trail.

As these examples illustrate, the idea with titled framing is usually either to capture a sense of fun or to exaggerate action. In less dramatic situations it can look very contrived and sometimes even quite silly.

There is, however, one other application of tilting that may not be intended to create a "fun" atmosphere or record action. This is when a point-of-view angle is chosen. Often, in order to compose in such a way that all important elements are included in the shot, or that strong compositional "lines" are preserved, it may be necessary to tilt the camera appropriately. When such a need arises, and because point-of-view shots are spontaneous in some ways, this tilting almost always works well.

For example, say that you want to shoot past your legs dangling over a cliff to the valley below and mountains on the horizon. Using a wide lens, and holding your camera vertically, you may get a decent result. But the shot will likely look a little static; by tilting the camera somewhat, on the other hand, it might be greatly improved.

The trick with all tilting is to control it fairly carefully. If your tilts become too radical, your viewers will wonder what on earth you're trying to convey to them. The only exceptions to this rule are if your subjects are really close to the camera and the shot is for fun, or if your point-of-view angle is subject to intense motion—perhaps you've mounted a camera to the side of your mountain bike, for example, to capture the thrill of a downhill ride.

Tilting from either a horizontal or vertical framing work equally well. Just remember: before ever committing to a tilted angle know why you're doing so.

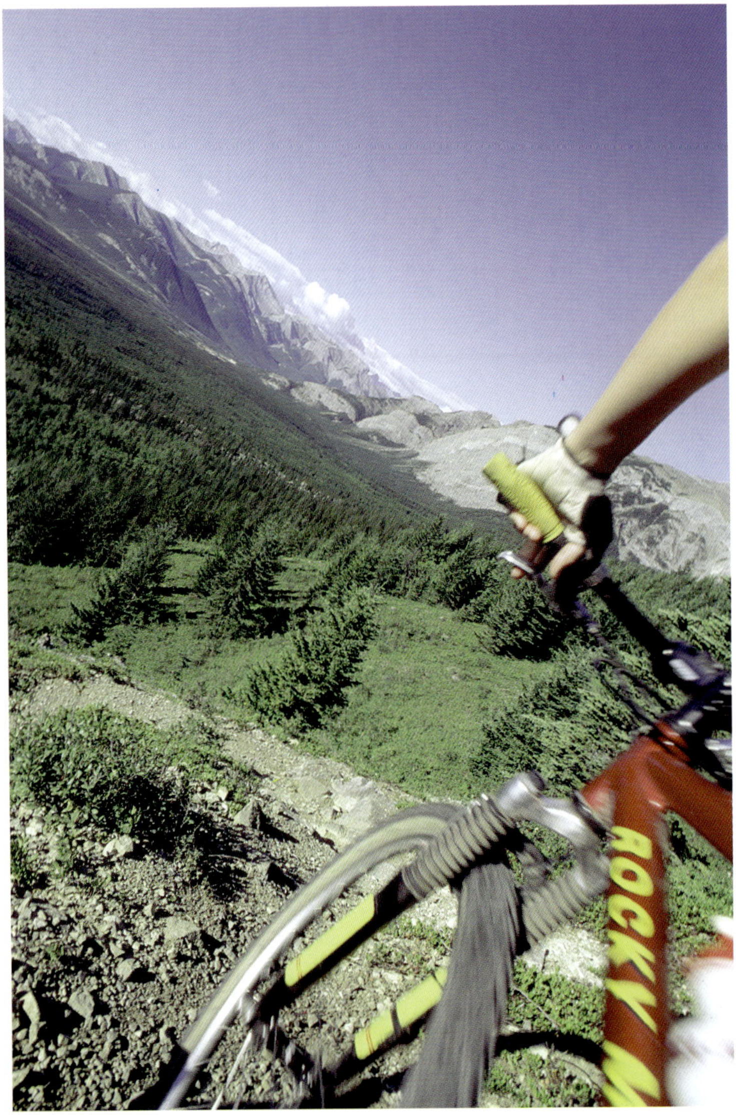

A strongly tilted horizon magnifies the biker's lean in this shot. Without the obvious motion it probably wouldn't have worked at all. Canadian Rockies. Fuji Velvia, 24 mm lens.

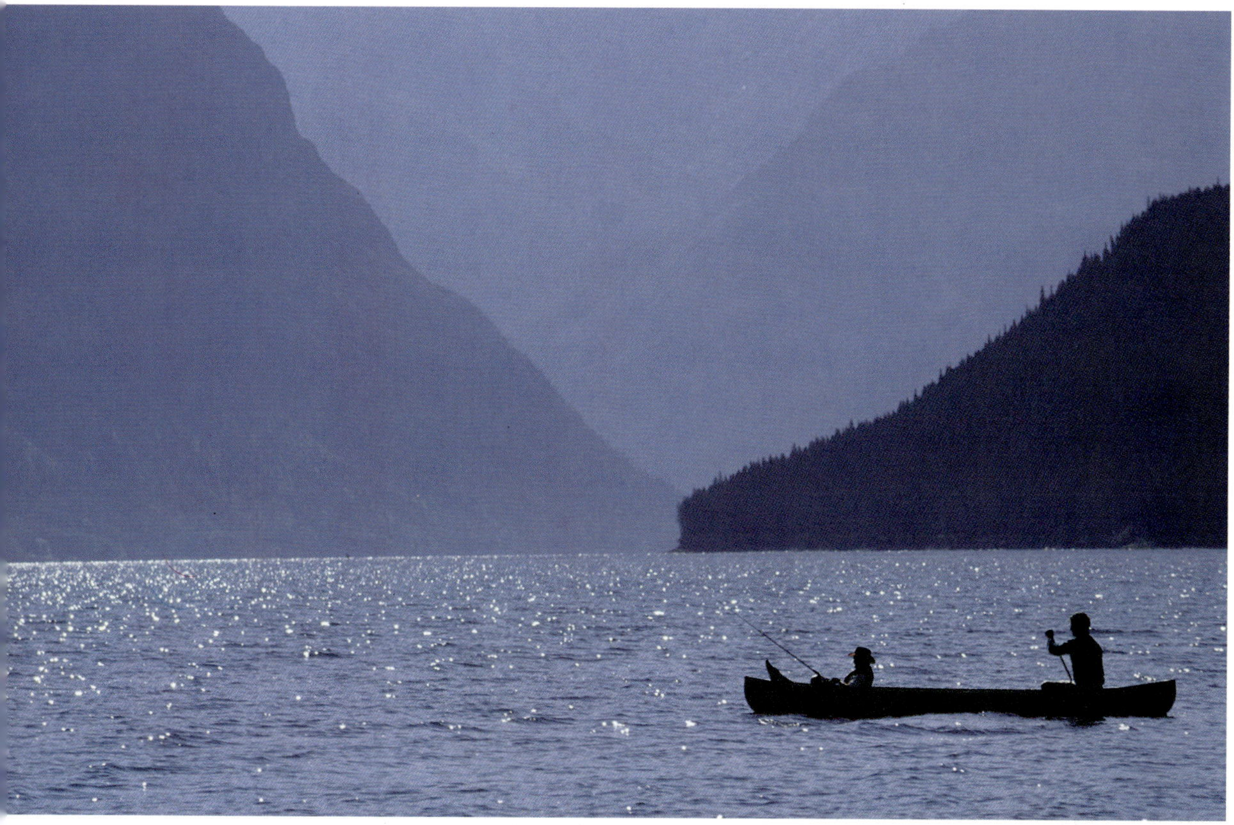

Owing to the lack of any horizon, the mountains seem to climb upwards forever in this shot. In fact, they were not much taller than pictured. Canadian Rockies. Fuji Velvia, 70-200 mm zoom lens.

Horizon, or Horizonless?

Mountain photographers have a particular penchant for showing horizons in their work, unless shooting downwards or very close to subjects. This undoubtedly has to do with the spectacular nature of most mountain horizons. Yet there are good arguments for avoiding horizons altogether in some shots.

This is particularly true during periods of bad weather, or when the landscape you're shooting in is dark relative to the sky. Even if you're properly exposing for your subject, not the entire scene, a bright sky will often overwhelm, rendering your subject and the scene powerless. By simply not including the horizon—i.e. shooting below it—your subject, or intended scene, is restored to full impact.

Note that it may be difficult, unless you are shooting downwards, to avoid horizons while shooting with wide lenses. With a telephoto lens, on the other hand, it's usually quite easy. And for this reason your decision to include a horizon or not may dictate your lens choice in some situations.

For example, let's say you want to shoot your family picnicking in an alpine meadow while the sun has slipped behind a large cloud. You'd like to include as much of the nearby mountain landscape as possible, yet not sacrifice the human elements.

A 35 mm lens, you determine, shows the entire scene nicely, but unfortunately also takes in a lot of white cloud horizon. By simply switching to a 50 mm or 75 mm lens, though, you may find that you can still preserve a good chunk of background without recording any horizon; thus, attention remains focused on your picnicking subjects.

Not that a bleached-out, or "burned"-out, background is always a bad thing. In fact, in many cases, it may be a desired effect, especially if you want to lighten the mood of a scene (see next section).

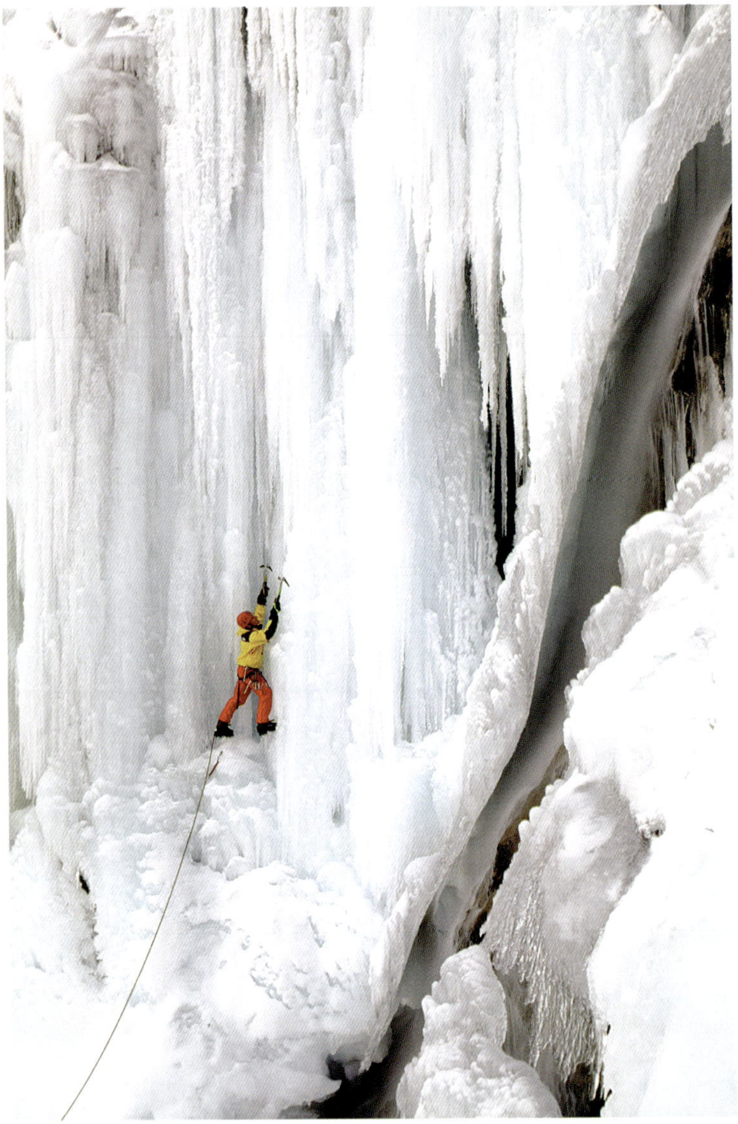

Likewise, this waterfall seems to stretch way beyond the frame's upper edge because of a lack of horizon. Sky above the waterfall was comparatively bright, and would have detracted from the composition if it had been included. Canadian Rockies. Fuji Velvia, 70-200 mm zoom lens.

But overexposed backgrounds should be created intentionally. There's almost nothing worse than seeing an exquisite mountain scene bleached beyond recognition when results return from the lab.

During a snowstorm the lack of any horizon can be especially dramatic, particularly if your backdrop is fairly dark. The falling snowflakes will contrast markedly against background objects and, by doing so, seem to gain intensity. Against a white winter sky above the horizon, however, they will almost certainly lose impact.

In these conditions, the combination of a telephoto lens with a horizonless background will probably be most effective. Photographing a group of Nordic skiers with conifer forest behind is a good example. If shot wide to include the horizon, the impact of the snowstorm might be totally lost. With a telephoto lens, however, and no horizon showing, the snowstorm will seem to gain extra intensity.

Light and Dark Backgrounds

As mentioned earlier, the use of light or dark backgrounds will change the feeling of almost any composition. Depending on what you're trying to capture or achieve, the mood swing can range from light and airy, and even ethereal if you really bleach the background out, to dark, sombre and sometimes foreboding.

On the other hand, both types of backgrounds can also simply make your well-lit subjects really "pop" out. In some cases, this may be your only criteria for choosing one or the other, especially if your subjects are mainly of interest on their own.

The lightest backgrounds are well suited to fun shots, whether it be young family members cavorting in the alpine, say, or skiing friends enjoying an outing in the piste. Lighter than normal backgrounds, on the other hand, can be effectively used just to describe location. Showing a mountain goat perched against a snowy mountain wall is a good example.

Dark settings create drama and power. A scene showing hikers illuminated on a ridge crest with black storm clouds brooding behind has plenty of both. So does one depicting a brightly lit climber scaling a shadowy granite wall of giant proportions.

Often, as in these examples, you will simply recognize great backdrops that suit the mood or effect you want to record on film, especially if you've really perfected your personal "art of seeing". At other times, you may want to position your subjects in bright or dark settings to create a desired effect.
If you do, and the resulting look is then too subtle, consider changing your lighting angle. Really dramatic background bleaching effects usually rely on strong backlighting; the most ethereal effects are achieved by shooting directly into a low sun and bright backdrop. Recording your subject faithfully against a dark background, on the other hand (as opposed to capturing him/or her as a silhouette) will necessitate strong frontal or sidelighting.

Lighting issues, such as these, will be fully discussed in a next section. Keep in mind, though, that in order to render your subjects faithfully against either very light or very dark backgrounds, you must first determine an exposure reading specifically for them—not for the entire scene. Otherwise both your subjects, and the scenes themselves, will sacrifice any mood they may have possessed.

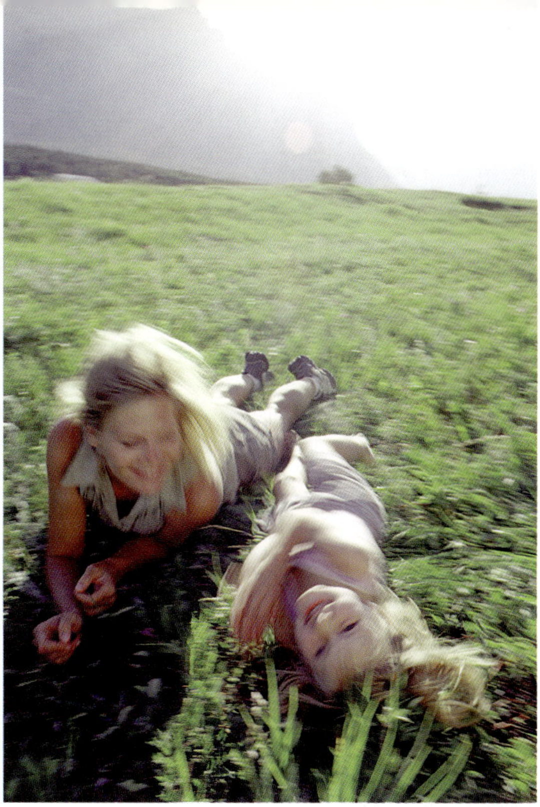

A light background compliments the fun feeling of this shot. I exposed for prominent skin tones, while knowing that other parts of the composition would be "blown" out. Canadian Rockies. Kodak E100VS, 28 mm lens.

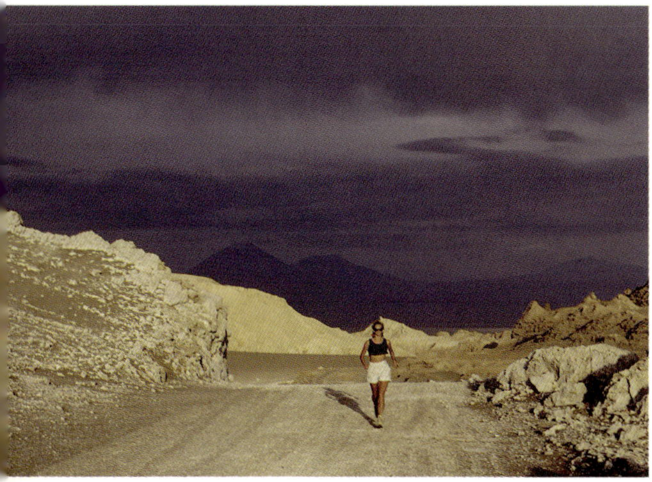

A dark, forbidding backdrop helps to establish a certain mood in this shot, one that speaks of both drama and power. Valley of the Moon, Chile. Fuji film, 35-70 mm zoom lens.

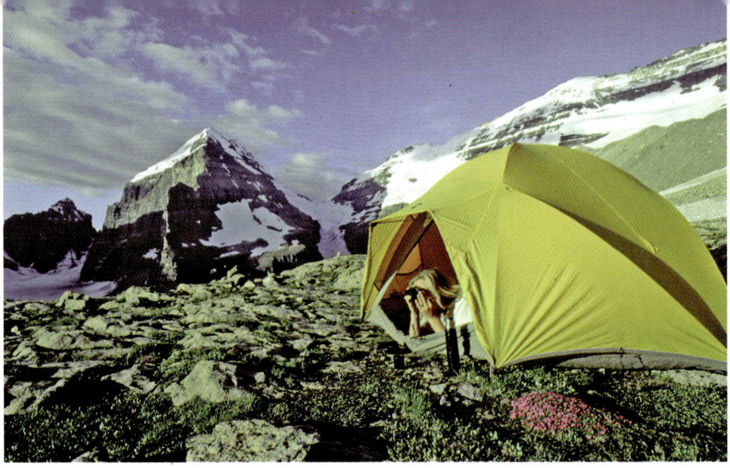

I wanted to render background elements in focus with this shot, since they were interesting and quite complex. A wide depth of field guaranteed that both they and the foreground would be sharp. Canadian Rockies. Fuji Velvia, 28 mm lens.

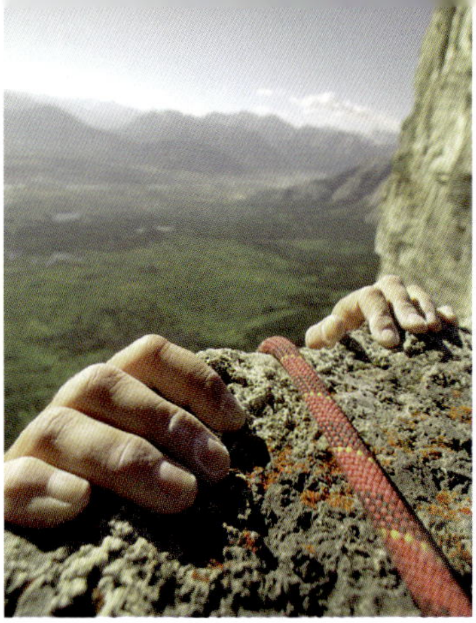

The climber's hands are of chief interest in this composition, and were therefore rendered in focus. The backdrop needed to be recognizable, but not so sharply that it would compete with the hands. Canadian Rockies. Fuji Velvia, 180 mm lens.

Sharp or Fuzzy Backgrounds

Just as light and dark backgrounds effect the mood of your compositions, so too the choice of a sharp or fuzzy background will influence their character. Good practical reasons for choosing a wide versus narrow depth of field have already been discussed. But compositional merit may often have more to do with what, and how much, you'll plan to keep in focus.

Simply put, isolating your subject from its surroundings—whether foreground or background—by choosing a narrow depth of field makes it stand on its own and command attention. Widening the depth of field has the opposite effect; your subject then becomes part of the overall landscape.

Extremely wide depths of field, such as where you try to include the entire scene in focus, can have the effect of rendering your subject nearly indistinguishable from its surroundings, at least if it's small enough in the shot.

This can work in some situations, especially when you're really intent on mainly shooting scenics, or capturing "environmental" views of your mountain travels. But habitually choosing the widest depth of field settings your lenses allow doesn't encourage a terribly creative approach to photography.

With portraiture at least, you'll typically want to choose depth of field values that isolate your subject somewhat from its background, although usually not at your lenses' minimum settings. The best way to determine what works best, from a creative standpoint, is with the depth-of-field preview function available on most SLR cameras (see page 59). When you are using minimum f-stop values, remember to ensure that all physical features of your subjects that you want in focus, such as eyes, nose and ears, are kept that way.

More distant shots of human subjects sometimes work with fuzzy backgrounds, but in general are best captured against a sharp background. Even if you tried to isolate a distant climbing companion against a more distant mountain backdrop, for example, it probably wouldn't work. You'd simply "push" the mountains out of focus, potentially losing the value of the scene and without gaining anything creatively.

For more compositional interest, though, it may be worth recording some "fuzzy" foreground in certain distant scenes, as suggested in the next section on interference. Again, your depth-of-field preview selection can give you a good idea of whether a particular approach works, or not.

Wildlife photos, like portraits, are often best captured with a fuzzy background. Or, put another way, the long lenses needed to record tight views of wildlife may leave you no choice; often, in order to render your subject in focus with a minimum of movement blur, a sharp background is necessarily sacrificed.

When you can use wider lenses to safely photograph wildlife, though, it's often worth trying to record background elements in perfect focus. This way the environmental context is preserved, and your viewers can appreciate your wildlife subjects exactly as you saw them.

Foreground as Interference

"Interference" is a compositional device used to add complexity to photographs for a very specific purpose: to build meaning.

As the name implies, interference distracts. When foreground details are used as interference, even though they are almost always rendered out of focus, a viewer's eyes are drawn away from main subject areas for a split second or two. They will then likely return to the primary subject, at least if the interference was cleverly planned, or recognized, by the photographer at the time of shooting.

The point is that an entire story can be told in this simple, pictorial way. A subject is recognized by the viewer, then details that somehow relate to the subject are noticed, and finally the subject and the details are mentally connected in a way that establishes meaning.

Consider the following example. You want to somehow record the elation of finishing a big wall climb showing merely your climbing companions and gear. If you were to shoot past a heap of out-of-focus carabiners, cams, slings etc., to your friends behind in perfect focus, you might create a powerful visual message. The resulting photograph would not only describe the moment of reaching the top, but it would also infer how difficult the climb was, or at least how much gear was required to get to it.

Say, in a different example, you want to shoot a moose foraging in a swamp and convey an intimate sense of these surroundings to your viewers. By kneeling low to shoot past swamp grasses and reeds—"natural" interference—to the moose in focus behind, you'll likely achieve a lot more than by simply shooting the moose on its own. In fact, the final effect might be quite voyeuristic, if shot well.

The small area of interference on the right side of the frame lends a three-dimensional effect to this shot. It also communicates the photographer's exact shooting location. Canadian Rockies. Fuji Velvia, 105 mm lens.

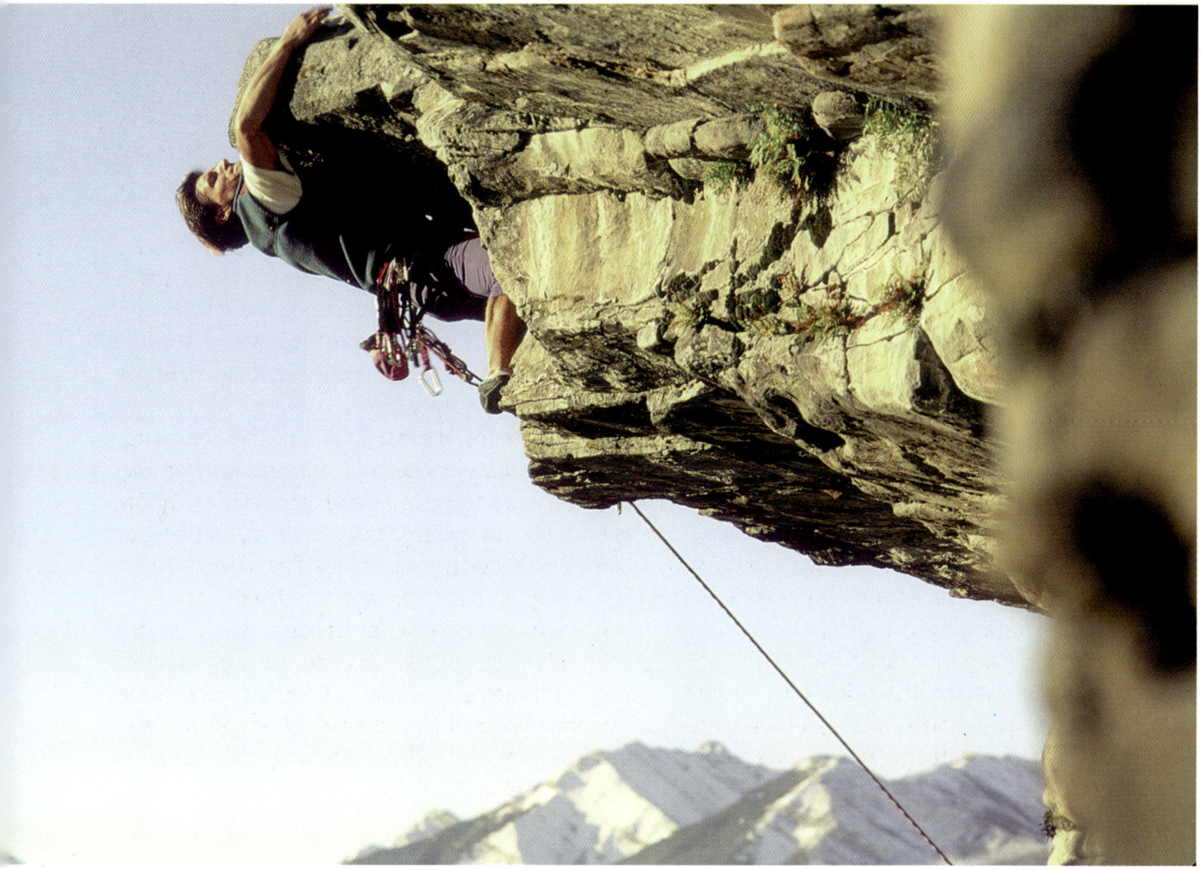

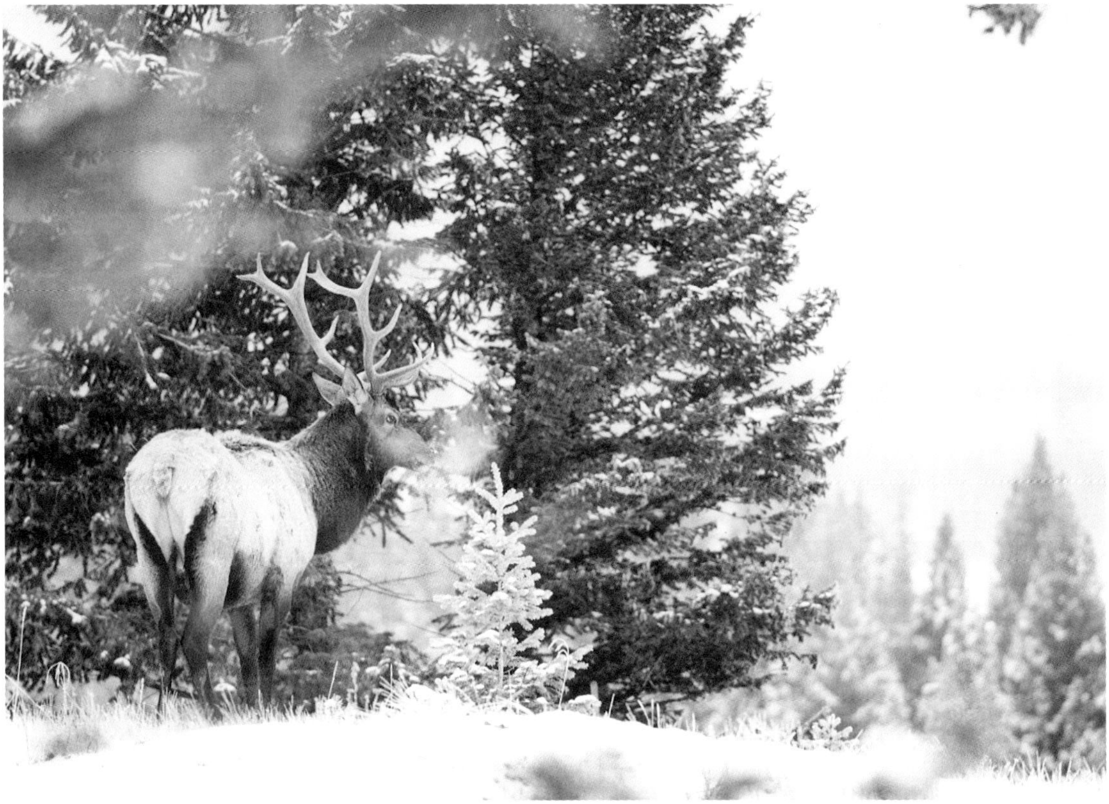

Interference in this shot suggests that the photographer is "peering in" on the bull elk from a hidden perspective. Since interfering elements are tree boughs, the strong environmental context has been maintained. Canadian Rockies. Fuji Velvia, 180 mm lens.

Note that you can also create specific foreground scenes to use as interference, usually by selecting and arranging foreground objects. Depending on what is involved, this can be fairly time-consuming, although often rewarding. If you have the time and the inclination, it may be well worth the effort.

For example, it would be fairly easy to create a map and compass "still-life" foreground to describe a scene where you and your companion are taking a break on a mountain trail. Although out of focus, the map could be made somewhat readable; thus, your photo would establish location, for your future reference or that of your viewers', as well as record details of the moment.

The importance of rendering foreground objects out of focus are threefold. First, this ensures they don't compete with the main subject or background areas. Second, it sets them well apart from a more distant subject, creating a strong sense of depth. Finally, soft foreground elements can be very pleasing visually, adding value to your composition.

Interference, as with all specialized compositional techniques, should probably be used sparingly. Too much of it, especially in a slide show or other visual presentation, would undermine the impact of its best uses.

Finding a Perspective

Mountain perspectives are amongst the most dramatic found anywhere. Whether a bird's-eye view from an overhanging crest downwards, a sunken vantage point peering upwards past a subject to a mountain summit, or simply a straight-on look at scenery, wildlife, or people at play, the options for finding a dramatic perspective are nearly endless here.

Often your choice of perspective will make all the difference between a ho-hum shot and a great photograph. For that reason, perspective should usually be chosen before exposure or shutter speed settings. Even if you have no intention of being creative with your camera, or when time constraints don't allow a great deal of thought on composition, it's worth giving at least a moment's attention to perspective.

With a little practise, determining the best, or at least an appropriate perspective becomes a nearly routine exercise, and an almost instantaneous one. You don't necessarily have to scramble up a cliff, for example, to get an overhead view of your subject, although often this will be a good choice if time, and your subject, allows. Perhaps merely standing on your toes will suffice.

As with all compositional decisions, the "right" perspective has everything to do with what you want your photos to communicate; not necessarily the statement you want to make, but often just a feeling or sense of drama you want to build. Invest a little extra time and thought toward perspective, and you may be rewarded with some truly expressive, as well as impressive, photographic results.

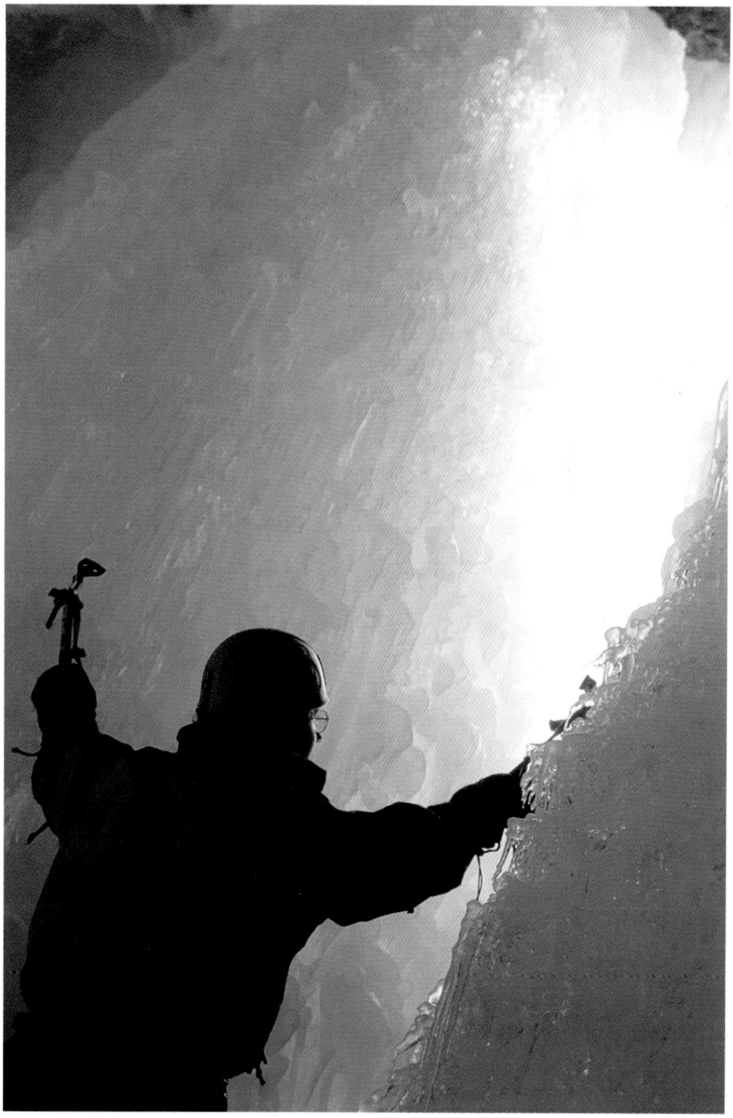

Here's an unusual perspective on ice climbing. The climber has reached a hole at the roof of a cave that is flooded by incoming light. Canadian Rockies. Fuji Velvia, 85 mm lens.

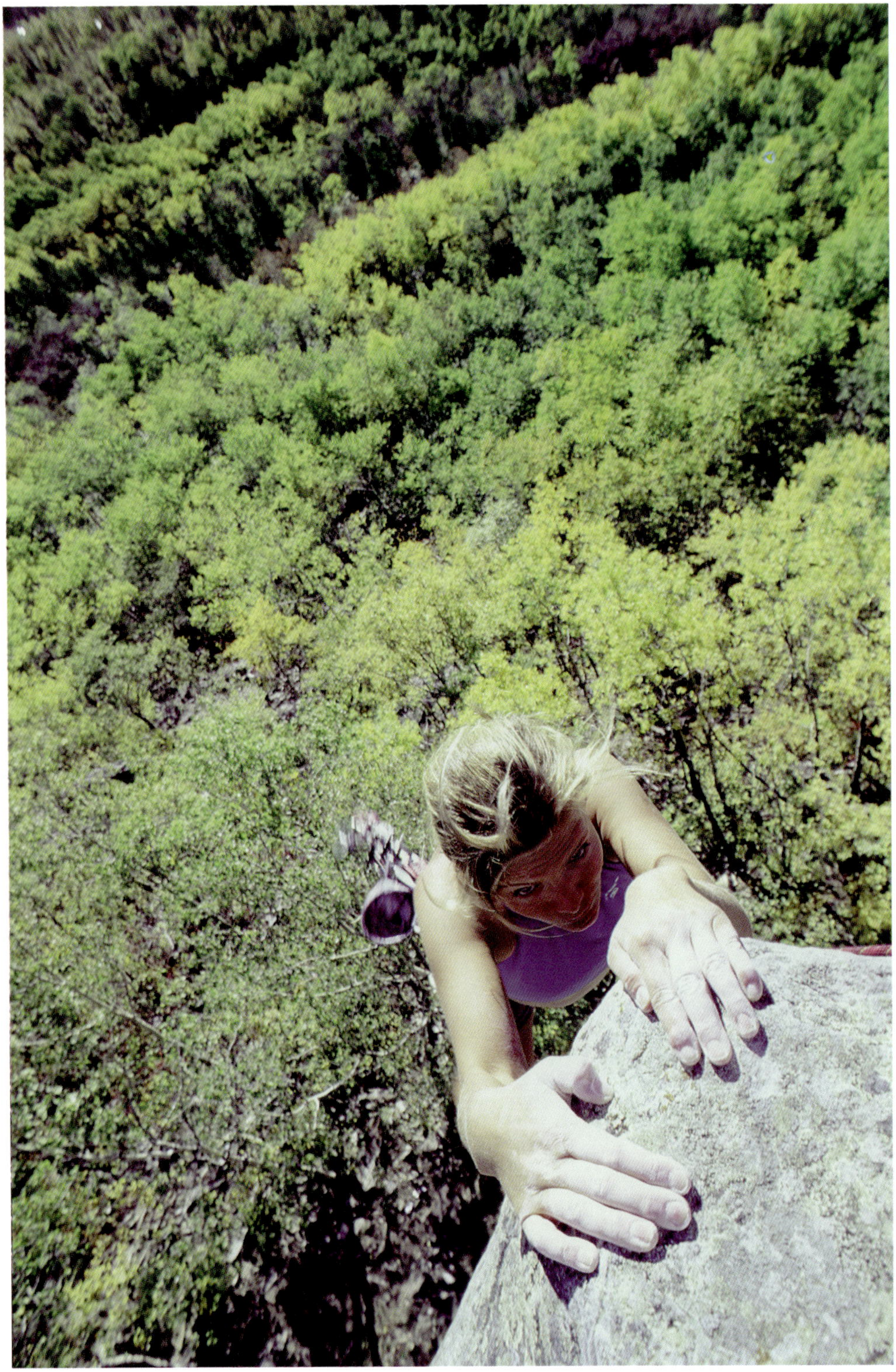

Downward perspectives are often exciting ones in a mountain context, particularly when they show action or expression.
Canadian Rockies. Fuji Velvia, 24 mm lens.

Level (normal) Perspective

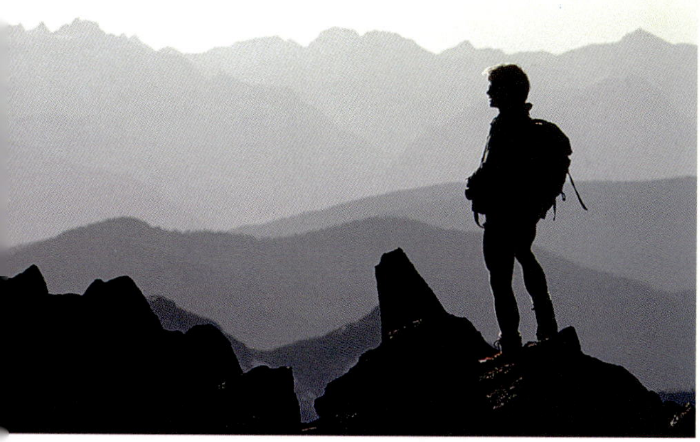

A level or normal perspective is usually the most honest one. Subjects are shown at exactly the same height and in the same context that they appear. Kokanee Peak, Canada. Kodachrome, 200 mm lens.

Most photos are shot from a standing position, by novices, amateurs and even professionals. This has as much to do with convenience as anything; the ease of simply standing firm and shooting subjects or scenes is hard to improve upon. It also has to do with speed, as photographing from a standing position is usually impossible to beat while shooting fast changing wildlife or sports-action scenes.

However, there is another good reason for selecting this perspective. Because it allows you to shoot directly towards a subject, of same height, on a horizontal plane (i.e. without either raising or lowering the camera lens), distortion is minimized. In fact, with a good portrait lens of say 90-150 mm on your 35 mm camera, you will record virtually no distortion when shooting level towards a subject's eyes.

If you've ever watched fashion photographers at work, either in real life or on TV, you might have noticed that they shoot with cameras level in relation to their subjects most of the time. Cameramen at sports events usually do the same. Although convenience is certainly one factor in choosing a level perspective, they've mainly done so to render their subjects with as little distortion as possible.

Minimizing distortion will likely be of significant value for you, as well, while photographing human or wildlife subjects. Chances are that you'll want to capture your mountain companions looking their best, especially close up. Eliminating or at least reducing distortion, particularly the kind that either elongates or squishes their torsos, will then be important.

You'll probably want to depict wildlife subjects as true to life as you can too, like most dedicated wildlife photographers. If you are really close to your subject, say a hoary marmot sunning on a rock a few feet away, even a camera perspective that's a little higher or lower than that of the marmot will distort him somewhat. A level plane between your camera and the marmot's eyes will, on the other hand, assure a natural and honest view.

Note that, as alluded to in this case, shooting "on the level" with shorter subjects may mean reducing your height, perhaps by squatting, sitting, or even lying down. Children will look distorted, for example, if they're photographed from an adult's standing position. By kneeling low enough you'll record them truthfully; in fact, you'll see them just as they see each other.

Sometimes a level perspective might demand instead that you somehow raise your shooting position in conjunction with the raised position of your subject. Say that you want to photograph a companion standing on top of a nearby pinnacle. To establish a level plane between yourselves you might first have to find a slope, or a pinnacle of the same height, to shoot from.

Just standing on your toes may make some difference in eliminating distortion with a nearby subject. The important thing to remember is that the closer your subject is to you, the more careful you'll have to be to keep your perspective level.

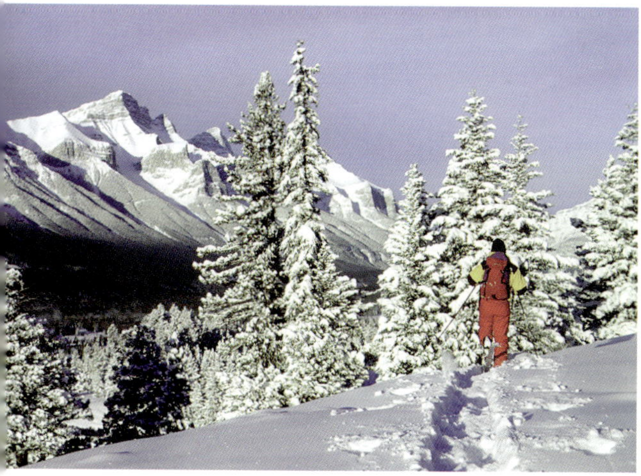

Level perspectives are often useful for showing a sense of scale between subjects and the landscapes they occupy. Canadian Rockies. Fuji Velvia, 35-70 mm zoom lens.

Direct Overhead Perspective

Overhead perspectives come naturally and easily in the mountains. Shooting downwards toward your climbing companions from a lofty perch is a fairly typical example of one. Photographing wild sheep from a high ridge, looking down, is another.

This perspective can be particularly dramatic, especially if you're a long ways up, or if the background is spectacular. It can also offer a great view of high-angle action or similar close-up activity, such as that of a climber struggling over an overhanging lip.

Although overhead perspectives are not unique to mountain environments, we alpine travellers have more exposure to them than most people. Hence, if you include a few good ones in a slide show before a non-mountain audience, you might hear some gasps and other sounds of incredulity. If your audience happens, on the other hand, to be composed of fellow climbers or trekkers, you'll likely see satisfying nods of appreciation instead.

Overhead views don't have to be sensational to be effective though. In an example mentioned earlier, just a simple shot of your companion from a slightly raised position, such as that offered by a nearby boulder, can be exciting if it includes a spectacular backdrop such as ranges of mountains below. Alternately, the same view can suggest "in-your-face" fun, particularly if a wide-angle lens is chosen and you close in tightly on your companion.

Some subject distortion is unavoidable with overhead perspectives. Looking straight down on nearly any subject will compress it, rendering it somewhat squatter and less vertical than it is. For example, if you're pointing your camera directly down toward a mountain goat standing on a ledge, looking up, it's back and face will appear enormous relative to the rest of its size. Its legs won't be visible at all, save for possibly just a hoof or two.

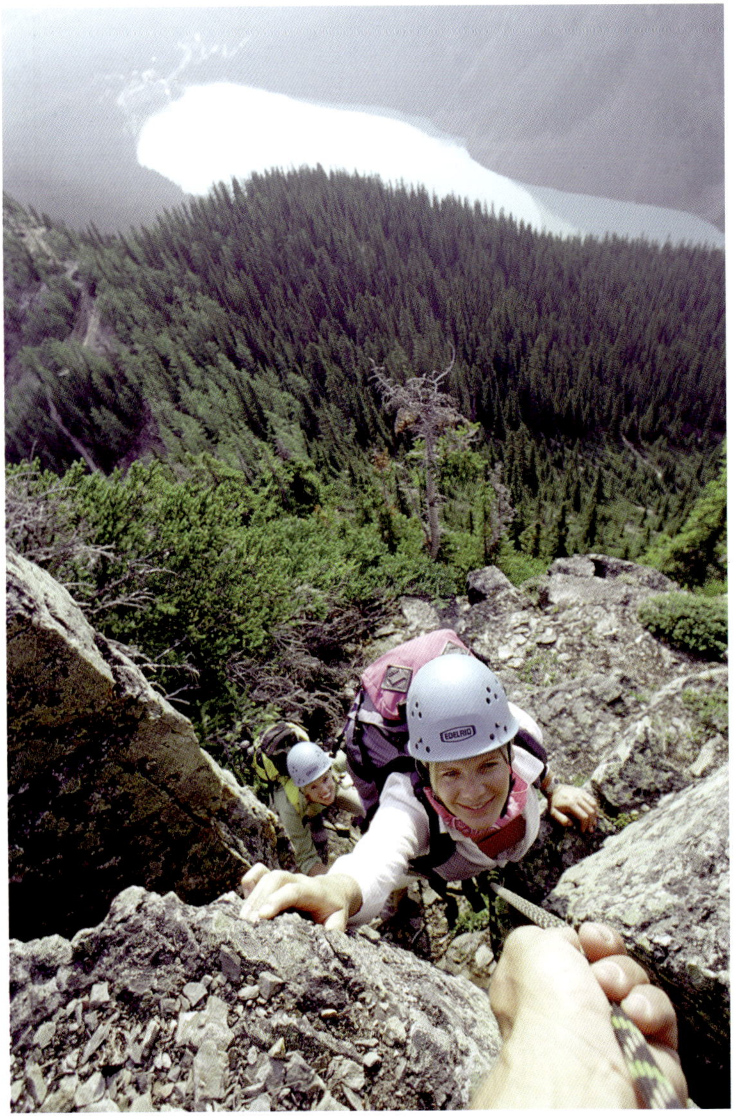

An overhead perspective can also be used to suggest leadership, as in this shot. Canadian Rockies. Kodak E100VS, 28 mm lens.

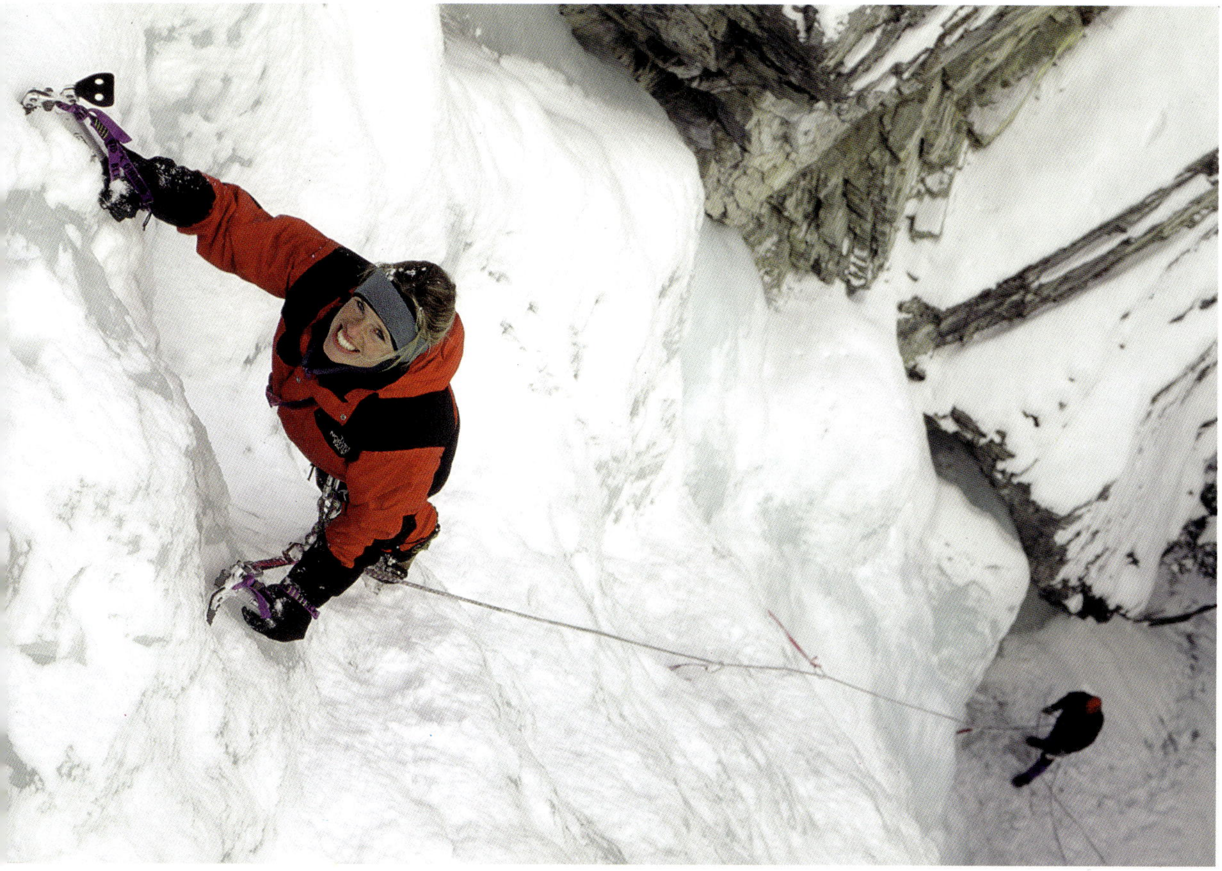

Overheard perspectives can give your viewers a great sense of the activity you're shooting. Here belayer, lead climber and rope connecting the two help to establish a three-dimensional perspective. Canadian Rockies. Fuji Velvia, 28 mm lens.

Similarly, a human subject will appear less vertical, and more two-dimensional, than it truly is when viewed from directly above. If your subject is wearing a backpack, this might look huge. Bare shoulders can also appear formidable in size, which may very well please the climbing companion you're snapping pictures of from your hanging belay.

This perspective also tends to give the impression to viewers that you, the photographer, have an enhanced role or position of "power". If you were to shoot straight down a rope towards your climbing partner, you would inadvertently establish a leadership role on film, even if you're not actually the leader. Likewise, in the mountain goat example above, you might suggest to your viewers a sense of mastery over nature by showing yourself to be up higher than the goat.

As unlikely as it may sound, there are times when a subtly enhanced "power" position may be the message you want to communicate to viewers. It need not be overly serious; perhaps you just want to dramatize the moment that your snowball, thrown from above, strikes a fellow hiker.

Ground-Level Perspective

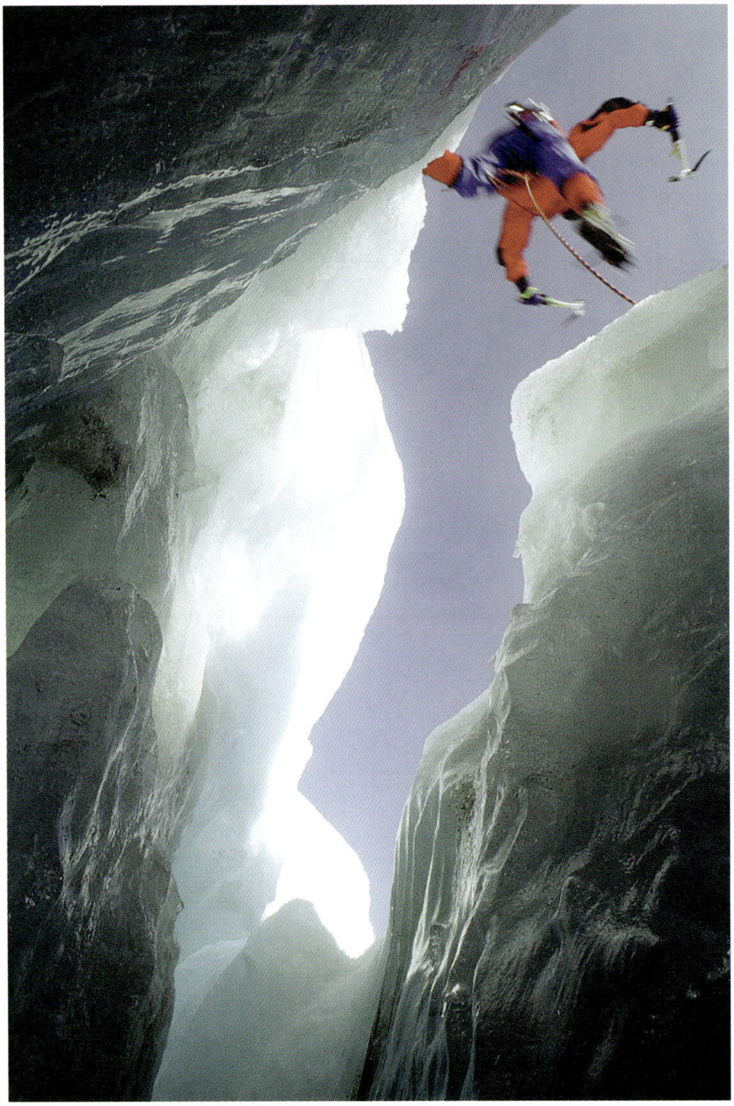

Ground-level perspectives are particularly powerful when taken from a very low shooting position. This photograph was shot from inside a crevasse, looking directly upwards. Canadian Rockies. Fuji Velvia, 28 mm lens.

Ground-level perspectives tend not to be as obvious, and therefore as commonly chosen, as either standing or overhead perspectives. Perhaps this has to do with reservations about grovelling in dirt or getting covered in grasses, which seems inevitable when trying to shoot really low down. However, often situations arise that make a few grass stains or dirt marks worthwhile.

In any event, there are ways of easily avoiding covering oneself in dirt. I often simply first throw a white sheet down, which I carry around and use for making reflection, or look for rocky terrain to squat or lie down on. Alternatively, I might keep my eyes open for sunken areas between boulders or rocky outcrops to sit down and shoot from.

The beauty of getting really low is that you often see things in a remarkably different way than while standing, or even squatting. When some activity takes place close to a ground-level position, say a runner in mid-stride or a mountain bike racing by, this perspective often best emphasizes the key moments of action.

Note that, for these kinds of situations at least, a wide-angle lens is absolutely essential for making best use of a low perspective. It's often important to include foreground objects such as grasses or rocks to give the viewer a sense of where you're shooting from, while, at the same time, including enough of your passing subject to describe the scene.

Because of the low perspective and wide-angle lens used, there will be a fair bit of distortion in any final rendering. Subjects will, opposite to the distortion created by overhead perspectives, become longer and more stretched out than they really are. All body or mechanical parts closest to the camera, such as the legs of the runner or wheel of the mountain bike, will appear huge by comparison to more distant things such as upper torsos and trees. The wider the lens chosen, the more this will be the case.

Distortion, though, is not only tolerable in many of these ground-level instances, but actually often the idea behind them. It's this distortion that dramatizes the moment a mountain biker almost (seemingly) runs over you, or which makes a hiker's stride so bold as he passes directly overhead.

Additionally, if you're gutsy and in a safe position—such as a hollow camouflaged and protected with willows or rocks—distortion can show moving wildlife in a greatly enlarged capacity. A ground-level view of them passing by even close to your camera will be dramatic to say the least, and possibly unique.

Ground-level perspectives don't always need to be chosen to dramatize close-up action though. Sometimes they're useful for just eliminating unwanted foreground or background elements in your composition.

I often employ a ground-level viewpoint while shooting in front of my house, perched in a mountain meadow above our town. From a standing or squatting position, the town is visible in any shot I take; when I get down in the grasses, on the other hand, I could be in perfect Rockies wilderness, a million miles from anywhere.

Skiing and mountain-biking action is often best recorded from a ground-level perspective. Flying snow, spray or debris will add credibility to any action you're trying to record. Canadian Rockies. Kodak E100VS, 28 mm lens.

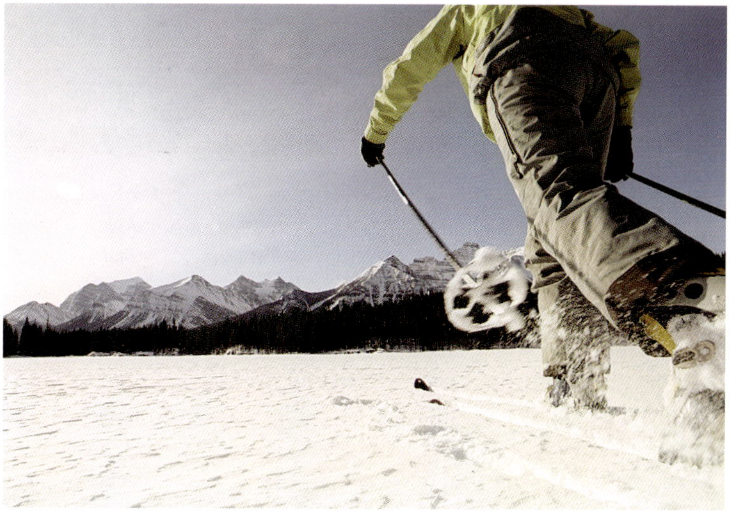

Oblique Perspectives

Oblique perspectives are often the best compromise between level and either overhead or ground-level perspectives. They can render some of the creative effect of high-or-low angle views while minimizing subject distortion.

Squatting or standing on a somewhat elevated platform from some distance away, such as a boulder or incline, will generally give you an oblique perspective of a subject you'd otherwise be level with. While shooting kids, of course, an oblique view can be created by just standing a few meters away on level ground.

As eluded to earlier, whether you choose an oblique upward, or downwards view really depends on a variety of things. First is your choice of background. If there are spires on a ridge crest, for example, that you want to include behind your hiking companion, you may have to shoot obliquely upwards to include them. On the other hand, if the background view desired is lower than, say, your climbing partner, an oblique downwards perspective might be required instead.

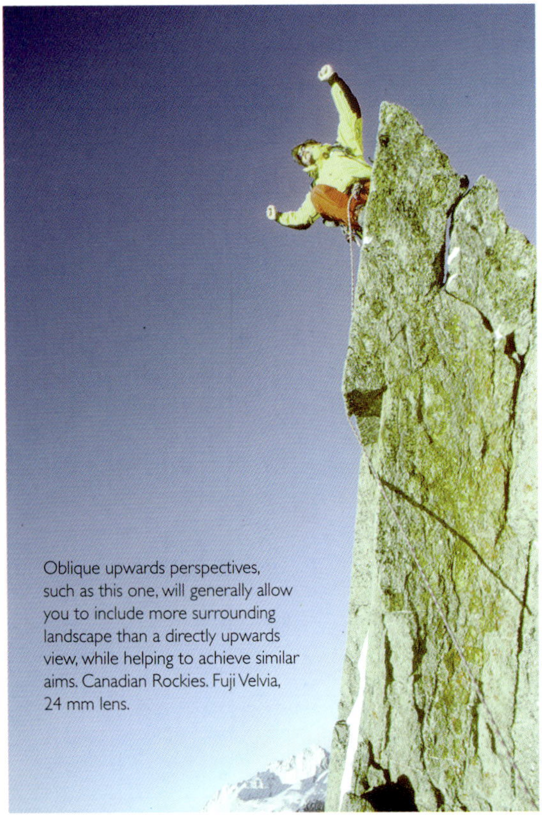

Oblique upwards perspectives, such as this one, will generally allow you to include more surrounding landscape than a directly upwards view, while helping to achieve similar aims. Canadian Rockies. Fuji Velvia, 24 mm lens.

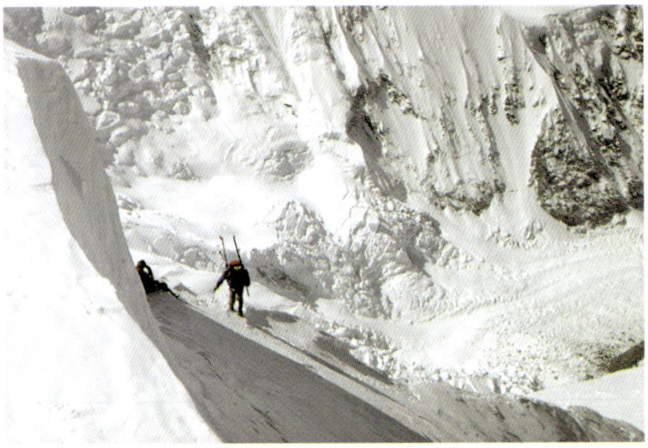

An oblique downwards perspective is likewise often better for capturing distant landscape. It also gives you more flexibility to compose either the subjects or background to your liking. St. Elias Mountains, Yukon, Canada. Kodachrome, 35 mm lens.

Next is any creative message you want to record or draw attention to. Shooting obliquely downwards to a backpacker struggling under his load will tend to emphasize the size of his burden; an oblique upwards view of kids running along an alpine trail will, on the other hand, suggest carefree abandon.

Finally, even though you may not want to distort your subject to the extent created by direct overhead or ground-level perspectives, you may nonetheless want to include some distortion, possibly even so little that it escapes your viewers' notice.

An oblique low perspective, for example, will record longer than normal hikers' legs, particularly with a vertically held camera. An oblique high perspective will exaggerate arms and shoulders instead, perhaps making your rock climbing companion look somewhat more muscular than he actually is. When subtly employed, the distortion created will completely escape your viewers' attention, and may earn you merit points from your hiking and climbing companions.

Mountains, thankfully, are well endowed with natural oblique perspectives. On the prairies or in coastal areas, oblique views might be restricted to what you can capture by simply standing on tippy-toes or squatting down low. In fact, many photographers working in these locations rely upon ladders for themselves, or raised platforms for subjects, in order to record oblique perspectives.

Rarely are these needed in alpine environments. The trick for mountain photographers is usually just spotting the best perspectives, or knowing how to use them. This takes a little practise, and time, but is always well worth any effort involved.

Dramatic Viewpoints

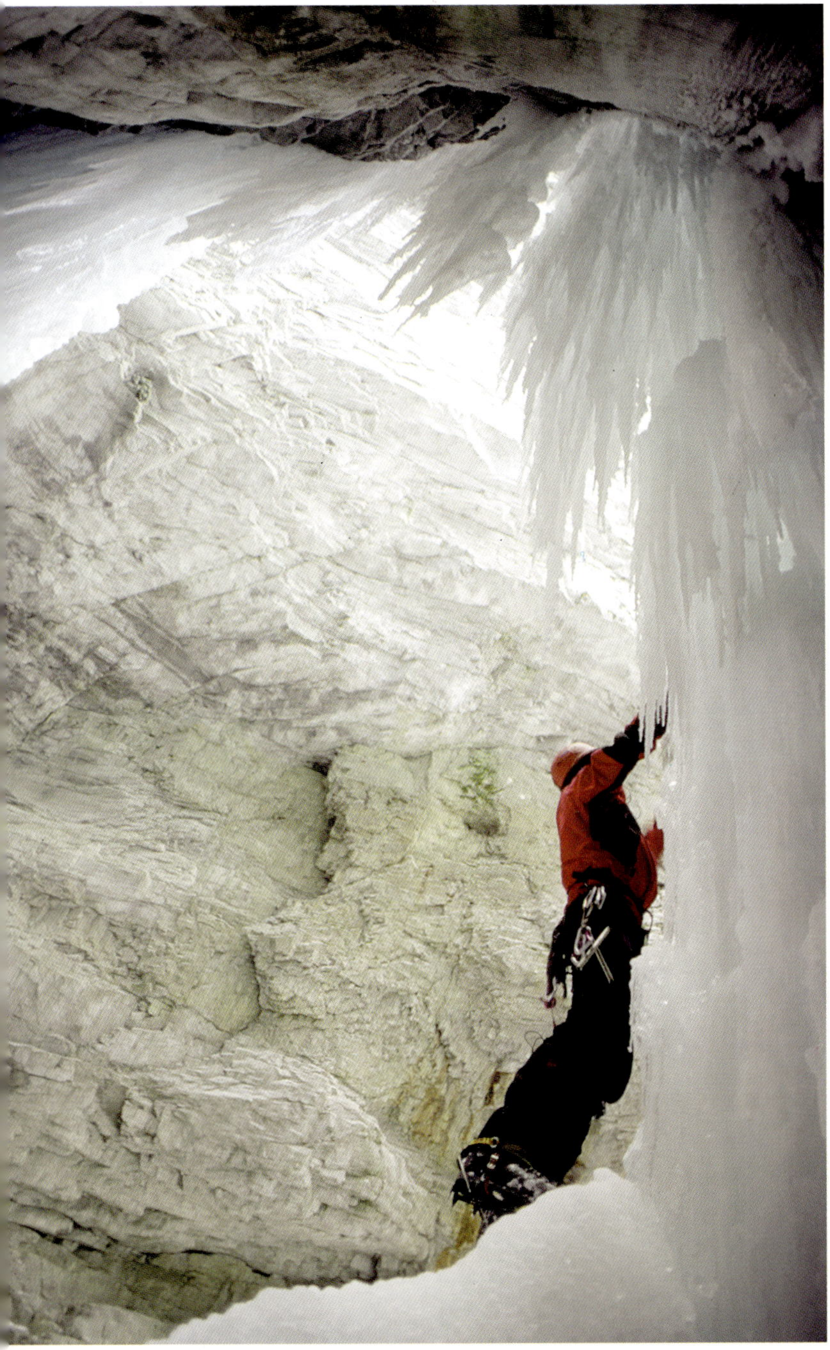

Try to pre-visualize any striking viewpoint for dramatic effect. This one seemed to have a natural curve, which I enhanced somewhat with a wide-angle lens. Canadian Rockies. Fuji Velvia, 20 mm lens.

Mountain environments possess a practically infinite number of dramatic viewpoints. Often all that is needed to take full advantage of them is a short scramble or ski from your chosen route, or from companions that you aim to include as subjects. Sometimes a little more pre-planning or physical effort is required.

Before racing all over the alpine in pursuit of elusive viewing perches, however, it's worth thinking a bit about characteristics that define the best ones. Try to envision an intended scene from a variety of different points of view. Consider where lighting angles might be best, or at least most complementary to your scene. If you're working with foreground subjects, think about how they'll be best positioned from different viewpoints.

I'm constantly on the lookout for dramatic viewpoints while on mountain forays. After choosing a scene I like, I'll often visually scan the nearby mountainsides above (and sometimes below) where I'm standing to see if I can spot anything really sensational. Such viewpoints are not always obvious; often, I'll make a mental note of something that looks good, and continue watching it as I hike, climb or ski closer towards it, or while I traverse by it en route to a further destination.

I discovered one of my favorite perches years ago in exactly this fashion. I'd already determined exactly the background view I was after to create a spectacular mountaineering scene. So then I checked the mountainside directly above me. I knew the morning light would be good there as the slope faces roughly southeast, and this light—I had concluded—also best suited my intended backdrop.

What I needed was a scouting trip. I recall setting off without any great expectations but, lo and behold, I discovered a perfect and accessible pinnacle a partway up a cliff face on that mountainside.

By standing back from it a ways to frame the pinnacle and mountain backdrop in a completely unobstructed way, I also found an ideal shooting stance. Although it was afternoon while I scouted, I knew that I could return to precisely this spot, with companions, for a spectacular morning shoot at some future date.

Since then, I've been back many times. I've tried different film stocks, created somewhat different mountaineering situations, and even tried shooting at different times of the day (although never so effectively as in early morning, as I first guessed).

This kind of discovery will reward every photographer, budding and professional, with great satisfaction and confidence. Any similarly spectacular viewpoints you find, independently of others, by simply combining thought with keen observation, become "yours" in a sense. Perhaps you'll even want to be unusually secretive about their location.

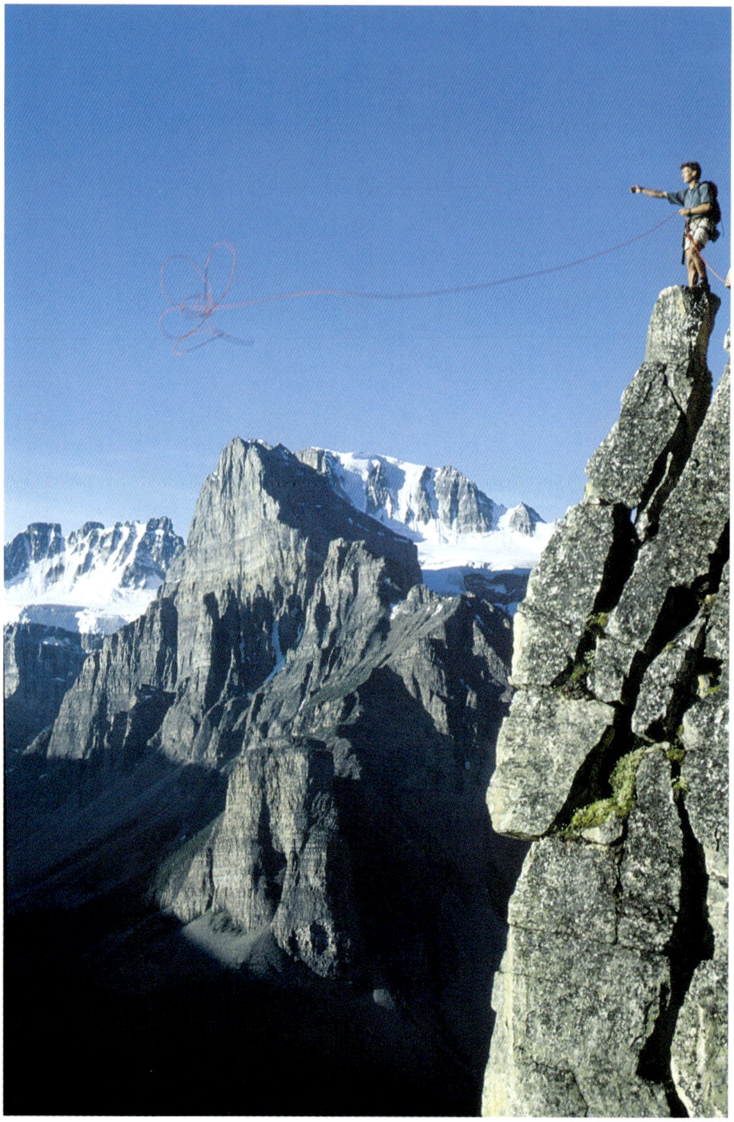

I'm always on the lookout for dramatic shooting locations. I came upon this one by chance while looking for a way to make use of the beautiful mountain backdrop. Canadian Rockies. Fuji Velvia, 70-200 mm zoom lens.

Most of all, you will realize that you can find other dramatic spots wherever you are. This, for me, is ultimate photographic freedom.

As well, the exercise involved will make you think about all the variables most important to exceptional photography: location, lighting and composition. By putting your eyes and brain to work, and not relying upon well-established location choices, or those made by more accomplished photographers, your photography skills will surge ahead.

Emphasizing Steepness

If you're like many other mountain photographers I've met, you've probably been disappointed more than once in the past when your photos haven't shown how steep something really was. Perhaps it's a picture that someone took of you, where you were climbing a dead vertical face (you'd swear it was), or skiing a 45 degree slope. The final results show a laid-back, and somewhat diminutive, rock face instead, or a ski slope that looks more like a bunny run than a spectacular chute.

There is, unfortunately, no simple formula for capturing steepness on film. There are, however, some basic points that, if observed, will help to improve results. And there are some tricks that can add steepness, and drama, to unspectacular situations.

To begin with, if a cliff face is truly vertical, make sure you're holding your camera likewise. It's very easy to get wrapped up in the activity at hand while photographing companions on a cliff face. Before doing so, though, find points at the edge of your frame that correspond to the exact camera orientation you want. Then make sure that framing doesn't deviate while you shoot away, oblivious to everything else.

Shooting straight up a vertical cliff can often underrate its steepness. This particular view tends to flatten three-dimensional space, sometimes even leaving the viewer wondering exactly what he or she is looking at.

Better to shoot from the side in situations where you're not sure what kind of rendering will be produced by a straight up, or straight down, perspective. Side views don't necessarily have to be straight on. Some of the best of these will be oblique, where you're looking slightly down, or slightly up, at a subject while viewing the cliff face in profile.

There are times, though, when looking straight up can render a strong sense of steepness. If prominent distant objects make the actual steepness of the slope obvious—an overhanging cornice, say, or hanging icicles—then the impact on film can be powerful. Even a foreground object can help to emphasize steepness, such as an ice axe clearly dangling under the influence of gravity towards the camera lens.

This latter device can help to effectively capture steepness looking down as well. In fact, nearly anything hanging by gravity alone, if conveyed obviously enough to your viewers, will trumpet steepness and drama. Without them, you will need to show a great expanse of vertical space to distant ground, or perhaps

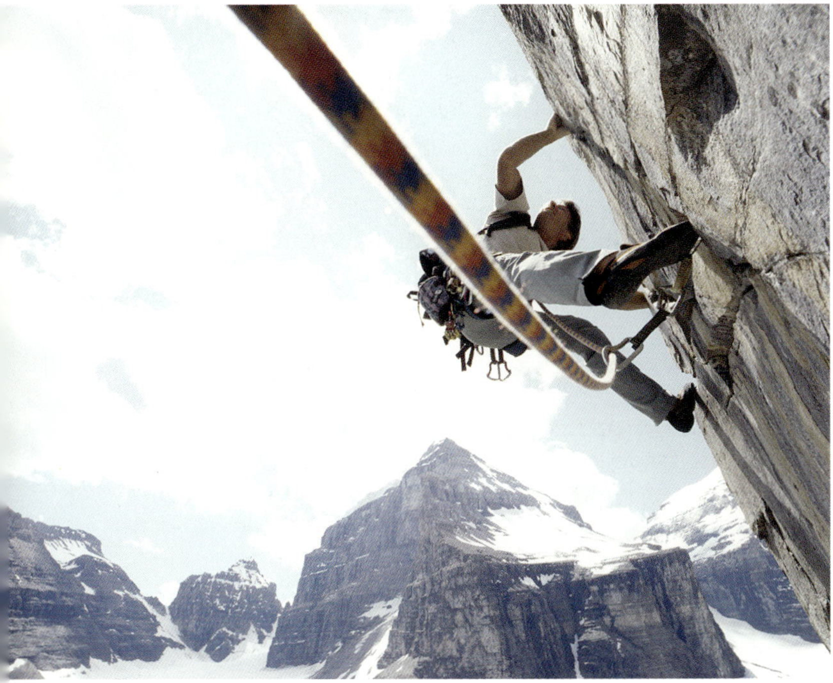

Shooting diagonally upwards is often the best way to capture - or exaggerate - steepness. In this shot, dangling quickdraws and other gear offer the best testimony to how steep the route truly is. Canadian Rockies, Kodak GX100.

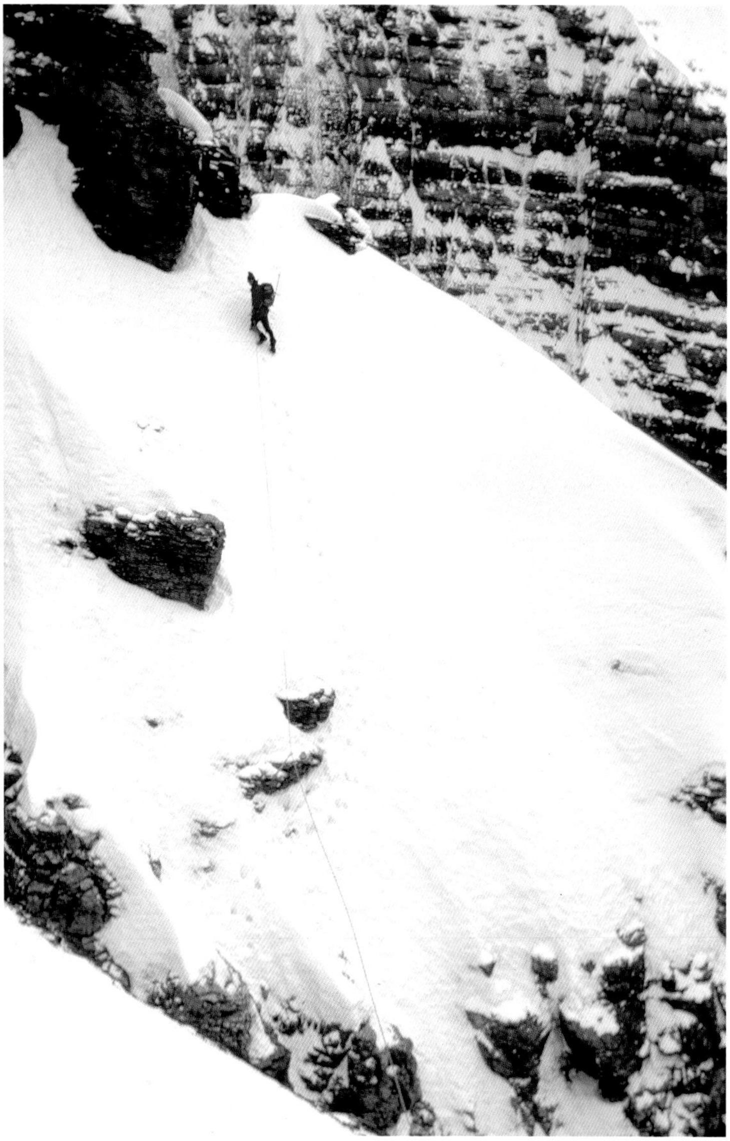

Straight-on climbing shots generally make things look more precipitous than they are. In this shot, the snow slope is probably only angled 50 degree or so, but it looks much steeper. Mount Robson, Canadian Rockies. Kodachrome, 85 mm lens.

an ominous crevasse or bergschrund below, to really dramatize the sheer cliff you're on.

Shooting perpendicular to a steep slope, especially from some distance away, is often the best way to emphasize steepness. You may have heard the truism, often uttered in the mountains, that slopes always look steeper when you view them straight on.

Consequently, if you were to photograph a skiing companion from this angle and at a distance, or a group of climbers roped together on a mountain face, they would always appear to be in far steeper terrain than it actually is. If cliffs or gullies of ice surround them, the slope angle would somehow appear to increase further.

Tricks for Enhancing Perspective

Photography tricks for the mountain shooter really come in two forms: there are ones used to exaggerate drama, and those used to minimize awkward angles, such as "bum" views. This section will look at both.

Probably the most common exaggeration trick has to do with adding more steepness to climbing and skiing views. In practice, it's generally fairly easy: you simply turn your camera beyond a strictly vertical (or horizontal) position until the angle of incline is appropriately steepened. The trick is in not being caught by your viewers.

Any number of things can give you away. An unnaturally tilted tree that appears in a corner of your frame, for example, or some loose rocks that inexplicably remain anchored to a steeply dipping ledge will not pass muster with most viewers. Nor will gear or hair that somehow hangs obliquely, not straight down.

The idea is to be subtle, as well as to watch for things like these that make your scene incomprehensible. Build a sense of realism by capturing foreground or background elements that substantiate the steepness of the perspective you've chosen. Use both wide-angle and telephoto lenses to magnify drama, and also to eliminate things like distant trees that might give you away.

Minimizing unkind subject angles, as with especially the infamous bum view, may rely at times as much on communicating with your subject as on camera technique. Again, subtlety is usually the key.

If your subjects were to, say, look out over a wide vista while you photographed from behind, you could ask them to simply shift their body positions to face you slightly on profile, thus reducing the full-on bum view. While climbing a rock wall directly above you, maybe ask them to simply draw a hip into the rock, again creating a somewhat sideways profile (doing so might better their climbing technique, too!).

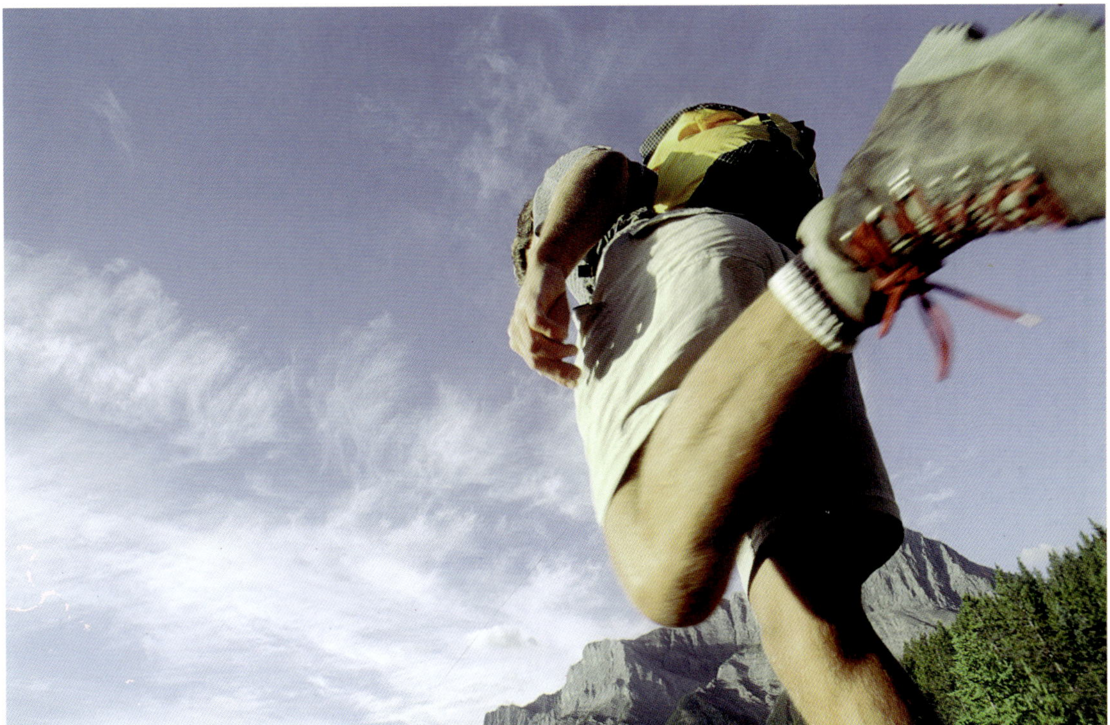

A low perspective, or high perspective, will help to reduce the bum view of a passing companion. In this shot a trailing leg blocks the hiker's bum almost completely. Canadian Rockies. Kodak E100VS, 28 mm lens.

If you can't, or don't want to, communicate with your subjects, there are a couple of devices you can almost always employ as a photographer to improve things significantly.

First, simply altering your position somewhat, or waiting until your subject shifts position, can be a great help. Whether you do one or the other depends, of course, on the exact situation. If you're photographing static subjects, such as hikers gazing across a mountain vista, you'll have to move; with dynamic subjects, it's probably better for them to go through their actions while you maintain what is likely a carefully chosen shooting position.

Altering your position may not just be from side to side either. A raised, or dramatically lowered, shooting position may make all the difference. Both perspectives de-emphasize the bum in relation to other areas of the rear torso; a raised perspective focuses more attention on back and shoulder areas, while a very low position highlights legs.

Note that it may not be your subject's bum that you want to de-emphasize. If he's balding, chances are he won't be thrilled with a straight-down view onto his head while, say, rock climbing. Unless, that is, you catch him throwing his head back, or have him twist it to the side where the bald area won't be as noticeable.

Alternatively, it may be best to change the shot completely, and try to photograph him from below on the next lead, or from the side on a traverse.

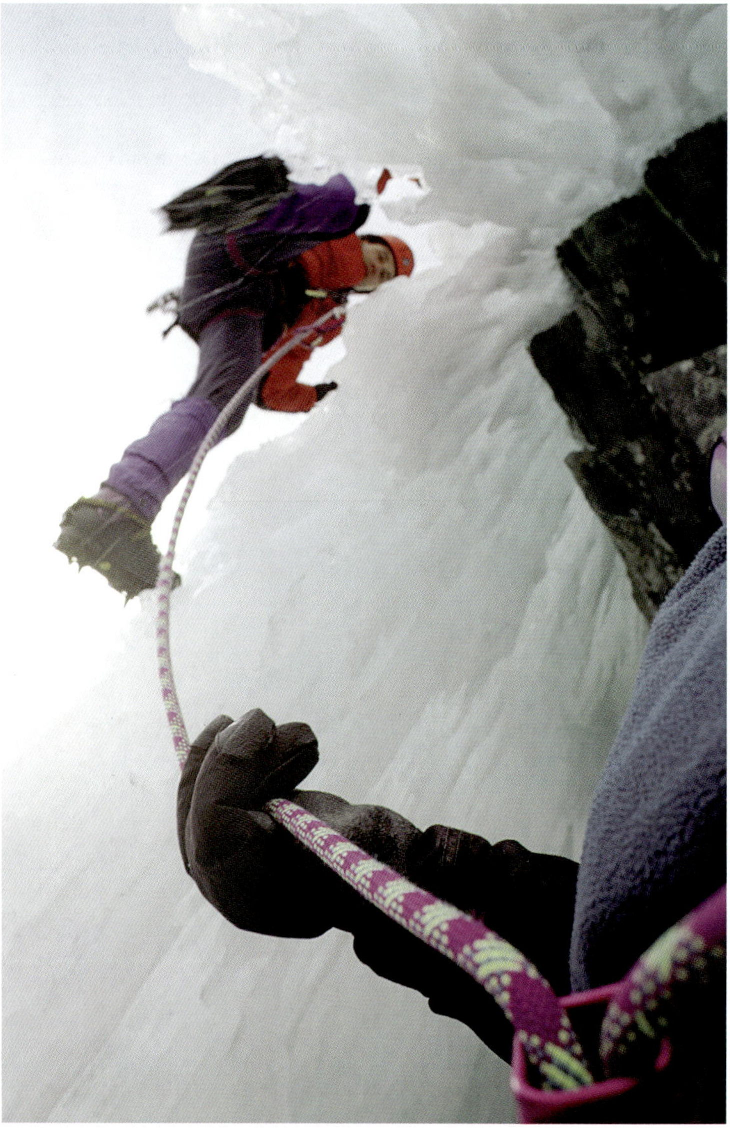

This view past a belayer's hands offers a bold perspective on ice climbing, while also describing the activity quite well. Strong foreground elements downplay the crotch view to an acceptable level. Canadian Rockies. Fuji Velvia, 24 mm lens.

Capturing and Creating Motion

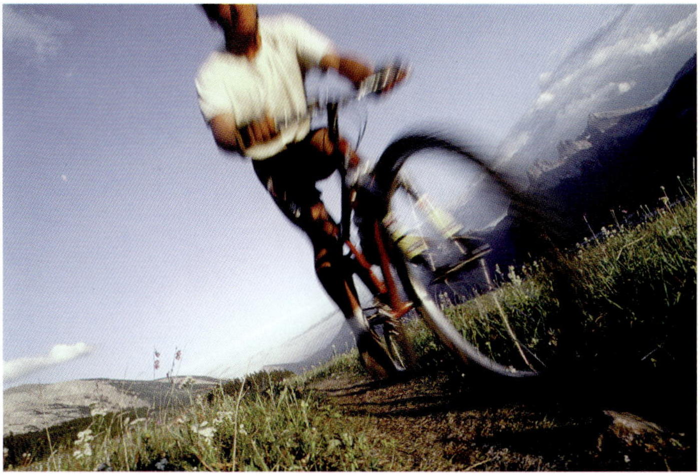

I selected shutter speeds that I thought would neither render the rider as a indiscernible blur nor frozen completely. This photo shows the best compromise. Canadian Rockies. Kodak E100VS, 24 mm lens.

Panning is a great way to show subject motion. If done well, your subject will remain sharp while other elements blur. Canadian Rockies. Kodak E100VS, 28 mm lens.

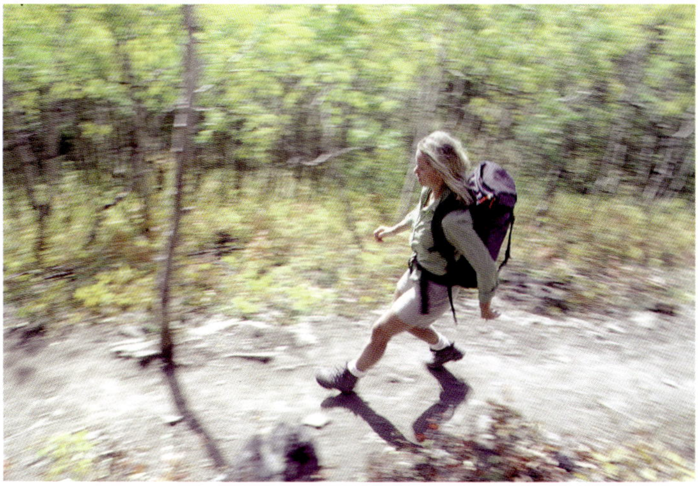

Contrary to notions expressed by some photographers, recording motion with a still camera is neither difficult nor something to perhaps try and then forget about.

Nearly every sports-action shot should have a dynamic feel. Blurred body parts, or an entirely blurred scene, can describe action more effectively on film than anything else. Panned or blurred views of wildlife, while not necessarily "better" than purely static shots, will often elicit way more interest from your viewers.

This is not to suggest that freezing motion entirely with a fast shutter speed isn't desirable at times. There are certainly good reasons for wanting to stop a skier in mid-air, for example, or freeze a bull moose as he thunders across a swamp (from a safe vantage point, of course). Just as often, though, these and similar scenes will be better photographed with motion shown explicitly, by panning or recording blur.

Motion, in any case, is generally not that hard to "create" with your camera. Often all that is needed is to choose a shutter speed that is slow enough to capture a sense of motion without rendering a scene incomprehensible or irritating. Pan shots require more technique, but nothing that can't be achieved with a little practise.

And here's the real clincher: just as subtle tricks with your camera can make a climbing shot appear steeper than it actually is, so too a disciplined control of motion can make an action shot appear to move faster than it actually does. Even educated viewers will be convinced of the apparently fast speeds recorded, if you've photographed well.

Control Motion with Shutter Speed Selection

Blurred motion, as suggested in the title, is most commonly controlled by your shutter speed selection. As a general rule, the amount of blurring recorded on film increases with decreasing shutter speeds. Hence, a 1/15 shutter speed will show more blurring than a 1/30 or 1/60 speed.

This may seem quite obvious, but it only holds true so long as other factors remain constant. If you were to move closer towards or farther away from your subject, change your shooting angle in relation to your subject's movement, use a longer or wider lens, or if your subject were to suddenly speed up or slow down, the apparent motion on film would also change.

Because of all these variables, there is no set rule for determining what shutter speed is best for recording any particular motion. All you can do is experiment with different settings in hopes of hitting just the right one.

Alpine skiing, for example, typically moves faster than Nordic skiing. Consequently, a higher shutter speed while photographing alpine skiers would likely create the same sense of motion that a lower speed would with Nordic skiers.

However, if even a fast downhill skier were to come obliquely towards you, instead of perpendicular to your camera, you would have to choose a lower speed to record significant blur. A Nordic skier passing by at right angles and close to your position, on the other hand, would blur at even a relatively fast shutter speed.

1/30 and 1/60 of a second tend to be good starting points for blurring most mountain activities. Hikers' legs, when viewed obliquely or at right angles, will invariably blur at either of these speeds, although usually not beyond recognition. A mountain biker or skier that races by an especially low camera position will also blur significantly (although perhaps too much

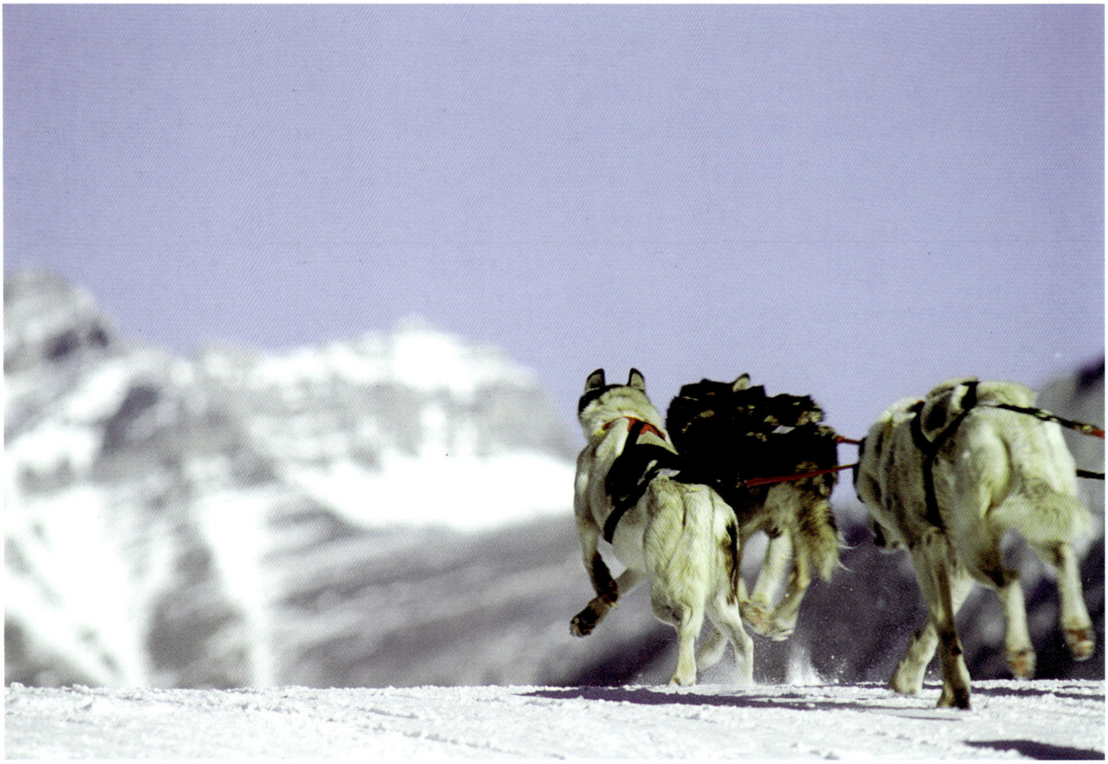

This photo was shot at a fast enough speed that the dogs themselves are arrested in motion, but their blurring legs show plenty of speed. Canadian Rockies. Fuji Velvia, 105 mm lens.

if you're striving for a subtle effect). Even details, such as a climber's sudden hand movements while reaching for a new hold, will probably record as a satisfying blur at one or the other setting.

If you choose a longer lens than 50 mm or so, either a faster speed will be needed to record an appropriate subject blur, or your shooting position will need to change.

With really long telephoto lenses, a great deal of care needs to be taken that the degree of blurring will not be over the top. In fact, any amount of blurring from a static shooting position might be undesirable with really long lenses. Generally you'd be better off panning your scene (see next section), or trying to arrest motion completely.

Some creative angles also work better than others in terms of recording blur, even with normal and wide lenses. Probably the best advice to dispense, since—to some extent anyway—personal taste will dictate what looks good and what doesn't, is just to experiment with a variety of approaches, lenses and speeds.

You'll likely get a pretty good sense of what speed works best after continually reviewing the results of such experimentation. Then, hopefully, all that will be required with any given activity, angle, or subject-to-camera distance, is to try one or two different speeds in order to nail the right one.

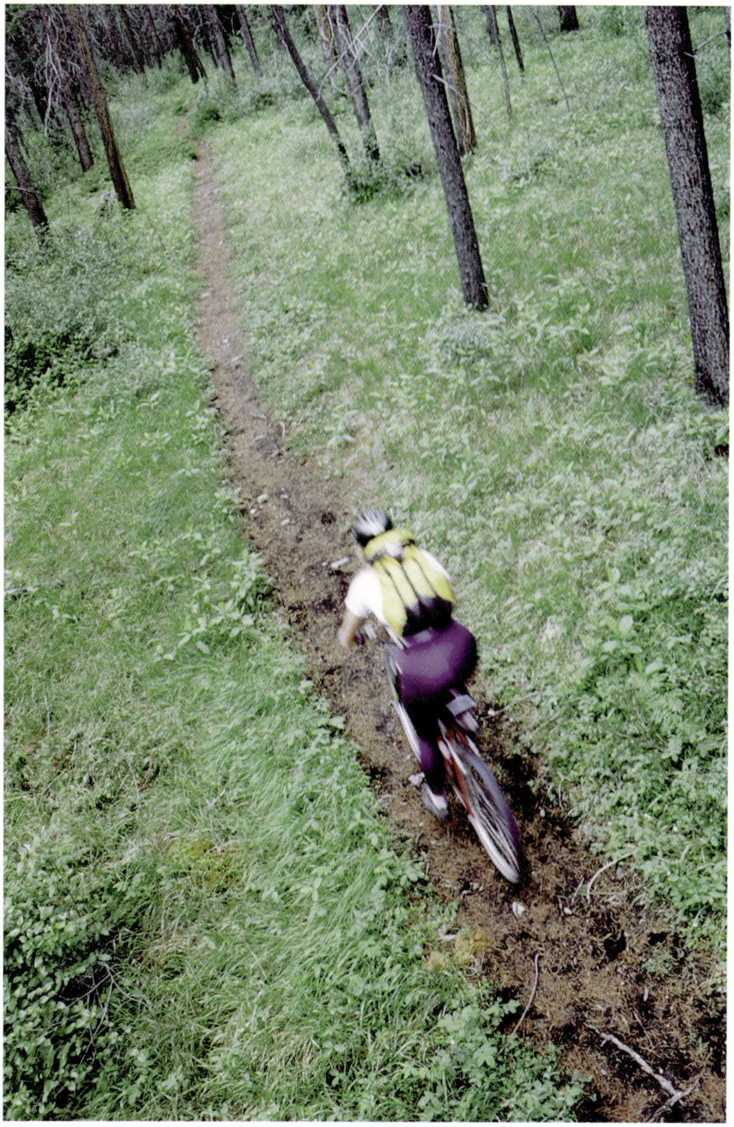

For this overhead perspective I wanted to include as much depth of field as I could. The speed I arrived at by default, 1/60 second, was fortunately exactly the one I needed to record some—but not too much—subject blur. Canadian Rockies. Fuji Velvia, 28 mm lens.

Panning Action Scenes

Panning, by definition, means moving a camera with a subject while releasing the shutter. Generally, camera movement is intended to correspond as closely to subject movement as possible, such that a resulting photograph shows a relatively well-focused subject and a blurry, streaking background.

Panning most commonly is practised in a horizontal fashion. This probably has to do with the fact that most rapid action operates from side to side. Panning horizontally is also fairly natural in practice and relatively easy to learn.

However, there are certainly applications for vertical panning too, especially in the mountains. A shot following a rappeler down a cliff, for example, could make an exciting pan, and would confer to any viewer a strong sense of the adrenaline that a rappeler might himself be experiencing. Even a tight shot of an ice climber, say, rapidly pulling himself up with axes, might make an interesting vertical pan if done well.

There are also possibilities for oblique panning. If you were to pan mountain goats jumping to a lower ledge on a cliff face, chances are the resulting shot would show oblique lines corresponding to the local rock strata. Following a skier schussing a steep slope with trees behind would likely record in a similar oblique fashion.

Here are the essential steps involved in good panning. First, select an appropriate shutter speed. Then, follow your moving subject in a smooth, fluid manner—without jerks—releasing the shutter either at the peak of action or at your most fluid moments.

A motor winder is a really nice accessory to have while panning. Without one, you'll have to interrupt the flow of panning movement to hand crank onto the next frame. A motor winder also allows you to shoot several frames while following any activity, and so helps you to catch the best moments continually.

Panning technique requires practise, more than anything else, to really master. Although a little odd, it would probably be worthwhile to try pans on different moving subjects without even shooting film, at least

Try to visualize whether your chosen background will suit a panned treatment, and ensure that the pan speed you select makes sense in terms of the activity you're panning. Canadian Rockies. Kodak E100VS, 28 mm lens.

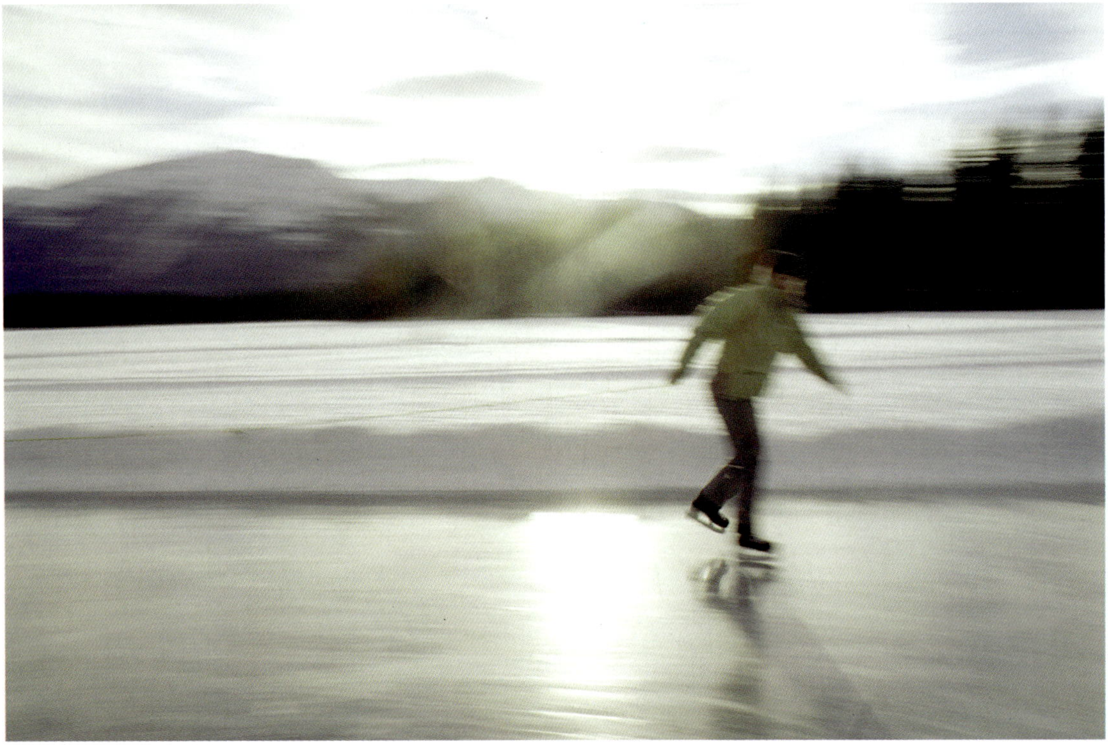

to begin with. This way you'll get a knack for following any movement smoothly with your camera without spending a dime on film or processing. Joggers, skiers—even cars—make easy neighborhood subjects for honing your panning technique.

Of course, if photographing with a digital camera, you'd might as well shoot your panned subjects and then check results. There is probably no better way to see what type of movement works best.

Once you have practised your technique, the trick is often just in choosing the right shutter speed for the action you're photographing, the lens you've chosen and background details. If it's too slow a speed, the setting might not be obvious to your viewers (often this will not be a problem, though, and may even be intentional). Also, your subject may not be as sharp as you'd like. If it's too fast, on the other hand, the pan might not attribute as much motion to your subject as you'd like, and the background won't be as textured or interesting as you'd planned.

As with all shutter settings for motion, getting the right ones for any given situation boils down to a combination of experimentation and experience. You might want to make written notes to begin with, and refer back to them whenever you're in doubt.

A general rule of thumb I follow, while panning, is to choose speeds that correspond with half the focal length of the lens I'm using if I want subjects to remain relatively sharp. Hence, with a 125 mm lens, I'll usually choose 1/60 of a second while panning relatively nearby subjects travelling at moderate speeds. With a 28 mm lens, I might choose 1/15 of a second instead.

However, if my subject is moving slowly, or if I want either my subject or background to blur excessively, I'll choose a lower speed. Likewise, if it's moving really fast, especially at relatively close range, I'll try a faster speed, although not usually faster than the lens focal length (i.e. 1/125 second with a 125 mm lens).

With lenses of, say, 180 mm and longer, it's usually best to mount the camera on a tripod to produce smoother pans. If you're using one without a pan head, try to lock down movement in one direction (say vertical) while freeing it up in the other (horizontal). There are no guarantees your pans will be flawless, but at least undesirable blurring from camera shake should be reduced.

Don't be limited by conventional ideas on panning. Try ones of your own. In some cases, your subject won't even have to move; a circular pan, for example, where you simply pivot your camera in an arc after composing, will give a strong impression of subject movement even though none is needed.

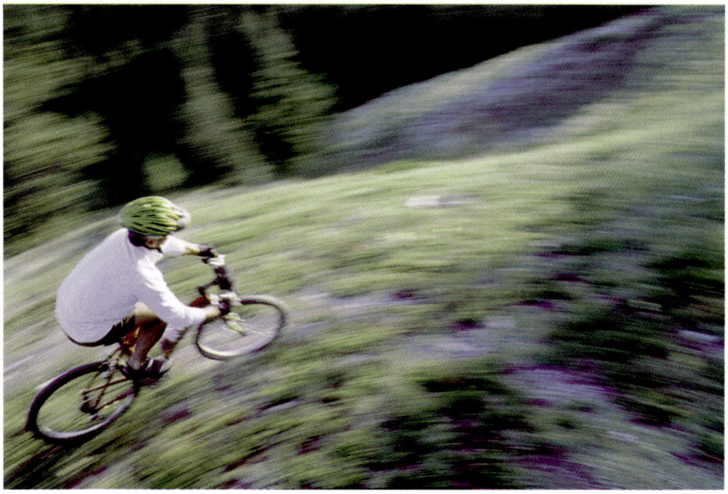

The rounded nature of this background encouraged me to try a slightly curving pan. For it to work, I had to get the biker to follow a similarly curving line. Canadian Rockies. Fuji Velvia, 35-70 mm zoom lens.

Attaching Your Camera to Moving Objects

Often the most exciting motion views in still photography are created by attaching your camera to moving objects. Such objects might even be a piece or extension of your principal subject. If so, the resulting image will have a strong point-of-view (POV) feel.

For example, consider mounting your camera to the side of a mountain bike, pointing forward past the handlebars to a trail ahead. When your shutter speed is set correctly, you should record hands, handlebars and other bike parts in relatively sharp focus, the trail as a recognizable feature, and the sides of your frame as streaks of motion. This combination can create a powerful image, especially if your background has been carefully chosen.

The possibilities are really endless for such moving POV creations. You could mount a camera on the side of a ski boot to show the ski ahead and sides of a ski run or Nordic track streaking by. Or you could strap a camera to the leg of a mountaineer and show his cramponed boot as it strides forward on an icy summit arête.

Not all views captured by mounting your camera to moving objects will be POV ones. Perhaps you simply want to record a distant subject from a moving object, without showing any of that object in the foreground. Consider, for example, the idea of shooting a whitewater kayaker following behind you. If your plan is to show him, alone, in the turbulence of a raging mountain river with froth streaking by at the sides of your frame, then this might be an unbeatable perspective.

Or perhaps you want to record both a distant subject and a nearby one from a POV standpoint. This can be a great way to show the dynamism of teamwork, or camaraderie, in the mountains.

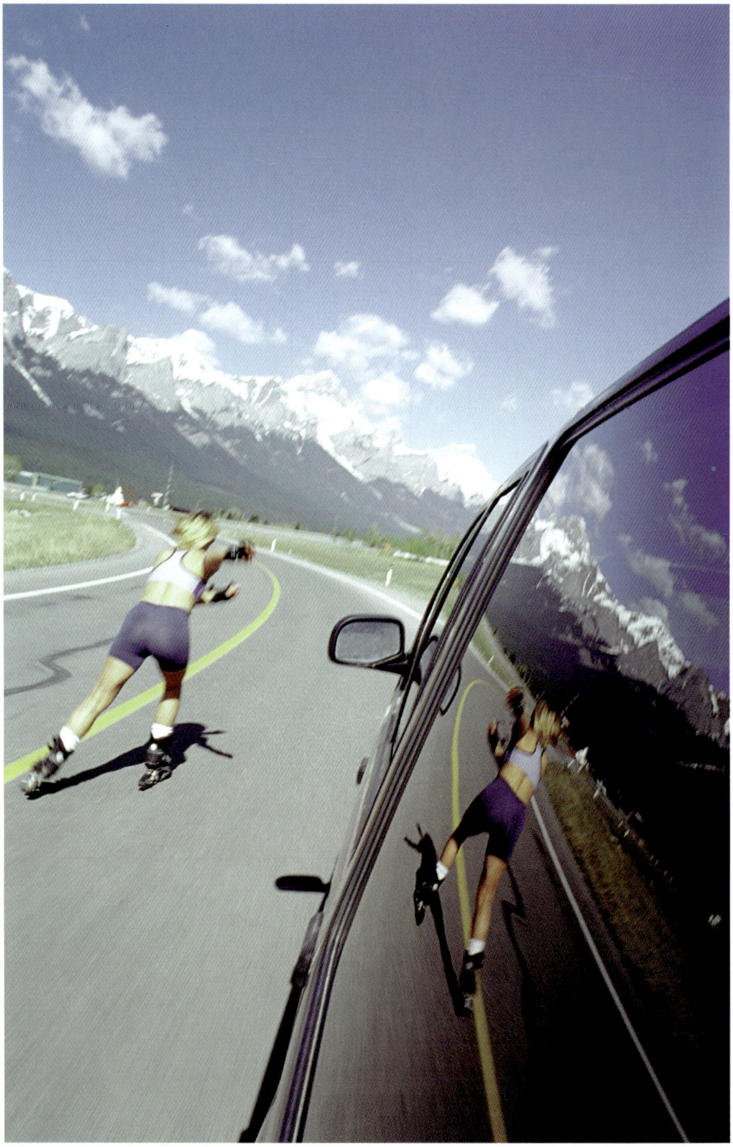

In this shot, both inline skater and the truck I was shooting from are moving at roughly the same speed. Consequently, the skater and vehicle appear quite sharp while other elements blur a bit. Canadian Rockies. Kodak E100VS, 28 mm lens.

Consider the above mountaineering boot and crampon example. If these foreground elements were joined to a somewhat distant mountaineer by a length of rope, a strong sense of teamwork would be created. Any foreground streaking movement recorded alongside the boot would simply imply or emphasize the idea of "work in progress", as the climbers draw nearer to their summit goal.

A mountain biker travelling at roughly the same speed as the one showing handlebar details will, likewise, create a sense of companionship on the trail. So would a skier racing alongside and maybe slightly ahead of foreground boot and ski details.

You don't always have to attach your camera to things in order to create moving POVs. Sometimes a handheld camera will suffice. For example, you could simply hold a camera down low (perhaps by peering through a top viewfinder, if you have one) to record your skis and a blurred horizon as you swoosh down the ski slope. Alternatively, you could hold your camera ahead and, again, low to record your hiking boots and maybe another hiker leading down a trail.

Nearly all such in-motion POVs will require a wide-angle lens. Sometimes the widest lens you have will work best. A 28 mm or even a 35 mm might be perfectly adequate though and perhaps even ideal. Try different lenses if in doubt to see what looks best.

Because a camera will likely get bumped and jerked around a fair bit when attached to fast moving bikes and skis, you might want to use any older or more durable one you may have in your possession. I have a dedicated "beater" camera for such POV shooting. Although it wouldn't have much value if I tried trading it for a newer, more sophisticated model, it's probably more dependable than any other for this kind of work.

Make sure that whatever camera you choose will support a fairly long cable release. You'll most likely have to run alongside the person or object it's mounted on while releasing the shutter. Unless it's mounted to you, that is, in which case a longer cable release will allow you to stand tall and pay attention to what you're doing, instead of fumbling with a shutter near your ankles.

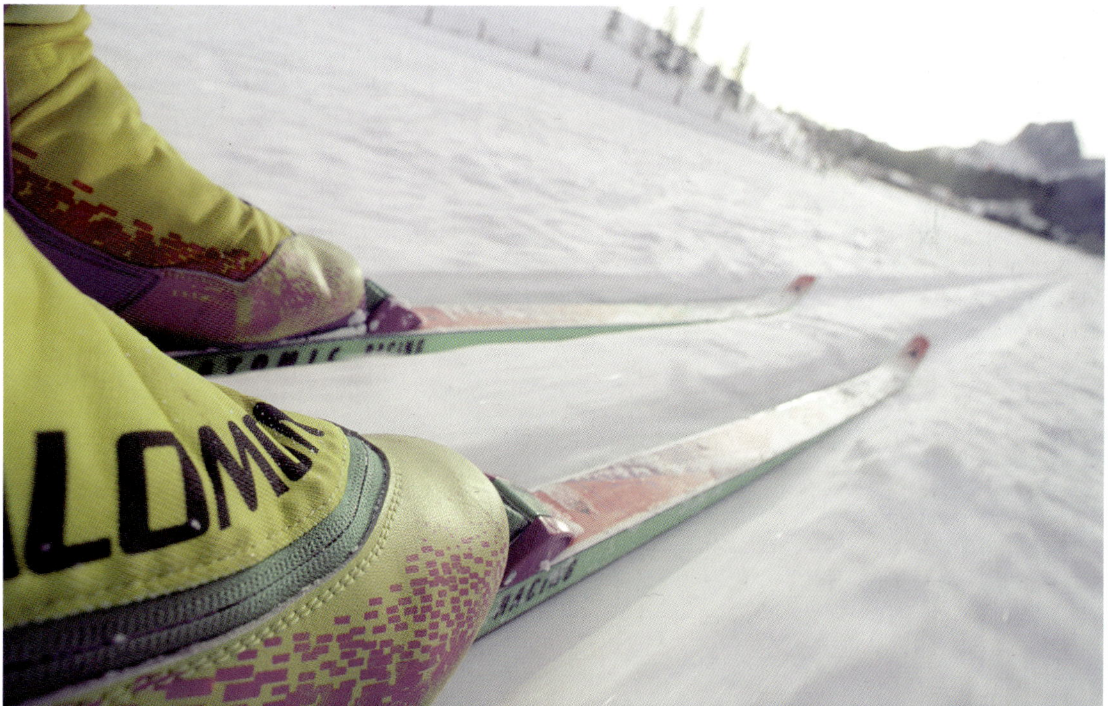

I strapped a camera to the skier's leg in this shot (and upside down in order to get it as close to the ground as possible). Although scenery blurs by with the skier's motion, boots and skis remain sharp. Canadian Rockies. Fuji Velvia, 24 mm lens.

Mountain Light

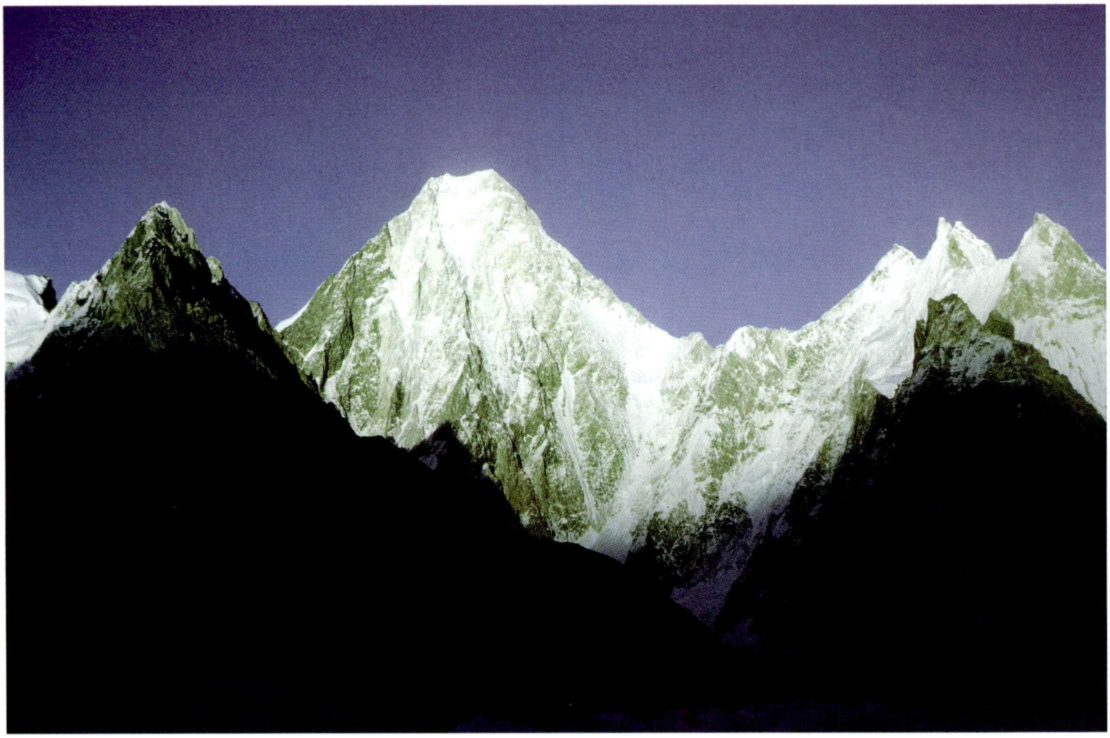

Mountain light is especially bold at high altitudes. Skies might look purple or blue–black at times, even though snow–capped mountains stand out brilliantly. Gasherbrum IV, Pakistan. Kodachrome, 85 mm lens.

Mountain light, put succinctly, is bold. In contrast to especially coastal or pastoral light, it tends to be far less subtle and muted. And the higher you travel into the mountains, the bolder it generally becomes.

At the highest altitudes, skies appear (and also record on film) incredibly blue and, sometimes, even purple in color. Rock and snow skylines etch against them ever so sharply. Long–range views of mountain ranges or valleys may be so clear that the minutest details stand out.

Good mountain photography doesn't always have to depict bold lighting though. There are a great number of subtleties that are always worth watching for. Sunset hues, for example, especially from mountain summits or in places that are lit by a setting or rising sun, can be as warm and muted as at any seaside place. Mists and fogs, commonplace in all alpine areas, often create beautifully subtle lighting conditions, as does a weak winter sun barely penetrating snowy gusts.

Bold light is, nonetheless, exciting to work with. It can be downright exhilarating, in fact, especially when dramatic rays of light illuminate a scene, or frame a spectacular backdrop. It's certainly something you should never need to contend with. Indeed, the point for any mountain photographer is to make the best use of it possible.

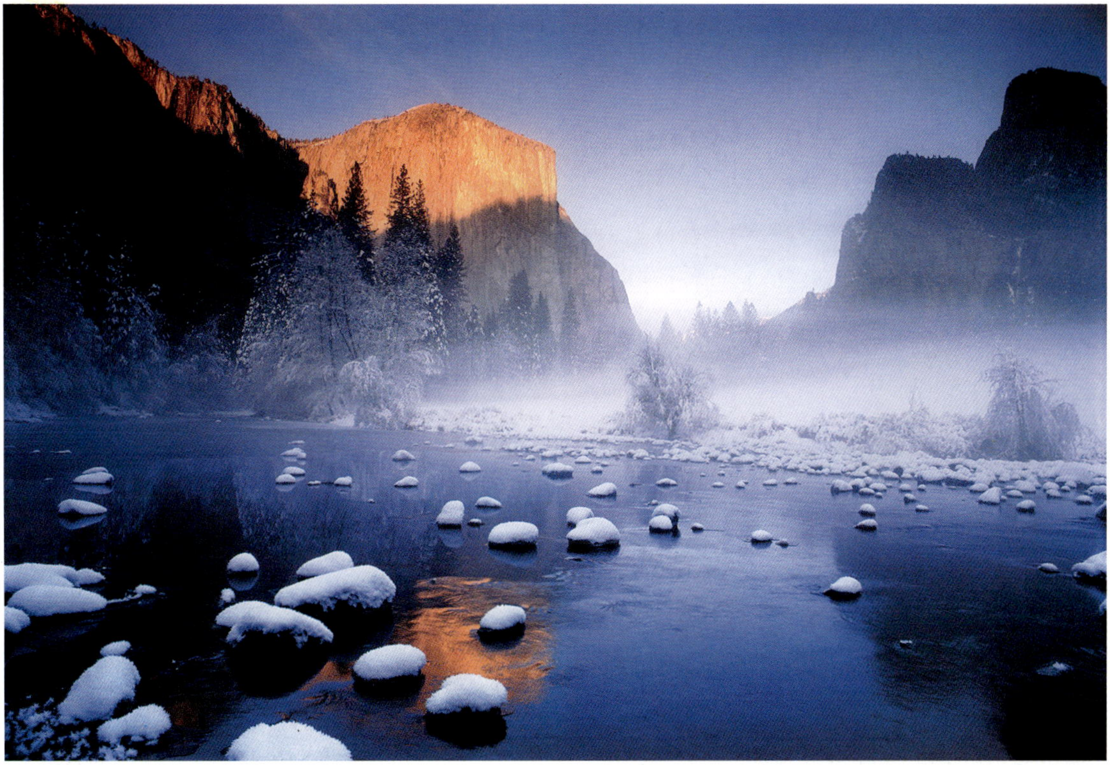

"Twice each day the cool, blue light of night interacts with the warm tones of daylight. Luckily for color photographers, these events, though predictable, are inconsistent. For a full hour at either end of the day colors of light mix together in endless combinations, as if someone in the sky were shaking a kaleidoscope."
From *Mountain Light – In Search of the Dynamic Landscape*. Photo by Galen Rowell.

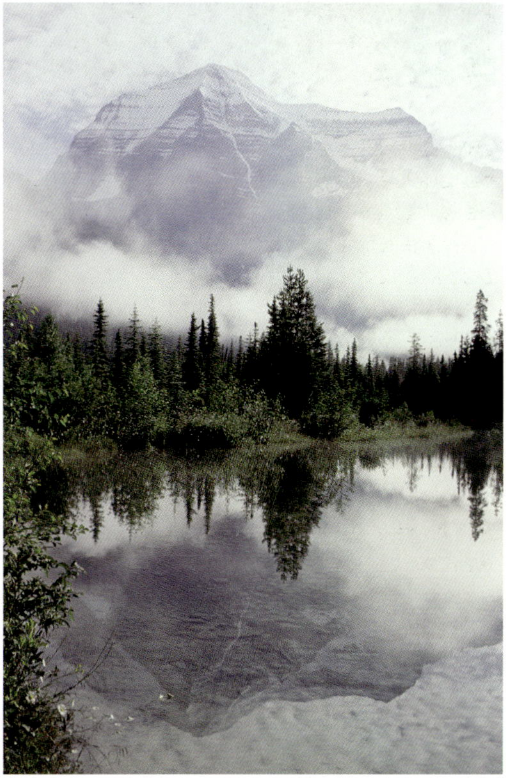

Mists and fogs create wonderful lighting subtleties in low–lying areas such as this, and even at higher elevations during or immediately after a storm. Mount Robson, Canadian Rockies. Fuji film, 28 mm lens.

Radiant Light: an Overview

To understand why mountain light is characteristically bold first requires a look at altitude effects on our main radiant light source: the sun.

As you climb steadily higher from sea level, the relative intensity of radiant sunlight increases, owing to decreasing amounts of particles and humidity, which scatter the sun's rays down below. This intensity translates, from a photography standpoint, into both enhanced clarity and higher than typical contrasts between lit and shaded areas.

Solar intensities are most marked at high altitudes in equatorial areas. At higher latitudes, the sun's intensity is more muted. This is because the earth's curvature forces incoming rays of sunlight to bend, lessening their strength. During winter at very high latitudes, the effect of curvature is particularly dramatic. Here, even high-altitude light remains muted, or nonexistent, most of the time.

For a similar reason, and at any latitude, the intensity of light diminishes before sunset and increases after sunrise. Because of the low-angled sun at these times of day, light rays are screened through a thicker atmosphere than at any other.

This screening scatters blue and ultraviolet wavelengths and allows longer red and yellow ones through. Color temperatures decrease markedly at the same time, from around 5500 degrees Kelvin, to values approaching 3400 degrees. The effect, as seen through eyes or on film, is "softened" or "warmed" sunlight.

Some artificial light sources, such as a tungsten strobe or simple flashlight, come close to emulating the color characteristics of soft sunlight. Others, like typical camera-mounted flash units, aim at reproducing full daylight conditions. Importantly, any artificial light source is, like the sun, a provider of radiant—not passive—light.

And, like sunlight at various times of the day, both warm and bright light accessories can be useful to the mountain photographer. In many cases, you'll have to simply make do with whatever ones you have on hand. Perhaps all you've packed on an outing is a headlamp, for example, or a flashlight.

More will be said, later, about artificially illuminating subjects when sunlight is insufficient for doing so, such as at night. Keep in mind for the moment, though, that whatever accessory you choose it should be capable of producing light of appropriate quality for the scene you're shooting, neither too warm nor too bright.

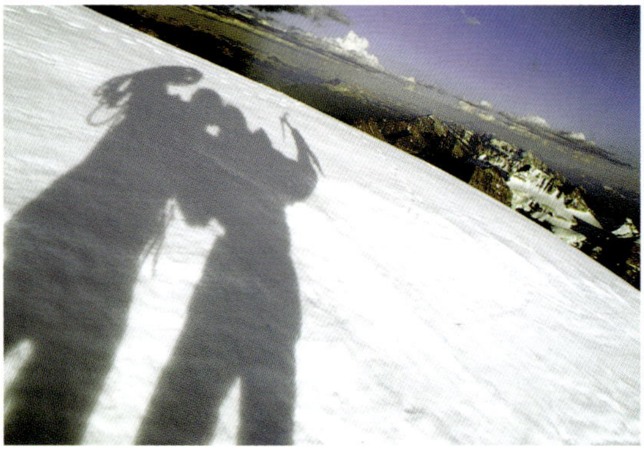

At early and late times of the day—especially at higher latitudes—a low angled sun creates long shadows. These are sometimes worthy photography subjects on their own. Canadian Rockies. Fuji Velvia, 24 mm lens.

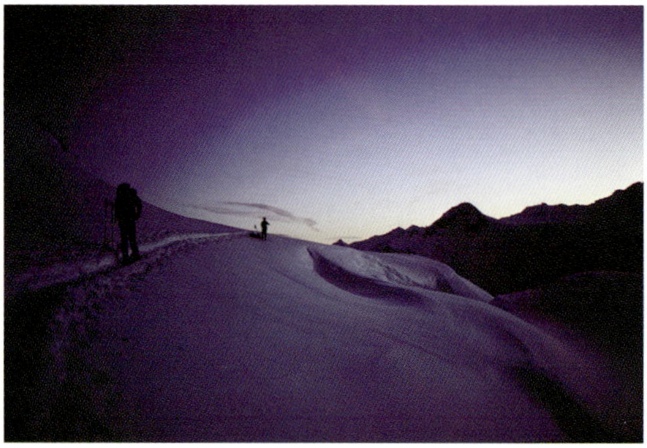

If atmospheric conditions are right, a beautiful glow will remain in the sky long after the sun has set, or well before it rises. This might just perfectly outline distant mountains. Coast Mountains, Canada. Kodachrome, 35 mm lens.

Choosing Time of Day and Time of Year to Shoot

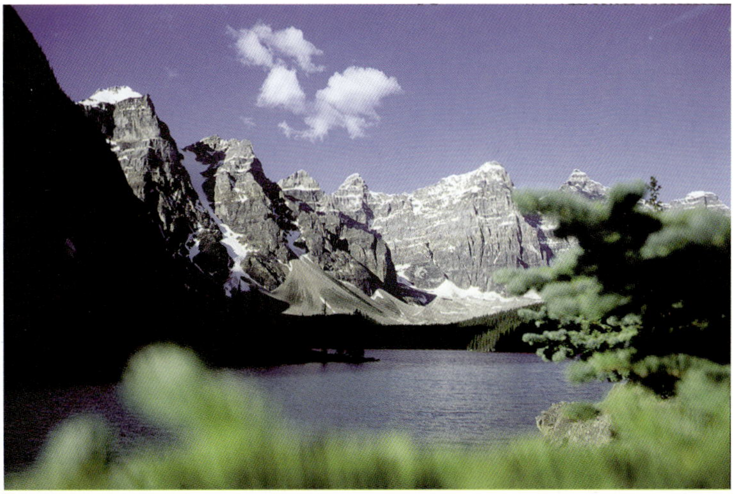

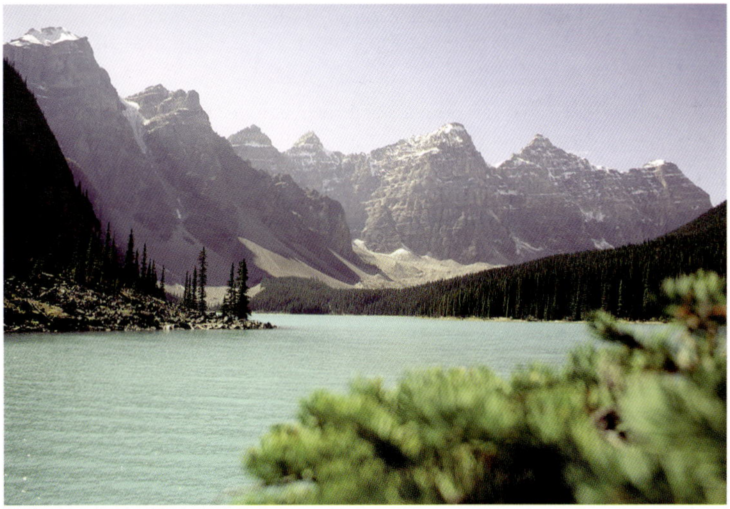

Mountain views change radically throughout the day and at different times of the year. The three shots in this section were all taken in essentially the same location; in early morning, mid–afternoon and in late winter (see next page). Moraine Lake, Canadian Rockies. Fuji Velvia, 28 mm lens.

The warm and soft characteristics of early morning and late evening light are what generally make these times the nicest to shoot in. The often cold colors and harsh shadows of mid-day dissipate and surroundings look their most inviting. Skin tones are much healthier looking; dark shadow areas on faces, especially around eyes and noses, become evenly illuminated as the sun sinks towards the horizon.

Not always are they best, though. Sometimes the relative harshness of mid-day high–altitude light can be more appropriate. If you want to show the absolute brilliance of a high mountain environment, there's no better time to shoot. Or, if you want to reduce shadow areas to a minimal size (i.e. not depth)—either those created by your subjects or by distant mountain features it may also be the preferred time of day to shoot.

There is sometimes another reason for avoiding very early morning or late evening sunlight: it may warm things too much. Deep orange and even red skin tones will result from shooting right at sunrise or sunset, especially with more saturated types of color film stock. These generally don't look great in review later, nor do radically discolored green anoraks or blue sweaters, for example.

The trick is often in choosing the right quantity and quality of radiant light for your intended shoot. Often the best solution is to try a late afternoon or early morning time that corresponds with some softening of light, but nothing too dramatic. Roughly an hour after sunrise or before sunset is one of my favorite times for shooting with human subjects, but this will vary with the specific demands and positioning of a shoot.

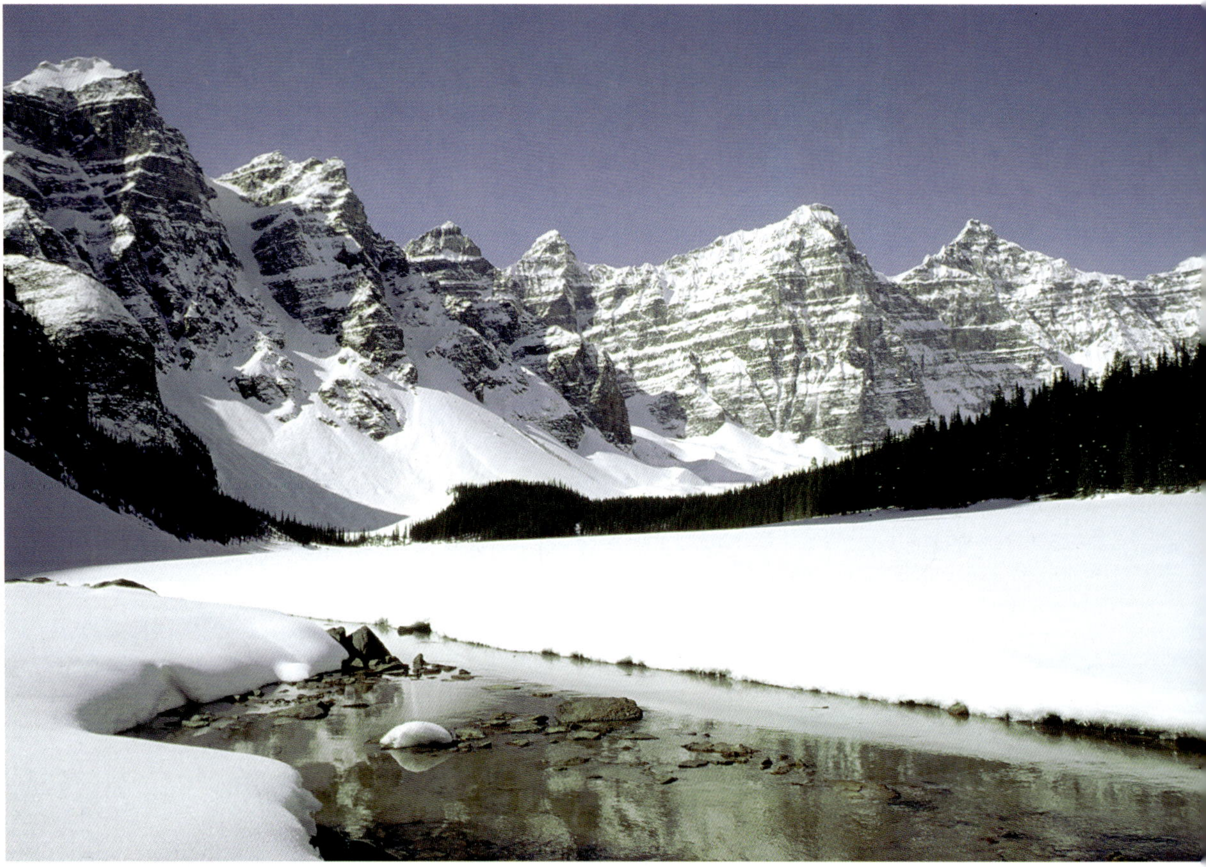

In some cases, radiant light won't even reach your subject an hour or two before sunset, even on a perfectly clear day. This is particularly true in the mountains where, for example, an east–facing slope might lose sunlight by mid-afternoon, or a west–facing slope may not see it until mid-day. Sometimes natural features near your chosen location will block sunlight for most of the day, such as trees, canyon walls, or nearby peaks.

The same argument will dictate what time of year is best for a given shoot. At moderate to high latitudes, the winter sun will not reach many of the places that you might have photographed during summer. Mountains, forests or even nearby rocks and trees may prevent the sun from striking an intended foreground, or any part of a larger view.

One of my favorite shoot destinations, an alpine lake in the Canadian Rockies, is only fully illuminated for about two months of the year. Because it's so high and shadowed it's generally ice covered for most of the month leading up to summer solstice (June 21). Consequently, my shooting forays there are pretty much limited to one month out of the entire year.

The opposite can hold true as well though. Another of my favorite background scenes is best photographed in early morning on the shortest days of winter. At any other time of year, the sun rises less to the south and more in the west, where it's blocked by a range of tall mountains until mid-morning.

Opposite: Frontal lighting can be as soft as the most subtle backlighting at times. Such light is especially good for photographing people or animal subjects, as well as the nearby environment. Sheep on hillside, Crete, Greece. Kodachrome, 85 mm lens.

Opposite: More commonly, though, frontal lighting emphasizes the power and boldness of things. Avalanches, waterfalls, storms and strong landscapes are often best photographed frontally, sometimes at mid-day. St. Elias Mountains, Yukon. Kodachrome, 35 mm lens.

Frontal Lighting

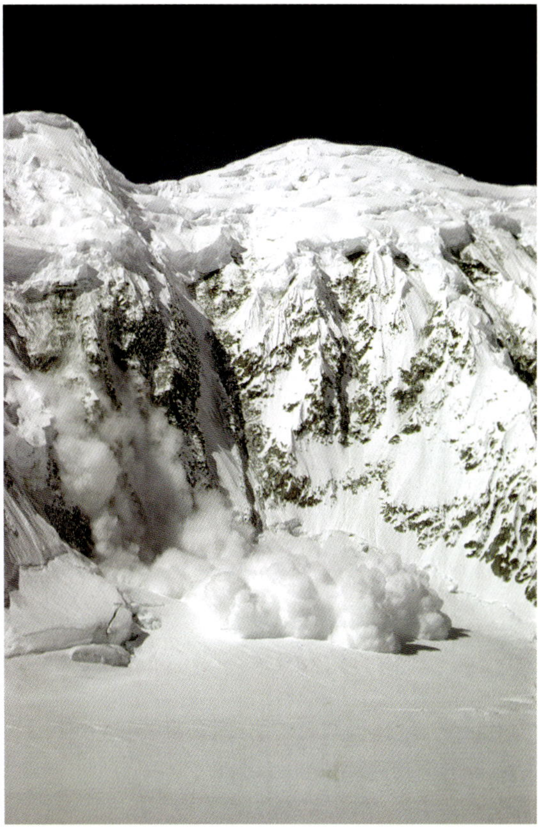

As suggested by the name, frontal lighting predominates when photographing a subject or scene with the sun behind your back. Illumination is more or less direct. Shadows, except ones caused by a partially overhead sun at mid-day, are thereby kept to a minimum, sometimes even eliminated completely.

Frontal lighting is, like mountain light itself, bold. Consequently, it's best used to emphasize drama, to suggest power, or to draw immediate attention to a subject. The best views of distant thunderheads looming over peaks, for example, are often frontally lit. So are waterfall scenes and avalanches roaring down mountainsides.

With human or wildlife subjects, frontal lighting can be quite complementary, especially if the ambient light is soft. Often, though, the look is either flat or quite harsh, and maybe even downright unattractive if chosen in conjunction with a mid-day sun. Attention has to be focused on shadow areas under the eyes and nose caused by an overhead sun; these can otherwise make your subjects look absolutely skeletal at times.

In winter, though, especially at higher latitudes, frontal lighting is often much more agreeable. Since the sun stays fairly low on the horizon for much of the day, facial shadows are not nearly as marked and ambient midday lighting is softer. The winter landscape, particularly open and completely snow-covered areas, is generally replete with suitable backgrounds for frontally lit subjects, owing to its inherent boldness.

The winter environment also provides natural reflection to fill facial shadow areas. More will be said about reflection and artificial lighting later. Keep in mind for now, though, that when you have no alternative but to shoot subjects frontally lit in full mid-day conditions—even in summer—you can improve things greatly by either reflecting light or by using a flash to fill shadow areas below noses and eyes.

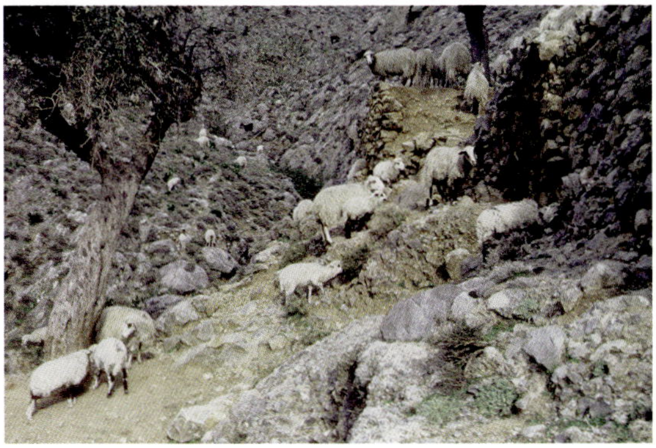

Since frontal lighting minimizes shadow areas in distant landscapes, it's often the best way to record these faithfully in all their detail. This is especially true early in the morning or late in the day, when even smaller overhead shadows disappear and the low-angled sun illuminates nearly every landscape feature.

In a high mountain meadow, for example, frontal lighting an hour or so before sunset will render the scene practically devoid of shadows and colors more or less truthfully. Distant details, such as mountain ledges or stunted trees, typically show up clearly on film, sometimes remarkably so.

Frontal lighting often provides the best illumination for wildlife too. Again, a low-angled sun in early morning and late evening will usually be most complementary, both to the wildlife subject and to the background scene. At these times of day you might also be lucky enough to record a glint of sunlight reflecting from an eye or bouncing off a canine tooth.

Sidelighting

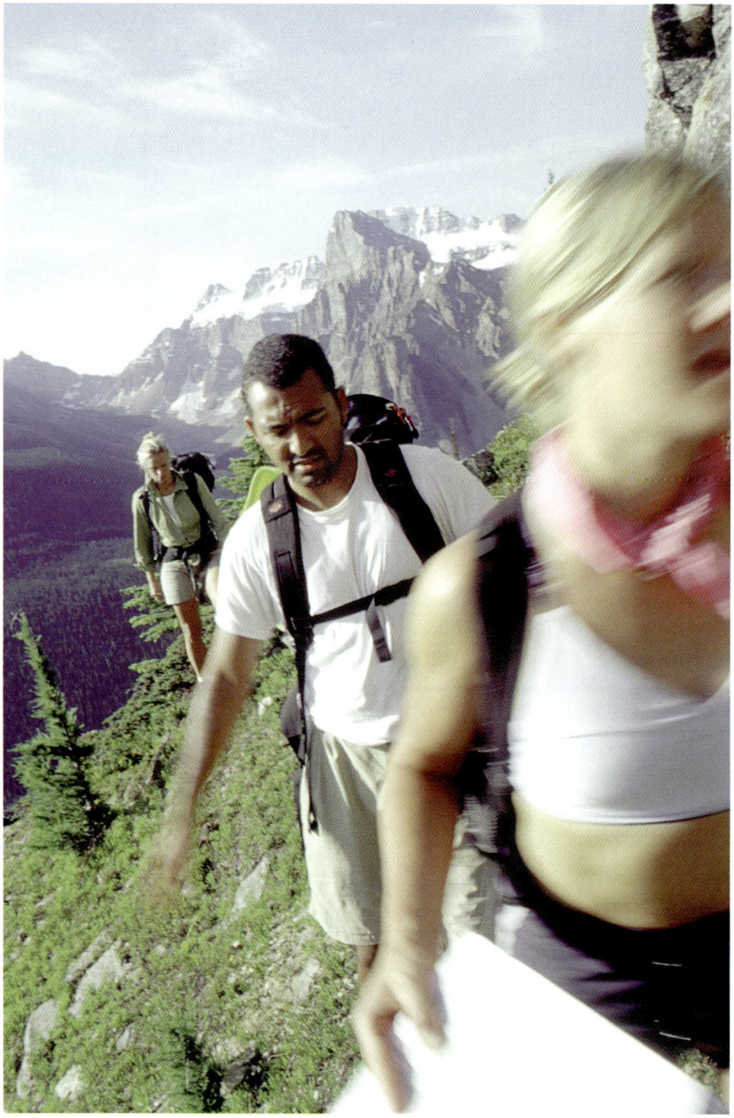

Side lighting, more than frontal or backlighting, gives definition to profiles of animal or human subjects, as in this example. Canadian Rockies. Kodak E100VS, 28 mm lens.

Sidelighting predominates when a radiant light source, such as the sun, strikes an object or scene at an angle, at least from the perspective of the viewer. When photographing sidelit scenes, the sun is neither behind you nor directly in front of you, but off to one side or the other.

There is a lot of variation in sidelighting. If the sun (or other radiant light source) is more behind you than in front, for example, some of the features of frontal lighting might be evident. Nonetheless, unless the sun is almost completely behind you, the characteristics of sidelighting will be more pronounced: your subject or scene will show more definition owing to bright and shaded areas, and therefore it will possess a more three-dimensional quality than with frontal lighting.

Similarly, if the sun is more in front than behind, your scene will start to resemble a backlit one (discussed in the next section). But, again, the three-dimensional and angular nature of sidelighting will outweigh the characteristics of backlighting, unless the sun is nearly right in front of you.

Sidelighting, especially early or late in the day, is often useful for emphasizing a subject's profile. If your subject is, for example, a male companion with a fairly well chiselled face, sidelighting will tend to enhance his angular features. This effect might then be heightened further in combination with an appropriate shoot location, say a high overlook with distant ranges of mountains below.

Likewise, with wildlife subjects sidelighting often creates a far more dramatic profile than frontal lighting does. The face of a grizzly bear, for example, that's half lit by a shaft of sunlight and half in shadow, will appear more menacing or mysterious than if fully lit. That of an elk or mountain goat will look more three–dimensional, more sculpted.

Sidelighting can also effectively dramatize the three–dimensional aspect of an alpine scene, even during mid-day. A view of mountain ranges towering over a lake is a good example. The mountain faces on one side will be strongly illuminated by sunlight, whereas slopes will be mainly shaded on the other. Depth is thus created in the scene, as eyes record distance between lit and shaded areas.

Many well known postcard scenic views of mountains show some degree of sidelighting. Often the success of these depends on having the right amount of sidelighting and choosing the best times of day to shoot. Late and early will not always work well. In some places, shadows fall so deeply at these times of day that any photo taken will record as much black as nicely lit landscape.

Consider the lake example shown here. If this were a narrow lake, hemmed in tightly by mountains, it might not even see any sunlight during the first few or last few hours of the day. An early morning or late day shot would therefore do little for the scene. Were you to photograph it sidelit at a time of day and time of year when sunlight strikes the lake's surface, on the other hand, you might just have a stellar shot.

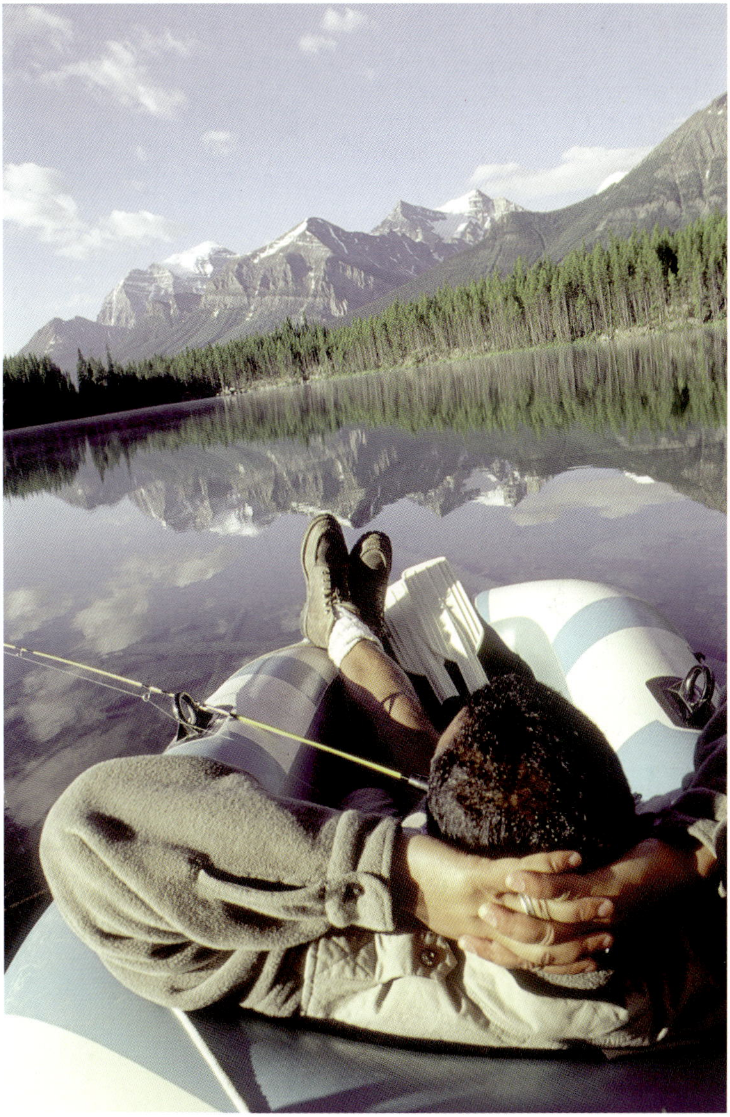

Side lighting also emphasizes the three–dimensional character of the natural world. For this reason, it is often the best form of lighting while shooting mountain landscapes. Canadian Rockies. Kodak E100VS, 20 mm lens.

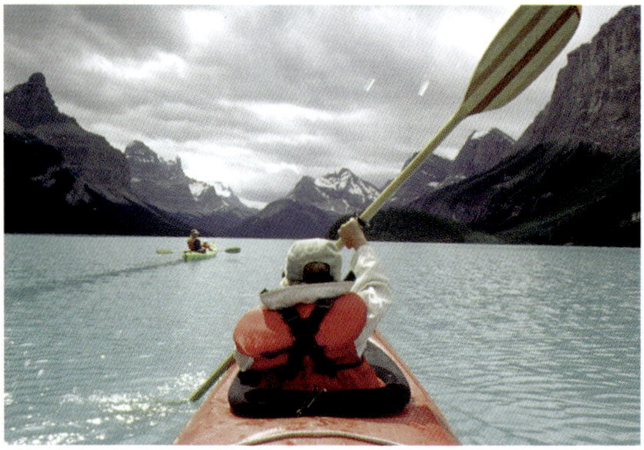

Backlit subjects are rendered softly by comparison to most frontally or sidelit ones. Water and other light–colored or reflective surfaces become ultra bright, sometimes bleaching out entirely on film. Maligne Lake, Canadian Rockies. Fuji Velvia, 28 mm lens.

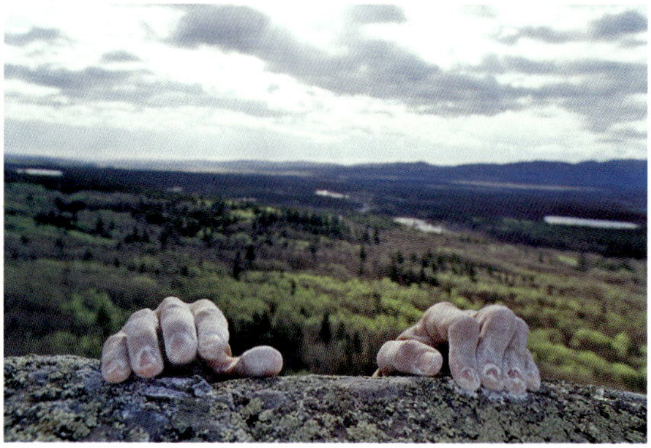

I backlit these climber's hands so that the knuckles would stand out in bold contrast to the forest areas below. The distant mountains also benefit from backlighting in this composition. Canadian Rockies. Agfa Scala, 24 mm lens.

Backlighting

When you shoot toward the sun, your subjects and the distant scene will be backlit. Depending how high the sun is relative to the horizon, backlighting effects will range from rear surface illumination to "halo" or rim illumination.

It is often the nicest lighting type of any while photographing human subjects, especially women and children. Facial features soften, lines and wrinkles are eliminated or at least subdued, and hair is brightened, sometimes to an almost ethereal point.

I remember having been told, when I picked up my first camera, to never point and shoot in the direction of the sun. I'm sure many others have received the same advice. What a mistake to follow it! Backlighting, carried out properly, is perhaps more satisfying to see in results than any other type of lighting.

Probably the best explanation for why this advice was frequently given can be summarized as follows: backlit subjects will generally turn out dark without reflection or metering; also, splotches of light–known as "lens flare"–may show up in pictures without proper shading of the camera lens.

The first issue can be rectified by simply positioning any subject near a natural reflector, such as a snow slope, or metering exposure from their faces. Alternatively, other sources of reflection and fill-in lighting can be called into use (see next sections).

To combat lens flare, all that's usually needed is a lens hood of the right size. Failing that, or to add more shielding if the sun is low on the horizon, simply holding your hand above the lens may work well. Just watch that no part of it appears through your viewfinder.

Generally speaking, backlit subjects look best against a relatively dark background. There are two reasons for this. First, any highlighted or rimlit details, such as the subject's hair, will stand out clearly, sometimes dramatically so. Second, brighter skin tones than background ones are almost always most complimentary to your subject.

Sometimes, however, a bright background might be more appropriate. If you want an entire scene to have a really ethereal, uplifting look, there is no better way to achieve that goal than to backlight a subject against a bright background. Meter exposure for the subject's face, and even overexpose beyond that reading by a 1/2 stop or so if you like.

When the sun is very low, or when your subjects are large in your frame, positioning them in a way such to block the sun can create a beautiful rimlit effect. The contours of their bodies, or edges of their garments, will be brightly lit, maybe with golden or orange hues if the sun has just risen or is about to set. You don't have to worry about lens flare at all with rimlit shots, provided, that is, that the sun is completely blocked by your subject.

Backlighting can be used to create beautiful scenics. The "layered" mountain effect that you may have seen in ads, postcards or your own photos is a result of backlighting. It is often easily achieved by simply pointing a camera in the direction of a low sun, from a vantage high above distant ranges of mountains. If there is ample atmospheric haze or humidity, layering will almost inevitably appear.

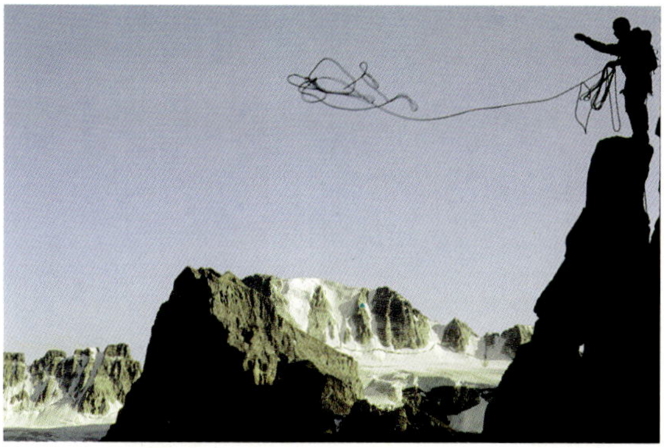

Because of a silhouette's inherent simplicity, activities are often clarified. This shot of a climber throwing his rope out before rappeling is likely more graphic than if he wasn't silhouetted. Canadian Rockies. Fuji Velvia, 105 mm lens.

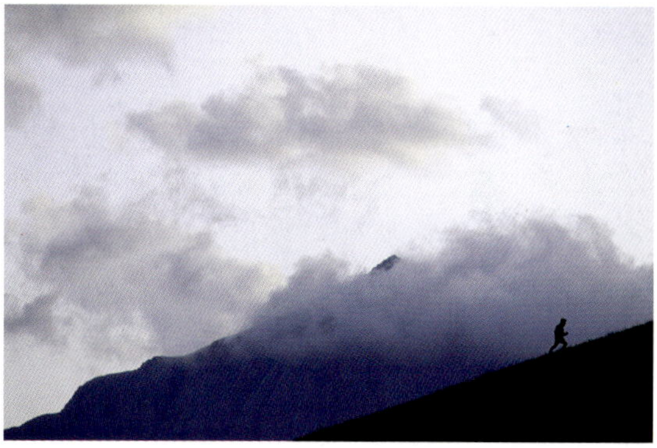

A subject usually needs to be silhouetted against sky, or some light–colored element, for it to work well. Here billowing clouds offer a barely light enough backdrop. Canadian Rockies. Fuji Velvia, 70-200 mm zoom lens.

Creating Silhouettes

Silhouettes are generally easy to find and shoot in the mountains, thanks to the availability of bright and shady areas nearly everywhere. If shot well, they can be powerful and graphic elements within a scene. Rendering subjects as silhouettes can also simplify a shoot, as exposure readings aren't required of them, of course, nor is additional lighting.

To make silhouette shots really effective, three things should be considered carefully. Does the silhouetted subject have an intriguing, or at least comprehensible, shape? Is the background interesting? And, finally, is the scene well enough lit so that your silhouettes stand in bold contrast to it (i.e. so they don't compete with other dark areas in the scene)?

The layered mountains described in the last section would be an especially nice backdrop for a silhouette of, say, a hiker enjoying the view from up high. Without enough atmospheric haze, however, or with poor timing—shooting the scene either too early or too late—dark areas of nearby mountains might not provide enough contrast to separate the silhouetted hiker from the scene.

Similarly, if the hiker was standing with legs together, and shot from behind, their profile might either be unreadable, or at least uncomplimentary. By turning the person sideways, on the other hand, or by asking them to separate their legs, the resulting silhouette would likely be more attractive and more obvious.

The very precise shape of a silhouette may, in fact, make all the difference between a good shot and a dud. The closer you get to your subject, in general, the more this holds true.

A close-up silhouetted view of a climber packing a rucksack at the base of a huge rock wall, for example, could be a very descriptive shot if done well. To make it so, the profile of the climber's face, positioning of their hands, and opening of the rucksack would all have to be clear and obvious to your viewers. If the subject was turned even slightly to one side or the other, such that their profile looked distorted, or if their hands or rucksack weren't perfectly positioned, the view would instead have little value.

In a slightly different way, silhouettes can be shot to either suggest motion or to actually depict it. Consider a silhouetted climber rappeling down a cliff. If the climber was photographed at the moment he was farthest from the rock, having pushed himself outwards, the motion of his descent might be nicely implied. So would that of a runner caught in mid-stride against a mountain backdrop.

Stop–motion of this kind relies, of course, on shooting at fairly fast shutter speeds. When photographing at slow speeds, moving parts will blur, even in silhouette. If your intent is to record this blur on film, while maintaining the shot's effectiveness, it's important that your background be simple, graphic and bright.

Shooting on Overcast Days

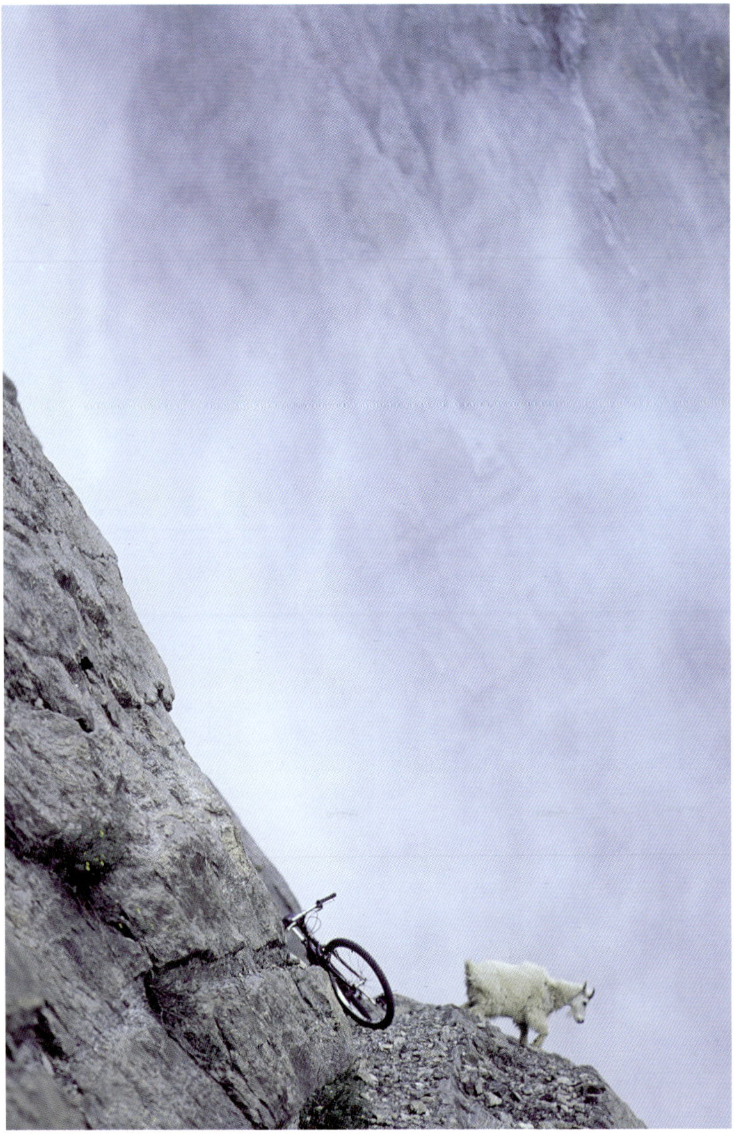

Contrasts are minimized on overcast days, at least when skies are eliminated while framing. The consequent uniformity and lack of shadows often creates an appealing simplicity. Canadian Rockies. Kodak E100VS, 28 mm lens.

The lack of sun, on any given day, is certainly no reason to keep your camera tucked away. Overcast light can be beautiful to work with, especially when your intent is to record mountain colors as faithfully as possible, or textures in all their subtlety. It can be great light with human subjects as well. There are, nonetheless, some things to watch for when shooting on overcast days.

First, it's important to realize that skies will be much brighter than anything else. Hence, if you take exposure readings for entire scenes, the result will likely be overexposed skies and underexposed foreground and background areas. Exposure readings must be geared instead to specific subjects or parts of scenes you have chosen to shoot.

A hiker, for example, crossing an alpine meadow on an overcast day will probably look disappointingly underexposed on film if a camera's light meter is used to determine exposure for the whole scene. How underexposed really depends on the composition of the scene. If it's mainly sky, and the surrounding mountains are quite small and distant, the hiker might be two or even three stops underexposed; in other words, not much more than a dark blob.

Say, however, you're lucky enough to record the person hemmed in against a background of relatively dark rock walls and little sky. The hiker might not be underexposed at all, or so slightly at least that they and the scene still look fine on film.

In effect, what you've done is to gear exposure to the hiker, which coincidentally, happens also to be the proper exposure for your scene. Of course you'd have been better off taking an exposure reading right from the hiker if your intent was to record just the hiker properly exposed. Or, better still, compare light readings from the hiker and average background surface to see if one setting would keep both nicely exposed.

This example points to one of the creative choices often made while shooting in overcast light: the elimination, or at least minimization, of sky areas. If you are properly exposing for a landscape or subject, the sky will always bleach out in any case. Such a stark whiteness often contrasts cruelly with important parts of a scene, drawing attention away from them.

Shooting below the horizon, so that the sky is eliminated, is generally not that difficult with a lens longer than 70 mm. With normal and especially wide–angle lenses it can sometimes be tricky. Often the best approach with wide lenses is to shoot slightly downwards onto a landscape or subject.

Say you want to shoot an entire aspen forest in beautiful autumn color during overcast weather. A slightly raised shooting position, perhaps offered by a nearby mountain slope, might reward you with a perfect perspective whereby you can employ a wide lens and still avoid recording any sky.

Or you may choose to shoot in the forest instead, maybe with a longer lens where foreground elements and background ones are selectively placed in and out of focus. Chances are, however, that you won't want to shoot looking even slightly upwards, or with a wide lens. Otherwise, a bleached-out overcast sky may dominate your scene.

Overcast weather softens portraits and renders landscape colors faithfully, as long as ambient light is strong enough. Canadian Rockies. Fuji Velvia, 105 mm lens.

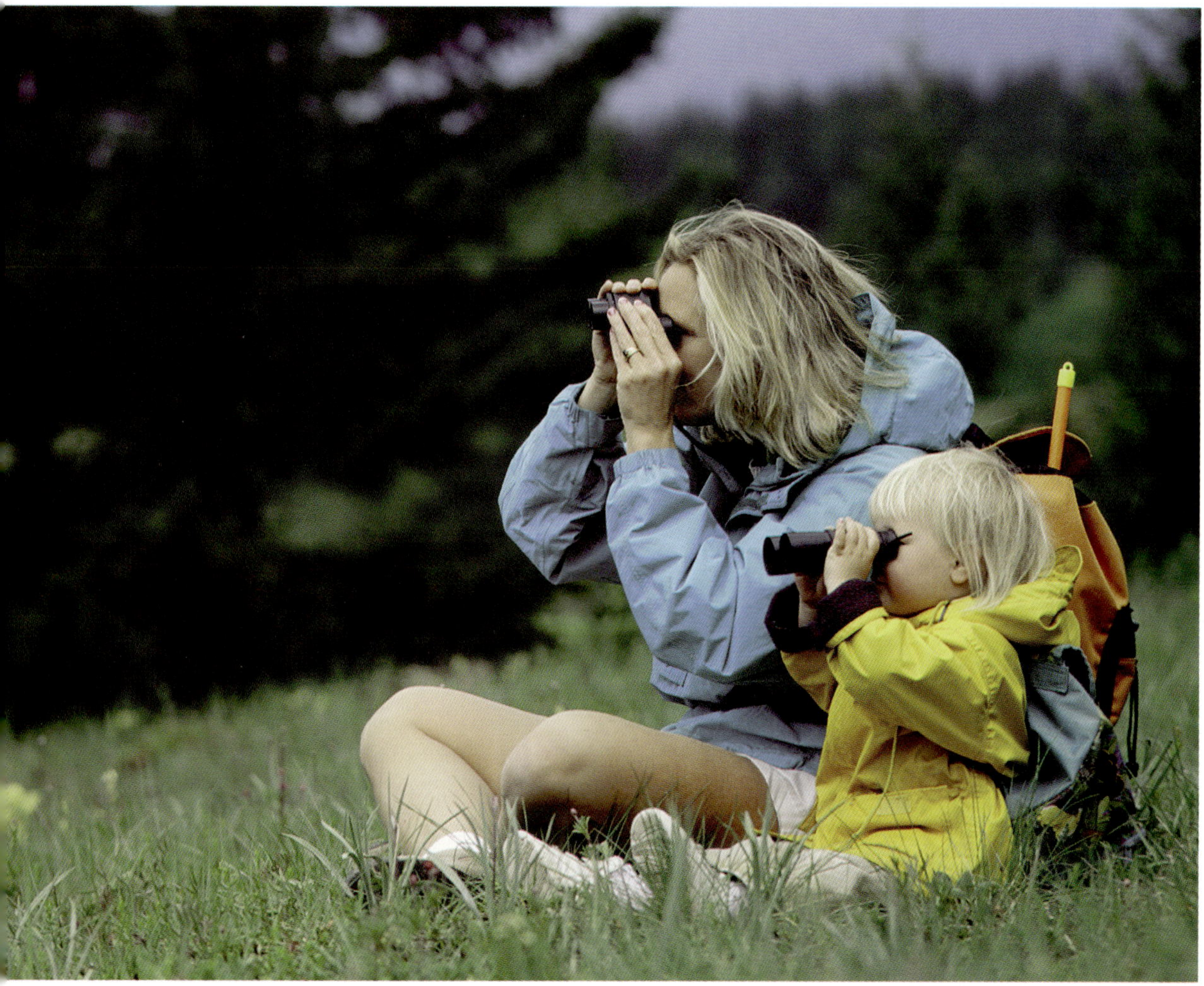

Bright Overcast Lighting

Bright overcast conditions predominate when there is some sun filtering through the clouds. They provide some of the nicest lighting for human, wildlife and other nature subjects, especially when there's a uniform, but light, cloud cover across the sky

There are two reasons this kind of lighting works so well. First, ambient brightness is always strong enough to fully illuminate subjects and to provide muted backlighting, sidelighting and front lighting effects. Cold blue tones are minimized, as well, since the sky itself is more white than blue. The effect, on film, is much warmer–looking skin, fur and vegetation colors.

Note, however, that it is still generally wise to eliminate or minimize the sky from most compositions on bright overcast days. Even though contrast between the sky and subjects will be lower than on heavy overcast days, there is still more than your eyes will register. Such contrast will likely exceed film tolerances. Moreover, the sky is usually uninteresting on most bright overcast days, and therefore not worth emphasizing or even including in your shots.

Shooting from above is again often complimentary to a scene or to subjects in this kind of light. And, unlike photography on darker overcast days, you needn't shoot subjects at slow shutter speeds or narrow depths of field.

Consider, for example, photographing a climber struggling up to your belay perch. An overhead perspective could keep the climber and the distant ground both in relative focus if overcast light was bright enough. Yet, shadows, whether on the rock face or climber's face, would become soft and attractive. These might be quite unsightly if the sky was clear.

Or think about photographing a mountain biker tearing down a trail from above. Bright overcast light would allow you to shoot him at a speed that, even with slow film, would stop his motion, or at least show an acceptable amount of blurring. Both he, and the surrounding terrain would also be rendered in a fairly monochromatic way, without deep shadow areas.

As mentioned earlier, this kind of light is also bright enough to provide subtle backlighting and sidelighting characteristics. These can be used to great effect with both human and wildlife subjects, in the same ways, although more delicately than with a full sun. Everything is less contrasty than on really sunny days, including background features.

It can be the best light for close-up nature photography as well. Because the sky is like a great white dome on bright overcast days, the greens of vegetation and vivid colors of flowers record honestly. They possess neither the blue tones from a reflected sky nor the overly warm tones from a setting sun. Yet bright overcast weather provides enough light that a reasonable depth of field may be chosen while using slow film, often an important consideration for this kind of shooting (see later section on close-up photography).

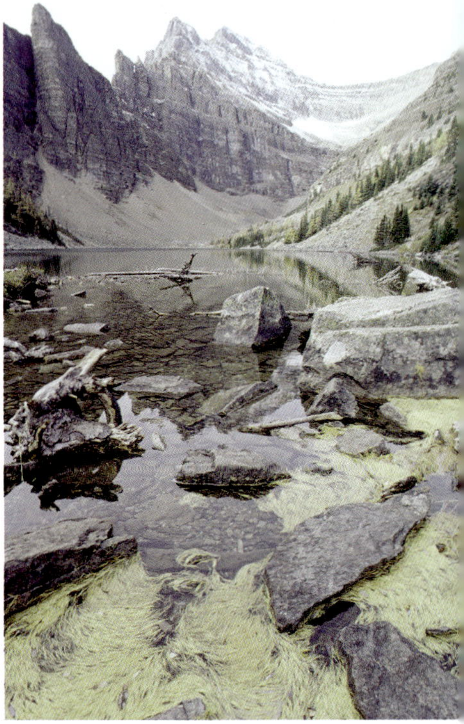

When overcast light is bright enough, both foreground details and distant mountains will be within acceptable contrast tolerance ranges for most films. Lake Agnes, Canadian Rockies. Kodak E100VS, 20 mm lens.

Bright overcast light is often best while shooting alpine flowers. Colors are rendered truthfully, without unkind blue tones, and higher shutter speeds or wider depth of fields can be chosen. Alpenrose, Austria. Fuji Velvia, 55 mm lens.

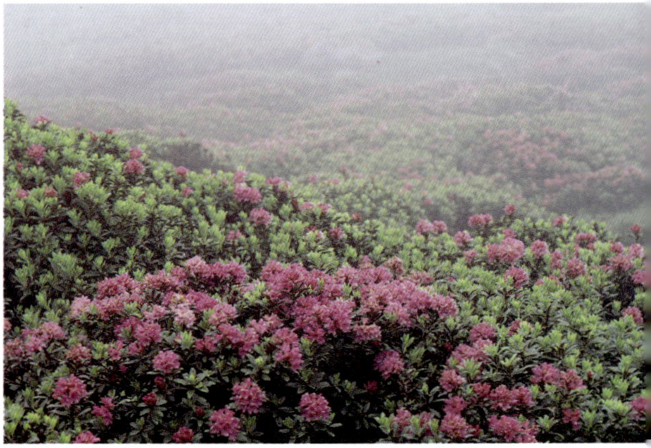

Partially Cloudy Weather

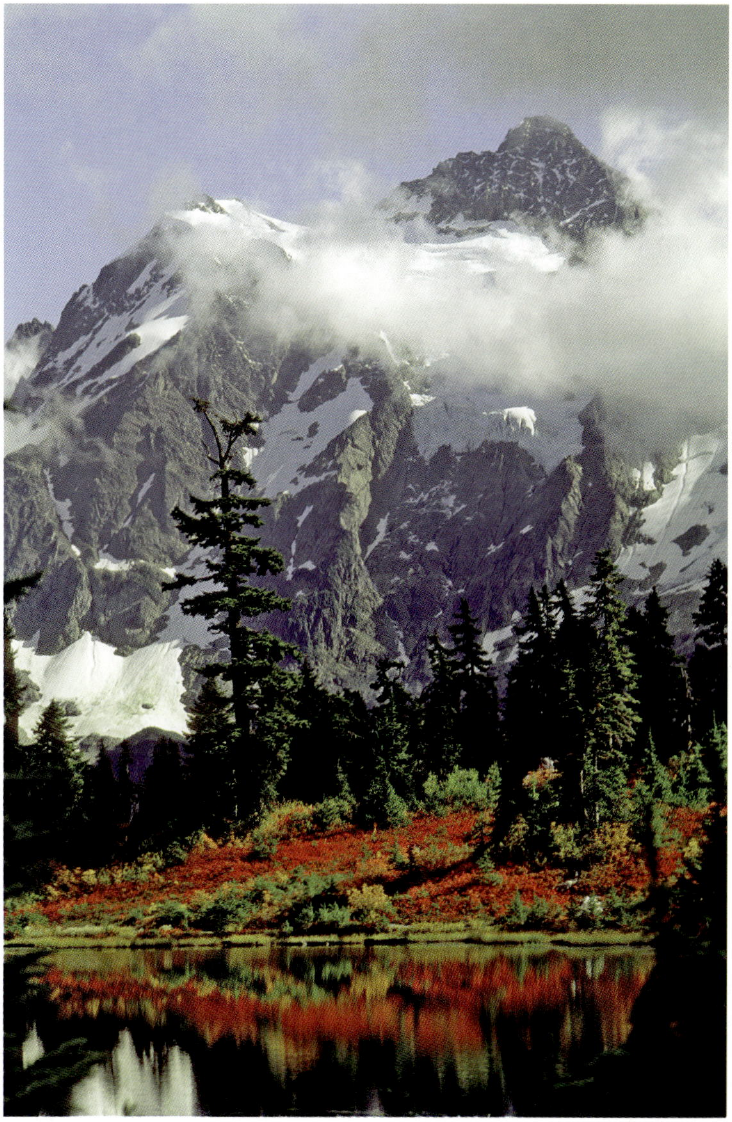

Partly cloudy weather is often best for shooting mountain landscapes. Clouds might either be low and billowy such as these, or higher with spectacular streaks and other patterns. Mount Shuksan, Washington. Fuji Velvia, 35-70 mm zoom lens.

A mix of sun and clouds is generally much more dramatic, especially when shooting scenics, than a perfectly clear sky. This is particularly true when clouds are either big billowy puffballs, menacing thunderheads, or wispy cirrus formations.

In many cases, the presence of interesting clouds will be reason enough to photograph a scene. In others, they might simply complement an already beautiful mountain view, making a photographic record of it more enticing.

Dramatic or picturesque clouds might also add the requisite degree of drama to make a sports action or wildlife shoot worthwhile. Consider the effect rendered by billowing clouds behind a lone mountain biker descending a steep mountain slope, for example, or by wispy streaks above a ground–level perspective as he races past. Or, similarly, that created by lofty clouds clinging to a mountain face just above a herd of wild sheep.

The important thing to watch for while shooting under a partially cloudy sky are cloud shadows. Often these can be used to benefit such as when, for example, dark distant shadows highlight foreground subjects. As often, however, they become problematic.

If cloud shadows fall on already dark areas of a scene, such as an evergreen forest, black or nearly black areas on film may result. Eyes can't always be relied upon to judge how dark such areas are relative to the rest of the scene; film, especially contrasty types, will exaggerate these. When in doubt, the best advice is to try metering off dark and bright areas in your scene. If the difference is more than four stops, you may want to try recomposing to avoid the darkest areas.

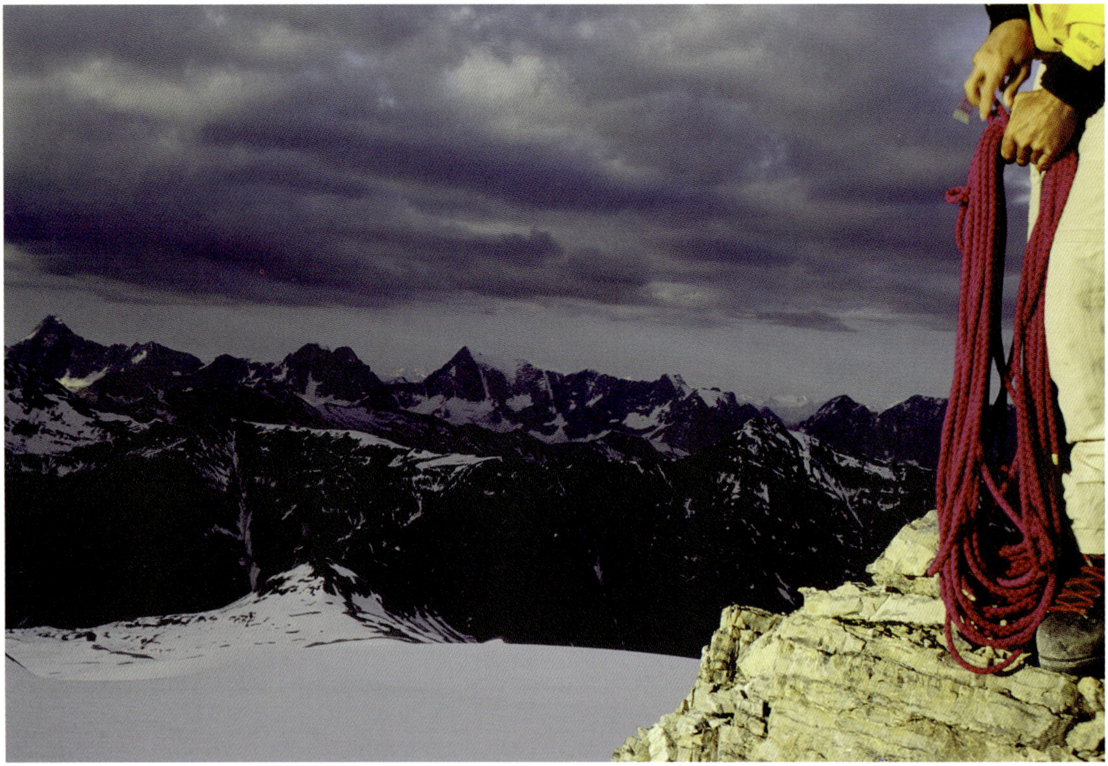

Clouds that cast shadows over foreground areas of interest can be problematic. The opposite, where shadows are cast over distant mountains and foreground areas are well lit, usually works better. Canadian Rockies. Fuji Velvia, 105 mm lens.

Cloud shadows may also give rise to harsh, cold tones from reflected blue sky. With foreground subjects, especially human or wildlife ones, these can be very unattractive. Skin tones are particularly vulnerable to a cold rendering. Even scenic features, though, such as alpine foliage, can easily lose any warmth they possess when cast in a blue–tinged shadow.

Of course, this cold blue light can be used to a positive effect at times as well. If your intent is to exaggerate the cold look of a scene, it might work wonders. For example, if you were to shoot past snow-covered rocks or trees to distant snowy peaks in the shade of a mainly clear day, the overall feeling would be very northern, very chilly. A closer view, say of an ice climber ascending a frozen waterfall, would likewise look perhaps colder than it actually was.

Fill-in Light

Reflected light is often as important to the creation of successful photographs as radiant light. Although generally more subtle in nature, it can be used powerfully to illuminate shadow areas that might otherwise record black or deeply underexposed. In some cases, it may—by default—even assume the role of primary illumination source.

Anything that doesn't actually emit light, but merely redirects it, could be considered a reflected light source. This really means nearly any surface, though, of course, some will reflect a lot more light than others.

In the mountains, good reflected light sources are unusually easy to come by. Snow, naturally, is one of the best ones. Water surfaces may also reflect light strongly, depending on the angle of the sun. Even rocks, especially light-colored ones, can be powerful light reflectors.

Our eyes routinely observe the effect of reflected sunlight, even if no mental notes are taken. A hiking companion's face, for example, may appear suddenly well illuminated as she stops to fill her water bottle in a creek, though the sun remains behind her and doesn't change in intensity. Likewise, a mountaineering partner may become completely illuminated, although still in deep shadow, as he passes close to an ice gully catching the full force of the sun's rays.

The trick is simply to "see" beautifully reflected natural light. Subject placement and lighting angle choices will generally follow quite easily.

Watch for exceptional opportunities created by natural reflections. Say, for example, you notice great reflected sunlight on a nearby knoll, created by the glint from a large cascade of water. If you're with several companions, this may be an ideal location for a group shot. You will likely be able to keep subjects small in the shot relative to surroundings, if you want, since the isolated area of bright reflected light will act as a sort of large spotlight.

Naturally reflected light, from a nearby snowbank, brightens dark areas in the woman's face and improves shadow details across the feeding gray jay. Coast Mountains, Canada. Fuji film, 85 mm lens.

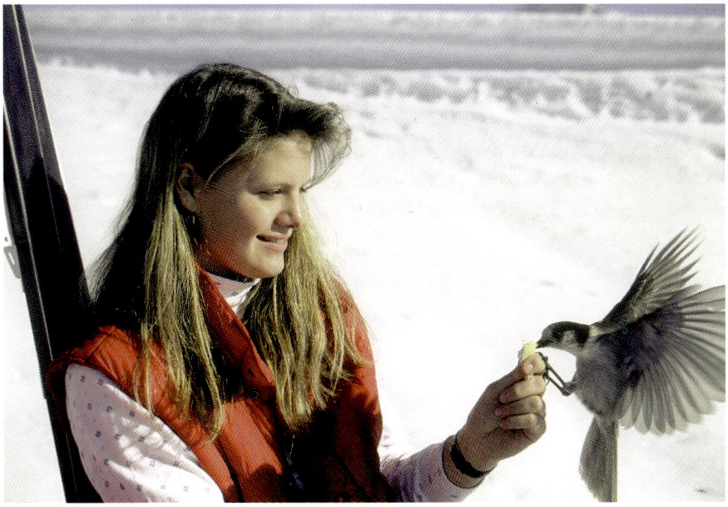

These illustrations might suggest that good reflective surfaces will be readily available in the natural landscape and will show up exactly where you want them. More often, though, they won't. When they're not, a simple handheld reflector is an invaluable accessory, especially for illuminating smallish subjects.

I keep a couple of these always handy amongst my camera gear. One is a small, fold-up device that fits neatly inside the flap of my camera bag and goes with me almost everywhere. Very light in weight, it has one white side and the other gold, in the event I need to add "warmth" to a chosen subject or scene. My bigger reflector is, quite simply, a whitish sheet that I use to illuminate larger areas or bigger subjects.

Almost any neutral-colored thing will do in a pinch though. A light-toned jacket, a white T-shirt, or even the back of a map can be improvised in the absence of a dedicated reflector. The larger the item, of course, the more reflecting surface you have. But even a T-shirt or map would be adequate to reflect light neatly into a subject's face.

Reflected light is most commonly used by photographers to "fill", or brighten, dark areas when backlighting or sidelighting subjects. Faces particularly benefit from good light reflection. Dark areas below noses and eyes can be reduced or even eliminated completely while sidelighting; a backlit face can be rendered two or three stops lighter with good reflection.

Other body parts may benefit from reflection too. A hand stretching onto a tenuous hold might not look really dramatic when viewed through your lens if poorly lit. By reflecting sunlight onto it, either to illuminate the whole hand better or simply to reduce shadow areas created by the fingers, it should command a lot more attention.

Sometimes it will be wildlife subjects or inanimate objects that you'll want to reflect light towards. Although large mammals may not typically be the best subjects for practising your reflection techniques on, smaller animals are certainly fair game, especially the slower moving ones.

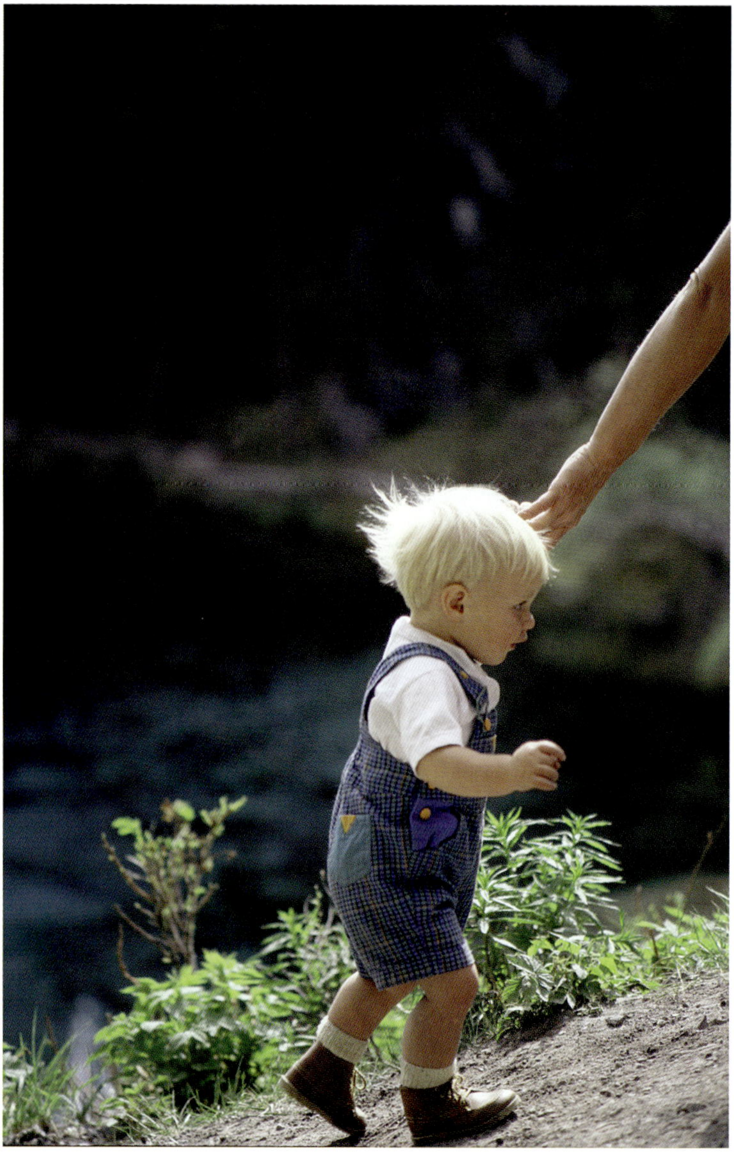

A yellow-gray rock wall bounced light onto the arm and young hiker in this shot, warming them more than if a pure white reflector had been used. Canadian Rockies. Fuji Velvia, 105 mm lens.

Wildflower shots usually benefit from ample light reflection. And interesting foreground rocks, or other smallish landforms, also can be made more prominent and eye-catching with additional reflected light.

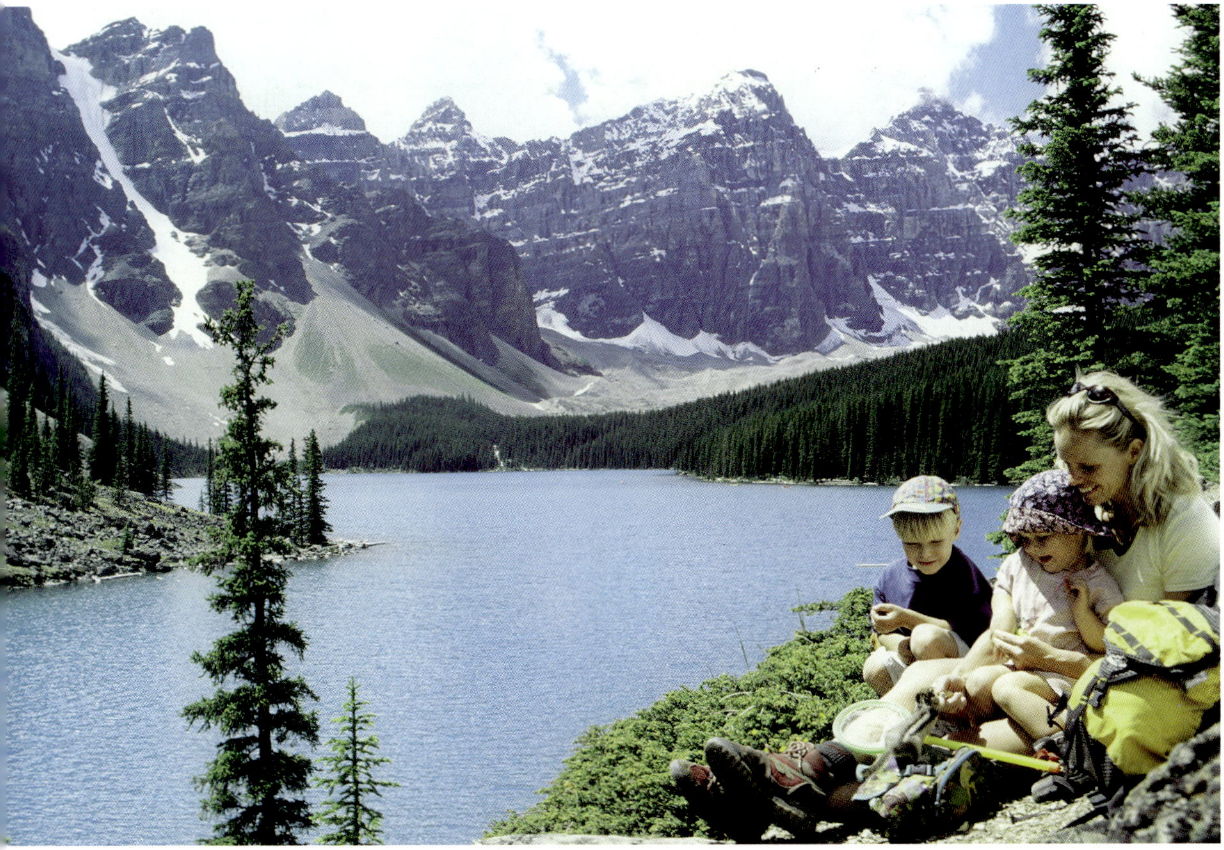

To reduce contrast between the bright areas of this scene and the darker faces, I employed a white sheet for reflection. It was strung up in a tree just off the right side of the frame. Moraine Lake, Canadian Rockies. Fuji Velvia, 28 mm lens.

Reflecting Light Purposely

How much reflected light is desirable really depends on the specific intent of a photograph. If your main purpose is just to evenly light an area of a shot, or to balance subject tones with those of the background, then your eyes can best tell you whether you're reflecting enough light or not.

If, however, you decide you'd like a subject to either stand out from its surroundings, or to show up darker than other elements, then reflection should be varied accordingly.

For example, if you want a sidelit subject's face to be prominent against a busy or complex backdrop, more pronounced reflection might provide suitably exaggerated brightness. On the other hand, if the gleam of a subject's eye is all you want to show against a dark backdrop, then only very subtle reflection would probably work best.

The point is that reflection should be used with intention. Just as choosing a certain lighting angle or creative style will substantially alter the mood of a given composition, so too will the quantity of reflected light.

And the quality of it. Natural reflectors, such as snow, rock and water, reflect light in subtly different color tones and, sometimes, textures. A yellowish rock wall, for example, will reflect light with an overall yellow tone. A rippled water surface will reflect light with an uneven texture.

These tones and textures may or may not suit skin and clothing features. In general, off-white smooth surfaces reflect the most complimentary light into faces and other areas of skin. Ripple patterns reflected onto a subject's face, by contrast, often look unsightly, or overly busy. And a strong yellow color cast might make a subject look jaundiced.

Sometimes, however, the reverse is true. A simply warmer than normal skin tone generally looks great, and reflected light patterns can add intrigue and mystery to a shot. When in doubt, stop for a moment to consider whether the effect you've created, or observed, is in fact well suited to the scene about to be photographed. Alternatively, shoot the scene and study the effect later.

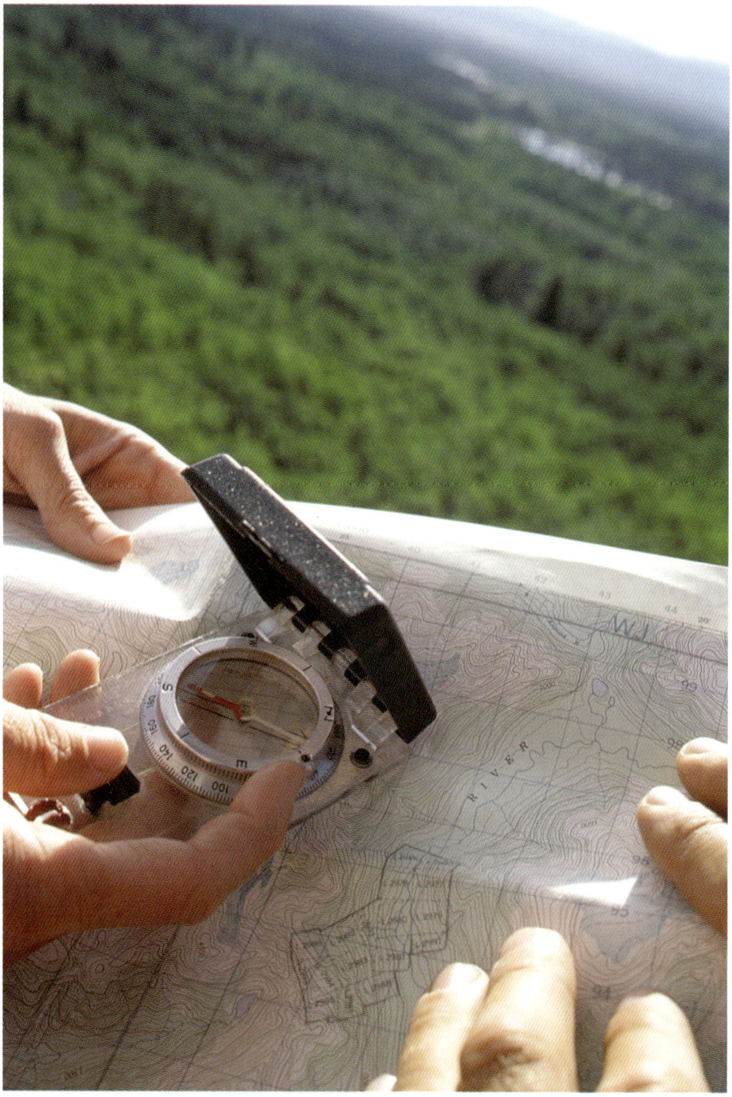

I used a small foldable reflector to add a little light to this shot, both to reduce contrast between light and dark finger areas and also to make the map more readable. Canadian Rockies. Fuji Velvia, 24 mm lens.

Opposite, left: A subtle flash could have been called upon to brighten skin areas a little more in this infrared composition. The greenish tones would then likely have disappeared altogether. Moraine Lake, Canadian Rockies. Kodak EIR, 28 mm lens, yellow 15 filter.

Opposite, right: I used a flash to subtly backlight this shot, mainly because of the awkwardness of trying to string up a large enough reflector to illuminate my subjects in their entirety. Canadian Rockies, Fuji Velvia, 70-200 mm zoom lens.

Filling with a Flash

In addition to its role as a primary light source, a flash accessory can also be used to "backfill" light onto a subject's face or over larger areas.

Unless the flash is used carefully and sparingly, however, the effect rendered might be quite artificial looking. Instead of recording subjects as though belonging to the surrounding environment, they may appear to stand radically apart from it.

This is especially true when shooting near sunset or sunrise. Most camera flashes are intended to closely replicate full daylight conditions. Hence, their illumination lacks any of the warmth that characterizes these times of day. Foreground objects illuminated by a flash will appear harsh and overbright in comparison to naturally lit background scenery.

The intense quality of direct flashed light might also be problematic during mid-day hours. It tends to make skin shiny looking, and at times overblown. Surfaces closer to or more perpendicular to, a flash will be especially illuminated, and vice-versa for ones farther away or parallel to the flash direction. Hence, even across a subject's face, for example, a camera's flash may create unacceptable areas of contrast.

These problems can largely be overcome with additional accessories or techniques. When shooting around sunrise or sunset, all that is generally required to more closely replicate the existing quality of light is to place an orange-colored filter over the flash lens (note, however, that doing so will reduce the flash's light output. Hence, flash settings will have to be adjusted to increase the amount of illumination).

In the absence of a proper filter, colored garments can also be strapped over the flash lens to change the color of flashed light. The color of such garments obviously has to be chosen carefully to approximate ambient light tones. Also, the thicker the garment material is, the more upwards adjustment is needed in flash output.

While shooting during mid-day, a "diffusion" filter can be added to the flash lens to reduce the harsh quality of flashed light. These are uncolored, somewhat opaque, and usually have a textured lens surface. White gauze material, such as that from your medical kit, will likely suffice if you don't have one. Again, a flash's output has to be increased to compensate for lost light with filtration.

Alternatively, flashed light can be bounced off a bright surface that is either angled towards, or perpendicular to, a subject. As with the filters discussed above, a flash's output will have to be increased while bouncing. How much depends on the brightness of the bounce surface, as well as the distance from this surface to the subject. In most cases, however, the increase will be significant, more than if you simply add a filter to the flash lens.

A problem with all these approaches is that they're somewhat hit and miss. It's difficult, especially on the spur of the moment, to perfectly match a flash's colored filter (or the color of a chosen garment) to soft, ambient light tones. And it's even harder to gauge the brightness of bounced light, unless, of course, you're bouncing off a known reflector at a measured distance.

If you are, and there exists even muted sunlight, then the question that must be asked is, why use a flash at all? Naturally reflected light can be easily controlled and measured with the simplest of accessories. This is why, when shooting in the mountains, I'll almost always take along a lightweight reflector, but often leave my flash at home.

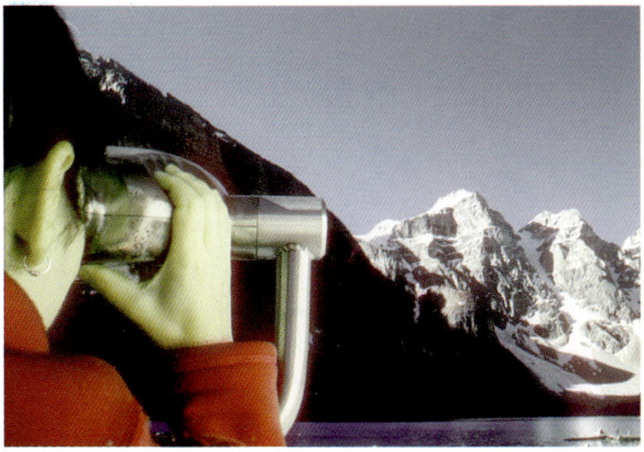

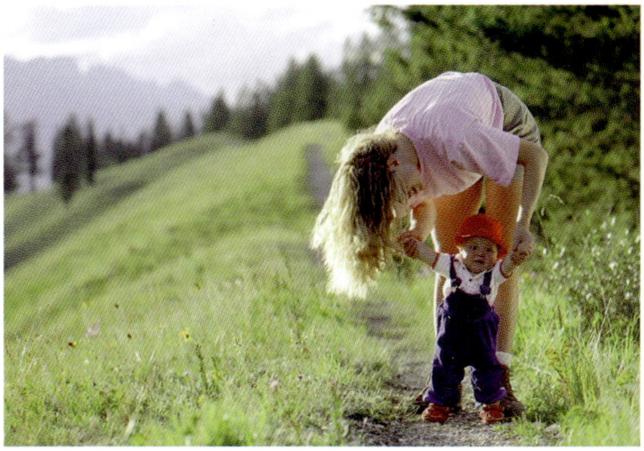

Creative Flash Use

Opposite: The tent was illuminated by a flash in this photograph. A lantern could also probably have been used, and perhaps with more accuracy. Canadian Rockies. Kodak E100VS, 28 mm lens.

Your flash doesn't always have to be used in a basic capacity as either a primary or secondary light source though. Sometimes it can be put to pure creative effect, or it can be utilized to just accent an otherwise photo-worthy occurrence.

Consider a really intense snowstorm in the mountains, where the flakes are big and flying furiously. A scenic shot of this or one of, say, a distant backcountry skier amongst trees, should show some of the snowfall's intensity. But using a flash to illuminate the closest flakes may render the photo absolutely eye-catching instead.

Highlighting with a flash is very easy at times like this. Once you've determined the exposure and depth of field you want, simply attach the flash either directly to your camera or via a cable attachment, turn it on and take the shot. The flash does the rest. If you use a slow shutter speed in conjunction with a flash, you will dramatize the falling flakes even more.

Your flash can also be used to highlight certain areas of a shot while leaving the rest comparatively dark. This is a great way of drawing attention to a subject that would otherwise be unnoticeable, or simply nondescript.

For example, a pair of hands gripping the lip of a cliff might make an interesting photographic study, particularly if warranted by a spectacular background. However, unless natural illumination on the hands was strong enough, they would probably just fade into the background, maybe eluding your viewers' attention altogether.

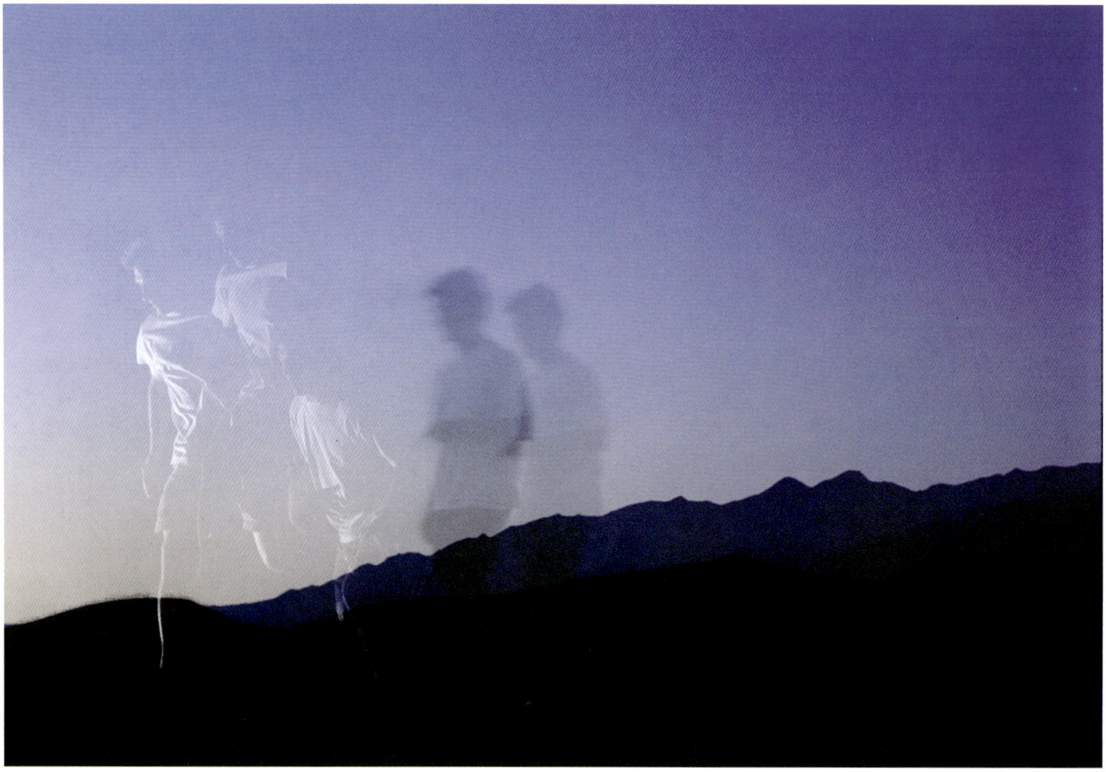

The runner's "ghost" effect was created by firing a flash several times during the long exposure required for this shot. Such experimental flash photography will commonly reward you with unique results, although not always successful ones. Death Valley, California. Fuji Velvia, 35 mm lens.

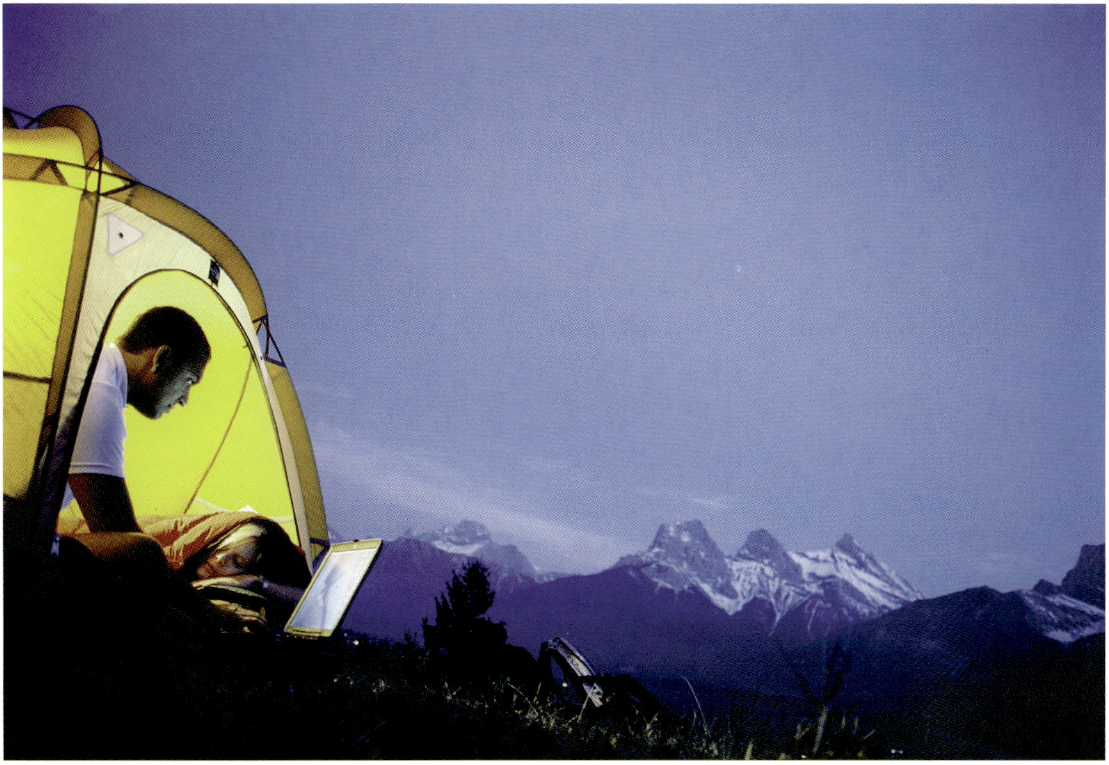

Careful flashing could have them "pop" out without discrediting the rest of the scene. It could also subdue confusing shadow areas created by fingers.

The trick, just as with fill-in lighting, is not to go overboard with your flash. Trying to eliminate shadows completely, or to brighten the hands excessively, will likely do more harm than bring credit to your composition.

Sometimes "going over the top" with your flash may not be a bad thing though. If your location or the existing illumination are unusual in any way, a flash can add a bizarre, yet somehow believable, effect.

For example, say you and your companions happen to be descending from a climb through gargoyles or pinnacles of ice around twilight. You notice that their headlamps cast an eerie glow amongst the surroundings, giving the whole scene an other-worldly effect. You determine, however, that there's not enough light illuminating faces to show their identities, especially from the somewhat distant perspective you've chosen. Flashing one or more of their faces during a time exposure may be exactly what's needed. Once you've set your camera on a tripod, give one of your companions a flash and instructions to trigger it back toward his/her face when you give the word. Then simply start the shot, yell "fire" and wait for the time exposure to end.

Of course any such flash will need a manual trigger that can be tripped when taken off a camera. You will probably want to turn the flash intensity down to its lowest level, both for the comfort of your friends (a full flash burst at short range is painful!) and also so that their faces don't bleach out too much. If you want, you can cover the flash head with gauze or colored fabric to change the quality of output (see page 169).

Note that your flash can be used as a spot lighting source in other situations too. Try illuminating different parts of a scene while your camera is set-up for a time exposure. You can literally walk around triggering it throughout the exposure and, unless you point it at yourself, no one will even know you were in the shot.

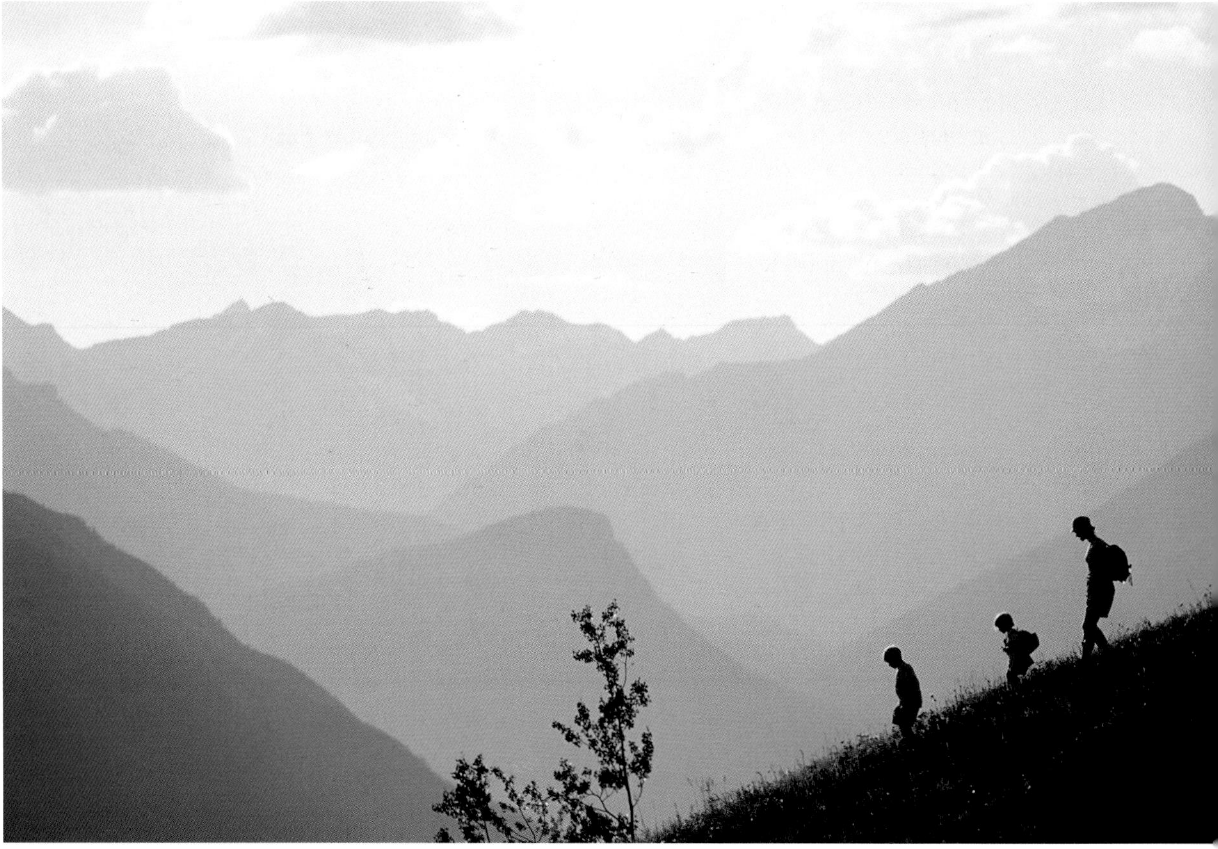

Atmospheric haze really makes this shot. Without it, the hikers would not stand out anywhere as clearly and the mountains would lack their moodiness. Canadian Rockies. Fuji Velvia, 180 mm lens.

Dealing with Haze and Lens Flare

Atmospheric, or ultraviolet (UV), haze and lens flare crop up routinely, at times ruining otherwise "perfect" photographs. Too much atmospheric haze results in photographs with an overly bluish tone, and somewhat diffused looking distant vistas. Lens flare shows up as colored blotches, usually oblique circles or hexagons, where the sun strikes the lens surface and causes distortion.

Both can be dealt with—to some extent at least—by selecting appropriate filters or lens hoods. But, as with many other things in photography, what appear to be problems at first can often be utilized, after a little thought, to heighten creativity.

First to the technical solutions though. UV filters, attached in front of virtually any camera lens, usually reduce atmospheric haze substantially, although they probably won't eliminate it entirely. How much reduction depends mainly on your lens choice, the height of the sun and the shooting angle you select.

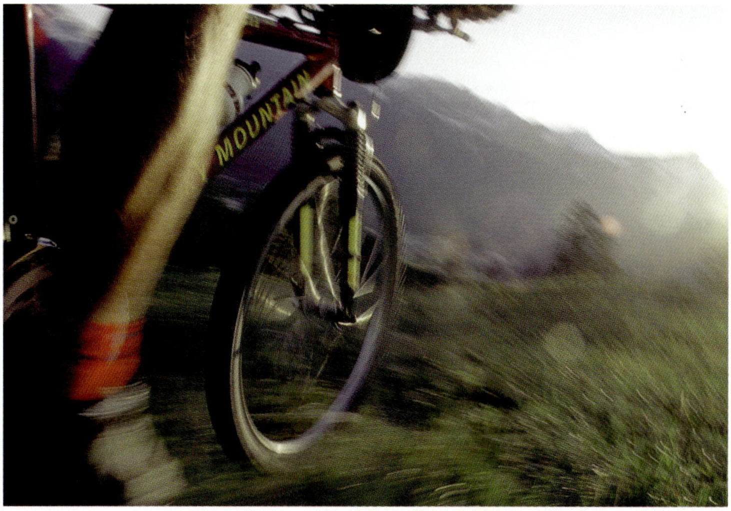

Lens flare on the right side of the frame adds to the sense of speed created by the biker. Even if I had wanted to, it's unlikely that I could have eliminated the flare with a lens hood, since the shot very nearly includes the sun. Canadian Rockies. Fuji Velvia, 24 mm lens.

Lens flare can be similarly reduced, although again not eliminated, by using a hood appropriate to the manufacture and focal length of a given lens. Except with very wide lenses, flare should be virtually nonexistent. Unless, that is, you're shooting directly into the sun, in which case it's nearly impossible to avoid recording some flare.

In the absence of a proper lens hood, a hand held against the lens in a shielding fashion will probably suffice. When blocking the sun in this way, it's important to ensure that your fingers don't fall into the field of view. As long as you're careful, with an SLR camera at least, this is never an issue: if you can't see any of your hand through the viewfinder at the time of shooting, it won't appear on film later.

With a rangefinder camera, however, it's quite another story. The best advice if you're using one of these is to stick to proper lens hoods at all times.

In some cases, you might decide that you don't want to eliminate all, or even most of, the ambient UV haze or lens flare. Consider, for example, a scene showing your hiking companion standing on a ridge crest with range upon range of peaks in the distance. There is substantial haze in the view that builds with each more distant range. You notice, while looking through your viewfinder, that your companion seems literally to be perched above a "sea of peaks". Why would you want to reduce that impression by filtering out haze?

Similarly, while shooting a fellow skier backlit on a slope, you notice flare marks through your viewfinder, which you know will translate onto film later. However, if anything, these marks intuitively seem to suggest more speed, or dynamic flow. Are you really sure you want to eliminate them?

The presence of lens flare will suggest something altogether different to your viewers than its absence. Most importantly, it draws attention to the very act of photography, thereby confirming the photographer's creative role.

Trumpeting your participation as a photographer is, of course, not always a positive thing. But if your intention, as much as anything else, is to leave the imprint of your creativity on a certain photograph, then this device, along with others, may be a useful way to achieve that aim.

Faithfully Recording Skies at Sunset and Sunrise

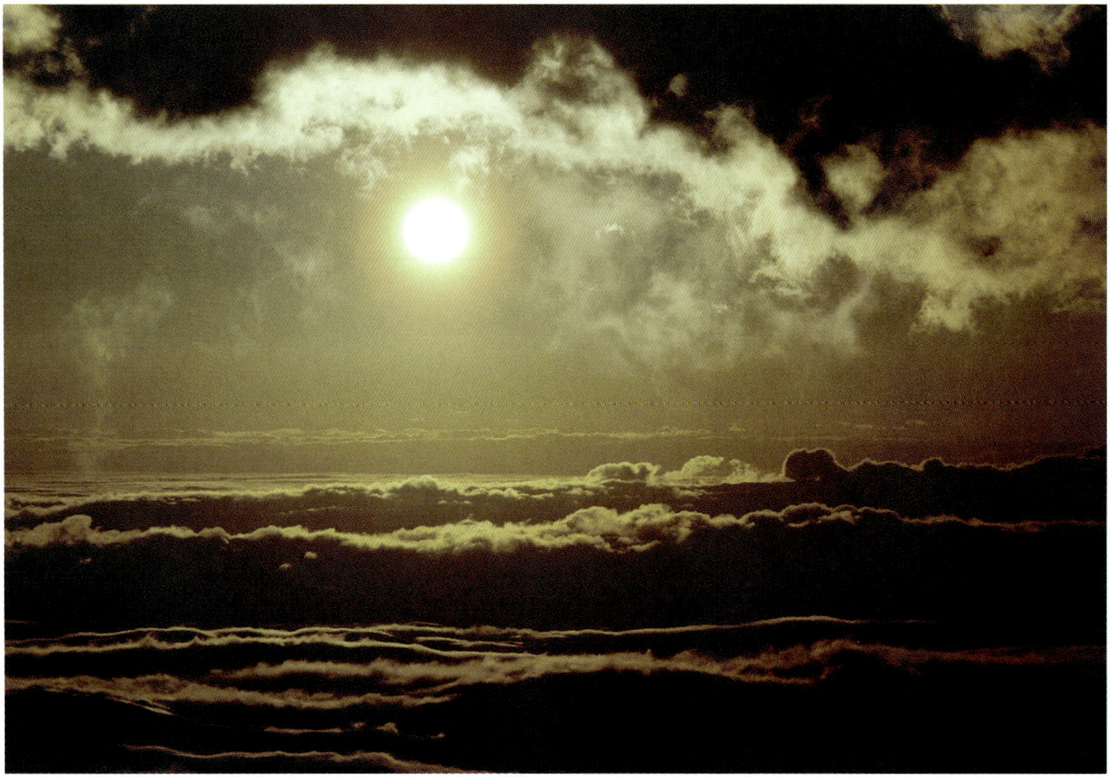

This photograph was snapped from an unplanned bivouac at nearly 14,000 feet. With the camera set on automatic, I simply pointed and shot, probably because I was too cold to do much else. Colorado Rockies. Kodachrome, 200 mm lens.

Recording the true colors of a beautiful sunrise or sunset is easier than most novice photographers are apt to believe. There is no real trick involved. All that's generally required is to point your camera towards the sky, take a light reading, set your camera at the determined setting and shoot.

Where most errors occur is in reading the scene as a whole, instead of just sky. Bear in mind that at the moment of sunrise or sunset, there is no light except in the sky. Hence, if you're taking a reading from a scene which is, say, half sky and half landscape, the light reading provided by your camera will inevitably overexpose the sky, while underexposing everything else.

Another typical mistake is to take a reading with the setting sun centered in your frame. Most camera light meters are centre weighted, that is, the bulk of a light reading will be determined by whatever is at the middle of your frame. Since the sun will always register considerably brighter than other parts of a sky, reading this way tends to underexpose final results, sometimes radically.

Getting around such snags is actually very easy. Point your camera at an area of sky that is neither brightest nor darkest, or take a reading from the most compelling part of it. If you're using a very wide lens, try to fill the frame with as much sky as you can.

Just be sure not to centre the sun in your frame. Unless, of course, you want to include it on its own, or as the major feature in a shot. Then, as long as the sun is at or close to the horizon, you should get a reasonably accurate reading while simply pointing your camera close to it, determining exposure and shooting.

Note that you'll probably want to use a fairly long lens, say 100 mm or longer, when shooting the rising or setting sun on its own. Anything much less than this tends to minimalize the sun, while allowing other elements in the frame to overwhelm.

Needless to say, be careful while doing so. Just as looking directly at the sun can blind you, so too can looking at it through your viewfinder. The sun's intensity will increase as your lens size elongates as well, such that as really long focal lengths, say 500 mm and up, blindness is an especially grave possibility.

Always wear sunglasses when shooting directly into the sun. And even while wearing them, try to glance only obliquely towards it while looking through your viewfinder.

Also, don't leave your camera pointed directly at the sun for any length of time, especially when a telephoto lens is mounted. The intensive radiation, conveyed through lens filaments, can burn a hole into your film, and then may go on to destroy your shutter mechanism.

The late evening color was the only thing of interest to me while composing this view. Consequently, I metered exposure from it only, using my camera and a medium length lens to do so. Purcell Mountains, Canada. Kodachrome, 135 mm lens.

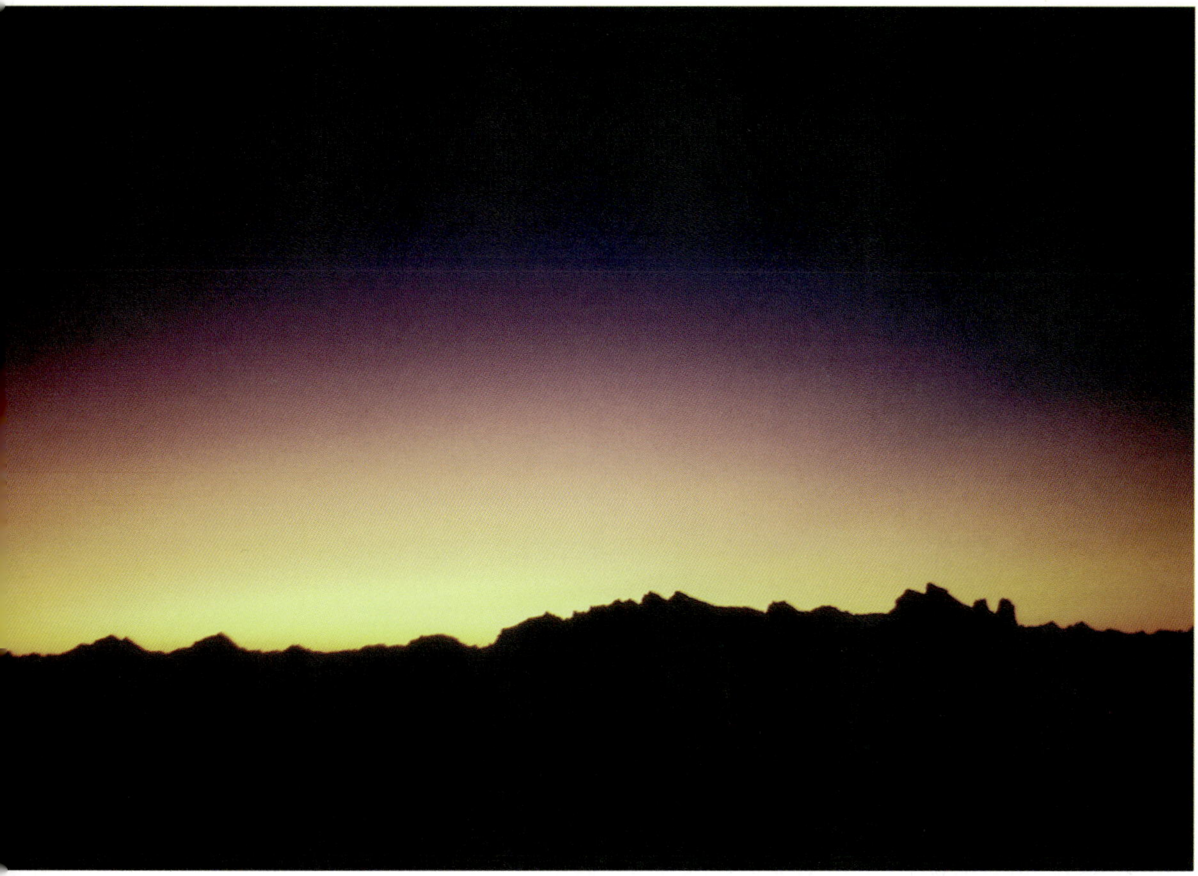

Shooting Comfortably (and Safely!) During Stormy Weather

Stormy weather presents a whole new set of challenges for us photographers. Yet successfully recording a stormy scene is immensely rewarding, particularly when the inclement conditions are really graphic, or when, for example, your subjects' grim expressions convey a picture of difficult moments that words can't describe.

Most precautions and techniques used when photographing in rain, snow, extreme wind or thunderstorms are fairly common sense, but often neglected in practise. It's well-worth considering, even before you head out on a mountain foray, what devices you'll have at your disposal to deal with stormy weather should it come about.

Rain, for example, will damage an exposed camera's circuitry over time and will leave spots on an uncovered lens. By simply providing protection, either by shielding it with your body or your anorak, you can prevent any serious damage. A small umbrella, whether held over the camera or mounted to a tripod and above your camera, may actually provide the best, and most convenient, protection of all.

Snow is generally not as troublesome as rain, unless it's wet. Still, it may be advisable to protect your camera in a similar way during a heavy snowstorm. Use a lens hood or keep lenses covered until you're ready to shoot. Also, as mentioned earlier, always protect against snow entering the camera housing while you change film or lenses.

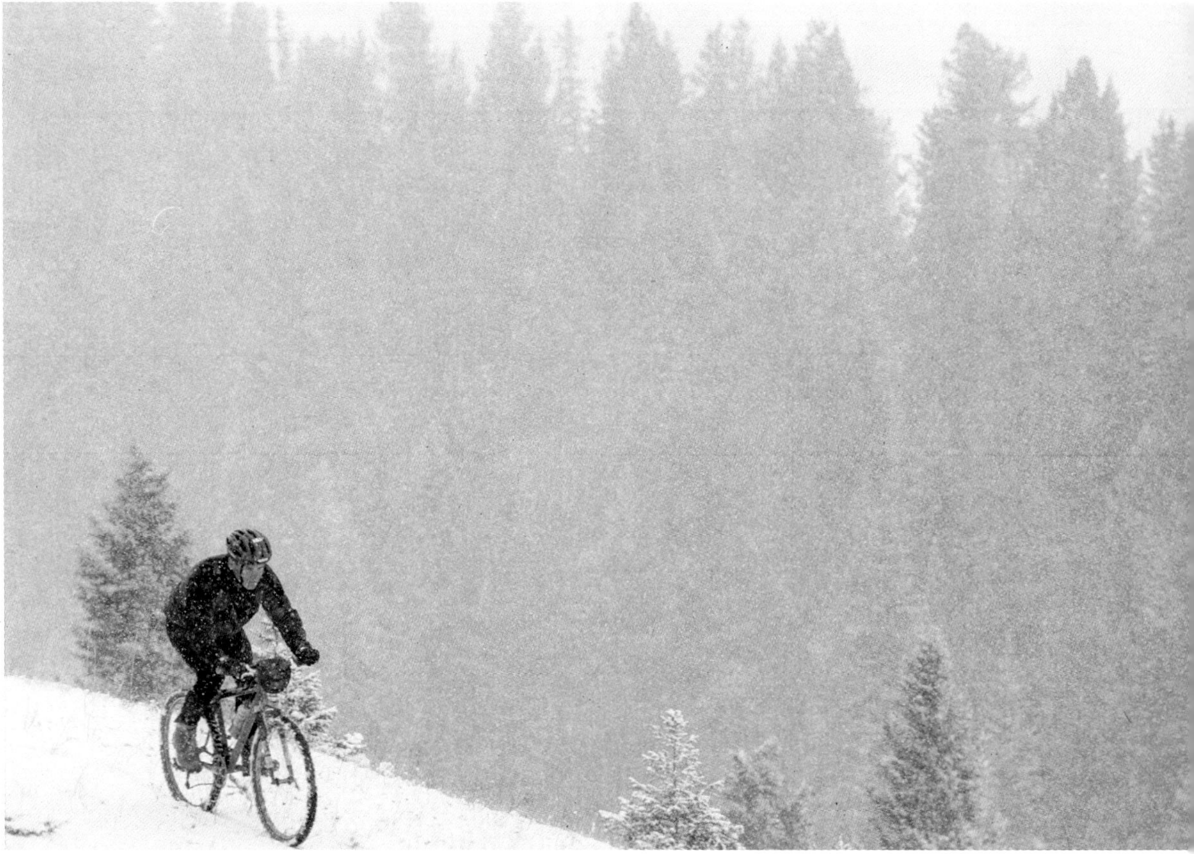

Snowstorms are wonderful events to record on film. Just make sure that your camera is protected from wet flakes of snow and that you stay warm while shooting. Canadian Rockies. Agfa SCALA, 105 mm lens.

Extreme wind can be particularly problematic, especially if dust or sand is blowing around in it. Try to shield your camera gear from wind gusts as much as possible, and remember to keep your camera case sealed so that lenses and accessories are also protected.

As much as anything, you want to keep yourself relatively comfortable while shooting in stormy weather. To this end, it may be advisable to put on an extra layer of clothing before taking any shots, particularly during cold temperatures. Or throw on a rain parka, even if it's only drizzling.

Thunderstorms come with their own unique challenges. As eluded to in an earlier section, they can be dangerous to shoot in, as well as difficult, if full of rain or wind. The obvious thing to watch for is that you are not in the firing line of thunderbolts while shooting. To this end, it's probably always advisable to photograph somewhat distant storms—not ones that are practically on top of you.

What makes matters riskiest while photographing lightning storms is the need, in most cases, to employ a tripod. Since it's impossible to tell exactly when a bolt might strike a particular scene, a commonly accepted shooting procedure is to open your lens for the longest possible duration. Full second or even longer exposures are often the result.

Your tripod, of course, will act as a lightening rod. How dangerous a one mainly depends on your location, as well as proximity to a storm. If on an exposed ridge crest, take extra care, and make sure to collapse your tripod fully as soon as ominous clouds move your way.

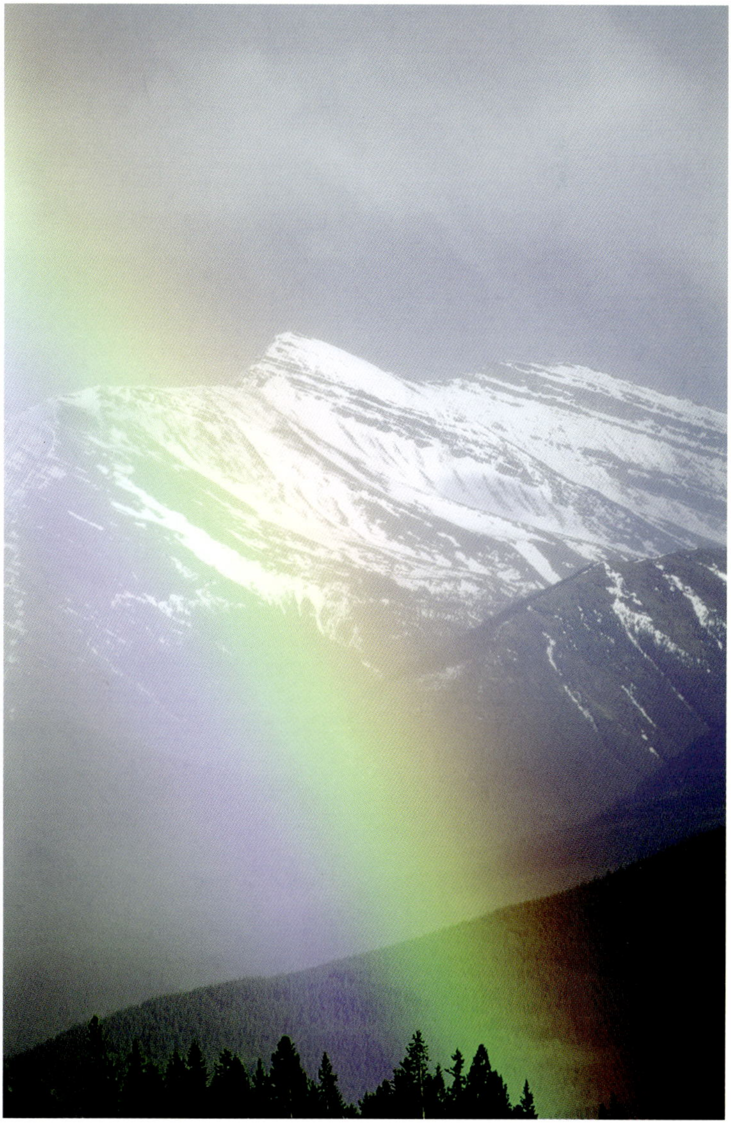

Beautiful rainbows and strikingly moody skies are among the rewards of shooting during, and immediately after, stormy weather. Canadian Rockies. Fuji Velvia, 180 mm lens.

Recording Twilight Glow, Lightning and Star Patterns

To reiterate again, long exposures are generally the rule when photographing lightning. So are they when photographing at twilight—unless you're using high speed-film—and for recording star "tracks" in the night sky.

The key to getting sharp pictures with all long time exposures starts with the camera-tripod assembly. Before heading out, make sure your tripod is sturdy enough for your camera's weight and size!

Choose a site to shoot from that is sheltered from breezes, and which appears to have a stable ground surface. Rock and compacted dirt tend to provide good ones; mud and spongy vegetated ones are generally poor. Attach your camera firmly to the tripod, and brace the legs of it with rocks to guard against unexpected movement, if any are easily accessible.

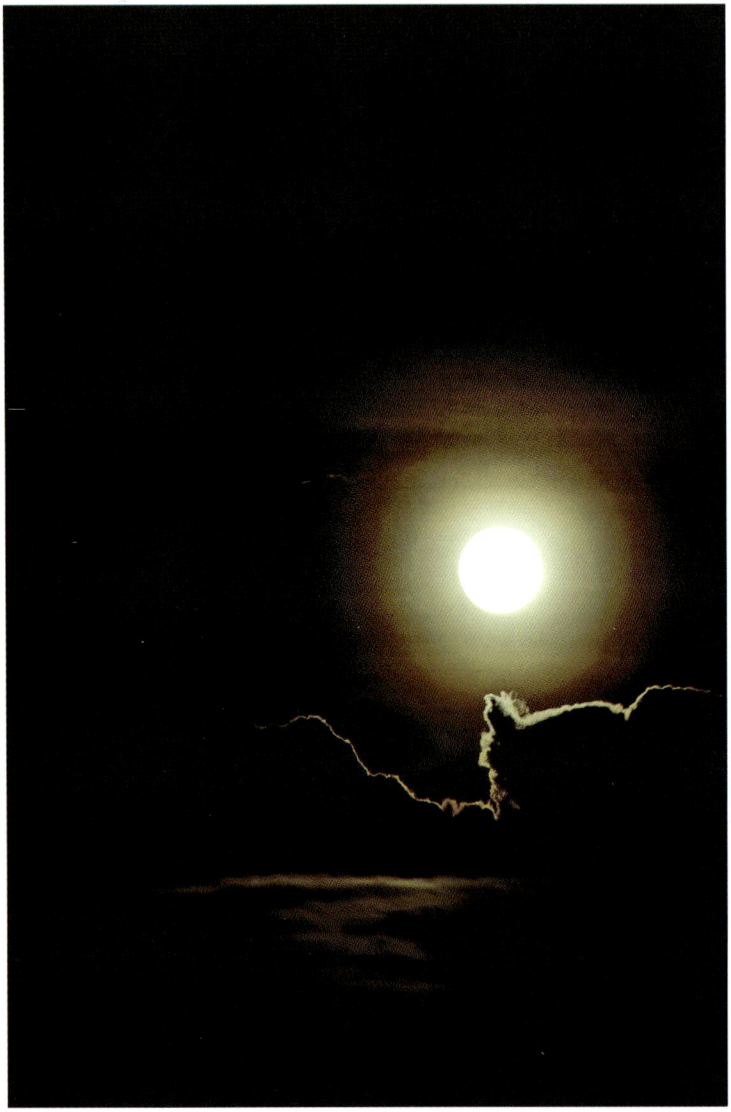

Shooting a full moon late at night requires a fairly long exposure, at least if you want to also record any of the glow that it casts onto surrounding objects. Canadian Rockies. Fuji Velvia, 200 mm lens.

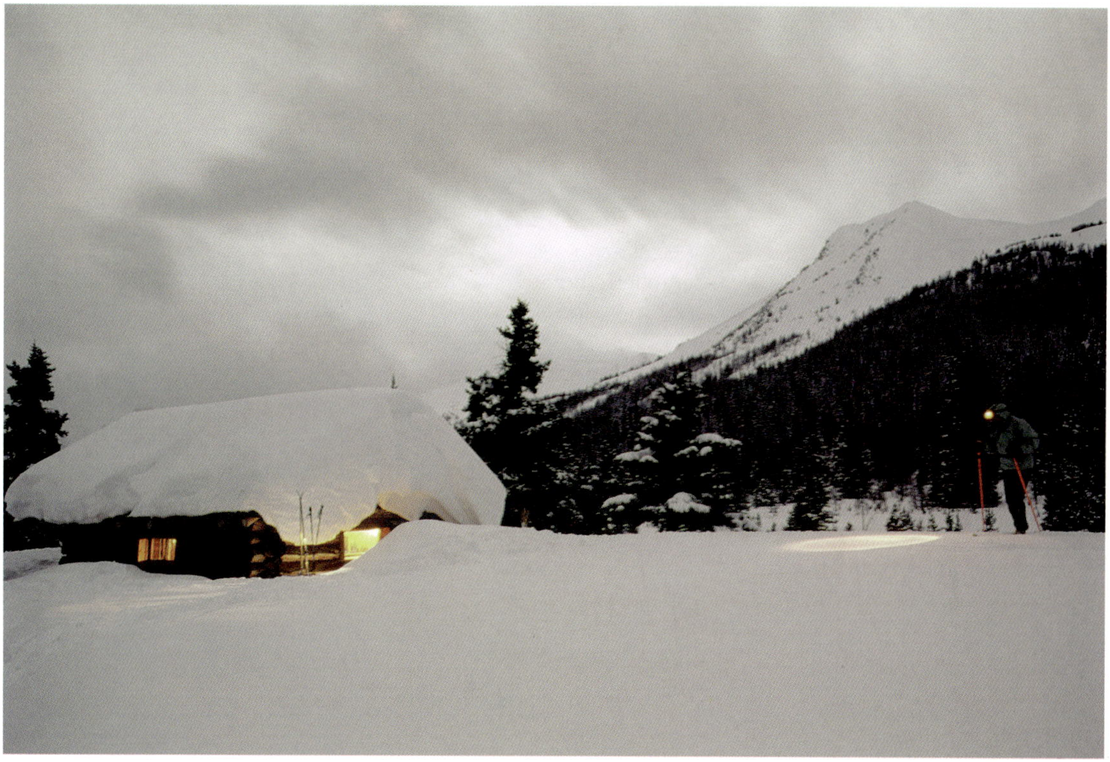

Opposite: I don't usually shoot twilight scenes until they possess a deep blue cast. Then, to intensify the sense of gathering darkness, I'll underexpose by 1/2 or one full stop from the exposure reading my camera's meter provides. Canadian Rockies. Fuji Velvia, 35-70 mm zoom lens.

After opening the camera's shutter, try not to move your feet at all. Don't hold onto your camera or tripod either, as even light touches may be enough to transmit vibration that will cause bluriness on film.

Even after observing all these precautions, it's unlikely that you will get perfectly sharp exposures if there's much of a wind blowing. This is particularly true with star patterns. Since these literally result from the earth's rotation, they may be hours in the making (if your intent is to record long, dramatic circular streaks).

For star shots, especially, choose a clear windless night. Ensure your camera has fresh batteries, set the exposure on "automatic", frame and shoot. You'll either need to use a cable release or, failing that, trip the shutter using your self-timer. The larger the f-stop value you choose, the longer the exposure will be and, consequently, the more dramatic the star tracks will look on film.

If you can identify the North star, while shooting in the northern hemisphere at least, try centering your frame on it. A very long exposure thus taken will show perfect concentric rings emanating outwards from both sides of this star. Again, watch the wind: anything more than a very slight breeze will reduce sharpness.

For lightning, your camera's shutter obviously does not have to be open nearly as long. How long really depends on the intensity of the lightning storm. If there's a jab of electricity every 30 seconds or so, then a two-minute exposure would probably land some good results.

Longer exposures might be needed though. This is generally not problematic while shooting in low light conditions, such as in twilight or at night, but during daylight hours slow film and a neutral density filter may be required to permit long enough exposures (see detailed description of neutral density filters on page 39).

Twilight shooting generally allows shorter exposures. However, you may want to include a wide depth of field to, say, keep the profile of a climbing partner in focus as well as distant mountain peaks. If so, many of the above suggestions will be worth observing.

Shooting In the Dark: Some Ad Hoc Lighting Ideas

As long as you have a tripod and cable release, you are never limited to flash photography at nighttime. All kinds of other things can provide illumination, often to greater creative effect than that achieved by a simple flash.

A headlamp can be an especially good choice. A shot of skiing or hiking companions wearing headlamps while travelling through, say, a twilit meadow is fairly easy to capture and very descriptive if carried out well. So is a downwards view of a climbing partner struggling up the last icy pitch of the day, under the glow of his headlamp.

The headlamp can also be easily used as a "spot" lighting source, since it's so mobile and allows your hands freedom to work the camera dials or move props around.

Consider, for example, photographing past an illuminated map and compass to distant mountains at twilight. Few other situations could describe the idea of routefinding, or being caught out after dark, better than this. To shoot it, simply mount your camera on a tripod, ensure the map and compass are on stable ground, cast your headlamp's beam onto it as you see fit, and trigger the shutter.

Of course, a flashlight could be improvised if you're without a headlamp. I always carry a small flashlight in my camera bag. In addition to providing spot lighting as needed, it has been indispensable on numerous dark eve-

Fireside views are often worth recording for the sake of memory, if nothing else. Red faces—one characteristic of shooting firelight glow on colour film—might not be too noticeable if you pull back from your subjects and shoot at some distance. Coast Mountains, Canada. Fuji film, 35-70 mm zoom lens.

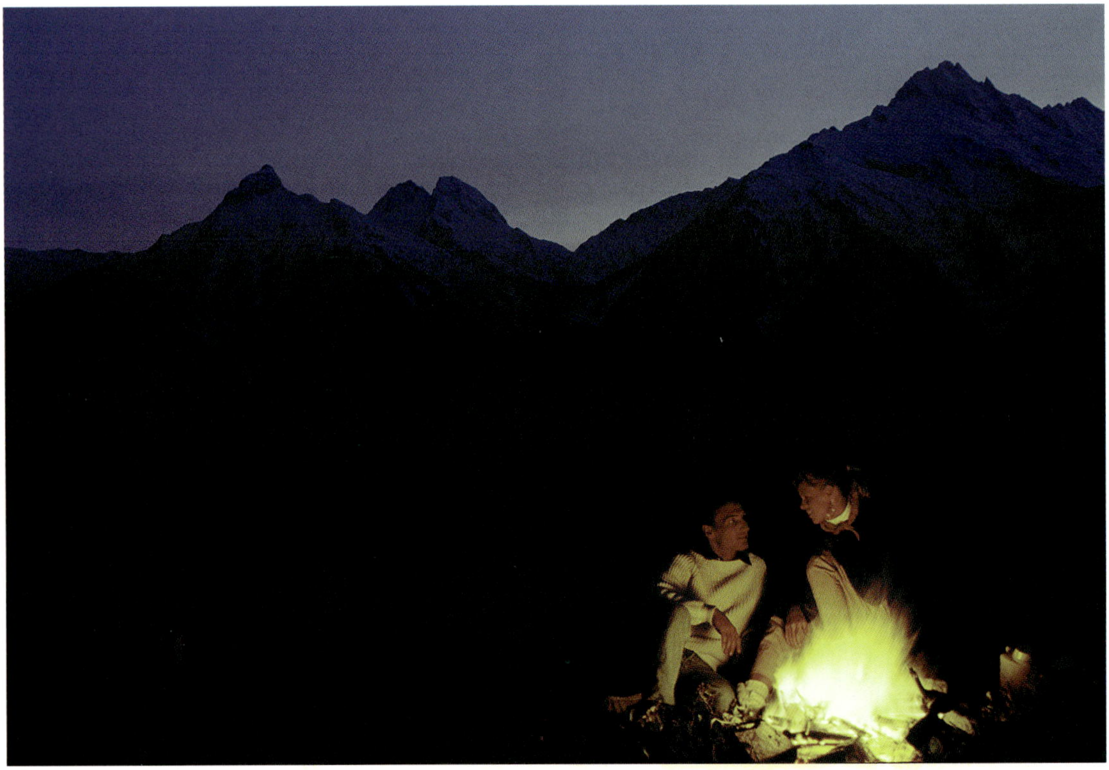

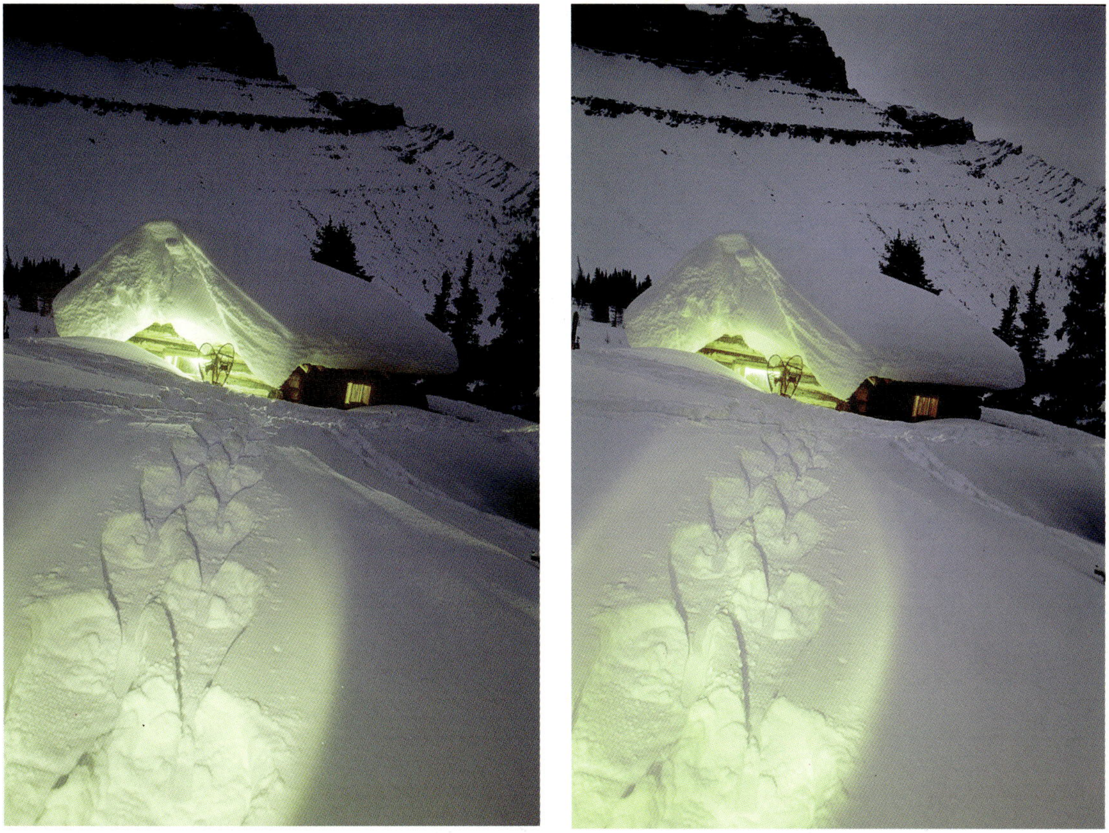

Getting exactly the right exposure while illuminating with a headlamp or something else is a little tricky. It's usually best to bracket by a few half-stop intervals, both above and below your best guess. Canadian Rockies, Fuji Velvia, 28 mm lens.

nings for reading camera dials and to locate the right film or accessory from deep inside my camera bag.

If you're close to a cabin or mountain hut, try shooting it as part of the evening landscape. You may find that the inside glow created by a lantern or propane lights registers beautifully on film. This is especially true in winter, if the glow illuminates the nearby snowy landscape or icicles hanging from eaves. With distant mountains fading into twilight, the effect can be quite arresting, providing a better visual description of cold and warm extremes than practically anything else.

Firelight glow, captured on film in juxtaposition to snowy mountains at twilight, can render a similar feeling. Even in summer, if recorded at the right time of evening, it will warm a setting tremendously.

Illuminating people outside a glowing hut, or around a campfire, is a little difficult, since exposures generally have to be long (unless you're using very high-speed film). Even if your human subjects are braced against a log wall or trees, for example, it may be difficult to stop eye movement completely for the minute or two an exposure might take.

Faces or other body parts might appear a little too red as well. This problem can be lessened, to some extent at least, by using appropriate filters to reduce the red cast, or by employing tungsten film, which will give a similar effect.

An off-camera flash will likely be the best solution of all, providing you have some way of filtering the quality of light it produces. But even if you don't have the required flash gizmos, or films or filters, it's well worth trying a simple time-exposed shot around the campfire.

Do it for experimental reasons, or just to record a great evening out. You may be pleasantly surprised. Make a note, too, that if your subjects are relatively small in your frame, their red faces might not look out of place at all.

Specialized Shoots

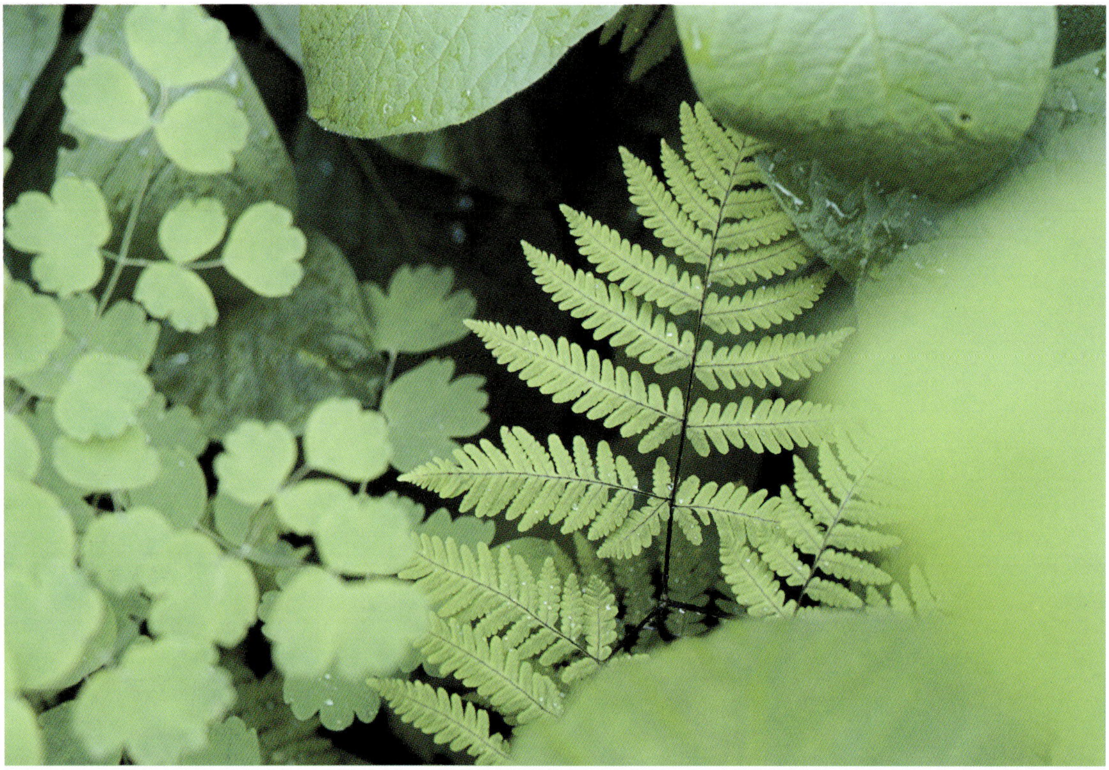

Close-up nature photography is a creative exploration unto itself. Shapes, forms and textures often look completely different through your camera lens than they do with the naked eye. Canadian Rockies, Fuji Velvia, 105 mm macro lens.

Most of us will master the basics of good photography—composition, focus, exposure control—with relatively straightforward subject matter, like mountain scenery and views of distant companions. Lots of creative variety can be discovered within such genre, if you look hard enough. For many people, though, the inclination to pursue more challenging content inevitably comes around sooner or later.

Photographers with a preference for nature subjects will most likely focus on wildlife, alpine flora and possibly panorama shooting. Those with a keener interest in mountain sports or human interactions will likely gravitate towards shooting activities with friends or family members who act as willing accomplices on photography outings.

This section will explore possibilities on both sides of the coin. It will try to explain how, and what might be necessary, to get the best results possible, and with the greatest of ease. Finally, it will address some of the inherent problems and risks associated with each creative enterprise, and the steps that can be taken to avoid serious pitfalls.

So, push the creative envelope! If you haven't tried shooting these more challenging subjects or situations before, by all means give them a shot. Don't forget, though, while you're doing so, to play it safe.

Opposite: Capturing climbing companions from best angles on film often involves using some rigging technique. Canadian Rockies. Fuji Velvia, 70-200 mm zoom lens.

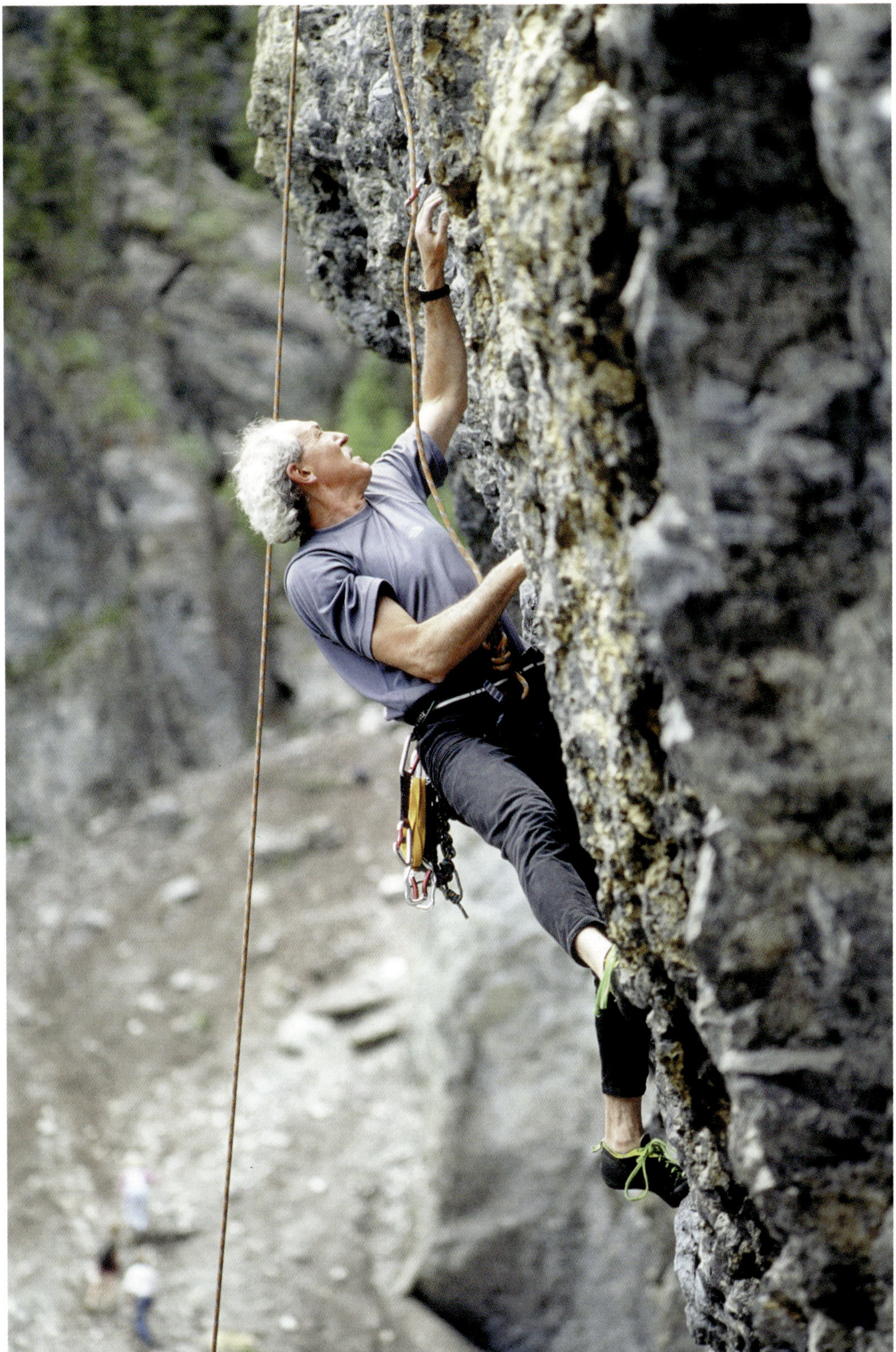

Photographing Wildlife

I've discussed photographing wildlife fleetingly thus far. This section will summarize all the important points to make your wildlife shooting as successful, and safe, as possible.

Most of all, keep your distance from wild animals! To do so, and yet get close enough visually, you'll need at least one long zoom lens. Alternatively, two or three long, fixed focal length lenses should be adequate most of the time, perhaps in 135 mm, 200 mm and 300 mm sizes or something similar.

A motor winder is also very useful. With one, you'll be able to record the subtle movements that wildlife make, some of which will be more photogenic than others. You'll have a better chance of recording fleeting opportunities as well, such as a view of some wild animal on the run. Remember that if you're shooting film with a motor winder, you'll likely need to carry lots with you.

Although it may seem contrary to natural impulse, it's often best to photograph wildlife in a relatively broad mountain context, especially when the landscape is spectacular. Really tight shots of wildlife—where the body or face fills more than half the frame—are generally best achieved in a zoo or game park.

This is a fine point though. A wild animal that appears as a speck or relatively insignificant part of your frame is generally not worth recording, unless silhouetted. But if it were to occupy a lower quarter, say, of a spectacular mountain view, the shot would be much more promising.

Wild animals are thankfully shy of human contact, so they usually

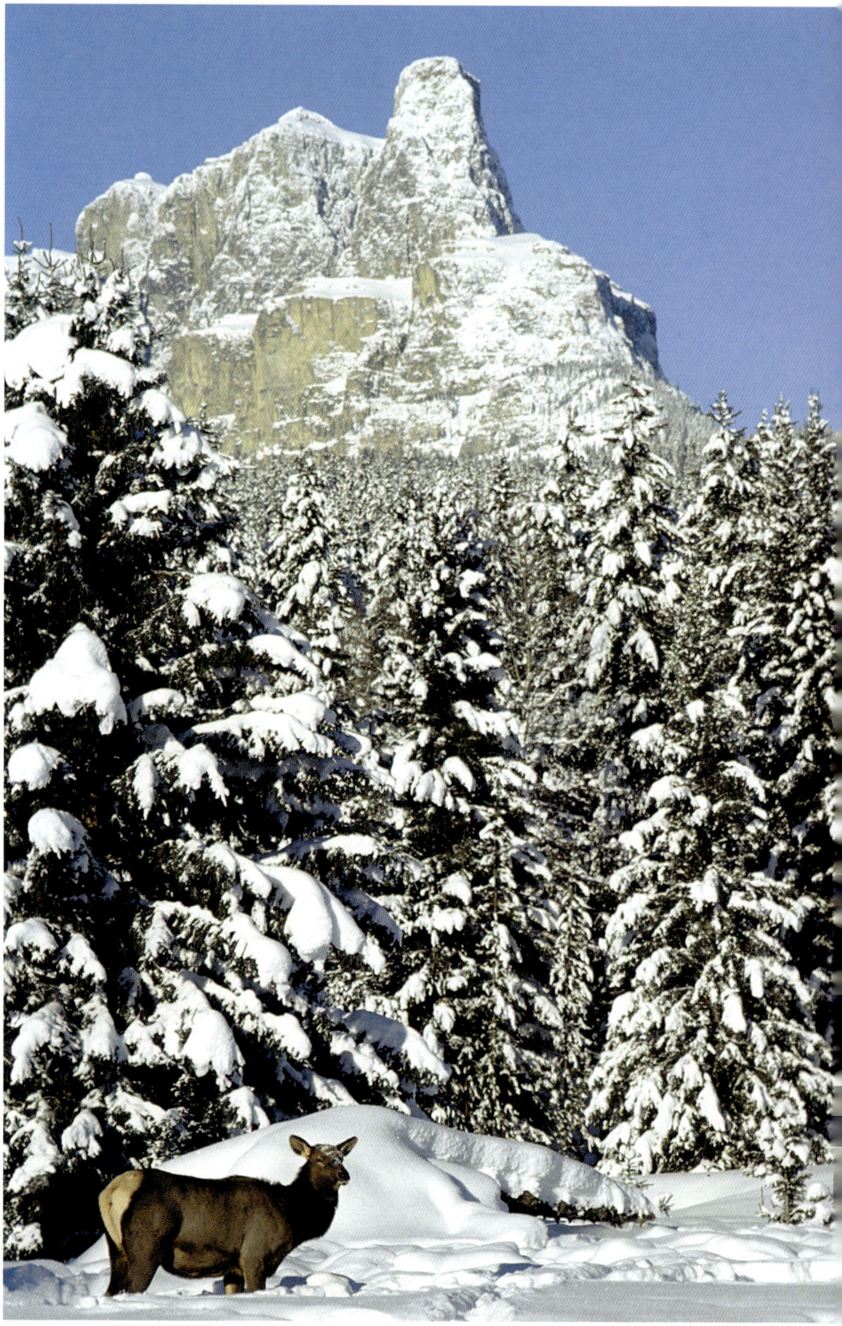

The best views of wildlife often show animals in the larger context of their environment. Although my main subject, this elk is just a small part of the overall scene. Canadian Rockies. Fuji Velvia, 85 mm lens.

will not allow really tight framing anyhow. When they do, look for an interesting backdrop to photograph them against, even if they happen to be close to the roadside, or dwellings. Usually you will have to act fast, as even animals habituated to humans tend to be a little skittish.

At times animal activities will be more photogenic than their settings. The rutting of bull elk during autumn is a familiar cliché, but also spectacular on film. Watch for behaviors that are perhaps not as often photographed, but which might speak volumes about your subject. Mountain goat kids engaged in a playful frolic, while mom feeds on alpine grasses, is one example.

Look for unusual angles while photographing wildlife. One of my favorite ones is a downward view of gliding falcons or eagles from the high purchase of a rock wall or mountain face. Just as birds are usually viewed from the ground looking up—not the other way around—so marmots and other small animals are generally seen from above, looking down. Try lying on your belly while shooting such subjects to see them from their own ground-level perspective.

Whatever you do, don't jeopardize the safety of your animal subjects. When spooked, animals often attempt maneuvers they wouldn't normally practise, such as jumping deep ravines or running across precarious ground. Sometimes these can lead to their injury or fatality. Close human intervention has also been known to influence mother birds to abandon their young.

Keep these points in mind before approaching too closely. Remember, too, that many wild animals are potentially dangerous, especially when you get between them and their young, or when you surprise them with sudden movement. If you can't get close enough to get the shot you want without risking life or limb, even with a long lens, let it go! Rely on your memory to preserve the moment instead.

Wildlife, like mountain companions, make great silhouetted subjects. Their features and relationship to other parts of a scene are often more recognizable than if non-silhouetted. Condor, Argentine Patagonia. Kodachrome, 200 mm lens.

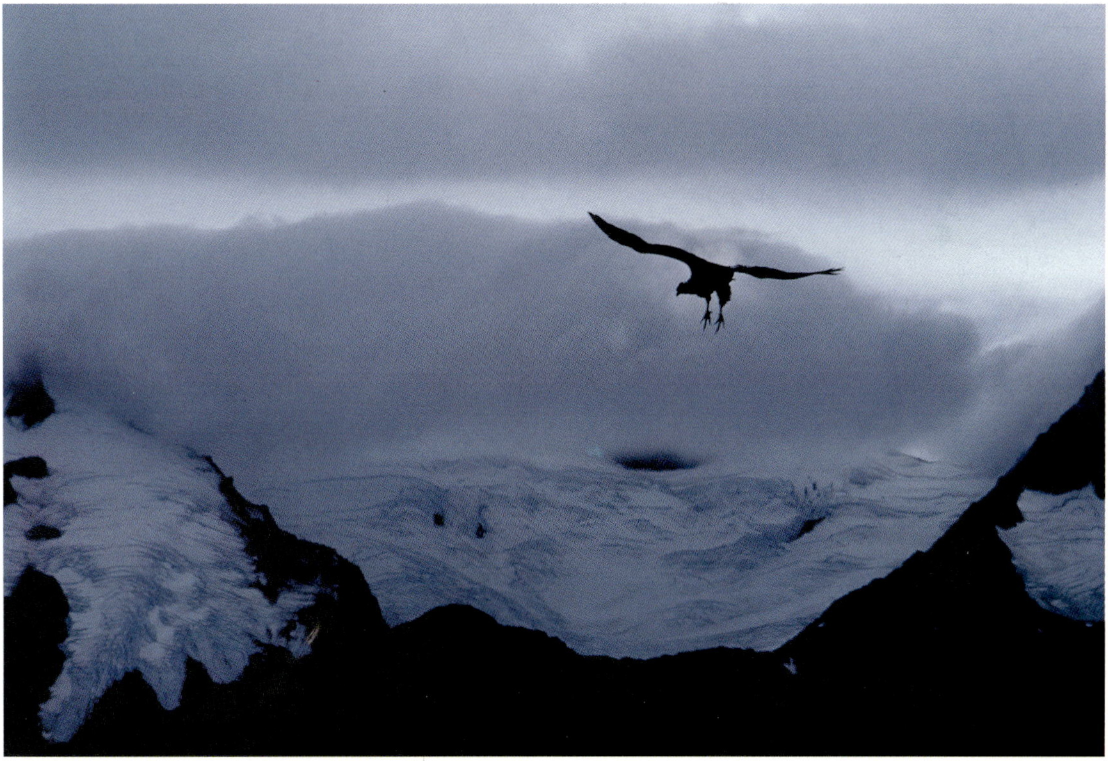

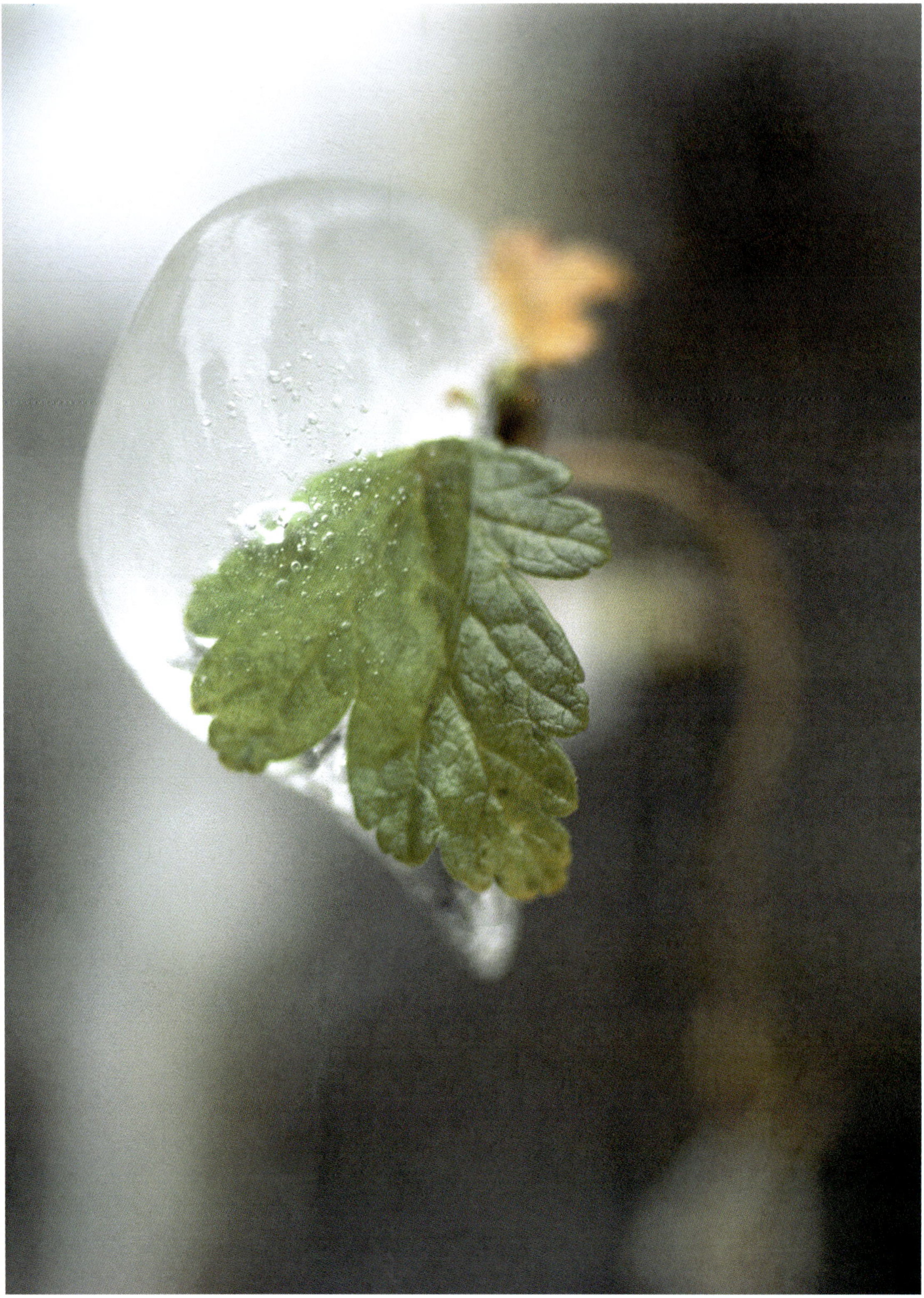

Close-up Photography

The mountains are filled with intriguing subjects for close-up photography. Many of the best of these will be ever colorful and varied alpine flowers, but rocks, water swirls, ice crystals and tree details all offer great possibilities too.

Perhaps the most interesting thing about alpine flora is its miniature size. Plants and blossoms simply don't grow very large, especially at, and above, treeline. Photography, therefore, has to be geared to small subjects usually growing very close to the ground.

A few pieces of equipment, and body maneuvers, need to be employed to get close enough. The first gear item will likely be a macro lens, or possibly a bellows attachment instead. Macro lenses are designed to focus at close range, so they literally allow you to move your camera far closer to your miniature subject than you could otherwise.

A bellows, which attaches between camera body and lens, uses a similar but different principle to accomplish the same thing. They are comparatively heavy, cumbersome and more difficult to work with, so most of us will likely stick with macros while doing close-up work in the mountains.

Macro lenses come in a variety of focal lengths, generally ranging from 35 mm through 200 mm. All can be quite useful in different creative ways, although I usually find I prefer ones on the longer end of the scale.

As mentioned earlier, they will be relatively expensive compared with normal lenses of the same fixed focal length. They will also be somewhat heavier and bulkier, though generally not dramatically so. You may sacrifice some speed by going with a macro lens, since many have to be slower to compensate for their extra optics. Consequently, any macro lens you invest in will probably not be the best lens to also shoot sports activities, where speed (i.e. wider maximum f-stop opening) is often important.

Another item of gear that you will need is a good tripod. Handheld photography is simply out of the question much of the time while shooting things close-up, especially in low light conditions. Macro settings exaggerate camera vibrations, so shots taken at even relatively fast shutter speeds may show some bluriness.

Make sure your tripod allows you to get your camera close to the ground. Although a downwards view of some subjects, especially flowers, will sometimes be best, you'll likely want to shoot from the side just as often, and even from below at times. Some tripods allow for the centre post to be flipped up-side-down to literally suspend your camera just above ground level (the images thus created will also be up-side-down, but this is generally of no real consequence, whether a digital or analog camera is used).

Sometimes the easiest and most effective tripods to use are the very lightweight, foldable varieties found at many climbing shops, most of which can be slipped into a large pocket. They will usually allow a low camera position while offering a fairly stable platform to shoot from. If they are not stable enough, say when a long lens is being used, an elbow can simply be rested on the ground while you focus and shoot.

Opposite: A very selective focus and a narrow depth of field will isolate things of interest from distracting parts of any close-up scene. Coast Mountains, Canada. Kodachrome, 55 mm macro lens.

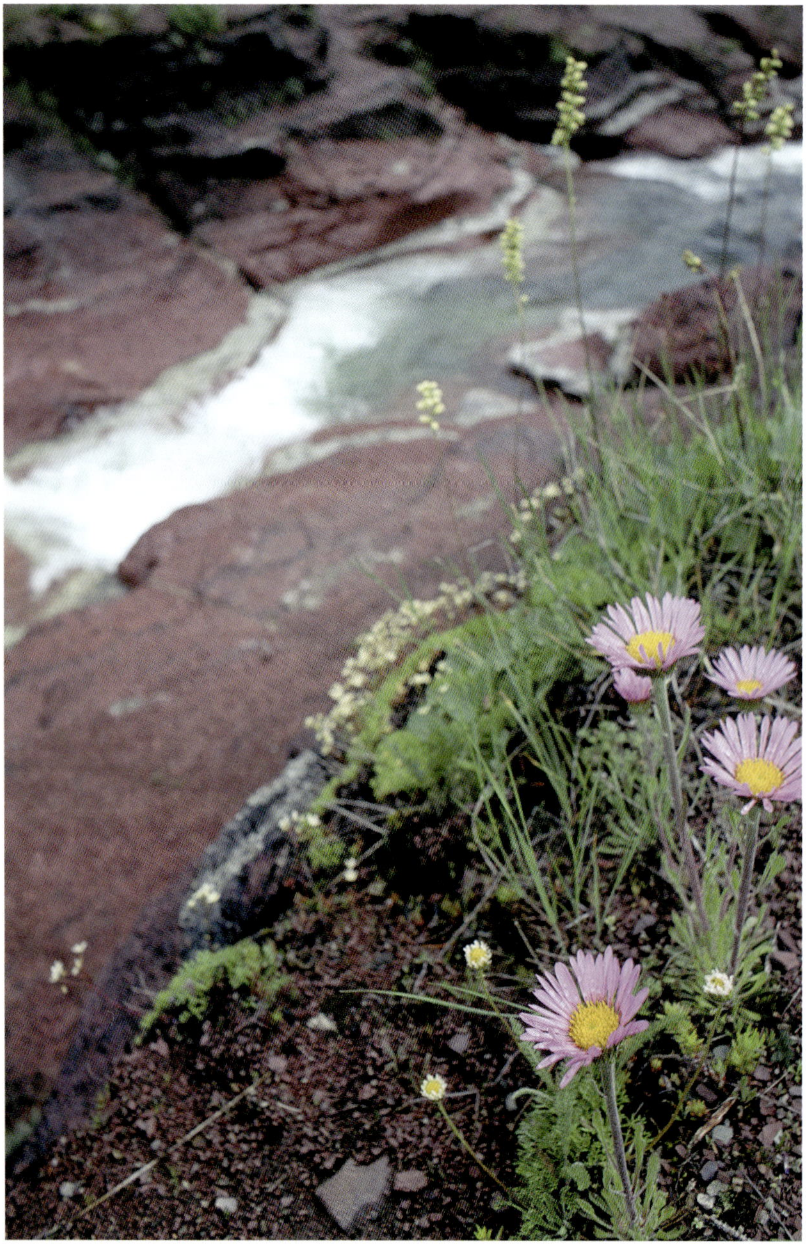

Using a wider depth of field will hint at the wider context a close-up subject occupies, but if slightly defocused background areas will not compete with the subject itself. Canadian Rockies, Fuji Velvia, 55 mm macro lens.

Use elbows, too, if you don't happen to be carrying a tripod. Lie on your belly with them resting in front of you. Hold your camera with one hand, and work the lens focusing ring with the other.

A flash or small reflector is essential with most close-up photography. Either it will enable you to backfill light into dark shadow areas or increase light over an entire composition so that a higher shutter speed or wider depth of field may be chosen. Unless you are really confident in your flash skills, I'd recommend using a reflector over a flash since you can easily control and readily see the extent of reflective illumination.

Bright overcast lighting is often best for close-up work. It tends to show colors in their truest shades, without the blue cast that sometimes results from shooting on a clear day. It will also illuminate subjects well and evenly enough that additional lighting may not be required, even while shooting with a wide depth of field. Try to take advantage of bright overcast conditions when you set out with your close-up equipment.

Watch depth of field carefully. At macro settings very little will be in focus unless you use a relatively high f-stop number (i.e. smaller aperture). Very tight focusing may be attractive creatively, but if you want to indicate the overall setting your subject occupies, a wider aperture will likely be ineffective.

If there's much wind, you'll probably have to sacrifice some depth of field for a higher shutter speed, or switch to a faster film if you have any. How fast is fast enough to arrest motion caused by the wind depends on several variables, including camera-to-subject distance, length of lens used and subject particulars like blossom size, etc. Whenever possible, try to wait for lulls between wind gusts before depressing the shutter.

Alternatively, try recording the blurring created by wind moving across your miniature subjects. It may well be the best creative option on breezy days, particularly if you're shooting with slow film and want to record a wide depth of field, say of wildflowers carpeting an expansive mountain slope.

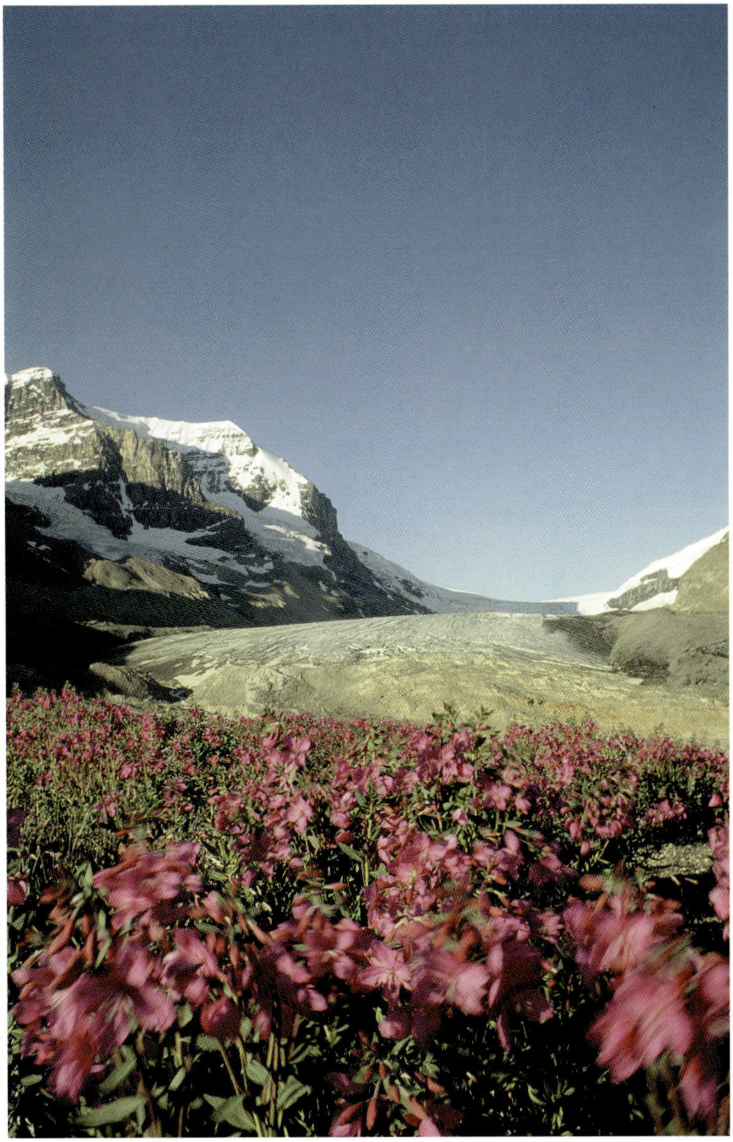

Windy weather, and a very wide depth of field, have meant that these wildflowers are not rendered sharply. But far from being problematic, the shot has a more dynamic look because of this. Canadian Rockies, Fuji Velvia, 28 mm lens.

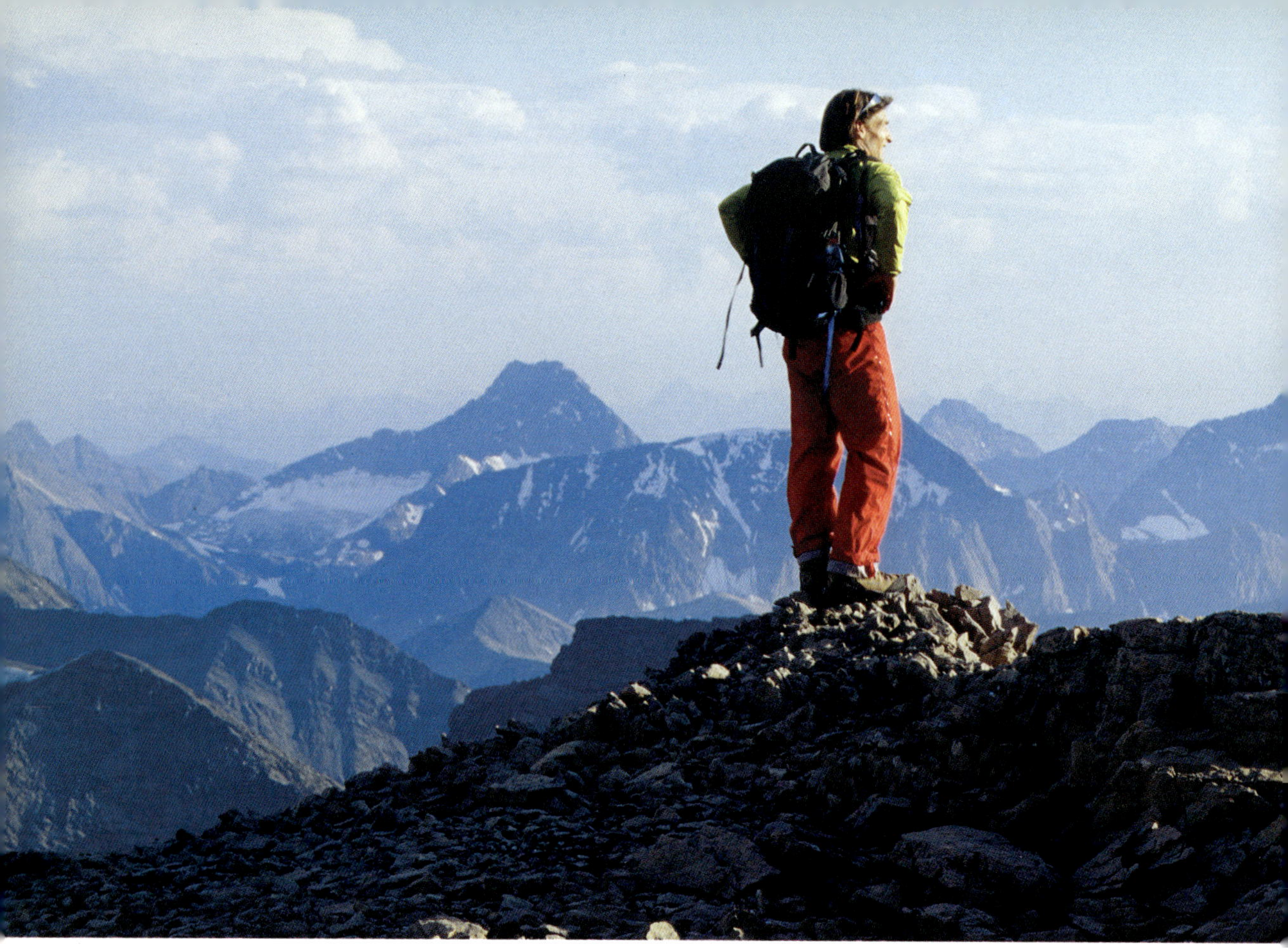

Here is an example of a "homemade" panorama shot. An 8x12 print was produced from a standard 35 mm negative, and top areas were then cut away. With this approach you always need to recognize, at the time of shooting, large areas on the vertical sides of your frame that you'll chop and discard later.
Canadian Rockies. Kodak E100VS, 28 mm lens.

Panorama Formats

"Mountain panoramas" are cliché for good reason. Whether a 360° view of distant ranges from the top of some peak or the wide sweep of a valley lower down, it seems that much of what we see in the mountains could be characterized by the word "panorama".

The standard 35 mm film format is often not wide enough to do justice to such sweeping views. Although not nearly square—as are some medium formats—it is nonetheless quite restricted in horizontal breadth.

If your chosen panorama view is relatively modest, a very straightforward approach can be taken while using any camera to create a wide, albeit not exactly "panorama", framing. Before attempting it though, make sure your camera is loaded with print film.

While composing a wide view, first predetermine areas at the top and/or bottom of your frame that are of no interest. Then shoot, print—usually into 8x10 format or larger—and simply eliminate those areas by cutting them out. You'll be left with a long, narrow print that you can either hang onto in its current state or scan into digital form.

The same discriminatory "cutting" can just as easily be done with images created by digital cameras and some basic computer software. Either way you get to choose, of course, the appropriate ratio of horizontal to vertical space for the finished image, as well as precisely where to make linear "cuts".

Once a chosen field of view exceeds 90° or so, another approach will almost certainly have to be taken. Wider lenses, needed to capture more horizontal space, create inevitable distortion; elements at the edges appear to either curve upwards or else become disproportionately large relative to ones closer to the centre. Also, main areas of interest, like distant mountains, become diminished in size.

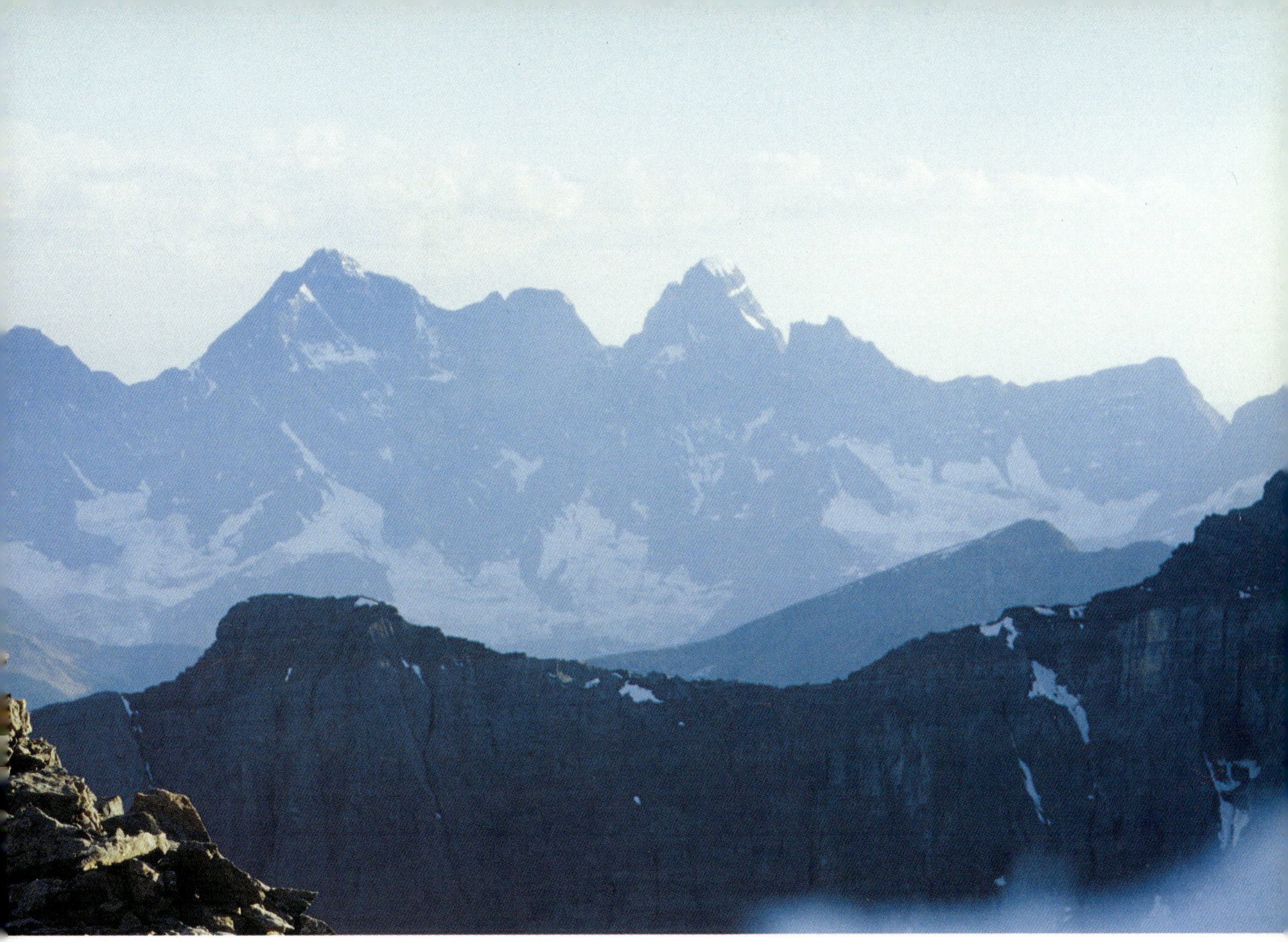

This very wide domain is perhaps best served by panorama cameras. Using pivoting lenses or some similar technology, they can scan across a very wide scene while recording it seamlessly on film. Some panorama cameras are capable of swivelling across a complete 360° span and recording the entire thing on a single long piece of film.

Panorama cameras will likely be too specialized—and expensive—for all but the most dedicated user, though. If your main interest is in simply recording ultra-wide views, say a complete panorama from the summit of a high mountain, try the following approach.

With print film loaded in your camera, position it and chosen lens securely on a tripod. Lock down the vertical adjustment lever on the tripod (it is nearly impossible to shoot with any accuracy if you don't have one). Then swivel the camera through a full 360° arc, making corrections in the vertical adjustment until you see exactly the panorama you want to record. Ensure that the final view looks the same as the first one.

Once these steps have been taken, you're ready to shoot. Make a careful mental note of each distant frame edge to match to adjacent frames. Overlap a little while shooting; it's always better to edit out bits of repeated scenery rather than coming up short.

Make sure that your film is printed in "full frame" size when you take it to the lab, so that the entire scene is reproduced just as you composed it. There will inevitably be minor variations in exposure between shots, but as long as you've trimmed and pasted each print carefully the final result should be quite satisfying.

Ironically, several old-style camera models may have a distinct advantage when it comes to photographing panoramas. Owing to their more rudimentary construction, the user is able to shoot and advance film without any frame separation. If one does so with great precision, and then processes exposed film strips (usually 120 size) as a single frame, it's possible to obtain an absolutely seamless panorama shot.

Who Wants to "Model"?

Who wants to "model"? Why bother looking for someone to "model", anyway?

Here's why: at some point, it may become more gratifying to actually organize a shoot with other people rather than to simply record them wherever they happen to be stationed against the mountain landscape. Such "directing" can be very casual, perhaps simply asking someone to turn a certain way, or stand up tall on a nearby ridge outcrop. Or it can be more serious, where you ask people to join you for the express purpose of photographing an outing or activity.

Of course, none of us wants to hire a real model; that is, unless we're working professionally. And nor should we have to, as long as we have willing friends or family members that don't mind being photographed.

Their willingness might just depend on what I refer to as "the fun factor" though. As long as any photographer remains lighthearted and not overly zealous while behind the camera, everybody should be deriving enjoyment from the shoot. Boring any participant by having them repeat scenes constantly or—probably worse—asking them to do things beyond their comfort zones would, in all likelihood, destroy the fun.

Kids are particularly sensitive to being asked to overperform in front of the camera. Try to work quickly as well as lightheartedly with any child or group of kids, and remember to show them the best shots afterwards. Digital cameras are particularly good for photo-

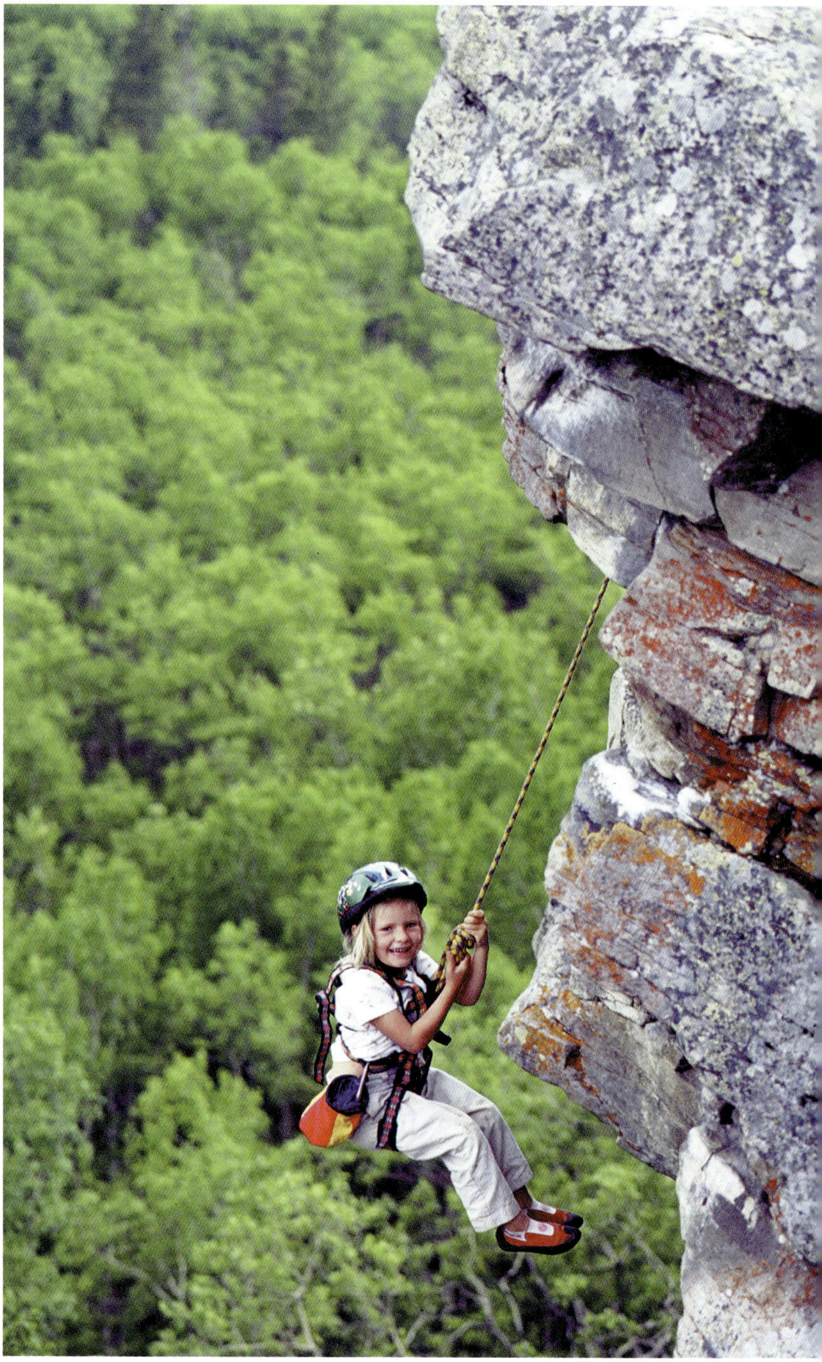

Kids love to be photographed—as long as they're having fun. More than adult subjects, they are rarely happy repeating some manoeuvre or performing in an unnatural way. Canadian Rockies, Fuji Velvia, 105 mm lens.

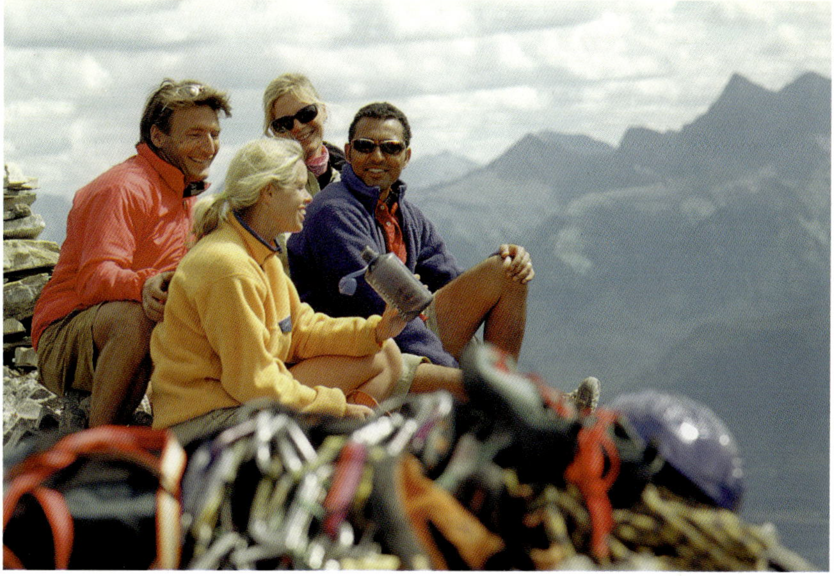

The best way to relax "models" so that they look as natural as the rest of your scene is to engage them in some activity or a conversation. Canadian Rockies. Kodak E100VS, 70-200 mm zoom lens.

graphing children, since shots can be reviewed almost instantly after having been taken. Providing the results are pleasing enough to your young subjects, they may pay you the ultimate compliment by suggesting to "model" for you more often.

Probably the best way that I've found to reward models of any age for their endeavors is by presenting a nice print of the event afterwards. I've also contributed a few photos to personal or business web pages at times. If your "models" insist upon being paid, ensure it makes good sense to you, and agree in writing on a price beforehand.

Who makes a good model? Surprisingly, many people do, albeit in different situations. The onus is really on you, the photographer, to determine the best of these to focus on with any individual, or group of people, you choose as models.

For example, some persons are just better geared to high-adrenaline sports activities, whereas others are more comfortable—and more photogenic—pursuing relatively tranquil activities. With the former group of people, facial and body expressions may be rigid, or simply look wrong, except when you catch them carving tight turns or pedaling at full speed down mountain trails. Any attempt at shooting the latter kind of person engaged in such fast-paced activity will likely look phony and forced instead.

It is difficult to find people who are really exceptional in front of the camera though. This is likely why many of us who shoot all the time continually return to the same models. You may do so as well.

With some people you try to photograph, either by choice or simply because they're the only ones around, getting the right facial expressions may become quite a chore. When this happens, photograph them from the side or behind, at an angle where faces aren't visible. If body posture is the issue, trying asking them to walk, ski or bike through a scene as per normal. By recording natural motion and perhaps a slight blur, posture problems will likely disappear altogether.

As with everything in photography, the only way to become accomplished at photographing with people is to experiment a lot. Don't be afraid to shoot several rolls of film while trying different angles and approaches.

Using a digital camera to shoot with models can save you considerable cost, especially during the most experimental stages. It will also give you instant feedback on results, which may help you push things creatively during a shoot.

Remember that, like any Hollywood director, you almost always have to take charge of your people subjects. They won't be able to envision things the way you do through your camera lens. So put on your director's cap and see what you can do with "models", whomever they happen to be. Be good to them, and you'll likely be rewarded with great shots and many more fun-filled outings.

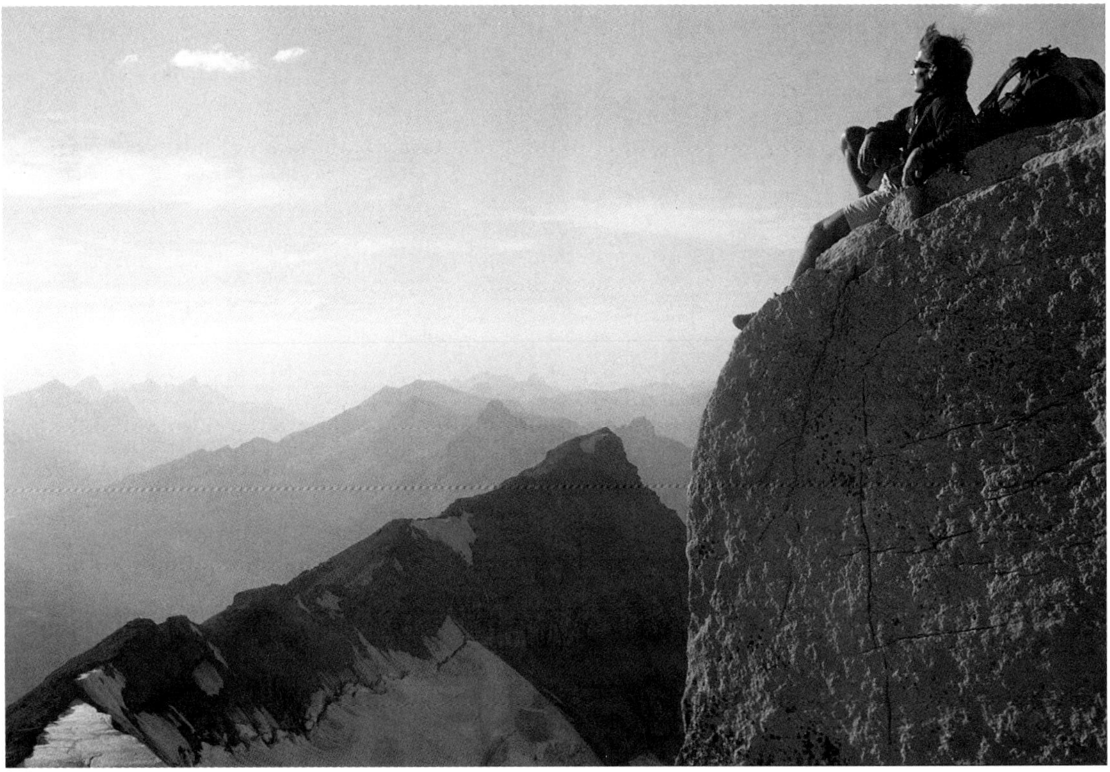

This is a fairly typical mountain self-portrait. I had spotted the boulder earlier and waited for the distant view to grow moodier. The only trick was to get into position in the 10 seconds my self-timer allowed me. Canadian Rockies, Agfa SCALA, 35-70 mm zoom lens.

Self-portrait Shooting

I find I include myself as a "model" in shots quite often. This is not because I travel alone in the mountains so much as it's because I simply like to have a visual record of myself on trips with companions, whenever possible.

Sometimes I'll just use a part of myself in the foreground of a shot, either as interference or as a sort of "lead in". For example, I've shot past my arm swinging into the frame with a companion ahead on the trail. I've also set my camera on a low tripod to show my foot stepping, or skiing, ahead while a fellow hiker or skier sets the pace in front.

These compositions often come off quite well, and without much set-up difficulty. Because they show fairly unusual angles and content, they're often well juxtaposed against typical straight-on views of companions or mountain activities, especially in slide shows and other multi-image presentations.

Of course, simple self-portrait shooting, where you mount your camera on a tripod and use a self-timer to trip the shutter, can be gratifying as well. If you are alone in a spectacular place, self-portraiture may help to establish essential scale or human warmth.

Along with a tripod, you'll need a self-timer or remote triggering device in order to shoot yourself at a distance. Most cameras come equipped with built-in self-timers. Some of these are adjustable, so that you can choose a setting of five or 10 seconds if you plan to pose close to your camera, or 20 to 60 seconds for more distant poses.

If your camera is an older version that doesn't include a self-timer, you can usually buy one that screws onto the shutter. These will generally accommodate remote control devices too, which allow you to stand a certain distant away from your camera—usually five to eight meters—and trigger the shutter whenever you like (remote controls are often packed with new cameras or are readily available from their manufacturers).

Remember, though, that self-portraiture need not show a simple, posed view of yourself standing at a viewpoint. With a little extra thought, and work, you can capture as dynamic a view of yourself as you can of anyone else. You may not even need a tripod to do so.

In fact, it's when I don't have a tripod that I usually think of relatively unusual angles and treatments if inclined towards self-portraiture (admittedly, this partly has to do with my utter disdain of trying to fudge stumps, say, or rocks in place of a tripod).

One angle that I've used on several occasions is to simple hold a camera, with 24 mm or wider lens attached, in front or above my face. Then, after selecting a slow shutter speed, I'll ski, run or bike (tricky!) forwards at a reasonable speed. If the camera is properly focused on my face beforehand, the result will show sharp facial features at the centre of the frame with side features streaking by.

The opposite angle has worked well too, at least sometimes. With the best shots, I've held my camera at eye or chest level and pointed across foreground skis or handlebars. These stayed in sharp focus, while side and background areas blurred to create effect.

The possibilities are nearly endless with self-portraiture when you allow your creative juices to flow. Your hands, feet, lower or upper torso and entire body can all be used in ingenious ways to draw attention to some activity or place. Perhaps the greatest thing about becoming adept at photographing yourself, though, is that you'll always have a willing subject to work with, even when others turn you down!

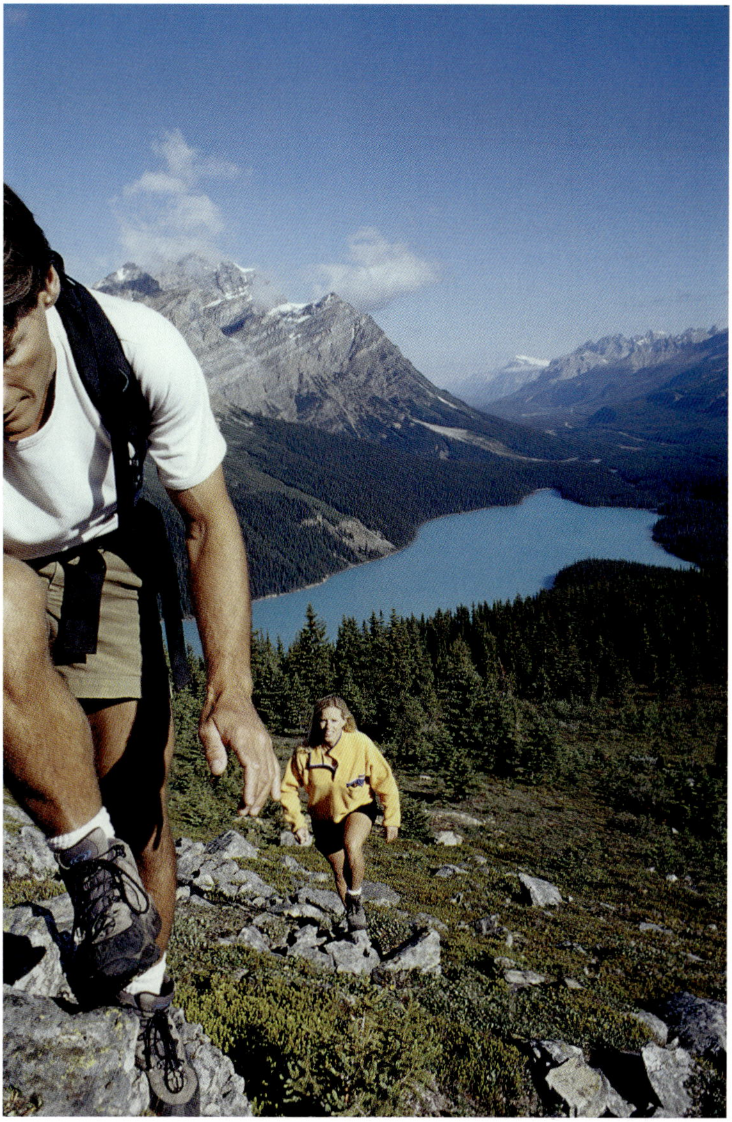

A self-portrait shot need not include all parts of you, nor you alone. In this shot I worked out positioning requirements with my companion before shooting. That way there was no risk of being in the wrong place when the shutter went off. Canadian Rockies. Kodak E100VS, 28 mm lens.

Rigging a Climbing Shot

Rigging properly to shoot climbing scenes may help you avoid serious injury, or possibly death. I'll go through some of the basic safety procedures in this section.

While I hope these pointers will be useful, the most important thing is to create a system of your own to follow, a safety checklist of sorts that you refer to religiously. Remember to always think through any set-up carefully before committing yourself on the end of a rope, or below someone else's.

Profile views of climbing are often the best ones on film. Unless you can get the shot you want from a gentle nearby slope, or an easily accessible ledge, chances are you'll have to suspend yourself from a second rope while shooting.

Quite possibly the greatest danger in doing so has to do with establishing that second rope. Make sure that your first priority during set-up is climbing, not photography.

Be especially careful while top-roping to gain a shooting position. An unbelievable number of accidents occur when climbers set up top ropes. If you do intend to drop a rope beside the one you're shooting, be extra careful not to drop loose rocks or ice on companions while doing so. Watch your footing on the approach too.

The best scenario while suspended from a rope with a camera is to have someone belaying you. Then you only need to ask for lowering, or tension, to improve or change your shooting position. If you don't have this additional person, you may be able to accomplish something similar with ascenders, or a "shunt", to keep you anchored.

Be sure to move ascenders up rope, or ask that slack rope be taken in by your belayer before advancing to a higher position. This may seem obvious enough, but in practise my tendency, at least, is to try to quickly move to a higher viewpoint without first ensuring all slack rope has been gathered up.

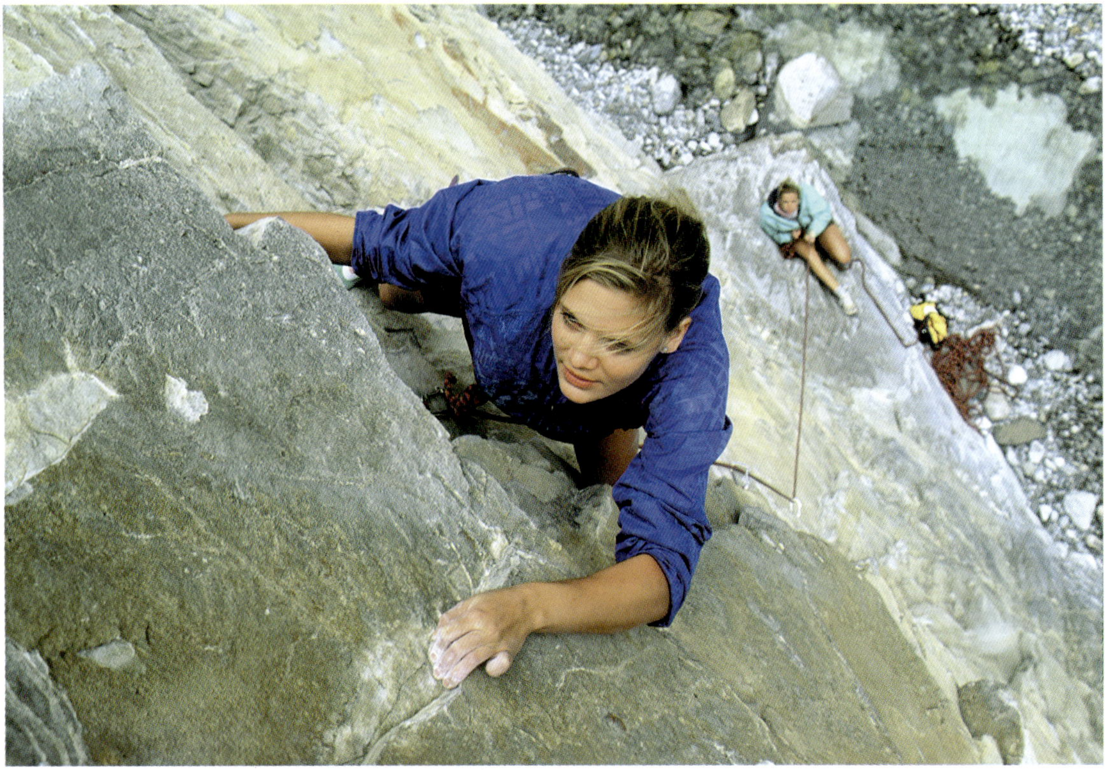

Overhead views of climbing are also often dramatic. You'll sometimes need to be well out from a rock or ice surface to get the best shots. Probably the easiest way is to push outwards with your feet as far as you can while using the tension of a rigging rope to keep you in place. Canadian Rockies. Fuji Velvia, 105 mm lens.

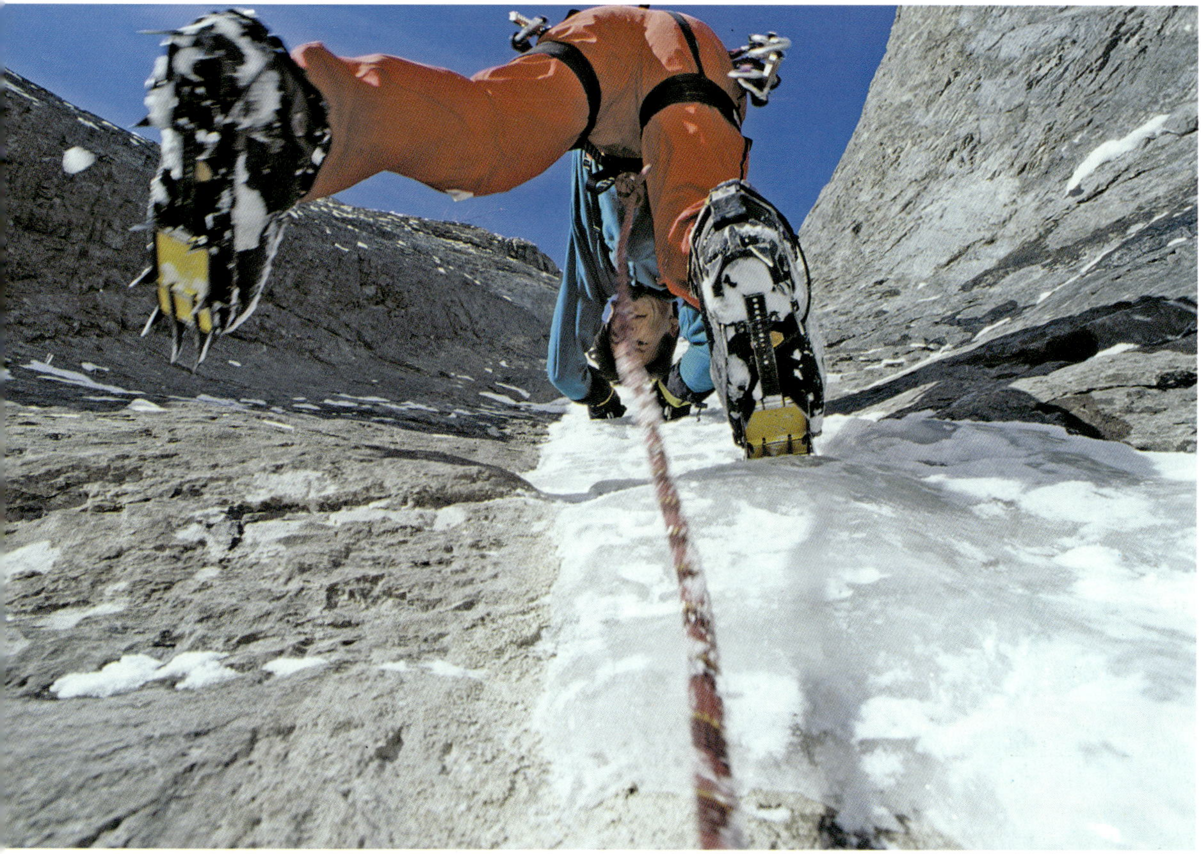

Climbing views that look straight up, such as this one, can be very effective. Just make sure your subject has a very secure stance before getting into shooting position. Crampons hurt! Canadian Rockies, Kodak E100VS, 28 mm lens.

You may find it difficult to establish a stable shooting posture while hanging below an overhanging lip. Try to shoot where you can at least gain some purchase with an extended foot. It is better still to brace the whole side of your body against solid rock, snow or ice, especially while using long lenses.

Straight up and down perspectives can be as, and sometimes more, exciting than profile ones. If you choose to shoot from below looking up, make sure you can do so safely. Never take your climbing partner off belay to grab a shot; use a device or technique that will keep him on belay while you free up your hands for photography.

Needless to say, be extra careful while shooting up towards a fellow ice climber, especially if he's only a few feet off the ground or from your belay. Crampons hurt, and they leave messy scars!

Similarly, watch that you don't drop rocks or ice on fellow climbers while shooting from above looking down. It's very easy to get caught up in the excitement of a potentially great shot and forget about the loose debris at feet level.

Of course, always keep an eye pealed and ear cocked for anything falling while shooting climbing scenes. Typically, a photographer's awareness of surroundings deteriorates somewhat while looking through his/her camera's viewfinder. While it's great to be totally attuned to the creative enterprise of the moment, this trait can be potentially lethal if left completely unbalanced.

Speed Kills! Protect Yourself

Mountain biking and skiing/snowboarding, in particular, come with hazards of their own for photography. In general, the closer you get to the action while shooting these activities, the better shots you'll get. But the risks run higher as well. A few safeguards can help to avoid painful injuries.

Probably the best cardinal rule is to shoot only those persons whose level of skill you can trust. I can imagine almost nothing worse than to be run into by a fast moving set of skis or mountain bike because the user was too incompetent to avoid hitting you.

Establish a safe photography position before shooting. If mountain biking is your chosen activity, have your biker subject cruise by a tentative spot before you occupy it. With skiing, try to pre-visualize the effects of terrain before setting up your camera.

Don't even attempt to shoot high-speed action without a motor winder. For one thing, you're unlikely to be successful. For another, you'll be tempted to request repeat performances from your subject, thus adding to the chance of his/her injury. Often it's the first take that proves to be the best one, particularly if your subject senses potential pain after making an initial effort and then tenses up.

Bear in mind that you don't always need to have your subjects move really fast in order to record the illusion of great speed. Sometimes all that is needed to blur subject motion effectively is to choose a slower speed setting than you might otherwise. 1/30 or 1/15 second exposures will blur all but the slowest activities.

When you don't want a blurry subject, you can always pan it to indicate speed. Again, by choosing a slow shutter setting, you will likely give a sense of rapid movement even when it's quite slow. The combination of a slow shutter speed and medium to long lens use will dramatize motion even more (although anything less than 1/30 second will likely be too slow to record your subject sharply).

You'll have to be in a very safe shooting position to get overhead action shots like this one. Given the right hollow or hideaway, it's a great perspective to record though. Canadian Rockies, Fuji Velvia, 28 mm lens.

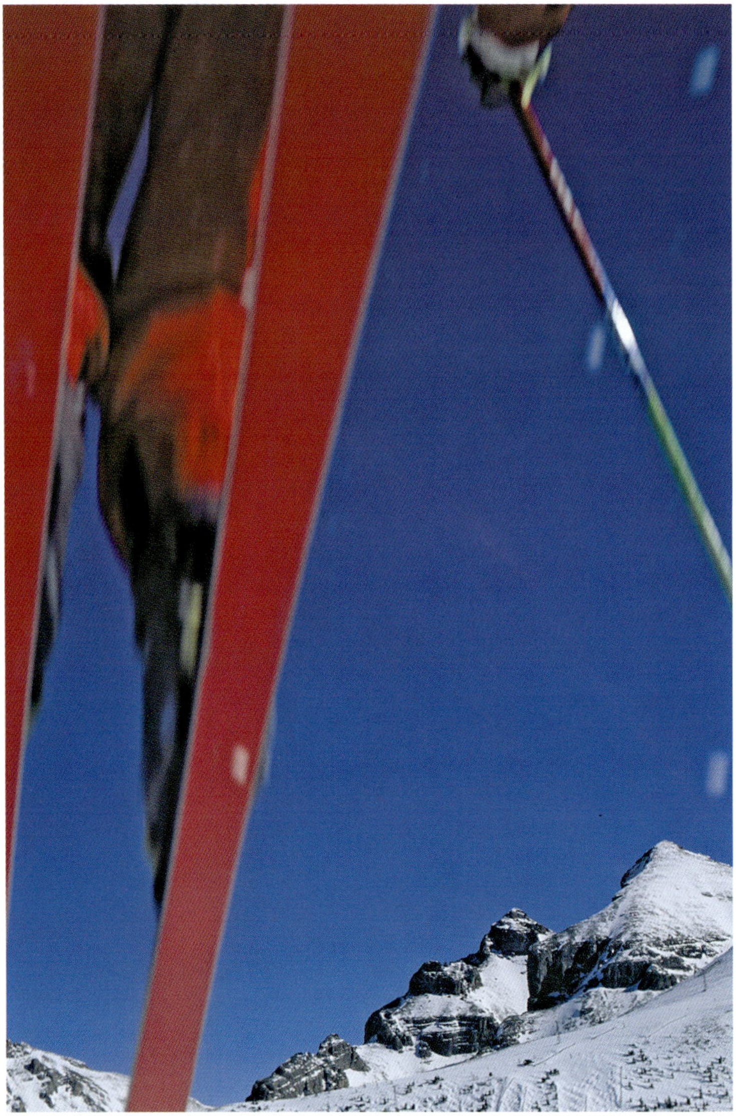

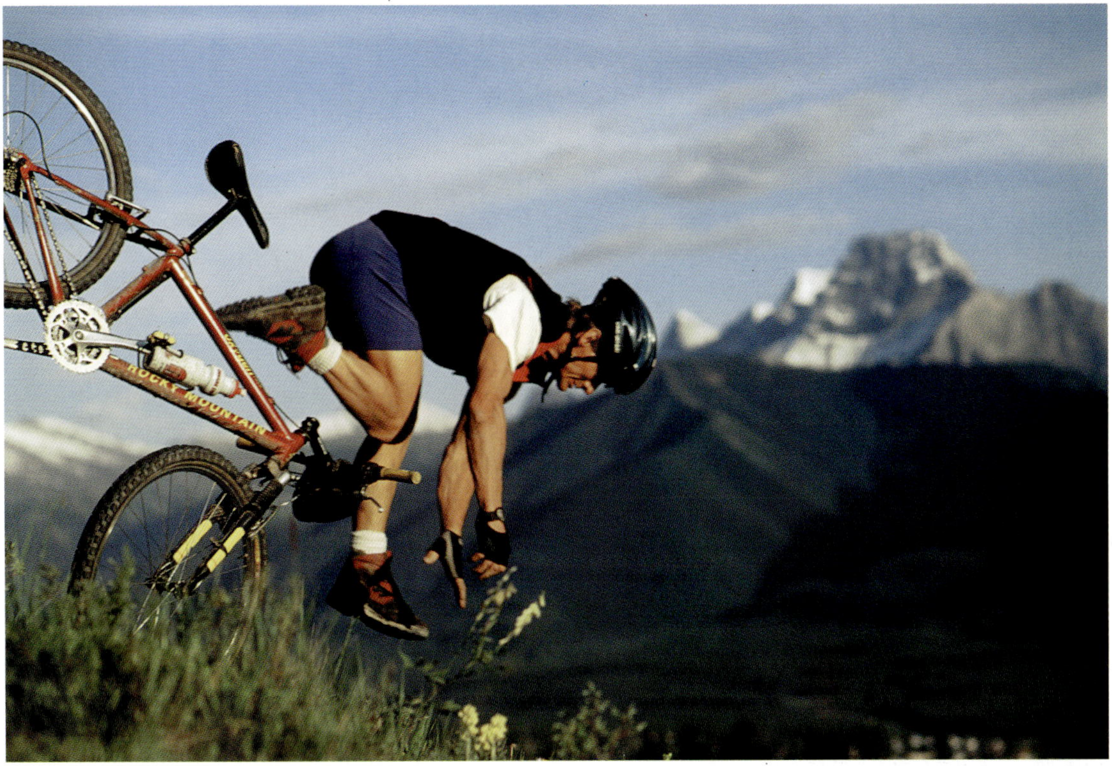

This biker's fall was intended. Even though I had placed a foam mattress on the hill below for him to land on, the impact still hurt. Consequently my "model" was hesitant to repeat the stunt. Canadian Rockies. Fuji Velvia, 105 mm lens.

If you're shooting ski or snowboard jumping, be extra careful to find a safe camera position. Your jumping subject may be unable to see you at all as he or she ramps up for the jump, especially if it's at the crest of a hill. In such cases it's very important to have good communication about where you'll stand or sit in relation to their line of descent.

One of the best shooting positions for any kind of jumping activity is right below the jump itself. This way you can shoot upwards toward your subject in mid-air, possibly with spectacular mountains or some other interesting scene behind.

Just make sure that any such jump won't collapse and bring a fast moving friend down on top of you. This has been known to happen. Also, make sure that you're tucked in below the jump far enough that you're not likely to be struck by a ski tail or back tire.

For this kind of shooting you'll pretty much need to have a wide-angle lens. Anything longer than, say, 35 mm will likely reward you with only a fractional view of your subject, but not the whole person.

Of course, for especially distant profile views of jumping you will probably need to employ longer lenses. There is rarely any danger of becoming a target of fast moving subjects when you choose this perspective. Consequently, it is probably the safest one if you want to avoid any risk of injury.

Big Trip Photography

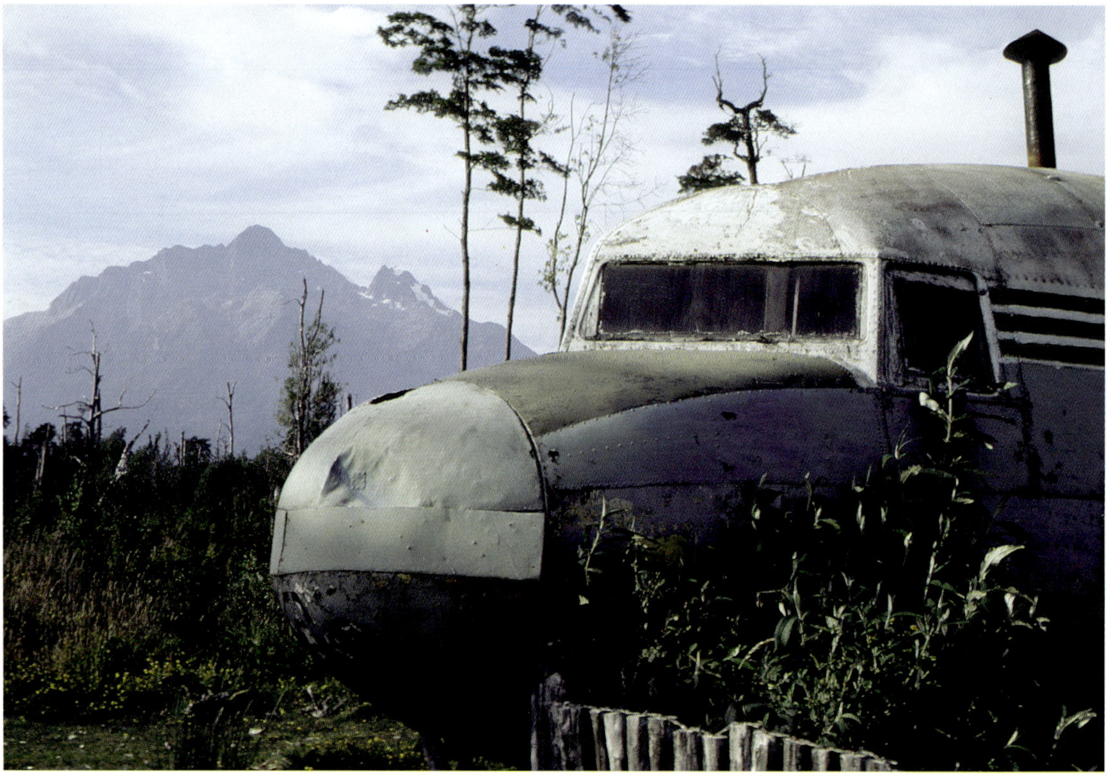

You never know what you might run into while travelling off the tourist track. I ran into this plane converted to someone's home in a remote part of Patagonia. Southern Chile. Kodachrome, 55 mm lens.

Whether you're planning to shoot while on high mountain expeditions, in ultra cold or tropically hot places, or during travels to mountainous places around the globe, things will have to be done a little differently than if on a simple outing to a favorite mountain haunt.

This section will look at the most important of those things. Since many of us like to show family, friends or the public at large the record of these trips afterwards, I'll also examine ways of most effectively putting together slide presentations, photo/text packages for publication and multimedia productions such as Powerpoint shows.

Be forewarned that these latter suggestions form merely an overview. Techniques will change—especially in the digital realm—with technology. My best advice is to consider some of these pointers and create experimental presentations yourself from your next big trip. Bon chance and bon voyage!

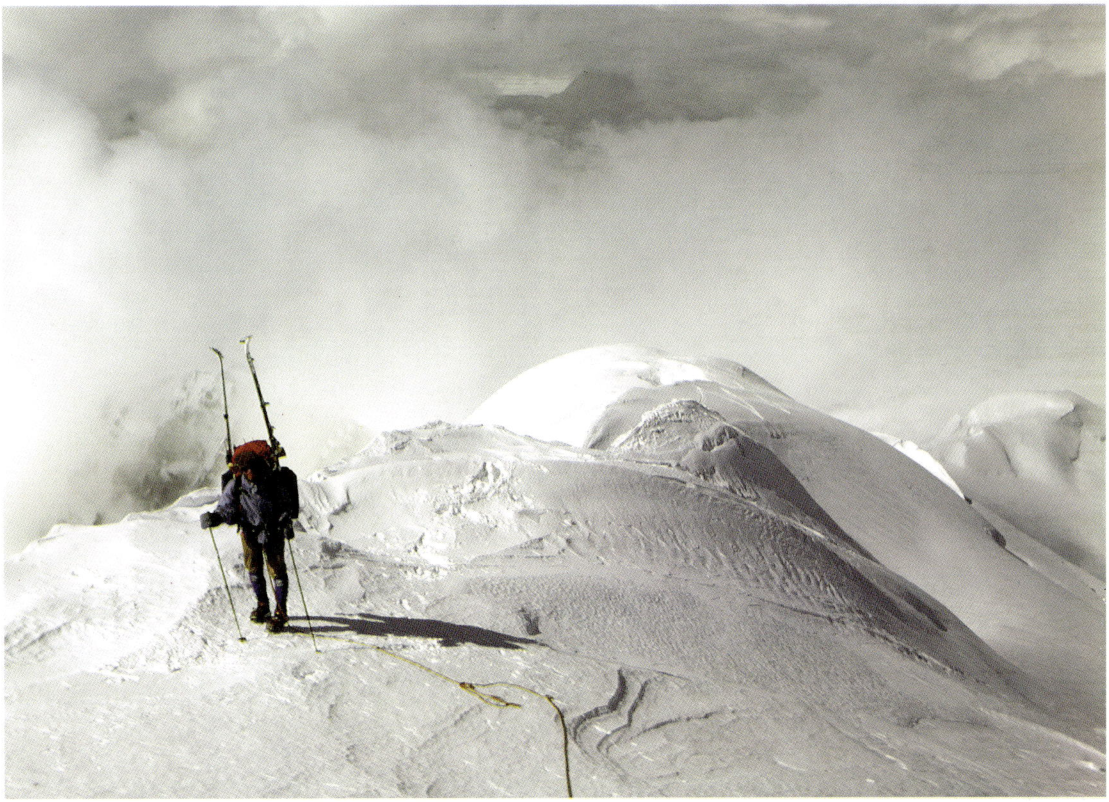

High–altitude photography, particularly in very cold weather, requires more tenacity—and pre-planning—than photography does in less arduous places. Mount Steele, St. Elias Mountains, Canada. Kodachrome, 85 mm lens.

High Mountain Expeditions

Some of us will embark upon expeditions into the most extreme mountain environments. Often these journeys will mean weeks or even months of travel away from civilization.

Extremes of both altitude and remoteness create hurdles for photography. Yet shooting while on the go is always worthwhile. The typically profound challenges inherent in expedition travel sometimes make phenomenal subjects on their own. At very least, its day–to–day progression—the expedition "story", if you like—needs visual documentation. Without it, rich and potent adventures and places are almost sure to fade from memory.

High mountain travel generally creates two constraints you have to operate under with camera gear. First is the limited weight requirement, meaning fewer pieces, less film and sometimes smaller cameras than you may be used to. Second is the need to have camera gear that will hold up well and be easy to work with in extremes of altitude and, often, cold (see following section).

Consider the first constraint. If you're travelling with porters or packtrains, heavier camera gear might not seem overly onerous. After all, at worst it may weigh in at the equivalent of two days worth of food for a party of four people.

In practise, though, heavy gear is a real pain. With certainty it will be considered amongst the most expendable items should weight need to be reduced. And, especially at the highest altitudes, it will feel weightier than ever.

This would seem to bode well for the employment of digital, rather than analog, cameras. Yet several things argue against them, at least for the moment. First is the battery issue; sometimes the weight you save by not having to carry film is more than compensated for by needing huge battery reserves.

More importantly, you need to ensure that your digital camera's electronics are not prone to failure while exposed to the enormous stresses of high mountain travel. Currently there is probably not a single digital camera on the market can match the toughness and rigorous performance of the older SLRs, such as Nikon's FE and F3 cameras. Until this changes, you might want to view digital camera use on expeditions with a healthy dose of skepticism.

Of course, if you have sponsors, or friends, back home that need constant visual updates, there is no contest between the two mediums. Digital cameras, in conjunction with a good satellite network connection, can provide continual up–to–the–moment reports on progress and events—something that no film camera could ever do.

Opposite, top: Cameras suitable for expeditions generally have to be smaller and more compact than for other mountain outings. Most of all they should be able to withstand rough handling. St. Elias Mountains, Canada. Kodachrome, 85 mm lens.

Opposite, bottom: "The old real estate adage location, location, location also holds true in mountain photography. I found just such a piece of real estate midway up the 2000 m west face of Denali in Alaska. All I needed was to step out of the tent and record our campsite's amazing location." Photo by Pat Morrow.

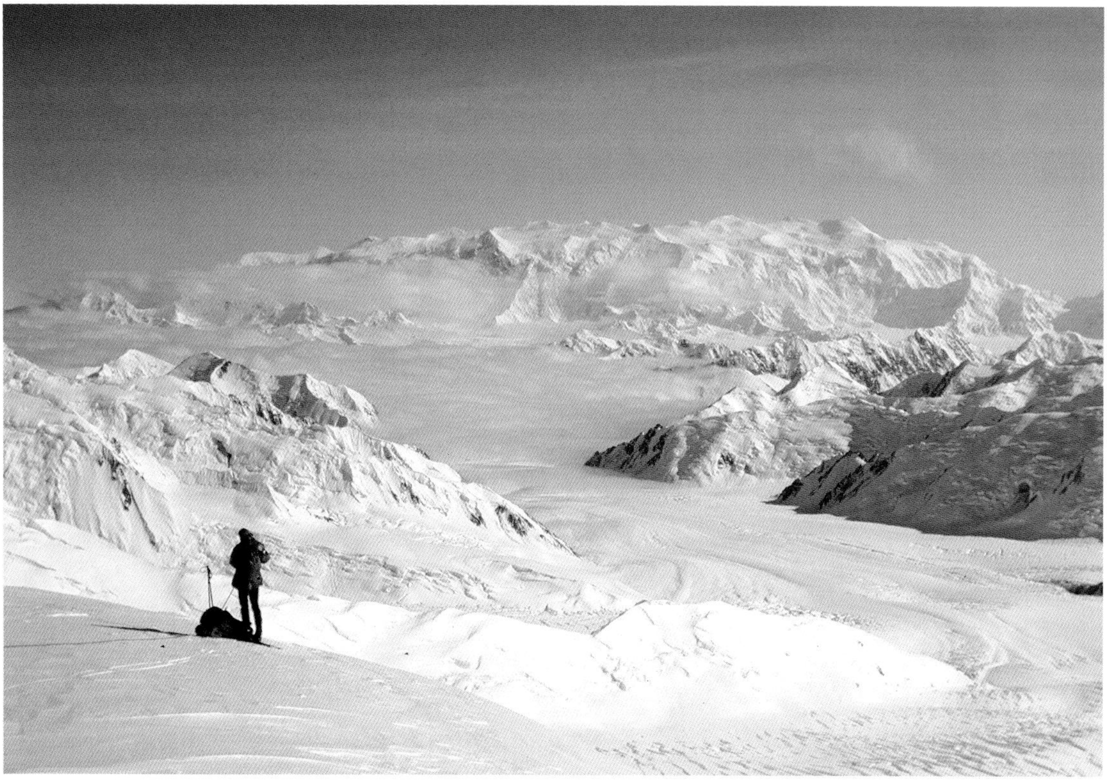

Having a good visual record of an expedition is intensely rewarding and almost always worth the difficulties that shooting on the go might present. St. Elias Mountains, Canada. Kodachrome, 35 mm lens.

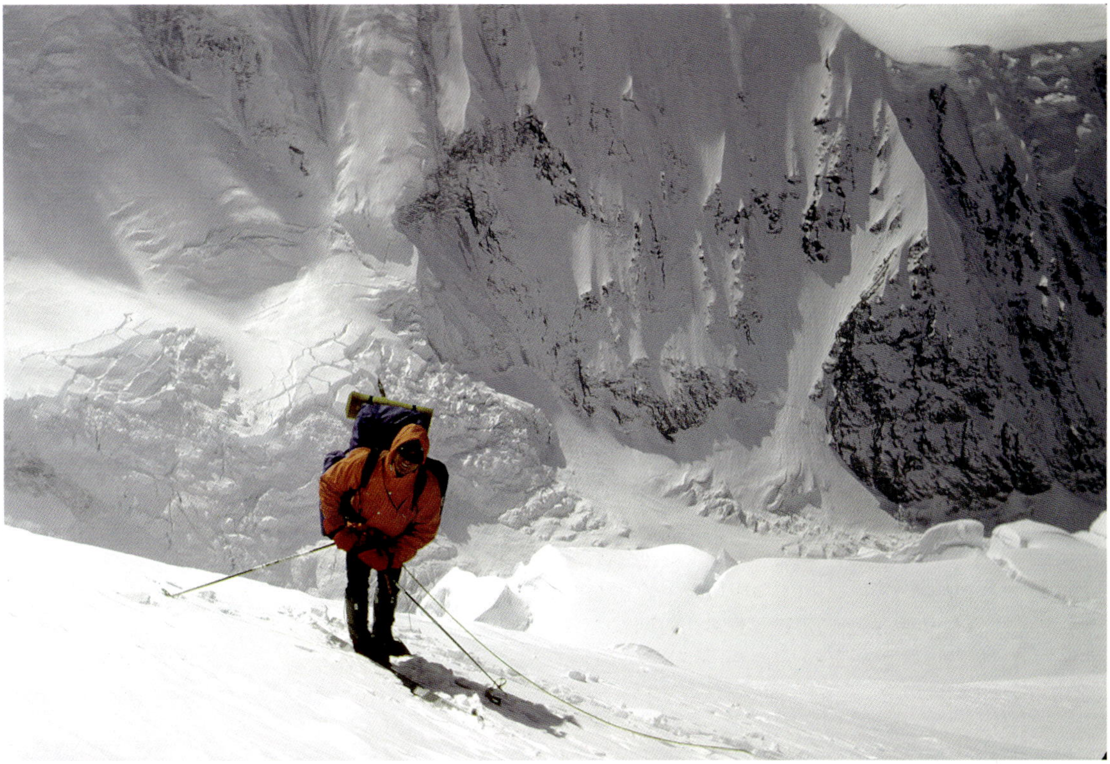

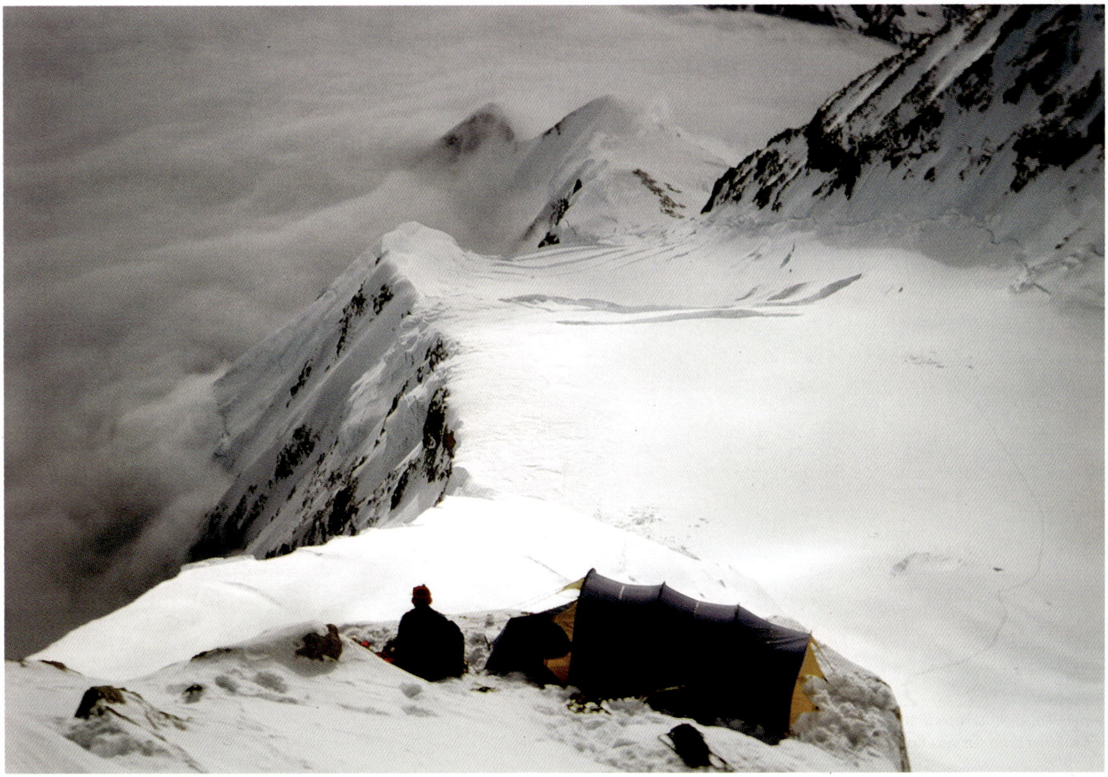

Shooting in Very Cold Weather

Mountain climates by nature are often cold, sometimes icily so. The coldest weather can easily snap film, and render batteries useless. It can also make using camera equipment extremely difficult because you fingers can easily freeze to the camera if they're unprotected. Heavy gloves may have to be worn, through which camera dials are nearly indistinguishable.

Shooting in extreme cold will never be easy. But there are a few precautions you can take and simple items of gear that you can acquire that will make it a whole lot easier.

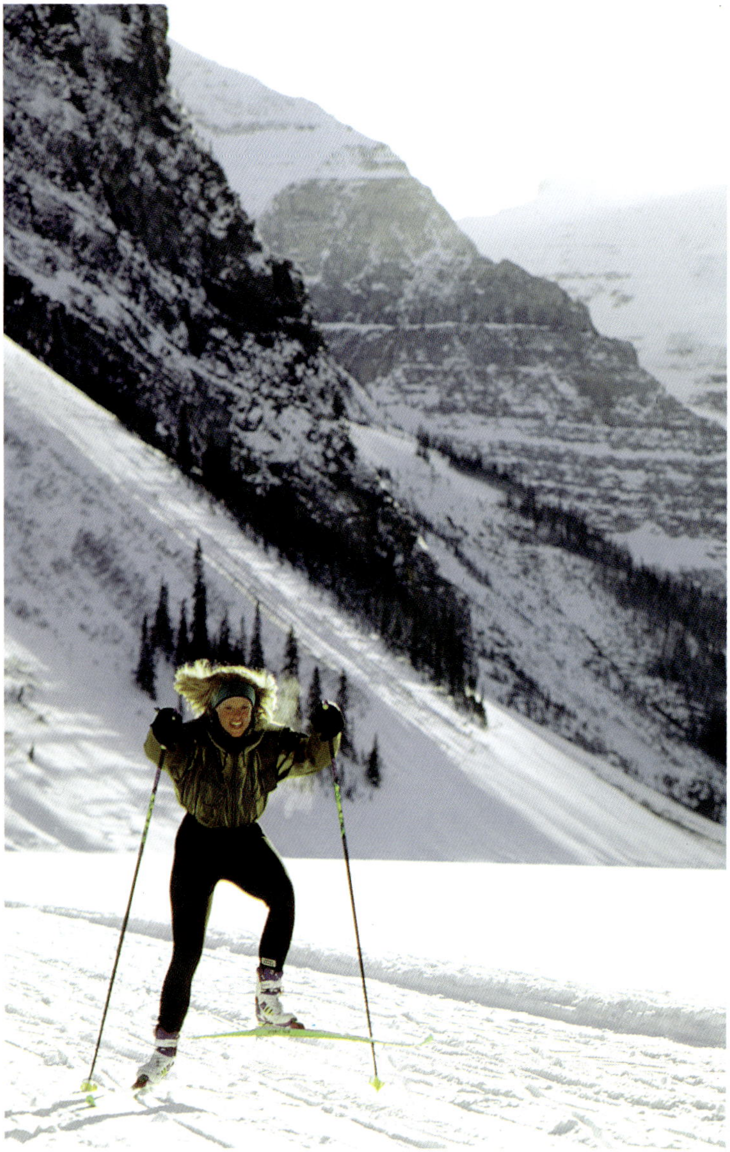

Remember to wear or take enough clothing to keep yourself—and your models—warm while shooting. Canadian Rockies, Fuji Velvia, 105 mm lens.

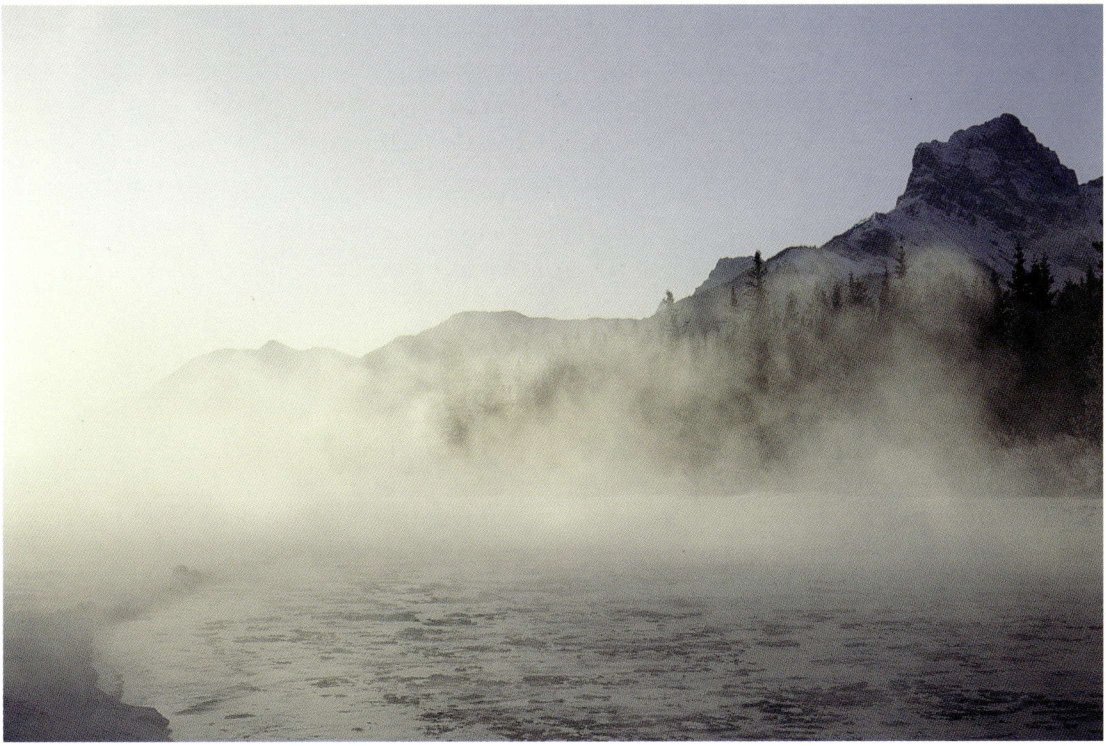

Ambient light is often strikingly beautiful in very cold weather, especially at early and late times of the day. Canadian Rockies, Fuji Velvia. 35-70 mm zoom lens.

The first of these is to protect your camera, and film, from the extreme cold, as you might also protect it from rain or excessive sun. Tuck it inside your parka, either while hanging from a strap around your neck or in a bag harnessed from your chest. Alternatively, place it in a part of your backpack that may receive a little ambient warmth, either from a hot thermos, say, or from your body during periods of exertion.

You should especially try to warm up new film spools before loading them into your camera. It's unlikely they'll snap at minus 20° C, but at minus 40° C film becomes very fragile. Even with slightly warmed film, exercise caution while loading if your camera has a manual winding lever.

With digital and automatic cameras the trick is to keep batteries functioning. Employ the same tactics as mentioned above. If you're not able to do an adequate job of warming with ambient body heat, try placing a "hot-shot", or similar packaged product, close to your equipment.

Use lithium batteries whenever possible; they'll likely outperform any NiCad product in very cold temperatures. If you have two battery packs, one can always be kept near your body, or some other external heating source, while the other is put to use.

Probably the best way to control camera function while also protecting your fingers in the extreme cold is to use a pair of glove liners. The best of these will allow outer gloves to be slipped on and off easily while providing fingers with both dexterity and warmth.

Remember that you have to keep yourself warm, too, when shooting in arctic weather, at least if it's to be even slightly enjoyable. To this end make sure that you wear adequate clothing. Invariably there will be periods of standing around while you compose or wait for just the right light, so make sure you have extra cold–weather gear in your pack too. The "hot-shots" mentioned earlier might make a useful and lightweight back–up item; buried perhaps in a chest pocket, in boots to keep feet warm, or tucked between inner and outer gloves.

Ultra-cold weather often creates intensely beautiful ambient conditions for shooting. These may well be your reward for braving the chills and heading into polar places, or at least their climates.

Hot Tropical Extremes

Although probably not as typical for most of us as shooting in cold weather is, very hot conditions might eventually become a fact of expedition travel. Sometimes they will be the preamble to higher, cooler and less humid weather, say while adventuring in Papua New Guinea, Africa and parts of South America.

Heat, especially in conjunction with high humidity, can wreak havoc on film. If left for a significant period of time in such conditions, colors deteriorate, clouding may occur and moulds sometimes begin to grow. The latter can render film absolutely useless and may not be observed until after processing.

These same conditions are horrible for other camera gear too, albeit probably not as catastrophic in the short term. Moulds might grow inside unprotected camera bodies, despite the somewhat toxic environment that usually exists there. Moisture can fog viewfinders and even coat the camera shutter itself.

Such persistent moisture will, if left unchecked, eventually disrupt all camera functions, starting with electronic ones. Hence, digital cameras do not necessarily offer a complete solution to the problem of shooting in the tropics.

Humidity is unbelievably pronounced while shooting in hot mountain jungles, particularly during wet times of year. Western Samoa. Fuji film, 35-70 mm zoom lens.

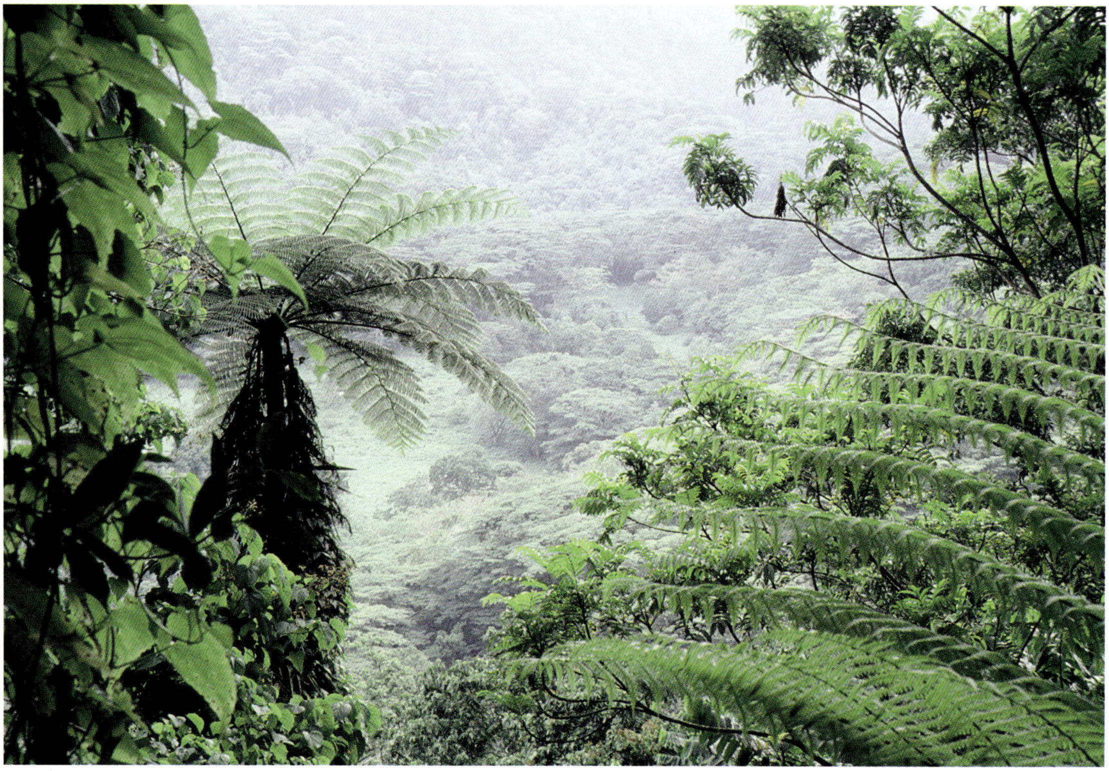

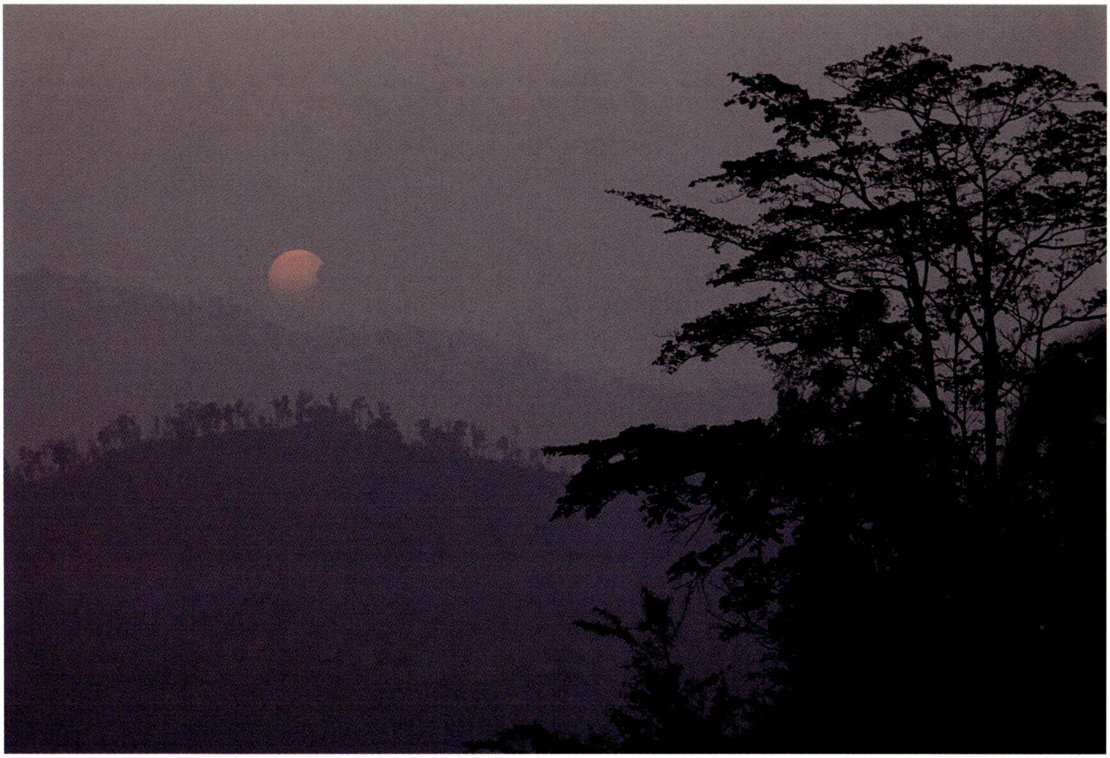

Intense heat and humidity create lighting conditions all of their own. As in other climates, light is usually best at early and late times of the day. Northern Thailand. Fuji film, 70-200 mm zoom lens.

The real trick is to plan a strategy in advance to protect both film and camera gear. Refrigeration is the best solution; literally placing one's cameras and film in refrigerated containers whenever they're not in use. Since such modern conveniences will likely be out of reach on almost any expedition to the tropics, other technology and techniques will have to suffice.

What you'll need to begin with is a good watertight case, such as those sold in camera stores for kayaking or canoe trips. Packages of silica gel should be liberally scattered inside; these will draw ambient moisture away from gear and film. Light–colored cases are preferable to dark ones, since they'll tend to reflect, not absorb, hot sunlight.

This case should be then stored and carried in whatever way attracts the least amount of heat. Keep it in the shade whenever you can. If the direct sun can't be avoided, throw a sleeping bag or blanket over it to provide some insulation while it sits.

Even after observing every possible precaution, film and gear will simply not last forever in the humid heat. If your trip is undertaken mainly for photography, you may simply have to limit your time in an unprotected tropical environment. When it's not, such as on a long jungle expedition, use as much ingenuity as you can.

World Travel

Journeying to mountainous places around the globe offers phenomenal opportunities for creative photography. Not only do landscapes and wildlife differ intriguingly from place to place, but so do the persons inhabiting such places. Mountain people and their cultural heritages in Asia, South America and Africa have indeed often been and remain the focus of illustrious photographic journeys.

You will almost always have to be sensitive to the cultural nuances of photographing in new places, though, most so in comparatively primitive ones. Not everyone wants their picture taken. In some places you are deemed to have stripped the very soul of anyone you snap a portrait of.

Some activities or places, such as festivals, temples or monasteries, may be off–limits to photography altogether. It's worth checking on this whenever you're not sure, whether in a travel guide book or with the local tourist office.

As mentioned in an earlier section, having an SLR with removable viewfinder can be an asset in such places, especially for recording candid snaps. With your viewfinder temporarily out of place, it's quite natural to keep your camera at waist level, or thereabouts, so you can look downwards to view a scene. Most people will be completely oblivious to a camera held this low, since they are accustomed to being photographed at eye level.

Wildlife varies remarkably between mountainous places around the world. Here my subjects are guanacos silhouetted against a very Patagonian backdrop. Southern Chile. Fuji film, 200 mm lens.

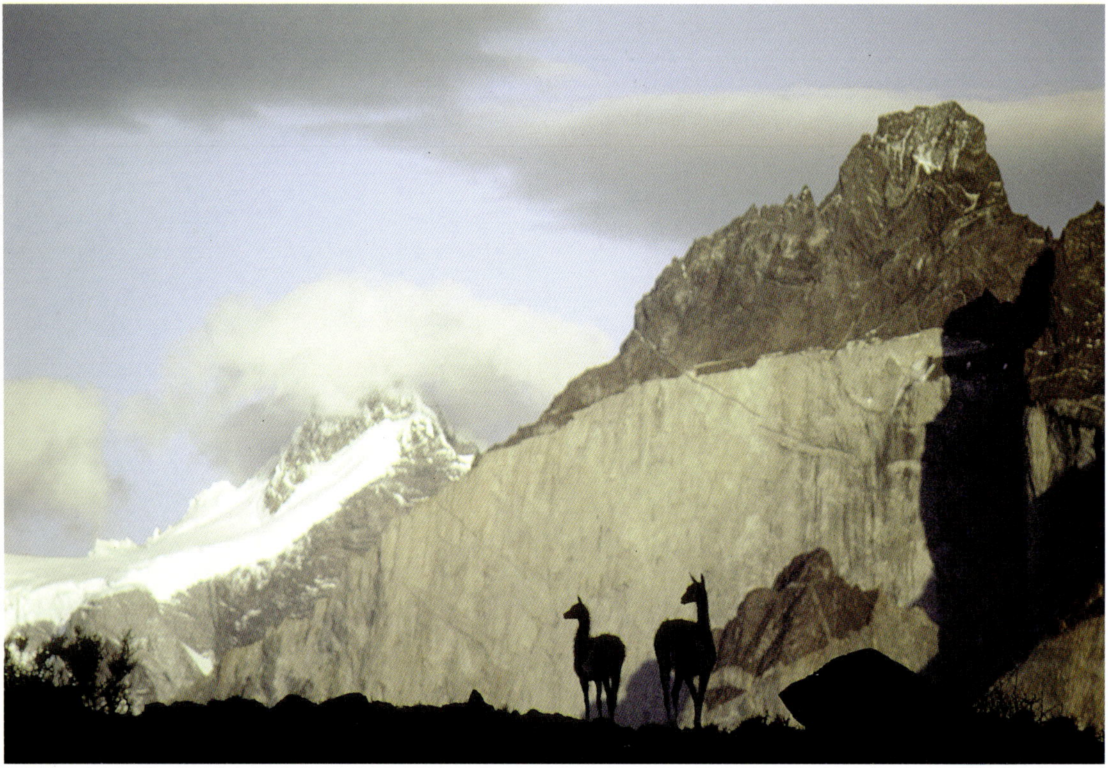

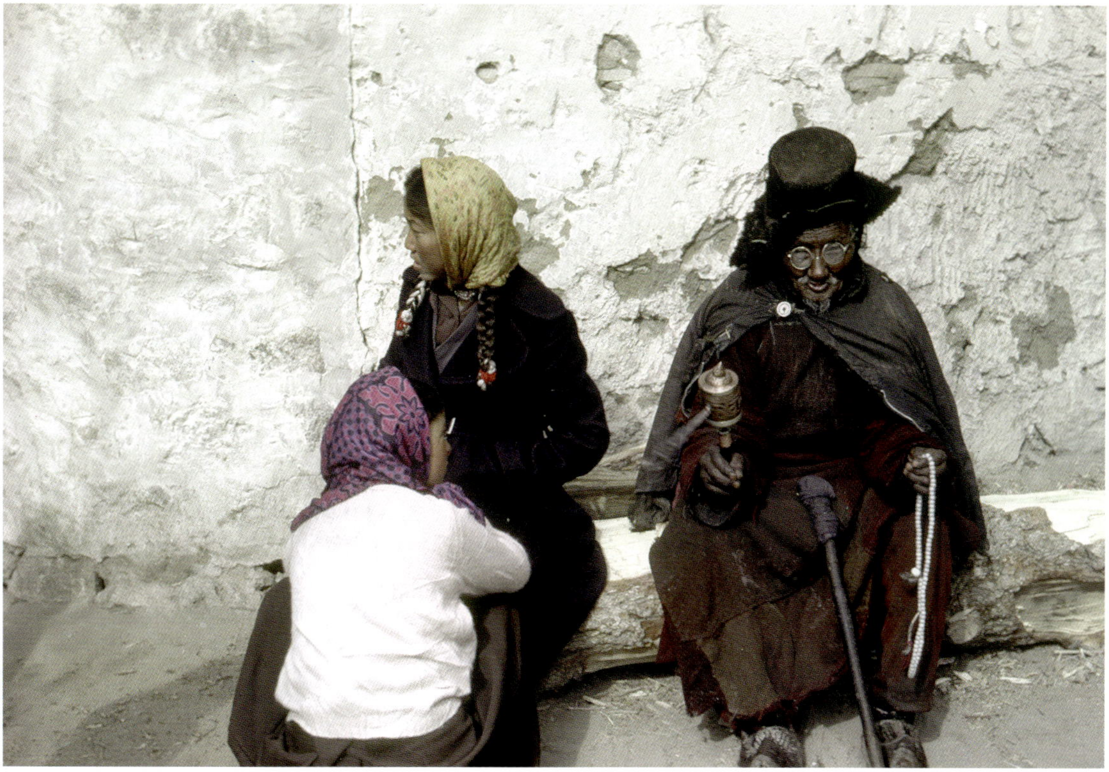

Being able to remove your viewfinder to look downwards while shooting can reward you with some great snaps. In this shot my subjects were completely unaware that I was photographing them. Ladakh, India. Kodachrome, 85 mm lens.

Exercise caution while shooting close to airports, railway lines, roadways or communication towers. These are considered strategic military installations in some countries and are protected as such by local law enforcement.

I was held at gunpoint years ago while photographing a piece of the scenic "toy" railway line snaking out of the Himalayas near Darjeeling, India. A police officer had me open my camera, then rip out and hand over the film inside before he would lower his gun from my right temple. Needless to say, since then I've been extra careful to learn what and where I can—and cannot—photograph.

Make sure to bring enough film from home. It can be both difficult to find and of dubious quality in many foreign countries. It may also be comparatively expensive.

Finally, ensure your film arrives at your destination safely and also at home afterwards. I always carry my film, along with the rest of my camera gear, on board with me when I travel by plane. Although it's probably safe enough to check it on if protected in a well-insulated case, I prefer the comfort of having it close to me while travelling. As we all know, checked baggage goes missing from time to time; to lose it for a period of days on a trip could be unfortunate at best, and potentially catastrophic.

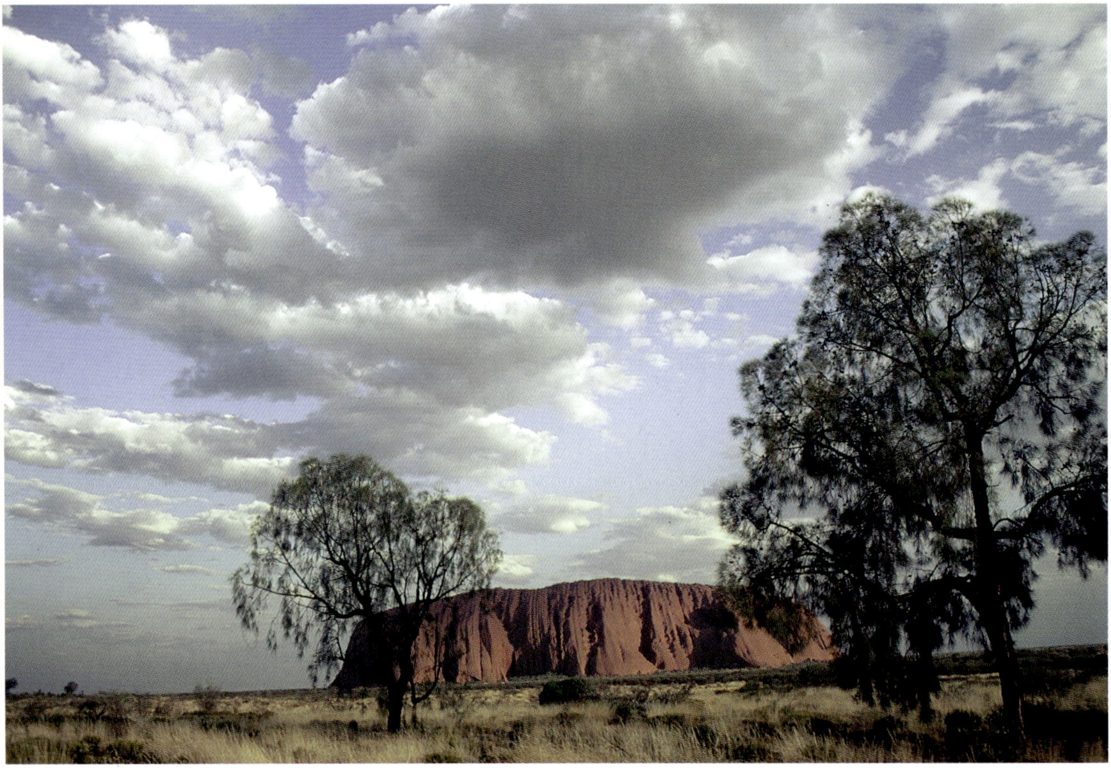

World travel offers countless opportunities for creative mountain photography. Uluru (Ayers Rock), Australia. Fuji Velvia, 28 mm lens.

While on the subject of airports, be careful with X-ray screening. Although airport officials may insist that their machines are film safe, this is simply not always true. Some are patently unsafe, and the problem is you never know which ones. I always request a manual inspection of my film instead of running it through the X-ray scanners: to date, I've only been denied once, while travelling through the Frankfurt airport.

Lead bags and containers especially designed to protect film from scanners may do more harm than good. Airport security personnel are trained to examine any unknown blobs appearing on their screens. Consequently, they will likely crank X-ray radiation levels even higher to learn what might be inside an apparently impenetrable bag or container.

After the tragic events of September 11, 2001, it may be inevitable that mandatory airport screening will be enlarged to include all types of film. If so, digital camera equipment will be more advantageous than ever. Just make sure that any you travel with will be up to the rigors of mountain travel in a foreign context, where replacement batteries or parts will be difficult—or impossible—to find.

Creating Effective Slide Shows

Mountain slide shows are a grand tradition. They have long been the forum for us mountain travellers to show our latest—or best—trips to family, friends and sometimes strangers. I vividly recall going to my first show nearly 30 years ago, and there were certainly many years of shows before that time.

These days they have been elevated to even higher and more sophisticated levels by professional speakers, who use slides of mountains and expedition travel in a metaphorical context for corporate or paying audiences.

Both a projector and screen are essential components of any slide show. Sometimes a white wall or bed sheet can be substituted if you don't have a screen, although usually at the expense of some image quality.

Projectors, in general, utilize trays, cubes and carousels. If shopping for one, keep in mind the probable length of your shows. It's a pain for you to be constantly changing trays or cubes, and your audience may lose interest too if the show is constantly disrupted.

Some projectors have better optics than others. The additional cost of these may be considerable, but possibly worthwhile if you plan to show your slides often.

There are two principal ways to organize your slides into a show. The first way is sequentially; slides are ordered starting with the beginning of the trip, and end with final stages, perhaps reaching base camp or a roadhead after weeks of travel. The other way is to think of a

Slide shows always benefit from shots linked in series, particularly when they "tell" a story. Here, the biker's fall is neatly described by two photos. A third shot that actually caught the beginning of his fall would have made the series even better. Canadian Rockies. Kodak 64T, 105 mm lens.

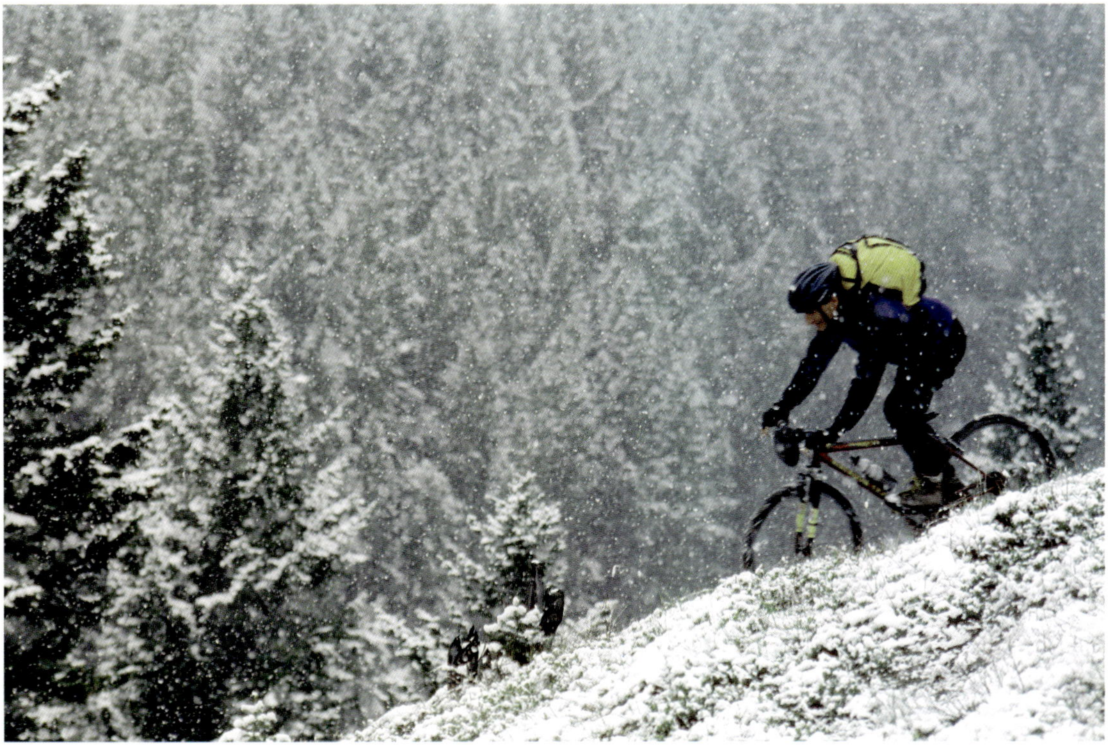

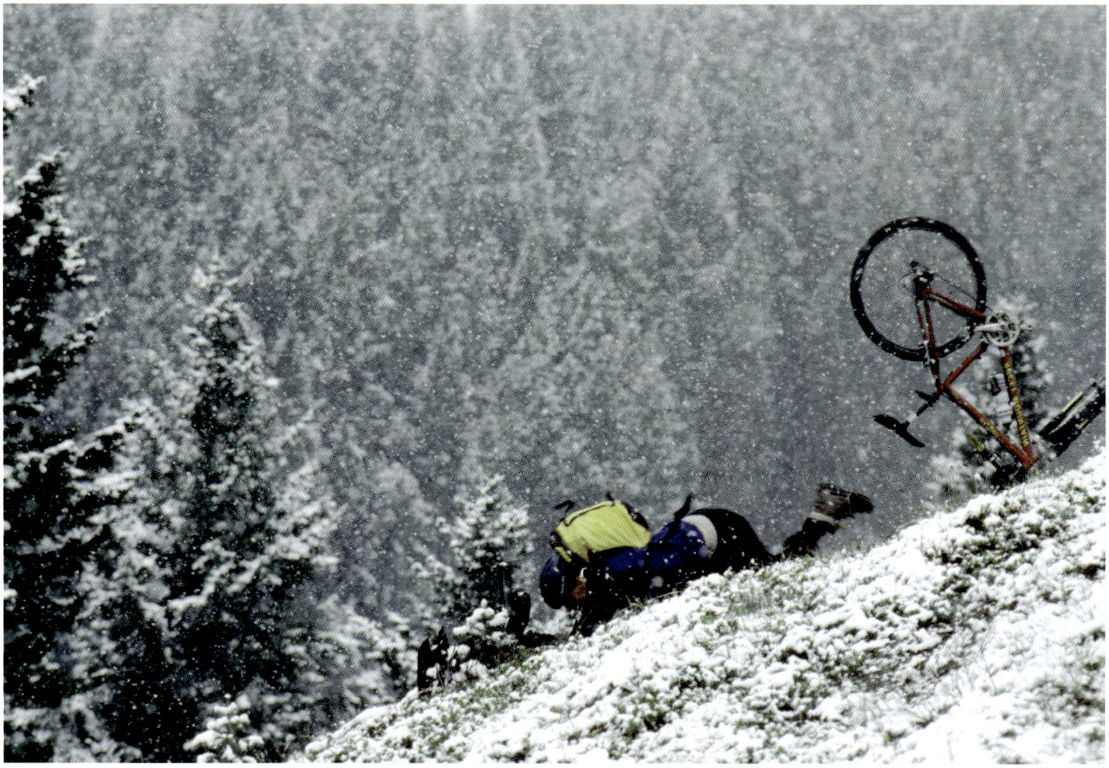

story before you construct your show and organize slides accordingly.

Neither is really better nor worse, although the latter approach is arguably more complex, and therefore more time consuming. Often, though, it provides a more intriguing presentation for your audience, especially when warranted by events that unfold.

Consider, for example, a trip to climb a high mountain, where the summit was reached after great struggle, and the descent was anticlimactic by comparison. Organizing slides sequentially would likely not be best, particularly if your final series of shots, showing the descent, was lengthy and relatively uninteresting.

Better to end the show just after the summit is reached. This may mean including some slides actually shot on the way down to illustrate the reverse, but why not? Call it creative license; only you, and your companions, will know differently in most cases.

Of course, there are circumstances where a sequential approach might still be the most exciting one. Say your main challenge, or misendeavor, occurred while on descent. Then this would become the natural climax of your story toward which the rest of it would build.

Some trips may have surprising highlights that have nothing to do with what you set out to accomplish, or see. I remember one such trip where two of us were forced to build a raft to cross a glacial lake in Argentine Patagonia. It took forever and was ultimately unsuccessful—it sunk and we had to climb a difficult mountain instead—yet it was by far and away the highlight of that trip.

Such stories are wonderfully told with slides. The trick in doing so effectively, though, is to give your audience the same sense of surprise and pure adventure you experienced at the time. Don't let the cat out of the hat, so to speak, until the last possible moment.

The greatest failing of any slide show is audience boredom. Along with arranging your photos for the greatest possible impact, you must be prepared to edit, edit and then edit some more. Consider each slide critically; if it's not either visually exciting or needed to tell your story, it should be left out.

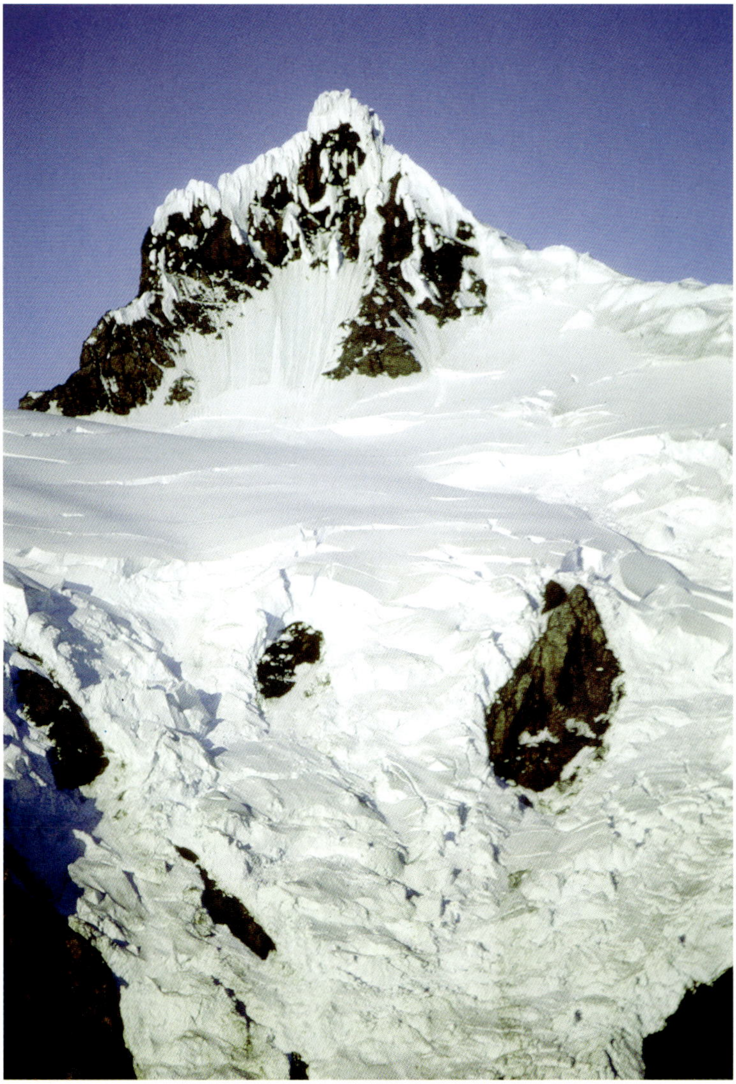

Vertical shots such as this one are particularly useful when seeking to publish mountain stories in a journal or magazine. As well as nicely showing the peak you climbed (or skied down), the vertical format fits magazine and book page layouts particularly well. Unnamed peak, Argentine Patagonia. Kodachrome, 55 mm lens.

Publishing Your Mountain Stories

The creation of photo and text packages for publication is particularly relevant with alpine travel. Mountain stories often need a visual component to make them really come alive, as well as to establish geographic or some other context.

Having your latest, or most cherished, mountain stories published in a magazine or alpine journal is more than simply satisfying. It can be downright exciting, particularly at the moment your piece first comes out in print.

If you have good writing skills and don't mind spending the time over your notepad or computer, your task is made quite simple. If not, but you know someone you can team up with to do the writing, then so much the better.

Remember the adage, "a picture is worth a thousand words". In many of the best pieces, photos will carry a story on their own. This is particularly true when you're the one writing the text and your photography skills are stronger than your writing. If writing skills are just as strong, or better, than photography ones, then shots should at least complement text, and hopefully enliven it.

It's always helpful to know before setting out on a trip if it is likely that you will be publishing an article on it so that you can gear your photography to a pre-developed storyline. Even if the storyline changes, owing to unforeseen adventures, say, or an improved understanding of the mountain areas you're exploring, chances are that pre-planned photography ideas will give you a better selection to choose from later on.

What you'll have to do in advance of writing any story is to approach the editor of the intended publication with a written proposal, or query. This can generally be done on-line, via snail mail, or perhaps by fax, but not over the phone; unless you're friends with the editor.

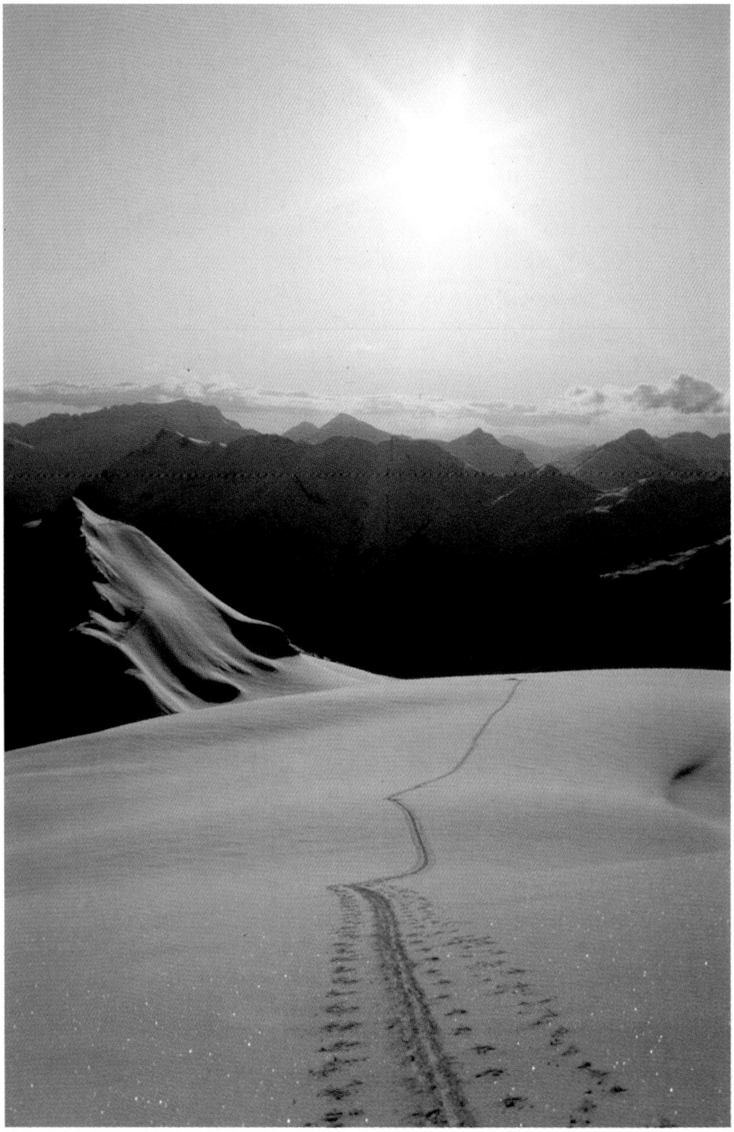

This kind of shot describes mountain travel in a particularly effective way. It will likely go further in telling the story of a trip than several written paragraphs. Cariboo Mountains, Canada. Kodachrome, 85 mm lens.

I won't delve into the logistics of proposal preparation here. There are several good books and courses that can take you through this process, if you're so interested. Check in the reference section for a few suggestions. Books and courses will also help you create, and finish, your story after receiving publisher approval. What they may not help you with, though, is selecting the best photos to send in with your finished manuscript.

Photos should be carefully edited to avoid dilution of your best work. They need not be only the best ones; in fact, you'll probably need a decent cross-section of images that may be illustrative as well as captivating. Whatever you do though, avoid adding shots that are neither particularly good, nor show anything that other photos depict better.

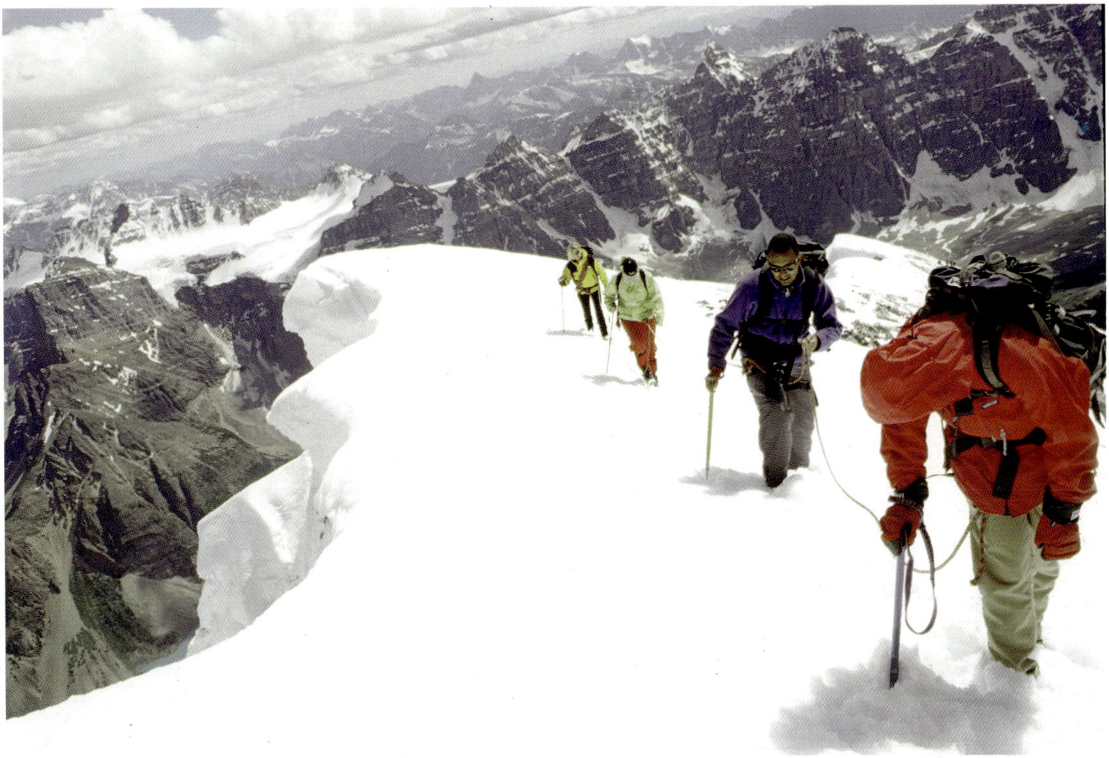

Building Multimedia and Digital Presentations

As with slide shows, photographs that connect details of a trip are especially useful in any multi-image presentation. In this series, the climbers are first shown struggling up a high ridge and then (next page) making a celebratory cell phone call from the mountain summit. Canadian Rockies. Kodak E100VS, 28 mm lens.

You don't need a lot of technology to create simple but professional looking multimedia productions, whether your camera happens to be analog or digital.

Both narration and music can be added to any slide show to give it a more polished touch. Adding sound is generally not that complex a procedure if your projection system allows for it. Check to see what's involved while buying any new equipment, or whether your existing projector will allow for it.

Powerpoint, Flash, After Effects and other similar software programs allow you to do the job even more easily, either while using a digital camera or after scanning your analog images onto your computer's hard drive. Images can be mixed not only with narration and music, but also with moving footage, text, illustration and other media.

The whole multimedia field has become more exciting than ever, thanks to such technology. It's one of those domains where sky is really the limit; your creativity can be absolutely boundless while experimenting in any one of a number of areas.

Learning the basic tools and procedures is actually quite straightforward. But, because multimedia technology is changing especially fast these days, you'll likely want to make yourself aware of the latest trends. Check the reference section for some suggestions on where to look.

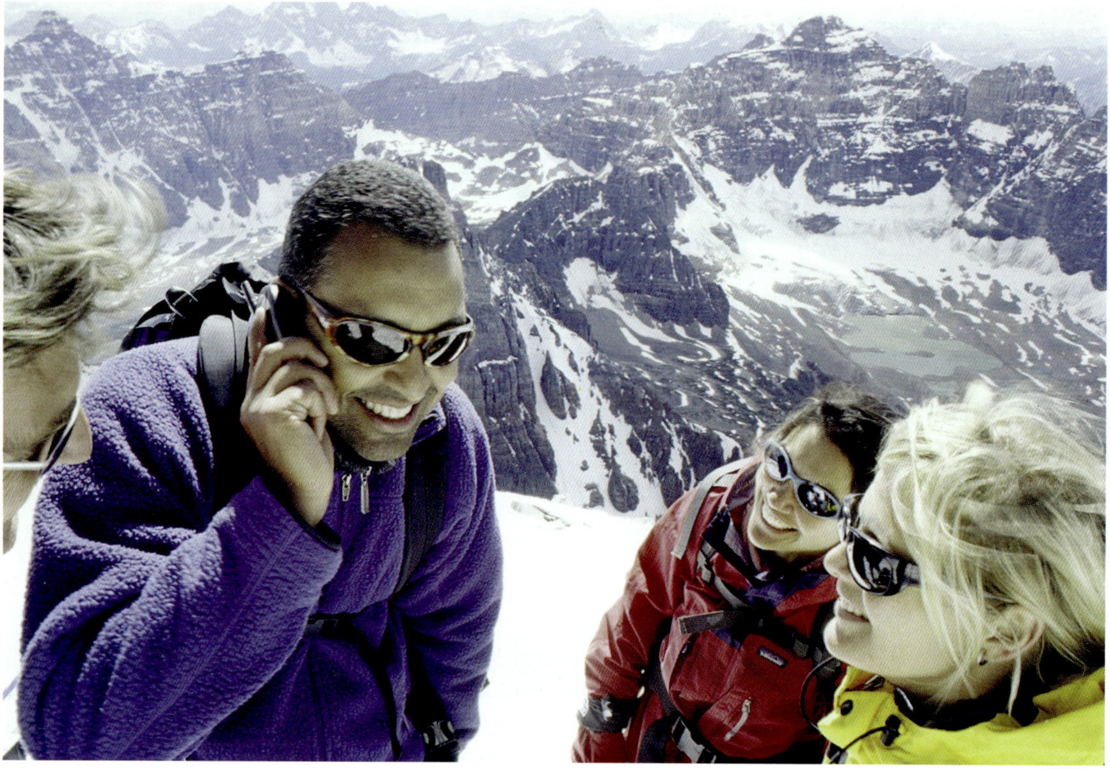

Note that what the latest technology won't change are the basic building blocks of story creation. No matter how good your technical knowledge or computer skills happen to be, any presentation will fall short if these are poorly applied.

Just as with putting on a good slide show, the starting point for building any presentation is to create a storyline of sorts. Hollywood producers normally create "storyboards", or sketches of intended scenes, before doing any filming. These can be very elaborate in some cases—the great film director, Alfred Hitchcock, liked to comment that his movies were complete before any film was shot, so comprehensive was his storyboarding. In other cases a rudimentary outline will suffice.

Most of us will likely be creating presentations after the fact; that is, choosing storylines after shooting, rather than before. The obvious advantage with this approach is that you know what you've got, photographically, before you plan any particular story or treatment.

From here it's mainly a matter of careful construction, always with an eye towards what your intended "audience" will be most entertained or intrigued by. And as you might show a slide presentation to a single viewer or two before airing it in front of a group of people, try your multimedia show on a friend or neighbour before making it public.

Troubleshooting

Camera

Problem: scratches are visible on the film surface, across most or all of the shots on a roll of film.

Solution: this indicates that grit has lodged itself onto the film camera's pressure plate (usually mounted on its hinged rear door). Inspect and clean it carefully before loading another roll of film. Try not to touch the pressure plate with fingers while doing so; otherwise it might pick up more grit or body oils.

Problem: an out-of-focus blemish occupies part of a frame edge.

Solution: chances are that a hair or filament has become stuck between lense and shutter, most likely on the bottom of the flip up mirror if your camera is a SLR. Inspect this area carefully, and perhaps both lense surfaces too. Use a blower brush to remove any obvious dirt, but be careful not to leave behind brush hairs while doing so.

Problem: an out-of-focus blemish shows up towards the middle of an image.

Solution: almost certainly this has resulted from dirt or hairs on a lense surface. Inspect and clean both thoroughly, especially the inside lense face (the one facing towards your camera).

Problem: a red or orange colored streak appears across one part of an image.

Solution: your film was inadvertently exposed to light before being rewound into its canister. Most likely the camera's door opened, even slightly, at some point while the roll was in use. Possibly your camera leaks light, in which case it should be thoroughly checked by a qualified technician.

Focusing Issues

Problem: everything is out of focus.

Solution: is camera shake the problem? If so, increase shutter speed or practice holding your camera more securely. Alternatively, use a tripod.

- If using an automatic camera, check to see that its focusing function is working properly.

- If focusing manually, ensure that your eyes are measuring things accurately. Ask a friend to focus on a chosen object, try doing so as well, and check that the focus setting you both select match.

Problem: subject is blurry and background elements are sharp.

Solution:this might occur if your subject is moving and your chosen shutter speed is too slow. If so, increase shutter speed and focus on your subject, at the expense of background elements.

- if using an automatic camera, review its instructions to learn how to focus on a chosen subject, not the entire scene. Alternatively, focus manually if your camera allows you to.

Problem: by selectively focusing, you'd like to isolate a subject from both foreground and background elements, and create a sense of "peering in" on your subject.

Solution: The device which best allows you to do this, while also helping you to create a three dimensional effect, is known as interference. Try shooting past an interesting foreground feature to a sharply focused subject and a defocused background. Use your camera's depth of field preview function, if available, to determine a best f-stop setting.

Depth of Field

Problem: only some parts of your subject are in focus when you want the whole thing to be sharp.

Solution: increase depth of field by choosing a larger f-stop number. This will mean either decreasing the shutter speed or using a faster film. If your camera has one, use the depth of field preview function to ensure that everything is sharp that you want to be.

Problem: many scene elements are sharp; you'd like to draw attention to particular parts of a subject by defocusing other things.

Solution:decrease depth of field by choosing a smaller f-stop number. To do so, either increase shutter speed, use a neutral density filter or a slower film. Depth of field preview will, if available, help you to fine tune your intended effect.

Problem: you'd like an entire scene to be sharp, including very nearby blossoms and distant mountains. How will you know whether it will be?

Solution: depth of field preview probably won't be of use in this case, even if you have it. Everything might be too dark to be readable. If your chosen lens has f-stop calibrations, try focusing first on the closest part of your intended scene. Match the reading thus determined to f-stop calibrations on your lense. Ensure that the corresponding calibration on the lense includes an infinity setting. If not, choose a larger f-stop number or move back from your intended foreground to a point where it does so.

Problem: a subject shows motion blurriness and background is unsharp.

Solution:you need to determine what you want sharply focused. If it's your background, choose a wider depth of field (larger f-stop number) to keep it in focus as well as intermediate parts of your frame. Your subject's motion blur might then look appropriate to the scene. If you want a sharp subject, however, and you don't care whether your background is sharp or not, choose a narrower depth of field (smaller f-stop number), a faster shutter speed, and then focus on the subject itself.

Exposure

Problem: entire scene is a little too dark.

Solution: decrease f-stop by 1 full setting, say from f-8 to f-5.6. Alternatively, decrease shutter speed by one full stop, such as from 1/250 second to 1/125 second.

Problem: entire scene is a little too bright.

Solution: reverse of above.

Problem: entire scene is far too dark.

Solution: decrease f-stop by 2 full settings, say from f-8 to f-4. Alternatively, decrease shutter speed by two full stops, such as from 1/500 second to 1/125 second. Or, decrease both f-stop and shutter speed by one setting each.

Problem: entire scene is far too bright.

Solution: reverse of above.

Problem: subject's faces, or other areas of main interest, are too dark; rest of the scene is well lit.

Solution:reflect or flash light onto dark areas so that exposure differences between them and the rest of the scene are lessened (anymore than 1 to 2 stops difference will generally look unacceptable in results).

Problem: subject's faces, or other areas of main interest, are well lit; rest of the scene is too bright.

Solution: as above, the best solution is increasing light on areas of main interest. Take a new light reading from both subject and background after having done so to confirm one to two stops difference at most between them. If in doubt about what exposure will give you the best results, try shooting 3 shots; one determined by the background exposure, one geared to subject exposure, and a third one in between these two settings.

Creative

Problem: your composition, which looked exciting and thus photoworthy at first, seems to lack those qualities when seen through your viewfinder.

Solution: analyse what aroused your enthusiasm to begin with. Was it foreground details? If so, pay more attention to them, either by including a larger foreground area in your shot than normal, focussing on it instead of background areas, or closing in tightly before shooting. If background elements were most captivating, think of ways to dramaticize them. If beautiful light was the key ingredient — and it has since faded — the shot may no longer be worth considering at all.

Problem: subjects appear uninteresting through your viewfinder, even though other compositional elements work.

Solution: often this is a result of a subject's relative size or placement in the overall composition. Try getting closer to your subject, perhaps even to the point of just showing body parts such as hands, feet or an upper torso (use a wide depth of field if you want to include these and background areas both in focus). Alternatively, make the subject small in your composition, by backing away from him, or by using a wide lens. If the distant scene is paramount to your shot, place your subject closer to the edge of the frame than you might otherwise. Keep trying new approaches until you see one you're satisfied with.

References

Here is an incomplete list of web sites and publications that I've found useful while hunting for new gear, for technical information and for inspiration. Hopefully you'll find them useful too.

Some web sites for cameras, lenses and flashes:

www.canon.com
www.contaxcameras.com
www.hasselblad.com
www.leica.com
www.minolta.com
www.nikon.com
www.olympus.com
www.pentax.com
www.sony.com
www.tamron.com
www.vivitar.com
www.yashica.com

Some web sites for film and accessories:

www.agfa.com
www.bogenphoto.com (for tripods and tripod heads)
www.fujifilm.com
www.ilford.com
www.kodak.com
www.lowepro.com (for camera bags)
www.manfrotto.com (for tripods and tripod heads)
www.tamrac.com (for camera bags)
www.tiffen.com (for filters)

Further reading:

35 mm Handbook, Michael Freeman, New Burlington Books, UK
Galen Rowell's Vision: The Art of Adventure Photography, by Galen Rowell, Sierra Club Books, USA
Guide to Climbing Photography, by Jeff Achey, Stackpole Books, USA
Handcoloring Photographs Step by Step, by Sandra Laird and Carey Chambers. Amherst Media, USA
Joy of Photography, by Freeman Patterson, Key Porter Books, Canada
Mountain Light, by Galen Rowell, Sierra Club Books, USA
Photographer's/Writer's market, by F&W Publications, USA
Photography and the Art of Seeing, by Freeman Patterson, Key Porter Books, Canada

Some useful magazines that feature great mountain photography:

Alp, Torino, Italy
Climbing Magazine, Colorado, USA
Desnivelle, Madrid, Spain
Klettern, Stuttgart, Germany
National Geographic Adventure, New York, USA
On the Edge, Derbyshire, UK
Outdoor Photography Magazine, Los Angeles, USA
Outside Magazine, New Mexico, USA
Rock and Ice Magazine, Colorado, USA
Vertical, Grenoble, France

Glossary

ASA – measure of a film's sensitivity to light. ASA is the acronym for American Standards Association. ASA ratings are arithmetically progressive, such that—for example—an ASA 100 film is twice as fast as an ASA 50 film.

Bracketing – a technique employed to reduce the likelihood of choosing a wrong exposure setting. The same subject or scene is photographed at different speeds or apertures, usually both above and below a best exposure guess.

Bounce flash – directing light onto a subject during flash photography, usually by reflecting it off a light colored surface such as a wall or handheld reflector.

Camera shake – unintended camera movement at the time of exposure that results in image blurriness.

Color compensating filter – filter employed to alter the color of light entering through a camera lens. Color compensating filters are available in all of the primary colors.

Color conversion filter – color conversion filters change the color temperature of light, either by warming it or by cooling it.

Contrast – variations in brightness across a subject or scene. High contrast means a large difference between brightest and darkest areas; low contrast means relatively small differences.

Depth of field – range of sharpness across a subject or scene. A wide depth of field can be created by reducing the lens aperture (choosing a higher f-stop number). A narrow depth of field is ascertained by doing the opposite.

DIN – like ASA, a measure of film speed. Unlike ASA ratings, DIN numbers are logarithmically progressive. DIN stands for Deutsch Industrie Norm.

Exposure latitude (of film) – the relative ability of a film to preserve detail in both shadow and highlight areas. High-exposure latitude films manage to do this better than ones which emphasize contrast.

f-stop – describes a lens' aperture opening. Small f-stop numbers correlate to a wide opening for more light-gathering power and a smaller depth of field. Large f-stop numbers relate to smaller openings, less light gathering, and a wider depth of field.

Film speed – the relative sensitivity of a film to light, generally expressed by an ASA or DIN number.

Fish-eye lens – extremely wide-angle lenses that cause significant distortion. A "fish-eye" shot is characterized by frame edges that curve dramatically away from the center.

Flare – scattered and reflected light that usually shows up as blotches, circles and hexagons on a photograph, often degrading image quality, but sometimes enhancing the overall creative impression.

Focal length – describes the size of a lens, either as wide angle, standard or telephoto, or with a numerical value. Focal length is technically the distance between the center of a lens and its focal point.

Graininess – relates to the "look" of an image, whether sharp (fine-grained) or "grainy" (coarse grained). The unassisted eye can't see individual grains on film—it resolves groupings of grains instead.

Incident light reading – incident meters record the amount of light actually reaching a subject or scene, not the amount of light being reflected from one.

Interference – out-of-focus foreground elements that visually and creatively distract attention from subject areas. Often they will help to describe a "story" about the subject or scene.

Lens flare – see Flare above.

Lens hood (or shade) – blocks unwanted angular light from striking the lens surface, especially the kind that causes lens flare. The hood is generally either an extension of the lens barrel or a separate device with a screw or bayonet mount.

Luminance – the amount of light being reflected from, or produced by, a surface.

Monopod – as opposed to the three legs of a tripod, a monopod only has one. Hence it cannot support a camera on it own. It may, however, help to neatly bridge the gap between handheld and tripod-assisted photography.

Negative – a photographic reversal. Negatives show reversed tones with black & white films, and reversed colors with color films. They are generally used to produce prints, but may also be projected or scanned in order to arrive at a positive image.

Neutral density filter – a filter that reduces the amount of incoming light through a camera lens. Neutral density filters lack any color, so will not change the appearance of an image, except for its brightness.

Panning – smoothly swinging the camera in unison with subject movement. Panning is usually practised in a horizontal fashion, although vertical and diagonal panning may also make sense in certain situations.

Parallax error – the difference between images seen at close distance from two slightly different positions. Rangefinder (or viewfinder) cameras are particularly prone to parallax error, since their viewing and lens positions are separate.

Polarization (polarizing filters) – polarizing literally restricts the directional vibration of light. The effect of a polarizing filter is to suppress white light reflection, sometimes improving the look of skies, water and other reflective surfaces.

Rangefinder cameras – also known as "viewfinder" cameras, rangefinder cameras have separate lens and viewing assemblies. The user does not actually see compositions through the camera lens, as is the case with SLR cameras.

Reciprocity failure – at very fast or slow shutter speeds (above 1/2000 second and below 1/4 second) film will not respond to light exactly as predicted. Extra exposure is needed, the amount dependent on film characteristics. Colors also shift somewhat, possibly requiring correction with filters.

Reflected light reading – unlike incident light readings, reflected readings depend on the light being reflected by a subject. As some surfaces are more reflective than others, these readings can vary greatly between objects, even though same amounts of light are striking them.

Reflector – any surface that is used to reflect light. The term is generally applied to items carried specifically for this purpose.

Reversal film – transparency film. It is called "reversal" because of a development process that reverses what otherwise would be a negative image.

Selective focus – literally as the term implies, focusing is chosen for selective elements of a scene. These might be close foreground subjects, one at a middle distance, or background elements.

Single-lens reflex (SLR) cameras – the mirror assembly of a SLR camera allows the user to look directly through a chosen lens while composing a scene. Consequently, problems with parallax error are eliminated.

Soft focus filter – soft focus filters are used purposely to dull image sharpness, primarily while shooting portraiture. They accomplish this with a rough or etched glass surface.

Telephoto lens – also known as "long focus" lenses, telephoto lenses are generally considered as those having a focal length roughly twice as long, or longer, than the film format. Hence, in 35 mm photography they include lenses of 70 mm and higher.

Through-the-lens (TTL) meter – a built-in exposure meter that takes readings through the camera lens. Many flash units have TTL settings, which allow for automatic flash output selection.

Transparencies – more commonly referred to as slides, they have a transparent film base, through which positive images can be viewed under light.

Tungsten film – film mainly intended for use with tungsten lighting sources, which operate at temperatures between 3200° K and 3400° K. When used in full daylight conditions, tungsten films require amber filtration if a blue color cast is to be avoided.

Wide-angle lens – lenses with an angle of view wider than roughly 50°. They are also referred to as "short focus" lenses and are generally defined as having a focal length no longer than the film format. Hence, in 35 mm photography wide-angle lenses are those of 35 mm and less.

Zoom lens – zoom lenses have a continuously variable focal length across their range. A 70-200 mm zoom, for example, permits the user to select any focal length from 70 to 200 mm without changing focus or aperture.

Acknowledgements

This book was years in the making, while I pondered countless questions friends asked about photography in the mountains. Many thanks to all of you for your often insightful queries and comments. Thanks also to Tony Daffern, the publisher of this book, for his inspiration and patience while I penned a response to these and still other questions.

My good friend and first "business" partner, the late Scott Duncan, was more enthusiastic and encouraging about photography than any other person I've met. His spirit continues to influence my work and life in powerful ways. Many thanks Scott.

Thanks also to other mountain friends and family members who have joined me on trips to the crags, and especially to those of you who have been willing accomplices on my mountain photography forays, often "modelling" and stunting for the pure fun of it. Thanks to my parents for introducing me at an early age to both mountains and photography.

Many thanks to those who have made direct contributions to this project, especially Pat Morrow, the late Galen Rowell and the Whyte Museum of the Canadian Rockies. Thanks also to Freeman Patterson, who inspired me to discover my personal "art of seeing" years ago, a theme still in progress.

And, finally, thanks most of all to my wife and career partner Karen. Not only is she responsible for many of the photos in this book, but she has also long been an endless source of ideas and creative innovation for my own photography. Her exacting standards have contributed enormously to the success of our partnership. I can't imagine planning a photography trip—or sitting down to write a book—without her.

Index

35 mm format 16
accessories 3,24,29
advanced exposure control 47
alternative film 93
analog cameras 13,14-17,30
aperture priority 64
art of seeing 100
ASA rating 30
backgrounds 125-126
backlighting 158
batteries 14,17,22-23
big–trip photography 200
black & white photography 79,90
black & white film 88
black & white filters 89
bracketing 3,46
bracketing dial 23
bright overcast 162,189
bulk film 30
c-clamp support 71
cable release 20,23,29,66,73
camera bags 3,27,28
camera shake 56
capturing motion 143
children 193
choosing a camera 10
close-up photography 187,188
cold weather 204
color films 85
color reproduction 13
complimentary colors 87
composition 23,26,34,45,48,50,59,61,63,70,72, 82-84,91,94,99,100,102-103,108,116,120,121,124-129,135,138,158,160,167,168,171,182,188,218
contrast 90,104-105
creating motion 143
creative eye 99
creative photography 20,23
cropping 112-114,116
cross-processing 93, 94,97
dark backgrounds 125
dead centre positioning 109
depth of field 217
depth of field 9,18-19,23,34,46,49,53,55,57-65
depth of field preview 59
digital camera 9,11,12,13,14,15,17,30
digital cameras 11,12,13
digital camera essentials 17
digital debate 11,12
digital technology 11,13
dramatic viewpoints 137
electronic release 23
emphasizing steepness 139
enhancing perspective 141
expiration date 31
exposing on snow and ice 49
exposure 218,220
fill–in light 165
film 30
film camera 12
film versus digital 14
filters 20,28,32,33,34,35
filters for black & white 35
flash 169,170,215
flash 21,23,29,56,168,169,170,171,180,181,188, 218,220,221
focusing 217
focusing 18,19,36,46,57,60,63
foreground 127
frontal lighting 155
fuzzy background 126
graduated tones 90
grain characteristics 30
ground-level perspective 134
hand-holding camera 40
hand coloring 92
harmonious colors 87
haze 172
high–altitude photography 201
high mountain expeditions 201
holding camera properly 40
horizon, or horizonless 123
horizontal framing 118
hot tropical extremes 206
humidity 206,207
incident meter 45
infrared film 97
infrared film 80,97,98
large format 16
lenses 24
lens flare 172
lens flare 172,173,220
lens hood, ... 173
lighting 102,125,155,162
lightning 178
light backgrounds 125
light leakage 39
loading and unloading film 37

macro capability 24
medium format 16
megapixel 17
mental flexibility 101
metering 3,43,44,52
metering exposures 43
meter calibration scale 43
mini-tripods 72
model 192,193,194,199
models 192
monopods 72
motion 111,143,144
motor winders 29
mountain camera features 22
mountain light 150,151
mountain safety 77
moving objects 148
multimedia presentation 215
neutral density filter 34
nighttime 180
night photography 23
normal perspective 131
oblique perspective 136
openness of mind 101
optical zoom 17
overcast days 160
overexposing 51
overhead perspective 132
panning 143,146
panning action 146
panoramas 190,191
parallax error 19
partially cloudy weather 163
patterns 103,104,105,111
perspective 129,131,132,134,141
photoshop 12
point-and-shoot 7,16,20,21,22
point-and-shoot cameras 20,21
point–and–shoot camera 16,20
polarizing filters 32
primary colors 87
protect yourself 198
publishing photos 213
radiant light 152
red eye 21
reflected light meter 45
reflecting light 167
reflector 165-169,188,220
remote flash 23
remote release 73
remote triggering 29
rigging 196
rule of thirds 106,107,108
saturated films 85
saturation rating 31
scanners 15
scratches 217
self-timer 23,29
self portraits 194
sepia printing 92
sepia toning 79
shapes and patterns 103
sharp backgrounds 126
shooting in the dark 180
shutter priority 65
shutter speed 53,144
sidelighting 156
silhouettes 159
single–lens reflex 3,16,18
slides vs. prints 81
slide shows 102,211
slow vs. fast film 83
small man–big environment 115
specialized shoots 182
star patterns 178
static shooting 109
steepness 139
stopping motion 55
stormy weather 176,177
sunset and sunrise 174
texture 104
thunderstorms 177
tilted framing 121
time of year 153
tonal range 90
tone 13,104
tripod 23,29,40,42,53,56,58,60,63,66-78,83-84,86,96,110-111,171,176,177,178,179,180,187-188,191,194-195,217,219-220
tripod head 70
tripod socket 23
tungsten film 95,96
twilight 178,179
underexposing 51
unsaturated films 85
UV filters 33
vertical framing 119
vests 28
visual communication 102
waterproof case 29
wildlife 166,182,184-185,208
world travel 208
zoom lenses 20,26